EMPIRE OF DESTRUCTION

EMPIRE OF DESTRUCTION

A History of Nazi Mass Killing

ALEX J. KAY

YALE UNIVERSITY PRESS
NEW HAVEN AND LONDON

For information about this and other Yale University Press publications, please contact:
U.S. Office: sales.press@yale.edu   yalebooks.com
Europe Office: sales@yaleup.co.uk   yalebooks.co.uk

Set in Minion Pro by IDSUK (DataConnection) Ltd
Printed in Great Britain by TJ Books, Padstow, Cornwall

Library of Congress Control Number: 2021936886

ISBN 978-0-300-23405-3

A catalogue record for this book is available from the British Library.

10 9 8 7 6 5 4 3 2 1

For Valentina and Cyrus

Everybody keeps on shouting 'Where was God?' I kept on saying 'Where was man?'

Josef Perl, Holocaust survivor[1]

And even if some proof should remain and some of you survive, people will say that the events you describe are too monstrous to be believed.

Primo Levi, quoting an SS guard at Auschwitz[2]

CONTENTS

CONTENTS

ILLUSTRATIONS

1. Smoke rises from the crematorium chimney at Hadamar Hospital, 1941. Diözesanarchiv Limburg, Papers of Father Hans Becker. Photographer: probably Wilhelm Reusch.
2. Group portrait of the staff of Hartheim Castle, near Linz, undated. United States Holocaust Memorial Museum, courtesy of National Archives and Records Administration, College Park; photograph number 31162.
3. Richard Jenne. United States Holocaust Memorial Museum, courtesy of National Archives and Records Administration, College Park; photograph number 78606.
4. SS personnel lead a group of blindfolded Polish prisoners to an execution site in the Kampinos Forest near Palmiry, Poland, autumn 1939. United States Holocaust Memorial Museum, courtesy of Instytut Pamieci Narodowej; photograph number 50649.
5. A German army firing squad shoots Polish civilians, undated. Granger Historical Picture Archive/Alamy Stock Photo.
6. German policemen search through piles of clothing belonging to the Jewish victims of the Babi Yar massacre, 1941. Archiv des Hamburger Instituts für Sozialforschung. Photographer: Johannes Hähle.
7. A man about to be shot by a member of the SD, Vinnitsa, Ukraine, 1942. United States Holocaust Memorial Museum, courtesy of Sharon Paquette; photograph number 64407.
8. Yura Ryabinkin and his classmates, 1937. Alexander Bogdanov, 'Yura Ryabinkin i ves' blokadnyy klass, v kotorom on uchilsya. Redkaya fotografiya, publikuyetsya vpervyye', 19 March 2015: https://sasha-bogdanov.livejournal.com/2529770.html.
9. Two women cut meat from a dead horse, Leningrad, early 1942. World History Archive/Alamy Stock Photo.

10. Bread is distributed to captured Soviet soldiers in a prisoner-of-war camp, Vinnitsa, Ukraine, 28 July 1941. Bundesarchiv, Bild 146-1979-113-04. Photographer: Hübner.

11. Soviet prisoners of war dig a burrow in Stalag XI D (321) Fallingbostel-Oerbke, province of Hanover, 1941. Stiftung niedersächsische Gedenkstätten/Dokumentationsstelle Celle; from the album of a Wehrmacht soldier; photograph number 40808.

12. A burrow for Soviet prisoners of war in Stalag XI D (321) Fallingbostel-Oerbke, province of Hanover, 1941. Stiftung niedersächsische Gedenkstätten/Dokumentationsstelle Celle; from the album of a Wehrmacht soldier; photograph number 42269.

13. Corpses of Soviet prisoners of war in Dulag 184, Vyazma, Russia, 19 November 1941. Stiftung niedersächsische Gedenkstätten/Dokument-ationsstelle Celle, Papers of Wehrmacht soldier Otto Dobberkau; photograph number 40617. Photographer: Otto Dobberkau.

14. Captured Soviet soldiers in a prisoner-of-war camp, 1942. Fortepan; photo ID 73897.

15. A soldier from a Wehrmacht security division secures the rope with which a man is hanged as a partisan, Vitebsk, Belarus, October 1941. Albatross/Alamy Stock Photo.

16. German paratroopers massacre the male inhabitants of the village of Kondomari, Crete, 2 June 1941. Bundesarchiv, Bild 101I-166-0525-30. Photographer: Franz Peter Weixler.

17. Children from the Łódź Ghetto are deported to Chełmno death camp, September 1942. Prisma by Dukas Presseagentur GmbH/Alamy Stock Photo.

18. Emaciated corpses in a mass grave at Bełżec extermination camp, 1942. Imagno/Getty Images.

19. Sobibór extermination camp, early summer 1943. United States Holocaust Memorial Museum, gift of Bildungswerk Stanislaw-Hantz; item number 2020.8.1_001_010_0007.

20. Hungarian Jews are selected at Auschwitz-Birkenau, 19 May 1944. Fortepan; photo ID 172032; donor Lili Jacob. Photographer: Bernhard Walter.

21. Women and children await selection following the arrival of Hungarian Jews at Auschwitz-Birkenau, late May 1944. Fortepan; photo ID 172050; donor Lili Jacob. Photographer: Bernhard Walter.

ABBREVIATIONS

AB	Außerordentliche Befriedungsaktion (Extraordinary Pacification Operation)
BArch	Bundesarchiv ([German] Federal Archives)
BArch-MA	Bundesarchiv-Militärarchiv ([German] Federal Military Archives)
BdS	Befehlshaber der Sicherheitspolizei und des SD (senior commander/s of the Security Police and the SD)
BLSA	British Library Sound Archive
Dulag	Durchgangslager (transit camp)
EK	Einsatzkommando (operational commando)
EM	Ereignismeldung (Incident Report)
Gestapo	Geheime Staatspolizei (Secret State Police)
Gulag	Glavnoe Upravlenie Lagerei ([Soviet] Main Directorate of Camps)
HLSL	Harvard Law School Library
HSSPF	Höhere/r SS- und Polizeiführer (higher SS and police leader/s)
IMG	Internationaler Militärgerichtshof (International Military Tribunal)
KdS	Kommandeur/e der Sicherheitspolizei und des SD (commander/s of the Security Police and the SD)
OKH	Oberkommando des Heeres (High Command of the [German] Army)
OKW	Oberkommando der Wehrmacht (High Command of the Wehrmacht)
Nbg. Doc.	Nuremberg Document
NCO	non-commissioned officer

NHCM	National Holocaust Centre and Museum, Laxton
NKVD	Narodnyy Komissariat Vnutrennikh Del ([Soviet] People's Commissariat for Internal Affairs)
POW	prisoner of war
RSHA	Reichssicherheitshauptamt (Reich Security Main Office)
SD	Sicherheitsdienst (Security Service [of the SS])
Sipo	Sicherheitspolizei (Security Police)
SK	Sonderkommando (special commando)
SS	Schutzstaffel (protective echelon)
Stalag	Stammlager (regular POW camp for enlisted men)
USHMM	United States Holocaust Memorial Museum
Wi Fü Stab Ost	Wirtschaftsführungsstab Ost (Economic Command Staff East)
Wi Rü Amt	Wehrwirtschafts- und Rüstungsamt (War Economy and Armaments Office [in the OKW])
Wi Stab Ost	Wirtschaftsstab Ost (Economic Staff East)
WVHA	Wirtschafts-Verwaltungshauptamt (Economic Administration Main Office [of the SS])
YVA	Yad Vashem Archives
z.b.V.	zur besonderen Verwendung (for special assignment)

NOTE ON PLACE NAMES AND CONVENTIONS

In order to ensure some uniformity in the use of place names in this book, I have adopted the name in use at the time of the respective German invasion. For example, for those Polish places whose names were changed during the German occupation from 1939 onwards, I have opted to use the Polish name, with the German name in parentheses at the first mention, thus Częstochowa (Tschenstochau), Dziekanka (Tiegenhof) and so on, and thereafter the Polish name only. Exceptions to this are Danzig (as the Free City of Danzig between 1920 and 1939), Cracow (as the commonly used English name) and camp names such as Auschwitz, Birkenau or Monowitz (as referring to the camp, not the place). By the same token, places that were part of Germany during the period in question until passing to Poland in 1945 are referred to by their German name, with the Polish name in parentheses at the first mention, for instance Breslau (now Wrocław). As Lithuania, Latvia, Estonia, Belarus and Ukraine belonged to the Soviet Union during the events in question, I have employed the Russian form of all Soviet place names, thus Lvov (not Lviv or – Polish – Lwów), Rovno (not Rivne), Kharkov (not Kharkiv) and so on. The Soviet administrative units *oblast* and *raion* are translated throughout as 'province' and 'district', respectively. I refer to the occupied Polish territories not annexed to the German Reich using the contemporary translation 'Government General' rather than 'General Government', which is more common in today's secondary literature.[1]

As use of the terms 'Nazi' and 'Nazis' was already widespread in both English and German during the period covered by this book, they will also be used here, where applicable. Throughout the text, most German military and paramilitary ranks are referred to by their British army equivalents. Where there was no equivalent, they are translated into English (see Appendix II: Comparative Ranks for 1942). In an effort to make the prose as reader-friendly as possible, I have opted to place references only at the end of paragraphs. This means, in some cases, that the reference for a direct quotation is not provided immediately after the quotation itself but rather at the end of the paragraph in question. Translations, except where otherwise noted, are my own.[2]

ACKNOWLEDGEMENTS

Books tend to be collaborative efforts, even when there is only a single author, and this one is no exception. A number of friends and colleagues kindly read one or more draft chapters at various stages of the writing process and made helpful suggestions for improvements: Paul Bartrop, Jochen Böhler, Robert Gerwarth, Gerrit Hohendorf, Martin Holler, Juliane Krause, Martijn Lak, Stephan Lehnstaedt, Peter Lieb, Darren O'Byrne, Reinhard Otto, Henning Pieper, Jeff Rutherford, Ben Shepherd, Christian Streit, Clemens Uhlig and Ulrike Winkler. I am grateful to all of them for giving their time and expertise. Nicholas Terry displayed a rare generosity by reading the entire draft manuscript and providing extensive feedback on the basis of his considerable knowledge of the relevant scholarship and historiographical debates in multiple languages. I am deeply indebted to him. My thanks also go to the two anonymous referees for their detailed and constructive feedback, and to David Stahel, Rolf Keller, Tal Bruttmann and Oleg Beyda for their help with images. I am obliged to the German Historical Institute in Moscow and the Holocaust Memorial Centre in Budapest for their invitations to present on themes covered in the book at conferences in September and November 2020, respectively.

My particular thanks go to the managing director and publisher of Yale University Press in London, Heather McCallum, whose positive response to my initial idea opened the way to me writing the book. Since then, she has enthusiastically guided and supported the process from start to finish. I am sincerely grateful to Marika Lysandrou, Rachael Lonsdale, Percie Edgeler and everyone else at Yale who worked on the book for their patience and attention to detail during the publication process. It has been a pleasure to work with the whole team. My appreciation also goes to copy-editor Robert Shore for 'exercising a light touch' on the manuscript. Here, again, I would like to thank Ben Shepherd, who first recommended Yale and put me in touch with Heather.

The supportive and generous working environment provided by my colleagues at the Chair of Military History/Cultural History of Violence in the Department of History at the University of Potsdam is proof that German academia need not be cut-throat or parochial. Discussions with students during classes I have taught in Potsdam since 2017 on genocide, the Holocaust and German mass violence have also been helpful and thought-provoking. On a more personal note, this seems like a fitting opportunity to thank my dad, Eddie, for all the long talks we have shared. The final phases of the writing process were carried out amidst the COVID-19 pandemic. This historic turn of events necessitated more than ever a kind and caring home environment. It was provided, as always, by Valentina and Cyrus. To both of them, I am eternally grateful.

Berlin/Potsdam, March 2021

Europe in 1941

INTRODUCTION

The Second World War is to date the deadliest armed confrontation in history. This distinction is a result not only of the huge number of military dead. It is also a consequence of the total nature of the conflict, whereby some of the belligerents used the opportunity to carry out the slaughter of entire ethnic and social groups under the cover of war, not because of anything the victims had actually done but because of what they represented for the perpetrators. This applies first and foremost to Nazi Germany, the main aggressor. Indeed, if we take only civilians and other non-combatants into account, the Nazis killed approximately 13 million people in deliberate policies of mass murder, almost all of them during the war years, 1939 to 1945, and the vast majority between mid-1941 and spring 1945, that is, in the space of only four years. These systematic killing programmes and their victims are the subject of the present book.

For perhaps the first time, all major victim groups where the death tolls reached at least into the tens of thousands will be considered together: Jewish and non-Jewish, Eastern European and Western European, internal and external. These victims encompassed the mentally and physically disabled within the German Reich and, later, in the occupied territories; the Polish ruling classes and elites; Jews across the length and breadth of Europe; captive and unarmed Red Army soldiers; the Soviet urban population; those civilians in primarily rural areas who fell victim to preventive terror and reprisals, especially in the Soviet Union, Yugoslavia, Greece and Poland; and Europe's Roma populations.

For all the differences in the nature of the victims and, frequently, the ways in which they were murdered, they had something fundamental in common. It is no coincidence that all these seven major Nazi killing programmes took place during the war years. The commonality shared by the different victim groups is closely related to the military conflict. While each of the killing programmes possessed a racial (and racist) component, the logic of war was central to the rationale for targeting each and every one of the victim groups, for they were regarded by the Nazi regime in one way or another as a potential threat to Germany's ability to fight and, ultimately, win a war for hegemony in Europe. This view was informed and justified by Nazi racial thinking, so it is difficult, if not impossible, to separate German wartime strategy from Nazi genocidal racial policies. Indeed, one might go so far as to argue that, in the case of the German Reich, genocide itself, and mass-killing policies in general, constituted a form of warfare. The disabled in Germany were seen as undermining the health and vitality of the German nation in wartime, while the disabled in the occupied territories were viewed as rivals for food and accommodation; the Polish ruling classes and elites were murdered as pillars of Polish national identity and potential focal points for resistance to the German occupation; as alleged leaders and revolutionaries pulling the strings behind the scenes, Jews everywhere were believed to pose a threat to the very existence of the German people; Soviet prisoners of war and urban dwellers were regarded as direct competitors of German troops and the German home front for precious food supplies; rural populations in Eastern and Southeast Europe were suspected of aiding and abetting partisans; Roma – whether itinerant or sedentary – were considered to be potential spies and a general factor of destabilisation behind German lines.

In view alone of this intertwinement of war and extermination, it makes a great deal of sense to consider the different strands of Nazi mass killing together rather than in isolation from one another. This of course means going against the grain of most scholarship on the subject by examining the genocide of the European Jews alongside other Nazi mass-murder campaigns. Some scholars repudiate the very notion that the Holocaust can be analysed within a broader framework. According to Saul Friedländer, for instance: 'The absolute character of the anti-Jewish drive of the Nazis makes it impossible to integrate the extermination of the Jews, not only within the general framework of Nazi persecutions, but even within the wider aspects of contemporary ideological-political behaviour such as fascism, totalitarianism, economic exploitation and so on.' I disagree. Taking an integrative approach to Nazi mass killing in no way contradicts the view – advocated here, too – that the Holocaust was an unprecedented phenomenon, not least in its comprehensive and systematic nature. Instead, it is possible to argue that the Holocaust was unprecedented yet simultaneously to regard it as one part of a wider process of demographic reconstruction and racial purification pursued by the Nazi regime, first in Germany itself and then, as the war progressed and the Nazi empire grew, in each and every one of the territories occupied by German forces.[1]

From today's perspective, more than seventy-five years after the events in question and with a wealth of historical research at our disposal, we are able to see how systematic Nazi mass killing often was. Aside from those in senior leadership positions within the Nazi regime, however, it is likely that most of the perpetrators themselves were quite atomised and had, at best, only a vague notion of their own role in a vast killing machine and, likewise, of the scale and exact nature of the Nazis' pan-European racial purification programme. An estimated total of between 200,000 and 250,000 Germans and Austrians – predominantly, though not exclusively, men – were directly involved in the mass murder of European Jewry. This particular estimate is limited to those involved in the actual killing of Jews and does not include other, related crimes, such as the theft of Jewish assets. If we consider all those who exercised functions of one sort or another in the machinery of annihilation, the total rises to more than 500,000 people for the Holocaust alone; many more were involved in policies of mass murder targeting other victim groups.[2]

The perpetrators of Nazi mass killing were spread across a number of state and party institutions. Some of these organisations were involved in several programmes of annihilation, often simultaneously. The Chancellery of the Führer, for instance, provided personnel for both the murder of psychiatric patients and the gassing of Polish Jews during Operation Reinhardt. The SS and police played a central role in the mass murder of Roma, psychiatric patients and Jews in the occupied territories. The Wehrmacht participated directly in the elimination of Polish elites, the genocides of Serbian and Soviet Jewry and of Roma, the starvation of captured Red Army soldiers and the Soviet urban population, and the brutal anti-partisan operations in Eastern and Southeast Europe. Viewing the entire range of Nazi mass-killing programmes, members of the Wehrmacht may in fact have constituted the majority of those responsible for large-scale crimes carried out on the part of the German Reich. As many as 18 million men served in the Wehrmacht during the Second World War, 10 million of whom were deployed at one time or another between 1941 and 1944 in the conflict against the Soviet Union, where German warfare and rule were saturated in violence, causing death and suffering on an unprecedented scale. The number of Wehrmacht divisions deployed on the eastern front in which no war crimes were committed was low. The implementation of Nazi mass-killing operations was assisted by the participation of substantial numbers of local collaborators, especially in parts of Eastern Europe. Rather than applying a broader brushstroke to paint a picture of violence committed by multiple nationalities across a given geographical space, as some have done, this book for the most part focuses specifically on by far the largest group of perpetrators of Nazi mass killing both in terms of their own numbers and the numbers of their victims: Germans (Reich and ethnic) and Austrians.[3]

While the six years of the war provide the temporal and contextual structure for this book, 'mass killing' offers a conceptual framework for its contents, hence the deliberate use of the term in its title: where hundreds of thousands or even millions of civilians and other non-combatants lose their lives, not as a result of natural catastrophes, unforeseen epidemics or general privation, but rather as a direct consequence of the conscious and wilful actions of other human beings, there can be no denying that we are talking about killing on a mass scale. Following sociologist Yang Su, I define mass killing as 'the intentional killing of a significant number of the members of any group (as a group and its membership is defined by the perpetrator) of non-combatants'. In a book addressing the massive, one-sided destruction of human life in a series of operations all planned, initiated and carried out by a single state and its institutions, the concept of 'mass killing' seems preferable to a range of alternative terms. It is broader, for instance, than 'genocide' and thus encompasses all seven programmes examined here. It is also less emotive, less politically contentious and less dependent on specific legal interpretations.[4]

According to the Convention on the Prevention and Punishment of the Crime of Genocide, which was adopted by the United Nations General Assembly in December 1948 and came into force in January 1951, the term applies to any 'acts committed with intent to destroy, in whole or in part, a national, ethnical, racial or religious group'. Naturally, diplomats, lawyers, historians and other actors have had a role in shaping the debates and the terminology itself ex post facto. As we know, the term 'genocide' was not even coined until 1944, by the Polish-Jewish lawyer Raphael Lemkin in his book *Axis Rule in Occupied Europe*, and only then used in the indictments of the German major war criminals in Nuremberg a year later. Having said that, we should keep in mind that Lemkin himself was influenced by the Ottoman destruction of the Armenians in 1915 and, especially, the mass murders in Nazi-occupied Europe; had he not (barely) evaded capture by the Germans, Lemkin might also have become a victim of either the extermination of the European Jews or the murder of the Polish elites.[5]

The definition offered by the UN Genocide Convention inevitably represents a diplomatic compromise that was acceptable to the largest possible number of signatory states at the time of its adoption. Most notably, political and social affiliations were rejected as criteria for inclusion in the list of potential victim groups. For this and other reasons, many scholars have questioned the value of the UN definition for understanding the nature of genocide. Furthermore, excessive use of the term since the late 1990s has led to its devaluation; 'genocide' has become an expression almost synonymous with mass violence. We are, therefore, in need of a scholarly definition to complement the legal definition, in order for us to gain an informed understanding of the crime. There appears, for instance, to be an emerging consensus among scholars that there are no objective criteria for membership in a group, but rather that the victim group is defined by the perpetrators. The victims do not have to belong to a particular 'national, ethnical, racial or religious group' to be subjected to a categorisation from which they cannot escape; it is sufficient – and indeed decisive – that the perpetrators include the victims in the target group. In spite of this modest progress, however, there is still little consensus on the applicability of the term to individual cases of mass violence, so that genocide remains an 'essentially contested concept'.[6]

Some scholars use the term 'mass killing' as distinct from 'genocide' to mean 'killing (or in other ways destroying) members of the group without the intention to eliminate the whole group, or killing large numbers of people without a focus on group membership'. The approach taken in this book differs insofar as mass killing and genocide are not regarded as mutually exclusive. Genocide is a very specific type of mass killing. The intention to 'destroy a group' is the crucial ingredient that sets genocide apart from other forms of mass killing. At its core, genocide is a historical process that is about group reproduction. Gender, therefore, is vital to our understanding of the crime, as the process of destruction permanently undermines the future survival of the victim group. If used accurately and consistently, then, genocide still deserves a place in the historian's conceptual, analytical and linguistic arsenal. The concept of mass killing is employed here as a means to augment and complement rather than supplant the concept of genocide. Where it is deemed applicable, therefore, the label of genocide is still used in this book, though no attempt is made to force all mass-killing programmes into the single definitional framework of genocide. As this is not a book on comparative genocide studies, this brief discussion of the concept of genocide will not be pursued in greater depth here.[7]

It is easy to get bogged down in terminology and the debates that abound over its usage and, in the process, to lose sight of the events themselves and the context in which they took place. Though these debates are necessary, because they help us to understand the similarities and differences between individual instances of state-sponsored mass killing, we must take care to avoid twisting the facts to suit our theoretical framework and instead adapt our theory to fit the facts. Naturally, there were substantial differences between the various Nazi killing campaigns examined here, but it is what unites them that is more important for understanding the nature of this unprecedented destruction of human life: each and every one of the victim groups was regarded by the Nazi regime in one way or another as a potential threat to Germany's ability successfully to wage a war for hegemony in Europe. For this and other reasons, they were systematically targeted and – in spite of their civilian and/or non-combatant status – deliberately murdered on a mass scale as part of the wider German wartime strategy.

The Nazis also saw war and conquest as a means to enable further waves of mass killing after the final military victory. Had Germany won the Second World War, plans already existed for violence on a scale that far surpassed anything that actually transpired. In other words, utopian plans in Nazi Germany generally *exceeded* the actual extent of the violence, horrific as that was. To cite just one example, the so-called General Plan East (*Generalplan Ost*) – no fewer than four versions of which were drawn up between early

1940 and mid-1942 – envisaged the long-term Germanisation of substantial swathes of territory in Eastern Europe and the expulsion of more than 30 million Slavs to western Siberia, including 80 to 85 per cent of all Poles in the settlement area, 65 per cent of western Ukrainians and 75 per cent of Belarusians. Those members of the local populations permitted to remain in the settlement area would be reduced to the status of slaves for their new German masters. This difference between what actually came to pass and the existence of even more far-reaching plans was one of several ways in which German violence differed fundamentally from, say, Soviet violence.[8]

No other regime in twentieth-century history deliberately ordered people to their deaths with comparable intensity and on the same scale as Adolf Hitler and the National Socialists. The starvation of tens of millions between 1958 and 1962 as a result of Mao Zedong's infamous experiment in social engineering, the Great Leap Forward, was not premeditated (though the same cannot be said of the killings carried out during the Cultural Revolution in China from 1966 to 1971, albeit on a much smaller scale). Notwithstanding the circulation of some overblown estimates, during almost thirty years of Stalinist rule in the Soviet Union, the number of victims of mass purposive killings amounted to something in the order of a million people – perhaps a thirteenth of the total murdered by the Nazi regime within a considerably shorter time span, namely in the space of only twelve years (the vast majority during the six years of the war). Admittedly, the figure for the Soviet Union does not include around 6 million people who starved to death during the famine of 1932–33, more than half of whom were inhabitants of Soviet Ukraine; though victims of the regime's criminal neglect and irresponsibility, there is no evidence to suggest that they succumbed to an intentional killing policy (in notable contrast to Germany's starvation of Soviet city dwellers and captured Red Army soldiers from 1941 onwards).[9]

It is not merely a question of figures, though – for the human beings concerned, each individual death is always singular. Nonetheless, a fundamental difference in the respective intentions of the perpetrators is clearly discernible. Rather than accepting widespread death resulting – without any initial, inherent intention of killing – from attempts to accomplish other goals, the Nazis actively planned the murder of millions *in order to achieve their goals* and then systematically implemented these plans in a way that neither the regime of Mao nor that of Joseph Stalin did, some exceptions aside. The Soviet Gulag network of forced-labour camps was comparable in some respects to the concentration-camp system under Hitler, but nothing akin to the Nazi *death* camps existed in Stalin's Soviet Union or Mao's China. From a total of 18 million prisoners who passed through the Gulag system between 1930 and 1953, when Stalin died, around 1.6 million lost their lives. This death toll owed much to the longevity of the Gulag complex; as the percentage of deaths among prisoners indicates, however, a general plan for their destruction did not exist. Other differences are worth pointing out, too. A far higher number of perpetrators were directly involved in mass-killing campaigns in Nazi Germany than in Stalin's USSR, where such operations were conducted almost exclusively by the police apparatus, principally the NKVD. The mass murder of children by the Nazi regime is particularly illustrative of how the regimes differed. Nothing analogous to the Nazis' deliberate and ruthless murder of millions of children is to be found either in the crimes of Mao and Stalin or any other twentieth-century campaign of mass killing. With the obvious exception of the elimination of the Polish intelligentsia and the starvation of captive Red Army soldiers, the murder of children on a huge scale (and often in disproportionately great numbers compared to adult victims) was a prominent feature in all the mass-killing programmes examined in this book.[10]

Clearly, the mass killing of the years 1939 to 1945 had a prehistory. What made the National Socialists – the most radical political movement to gain power in modern European history – believe that they had the right to eliminate so many human beings? They were convinced that some groups of people with particular characteristics, whether religious, cultural, racial or physical, were unalterably inferior to other groups. Of course, this was by no means a concoction of the National Socialists. In their case, however, this racist ideology was combined with an extreme form of ethnic nationalism directed not only outwards but also inwards – be it against political opponents, those considered antisocial or work-shy, Sinti and Roma or, especially, Jews – and a radical will to recast society in accordance with their own vision. The ultimate ideological aim of the Nazi movement was thus to secure the hegemony of what it regarded as a purified, racially superior national and ethnic community. It is tempting to dismiss Nazi ideology as irrational, as the product of delusional paranoia, pseudo-science and a crisis of meaning. From the perspective of those who devised and advocated it, however, Nazi racial doctrine was anything but irrational. Indeed, in the context of the war, the National Socialists developed their own inexorable logic of mass murder.[11]

Although National Socialist ideology had many sources and influences, it was also a product of specific circumstances. Germany's status as a delayed or belated nation-state affected its concept of citizenship and belonging. The inception of the idea of the nation before the state remained decisive. Germany's notion of a fixed national territory could only develop after unification in 1871. As a late colonial power, Germany ranked far behind its main European rivals, Britain and France, in the race for colonies. Overseas Germans living in distant foreign states therefore became the main point of reference for an ethnic-nationalist (*völkisch*) sentiment because the comparatively small German colonies offered only a weak territorial link. Ethnocultural ideas of the nation were thus quite clearly viewed and deployed as a means of compensating for the political weakness of the state. Military collapse and capitulation in the First World War were followed not only by the confiscation of those colonies Germany had managed to obtain since 1884 but also by the separation of substantial territory from the nation-state itself and the German citizens living there along with it. It was within this context that a radical ethnicisation occurred that led to the breakthrough of an ethnic-nationalist conception of citizenship, which in turn became an instrument of revisionist policy.[12]

The key to understanding and explaining the vision that Nazi ideology had of society and the violence it spawned is thus to be found in the First World War, its outcome and, above all, societal perceptions of this experience. According to Sebastian Haffner, one of the most perceptive contemporary commentators on National Socialism, the war years later became 'the positive underlying vision of Nazism'. Immediately after the First World War ended, scapegoats were sought for Germany's defeat, resulting in the stab-in-the-back myth (*Dolchstoßlegende*) of a betrayal by Jews, communists and pacifists on the home front. The defeat – and right-wing rationalisations for it – bred a traumatic fear of internal instability in times of war and crisis. Lessons were drawn from the constantly invoked crisis of 1918: a repetition was to be avoided at all costs. This called for radical preventive measures. Whatever was deemed necessary was also regarded as legitimate. Thus, in wartime, all real and prospective enemies (ideological opponents, racial undesirables, those considered unproductive, worthless or a burden, and other potential dissidents) were to be removed and eliminated with the goal, on the one hand, of preventing a recurrence of the defeat and turmoil of 1918–19 (street fighting in Berlin, Munich and the Ruhr region; efforts to establish revolutionary republics and the violent suppression of these attempts; extreme right-wing Freikorps paramilitaries continuing the fight against Bolsheviks and nationalists in the Baltic countries), and, on the other, of purifying and strengthening German society and, later, a German-dominated Europe in the name of the National Socialist utopia.[13]

National Socialist Germany could also draw on an undeniable tradition of lethal violence against defenceless people dating back at least to the colonial warfare of the first decade of the twentieth century. Between 1904 and 1907, deeply racist German colonial authorities and troops murdered or caused the deaths of between 70,000 and 100,000 people in German Southwest Africa (now Namibia). Military operations were carried out against women and children, people were driven into the Namib Desert, and men were starved in prison camps that served to subjugate the Herero and Nama peoples. Around the same time, the German suppression of the Maji Maji rebellion in German East Africa (now Tanzania, Burundi and Rwanda) claimed about 100,000 lives. Though not unique, German colonial atrocities were among the worst of their time. During the First World War, more than 70,000 patients of German psychiatric hospitals were allowed to die from starvation as a result of the reduction in daily food rations in favour of members of society considered more productive or worthy in wartime. In Belgium and France between August and October 1914, regular German troops killed around 6,500 civilians in mass executions for alleged (and largely imagined) irregular attacks. Of course, we cannot draw a straight line from Africa to Auschwitz. However, in spite of the evident discontinuities – prior to 1933, German mass violence carried out simultaneously against several victim groups was rare, and few of the victims of mass murder were Jews – there were clearly also important continuities between colonial times, the Great War and the Nazi regime. Such precedents later acted as a point of reference, and the National Socialists were able to call on these experiences of conceiving and committing mass murder against vulnerable internal and external groups.[14]

Notwithstanding the continuities between German colonial atrocities and the horrors of the Nazi era, any categorisation of the Holocaust – the most comprehensive and relentless of all Nazi mass-killing campaigns – as a 'colonial genocide' is very problematic. Colonial racism is an ideology of superiority; anti-Semitism is an ideology of inferiority. The Germans felt inferior to the Jews. Jews living in nineteenth-century Prussia and, from 1871, the German Reich exploited with extraordinary success the new opportunities offered them by the lifting of legal discrimination. They further emancipated themselves by means of their work ethic and the importance they attached to education and learning. As of 1886, the share of Jewish schoolchildren in Prussia educated to a level beyond primary school came to 46.5 per cent. The equivalent figure for non-Jewish children in Prussia was only 6.3 per cent. By 1901, these proportions had risen to 56.3 and 7.3 per cent, respectively. The emancipation of the Jews (and indeed the wider polit-ical emancipation of the middle classes) was driven by Enlightenment thought. The Nazis rejected Jews not least because they rejected the moder-nising forces of the Enlightenment, with its ideals of advancement and prog-ress. This alone should tell us that the Holocaust was something fundamentally different to, say, the genocide of the Herero and Nama in German Southwest Africa. In a speech he gave on 1 April 1933 entitled 'Against the Atrocity Stories of Global Jewry', Reich Minister of Propaganda Joseph Goebbels summed up the Nazis' antipathy towards Enlightenment thinking and the ideas that inspired the French Revolution of 1789:

> We want to do away with the ideology of liberalism and the adoration of the individual, and replace them with a sense of community that once again embraces the entire nation and once again aligns and subordinates the interests of the individual to the common interests of the nation. In this way, the year 1789 will be removed from our history.

The German Jews were among the biggest winners of the Enlightenment, which allowed them finally to escape the confines of the ghetto and seize the opportunity to demonstrate their abilities.[15]

While the Nazis felt inferior to the Jews, it is clear from National Socialist ideology and propaganda that they looked upon Slavs with very different eyes. For the Nazis, Slavic peoples such as Czechs, Poles, Russians and others were in themselves primitive, backward and passive 'sub-humans' who posed a threat only when led by supposedly cunning and nefarious Jews – as in the case of the Bolsheviks, who were viewed by National Socialists as the stooges of 'international Jewry'. In accordance with this way of thinking, Slavs were eminently expendable and formed a regional obstacle to the expansion of German power, but they did not constitute a real danger for the Germans as such. Jews, by contrast, were portrayed as *the* global enemy and a worldwide threat to the very existence of the German people. While the Slav masses were deemed fit, at best, for enslavement, the Nazis conferred agency on the Jews: they were the alleged leaders and revolutionaries pulling the strings behind the scenes. Even a comparison of Nazi Germany's treatment of Slavs with Imperial German colonial violence, however, has its limitations: the concepts of development, indirect rule and the training of local 'elites' inherent in late European colonialism were entirely absent from Nazi rule in Eastern Europe.[16]

Germany's late arrival in the race for colonies, the defeat of 1918 and the loss not only of its colonies but also of Reich territory in the north (to Denmark), the east (to Poland and Czechoslovakia) and the west (to France and Belgium) spawned an individual and collective inferiority complex in German society. This was characterised by resentment, pettiness and a strong yearning for status and affirmation, all characteristics of the future Nazi perpetrators. Not surprisingly, then, the Nazi regime's subsequent propagation of a veritable culture of resentment resonated widely among the population generally. The perpetrators' ambition and craving for recognition were strengthened and, significantly, justified by Nazi ideology and the belief that they belonged to a 'master race'. Their ideological convictions persuaded them that the career advancement, status and recognition they sought were no more than their due; they felt they had a right to success and power. Ideology and egotism were mutually reinforcing. This sense of superiority later manifested itself above all in German attitudes and policies towards 'Slavic sub-humans' in occupied Eastern Europe – the heart of the Nazi empire – from 1939 and, especially, 1941 onwards.[17]

The defeat of 1918 had always been and remained the Nazi movement's central point of reference. It was characteristic of the National Socialist regime to radicalise violently any policy in the face of a threat and frequently to stop at nothing to achieve its goals. This in no way means that Nazi violence was merely a reaction to an actual external danger. Violence was an integral and essential component of Nazi theory and practice from the start. The battles for the streets during the late Weimar years, the terror that accompanied the consolidation of Nazi rule in Germany in 1933 and 1934, the violence against Jews that continued in the provinces throughout the pre-war years, the expansion of the concentration-camp and prison system and the pogroms of November 1938, to name just a few examples, were all testament to this long before Germany launched a war of aggression against Poland, triggering what would become the Second World War. The centralised killing of psychiatric patients was instituted at a time when German troops had just overrun Poland. The Nazis were not reacting here to a genuine and imminent wartime danger posed by the mentally ill; instead, they were removing what they perceived as a potential threat by embarking on their programme of racial purification and applying the lessons they had drawn from the experiences of 1914–18. Of course, when an actual threat did emerge and a policy was then violently escalated – such as the radicalisation of anti-Jewish measures in early summer 1941 in response to the stuttering military campaign against the Soviet Union – this was merely consistent with the Nazi conviction that the only way to tackle difficulties was to up the ante and increase the severity of their approach. Only in this way, they believed, could they avoid a repetition of 1918.

As discussed above, the six years of war provide a framework for the progression of Nazi mass killing and, in turn, for this historical narrative, which accordingly takes a broadly chronological approach to events. Part I addresses the period from summer 1939 to summer 1941, and with it the murder of the mentally and physically handicapped in the German Reich and the annexed Polish territories, and the elimination of the Polish ruling classes and intelligentsia. The German invasion of the Soviet Union in summer 1941 marked a fundamental change in both the scope and systematic nature of Nazi mass violence. For the first time, mass murder of Jews and other racial and political opponents was the order of the day from the very outset of the military campaign, which was conducted in an unrestrained and blatantly ideological manner. Part II, therefore, covers the period from summer 1941 to spring 1942, taking the occupied Soviet territories as its geographical focal point and devoting individual chapters to the mass killing of Soviet Jews, psychiatric patients and Roma, the starvation of substantial sections of the Soviet urban population, the mass mortality of Red Army prisoners of war, and the preventive terror and reprisals directed against the rural civilian population. It seems fitting to include (male) Serbian Jews in the analysis in Part II, as they were murdered both systematically and in parallel with Soviet Jews. Similarly, the German invasion of the Soviet Union was also a turning point for anti-partisan warfare in Serbia; its victims will likewise be discussed in Part II. The chapter on preventive terror and reprisals also extends temporally beyond spring 1942 in order to include Greek civilian victims, who were often killed for similar reasons to their Soviet and Yugoslavian counterparts.

Part III examines the remaining years of the war, that is, the period from spring 1942 to spring 1945. It begins with two chapters on the genocide of European Jews in the Chełmno, Operation Reinhardt and Auschwitz-Birkenau death camps. The second of these includes a sub-section on the forced evacuations of concentration-camp inmates during the final phase of the war, commonly known as 'death marches'. The next two chapters also pick up where earlier chapters leave off: the first of these looks at the expansion of deportations and killings of Roma to include other territories under German occupation, while the second addresses the decentralised murder of the sick in mental asylums and concentration camps in the German Reich up to Germany's unconditional surrender in May 1945. The final chapter of Part III returns to the slaughter of civilians during German reprisals and so-called pacification operations, though this time focusing on the Polish *urban* population, specifically the huge loss of civilian life during and in the aftermath of the suppression of the Warsaw Uprising in the late summer and early autumn of 1944. A concluding chapter offers an explanation for what motivated the hundreds of thousands of perpetrators and how we can account for their actions.

A word of warning: some readers may find this work harrowing to read. This might appear to be a rather banal or unnecessary statement to make about a book with the subtitle 'A History of Nazi Mass Killing'. It is true, however, that I have not shied away from presenting the events in graphic detail. My purpose is not to shock or sensationalise. On the contrary: writing a sanitised version of these events would only succeed in making them appear more abstract; realism and accuracy would be sacrificed in favour of palatability. There is a moral obligation to the victims to tell their story as faithfully as possible. My extensive use of testimony from survivors and other victims hopefully goes some small way towards giving them a voice and treating them as individual human beings rather than as statistics. If this book is emotionally hard to read, let us for a moment imagine how infinitely more difficult it must have been for the victims to suffer the events described here.

Part I
SUMMER 1939–SUMMER 1941

CHAPTER 1
KILLING THE SICK IN THE GERMAN REICH AND POLAND

The First World War was a turning point for the German psychiatric profession. Many physicians lamented the devastating effect on the German nation of the deaths of millions of healthy young men on the battlefield, while those less physically fit and able survived back home. This argument knowingly ignored the death from starvation and diseases caused by undernourishment of at least 70,000 patients in German psychiatric hospitals between 1914 and 1918. This was not a centrally initiated and managed killing programme, but rather the unintended outcome of the reduction in the daily food rations of the vulnerable psychiatric patients and the conversion of many facilities into military hospitals. These measures and their devastating consequences were widely accepted by the general public and psychiatric professionals alike as a necessary sacrifice in times of war.[1]

Defeat in the Great War and the losses incurred in human life, especially among the young and the fit, triggered and appeared to justify a heated debate in post-war Germany over the legitimacy of eradicating life that was supposedly worthless. This debate was symptomatic of how received humanitarian values were being reconsidered in the wake of the war, with concern for the wider collective usurping the rights and value of the individual. Although the concepts of eugenics and racial hygiene were not limited to Germany, such a debate was nonetheless unique among countries involved in the war, so that we can already detect a specific radicalisation for Germany here. Even in neutral Sweden, which became the first country to set up an institute for racial biology in 1922, there was no counterpart to the German discussion of euthanasia. Although the debate receded somewhat during the mid-1920s, it resurfaced at the time of the Great Depression and the attendant mass unemployment, particularly with regard to possibilities for cost-cutting in asylums and hospitals. Even before the effects of the depression could be felt in Germany, however, Nazi Party leader Adolf Hitler declared in his closing speech at the Reich Party Rally in Nuremberg in August 1929, almost three-and-a-half years before his appointment as German chancellor: 'If Germany were to get a million children each year and eliminate 700,000 to 800,000 of the weakest, then the end result would perhaps even be an increase in strength.'[2]

Though 1933 did not mark a decisive break in the German medical profession, 'the barriers to state-sanctioned measures of gross inhumanity were removed almost overnight', in the words of Ian Kershaw. What had previously appeared to be little more than fanciful thinking suddenly became feasible. On 14 July, less than six months into Hitler's chancellorship, the legal basis for forced sterilisations was created by virtue of the Law for the Prevention of Offspring with Hereditary Diseases (*Gesetz zur Verhütung erbkranken Nachwuchses*). According to this law, which came into force on the first day of 1934, someone could be sterilised without their consent if their progeny were expected to have serious physical or mental hereditary defects. Between 1934 and 1945, more than 300,000 men and women in Germany and Austria – where the law came into force on 1 January 1940 – were forcibly sterilised by order of the hereditary health courts specially set up for this purpose. Around 5,000 of them, predominantly women, did not survive the surgery. It was not uncommon for people to commit suicide before or after the procedure. This was particularly true of women, in an evolving political climate that set great store by eugenically fit, prolific motherhood. These measures demonstrated an increased readiness to use violence against people regarded as genetically defective. Hitler evidently remained an advocate of the views he had publicly voiced in August 1929, as illustrated not only by the speed with which the Law for the Prevention of Offspring with Hereditary Diseases had been passed but also, and not least, by his comments to Reich Physicians' Leader Gerhard Wagner in September 1935, again on the occasion of the Reich Party Rally, to the effect that he intended 'to eradicate the incurably insane' in the event of a future war.[3]

From this point on, at the latest, the mass murder of the mentally and physically disabled was no longer a question of if but only of when. Following his discussion with Hitler in September 1935, Wagner repeatedly made it known within party physician circles that Hitler was planning to authorise 'the annihilation of worthless life' in the event of war. For instance, Paul

Nitsche, director of the Pirna-Sonnenstein mental asylum, one of the subsequent central killing centres, later claimed to have learned of Hitler's 'euthanasia' plans from Wagner in March 1937. As early as 5 April 1937, four days after his appointment to administer all state hospitals in the Prussian province of Hesse-Nassau, Fritz Bernotat made his position on the subject clear during a conference of asylum directors in Dehrn Castle: 'If I were a doctor, I would knock off these sick people.' This was not an isolated expression of murderous intent on the part of Bernotat. On another occasion, he urged doctors and nursing staff: 'Just beat them to death, then they're gone!' At a 1938 meeting of government officials responsible for the administration of mental institutions, one speaker concluded in less uncouth but no less deadly terms that 'a solution for the field of mental health would simply require that one eliminates these people'. The implementation of this 'solution' was not long in coming.[4]

Child 'Euthanasia'

Prior to the outbreak of war, preparations began for the murder of the weakest and most vulnerable of all Nazi victims: disabled children. In early 1939, the case of a severely disabled infant named Gerhard Kretschmar in the village of Pomßen, near Leipzig, was brought to the attention of Professor Werner Catel, director of Leipzig University's paediatric clinic. Catel prompted the parents to submit a written request to grant permission for a mercy killing – which was liable to prosecution under prevailing laws – to Hitler via the Chancellery of the Führer (*Kanzlei des Führers*, or KdF). This course of action was by no means uncommon; the Chancellery of the Führer received 2,000 such petitions every day. Upon receipt of the parents' request to kill their son ('this monster'), Hitler commissioned his escort physician, Karl Brandt, to examine the case. After visiting the parents in July, Brandt arranged for the child to be killed; Catel personally carried out the killing a few days later. Gerhard Kretschmar's case evidently caught the attention of the Nazi officials, perhaps due to the particular severity and plurality of the boy's disabilities, and subsequently led Hitler verbally to empower Brandt and the head of the Chancellery of the Führer, Philipp Bouhler, to take the same action in similar instances. This constituted the transition from the killing of unborn life, which had been legalised in June

1935 in the event of genetic disorders, to the murder of babies, children and adolescents, cynically referred to as child 'euthanasia'.[5]

In order to prevent public exposure of the involvement of the Chancellery of the Führer – whose principal function was in fact to deal with appeals and petitions addressed to Hitler by members of the German public – and, by extension, of Hitler himself, the planners established a front organisation for the child 'euthanasia' programme with the name Reich Committee for the Scientific Assessment of Serious Hereditary and Constitutional Suffering (*Reichsausschuss zur wissenschaftlichen Erfassung von erb- und anlagebedingten schweren Leiden*). Philipp Bouhler entrusted his deputy and head of Main Office II (State and Party Affairs) in the Chancellery of the Führer, Viktor Brack, with the overall organisation of the 'euthanasia' killing programme. Brack, in turn, assigned the day-to-day management of child 'euthanasia' to Hans Hefelmann, head of Office IIb within Brack's Main Office II, which was responsible for affairs relating to the Reich ministries but also for clemency petitions. The small planning group worked swiftly, for as early as 18 August 1939 a strictly confidential circular decree was issued by the Ministry of the Interior – the only state department to have a representative on the Reich Committee – to the regional governments. As it was intended that disabled children not in institutional care be killed in the framework of the child 'euthanasia', the Reich Committee was dependent on the cooperation of the public-health authorities for the seizure of the murder victims. The circular decree imposed on midwives, doctors in maternity hospitals and obstetric wards, as well as general practitioners, the obligation to register newborns and infants up to the age of three years suffering from 'imbecility', 'mongolism', deformities (especially missing limbs) and palsy. Notifications were to be sent to the responsible public-health authority and, from there, to the cover address of the Reich Committee. The three consultants of the Reich Committee – paediatrician Ernst Wentzler from Berlin, child and adolescent psychiatrist Hans Heinze from Brandenburg an der Havel and the aforementioned Werner Catel – decided solely on the basis of these registration forms whether the children would be transferred to a so-called special children's ward and thus included in the killing programme; they never saw the children and did not even consult existing medical case histories. The fact that no one from the Reich Ministry of Justice was involved at this early stage demonstrates that the planners had an extralegal solution in mind.[6]

Even before the first of the 'special children's wards' had been set up, the perpetrators made reference to the approaching 'euthanasia' with chilling audacity. At Eglfing-Haar mental hospital near Munich, director Hermann Pfannmüller conducted tours through his institution to illustrate the inherent uselessness of the patients. Between 1933 and 1939, over 21,000 people trooped through Eglfing-Haar, including 6,000 members of the SS, some of whom came out recommending that machine guns be set up at the entrance to mow down the inmates. After the war, Bavarian schoolteacher Ludwig Lehner vividly recalled a visit to Eglfing-Haar in the autumn of 1939, shortly after his release from incarceration in Dachau concentration camp for membership of an anti-fascist group:

In autumn 1939, I witnessed a crime that unsettled even me, in particular by the way it was carried out, although at that time I was already accustomed to many things, having left Dachau concentration camp only a few months earlier. The general public was given the opportunity at that time to visit lunatic asylums. As I had studied psychology in 1934–35 during my professional training and therefore possess some specialised knowledge, I was naturally particularly interested in the way an asylum was run. For this reason, I decided to take one of these tours through the lunatic asylums.

After visiting several other wards, the asylum director, who was called Pfannmüller, led us into a children's ward. This ward made a clean and well-kept impression. About fifteen to twenty-five beds contained the same number of children, aged between one and five years. In this ward, Pfannmüller explicated his intentions in particular detail.

I recall the gist of what Pfannmüller said as follows: 'These creatures (he meant the children) naturally represent to me as a National Socialist only a burden for our healthy racial corpus. We do not kill (he might also have used a euphemism instead of the word "kill") with poison, injections, etc., because that would only provide new hate-propaganda material for the foreign press and certain gentlemen in Switzerland. No, our method is, as you can see, much simpler and far more natural.' With these words, and assisted by a nurse from the ward, he pulled a child from its bed. Displaying the child like a dead rabbit, he stated, with a knowing look and a cynical grin: 'This one will last another two or three days.' The image of this fat, grinning man, with the whimpering skeleton in his fleshy hand, surrounded by other starving children, is still clear before my eyes. Furthermore, the murderer then pointed out that they did not suddenly withdraw food, but instead slowly reduced rations. A lady who also took part in the tour asked, with an outrage she had difficulty suppressing, whether a quick death by means of an injection would not be more merciful. Pfannmüller thereupon sang the praises of his methods once more, as being more practical in view of the foreign press. The openness with which Pfannmüller announced the methods of treatment mentioned above can only be explained as the product of cynicism or foolishness. Furthermore, Pfannmüller made no secret of the fact that among those children who were to be murdered according to the aforementioned method were some who were not mentally ill, namely the children of Jewish parents.

Even before child 'euthanasia' had officially commenced, then, Pfannmüller was murdering children at Eglfing-Haar. It is worth noting here that, in spite of her outrage at the treatment of the children, the suggestion made by the female visitor mentioned by Lehner is in itself disturbing – she questioned Pfannmüller's methods but not his goals.[7]

From 1940 onwards, more than thirty 'special children's wards' were established to receive the children approved for murder. The wards were set up for the most part in regular hospitals on Reich territory (including Austria); their directors worked closely with the Reich Committee. Except in cases where the children were already institutionalised, however, the programme could only work if parents surrendered their children to the killing wards. Usually this posed no problem: the parents were commonly left in the dark regarding the actual purpose of the transfers and the authorities obtained their consent under false pretences, telling them that their children could be cured in the wards. The public-health officials were initially instructed to abstain from coercive measures. Against those parents who steadfastly refused to part with their children, however, pressure was applied. From September 1941, in accordance with instructions issued by Reich Health Leader Leonardo Conti in his capacity as permanent secretary in the Reich Ministry of the Interior, the public-health officials were permitted to threaten parents who opposed the relocation of their children with the withdrawal of custody. This intimidation usually worked. In order to force especially working-class mothers whose husbands were absent as soldiers during the war to give up their children and consent to the treatment, the Reich Committee contacted the local employment offices to issue them with work assignments.[8]

The first 'special children's ward' was set up in summer 1940 in Görden, Brandenburg. Its director was the psychiatrist Hans Heinze, who – like Werner Catel – was one of the three consultants of the Reich Committee. The senior physician on the ward was Dr Friederike Pusch; she also trained doctors from other 'special children's wards' in the methods used to murder the patients. A total of 172 children were sent by the Reich Committee to the ward in Görden; 147 of them, or 85 per cent, were murdered there. In marked contrast to the circular decree issued by the Ministry of the Interior on 18 August 1939, which had stipulated that newborns and infants up to the age of three years be registered, more than 40 per cent of those murdered in Görden were aged between three and thirteen years. (At the aforementioned Eglfing-Haar mental hospital, almost 60 per cent of the victims were older than three years of age.) As a rule, the children were murdered one at a time. For the most part, the barbiturate phenobarbital was used, administered as tablets or by injection, to induce hypostatic pneumonia, from which the children died. In this way, death from 'natural causes' could be simulated. (At Eglfing-Haar, 93 per cent of the children were murdered in this way.) It took between two and five days for the children to die. By the end of the war, a total of 1,270 children had died in the 'special children's ward' in Görden, while another 430 had been transferred from Görden to the gassing facilities of the so-called Operation T4 (*Aktion T4*) and murdered there.[9]

The majority of parents were tricked, deceived, pressurised and threatened into surrendering their children. The psychological, social and existential strain resulting from the war, when fathers were often away serving in the Wehrmacht and some mothers were likewise obliged to work, was also an important factor in parents agreeing to or even requesting their children to be admitted into care. This should not, though, be equated with a desire to see them killed, as many parents genuinely hoped that in this way their children's suffering might be alleviated. However, there were also parents who voluntarily delivered their children to the 'euthanasia' programme, knowing full well what this meant. No small number acquiesced in the murder of their disabled children because they saw it as an opportunity to rid themselves of a burden. Other parents called for the death of their disabled child in the spirit of the times. One father of a patient at Eglfing-Haar mental hospital enquired, also on behalf of his wife, whether it 'would not perhaps be best to eliminate such a child from the racial corpus, as that, I think, would also be in the interests of the state'.[10]

As the aforementioned statistics from Görden illustrate, not all the children transferred to the special killing wards were in fact murdered. According to the surviving medical files from the 'special children's ward' in Eglfing-Haar, for instance, a total of 312 children and adolescents were murdered (of whom 26 were killed following their transfer to the 'special children's ward' in Kaufbeuren), while 91 survived, resulting in a survival rate of 22.58 per cent; in other words, more than three-quarters of the children transferred to the children's ward were murdered. For the vast majority who survived, the physicians on site concluded after an initial examination that the children in question were not 'unworthy of life' after all, and thereby overturned the earlier decisions made by consultants of the Reich Committee. These children were then promptly discharged in order to make room for new admissions. Even then, however, not all parents collected their children. Relatives of the residents of the institution for mentally disabled children in Mosbach, for instance, were told in no uncertain terms: 'By order of the Reich Ministry of the Interior, the Schwarzacherhof Mental Hospital must be emptied with immediate effect. Collect your child *immediately*, or it will be transferred to another institution.' The relatives of 71 children responded to this call and collected their offspring, while the relatives of the remaining 28 did nothing. The institution to which these 28 were then transferred was the Grafeneck killing centre.[11]

More than 5,000 children were murdered in the framework of the child 'euthanasia' programme – that is, in the 'special children's wards' of the Reich Committee scheme – between 1939 and 1945. It must be borne in mind, however, that this figure does not include those mentally and physically disabled children murdered in the context of other 'euthanasia' schemes. During Operation T4, and indeed after its official discontinuation, further children were killed in institutions other than the 'special children's wards'. They were murdered by means of drugs, starvation or deliberate neglect without notifying in advance the headquarters of the ongoing 'euthanasia' programme. In particular – though not exclusively – children over the age of fourteen were killed in the gassing facilities of Operation T4. Around 4,500 of the total number of victims of the T4 programme, that is, almost 6 per cent, were not adults. Factoring these in yields a probable total number of child and adolescent victims of the killing campaign against the mentally and physically disabled in the German Reich in excess of 10,000. Children were also among the Polish psychiatric patients murdered by German troops following the invasion of Poland in September 1939.[12]

Polish Psychiatric Patients

The baby boy murdered near Leipzig in July 1939 provided the impetus for, and was indeed the earliest victim of, the 'annihilation of worthless life' – Nazi Germany's first mass-killing programme. Even before the murder of children had begun in earnest, however, the decision had been taken in July 1939 to extend the killing operations to include adult psychiatric patients. Hitler initially entrusted Reich Health Leader Leonardo Conti with the implementation of this expanded 'euthanasia' programme but, following a power struggle within the Nazi leadership, the Chancellery of the Führer succeeded in procuring a retraction of the order and the reassignment of the task to the two plenipotentiaries of the child 'euthanasia', Brandt and Bouhler. As with the child 'euthanasia', administrative direction by the Chancellery of the Führer ensured that neither the party, through its visible SS formations, nor the state, subject to budgetary controls, would be openly involved. In October of the same year, after the end of the military campaign against Poland, Hitler signed a letter of authorisation that had been prepared by the Chancellery of the Führer on Hitler's personal stationery but was never promulgated or published in any legal gazette. Though it did not actually have the force of law, it would serve as the official basis for the killing operations and was used to convince physicians to collaborate in the murders. The single sentence read: 'Reichsleiter Bouhler and Dr Brandt are charged with the responsibility for extending the authority of physicians, to be designated by name, so that, after a most careful assessment of their medical condition, they can grant a mercy death to patients whom they judge to be incurable.' This written authorisation was backdated to 1 September 1939, the day the Second World War had begun, in order to link the murder of patients to the perceived exigencies of the war. Bouhler again charged Brack and his Main Office II, which already ran the child 'euthanasia' programme, with the administrative details.[13]

Hitler's letter of authorisation also served another purpose: to legitimate the murder of the sick already under way in occupied Poland. The start of the war had triggered a veritable contest over control of the mental hospitals in the annexed Polish territories. Wehrmacht, SS and other Nazi Party institutions laid claim to these buildings – preferably completely vacated – above all for war-related purposes. The murder of psychiatric patients in the northern and western Polish territories occupied by the Germans commenced on 22 September 1939 with the shooting of around 2,000 mentally disabled people from the Kocborowo (Conradstein) mental hospital in the town of Starogard (Preußisch Stargard; now Starogard Gdański), south of Danzig, by a battalion-sized unit under the command of SS Major Kurt Eimann. In October and November, the same formation also carried out the murder of 1,400 German psychiatric patients from Pomerania, the Prussian province bordering on Poland in the north. Provincial Governor Franz Schwede-Coburg instructed his staff: 'Pick out the most disgusting sick people.' Selections were carried out by the individual doctors on site at the Pomeranian institutions. The victims from institutions in Stralsund, Lauenburg, Ueckermünde and Treptow arrived by train in the town of Wejherowo (Neustadt) in neighbouring Danzig-West Prussia, a newly created German province – known as a Reich Gau – encompassing the former Free City of Danzig and the area of West Prussia seized from Poland. There, they were taken to a nearby forest, where they were shot into pits dug by Polish political prisoners from Stutthof concentration camp near Danzig. Eimann personally shot the first victim. After the shooting had finished, the Stutthof prisoners filled in the pits and were then also shot by Eimann's battalion. The vacated institutions in Lauenburg and Stralsund were placed at the disposal of the SS, while the institution in Treptow served thereafter as a Wehrmacht hospital.[14]

In another newly created Reich Gau, the Wartheland – named after the Warta river (German: Warthe) that flowed through it from the southeast to the northwest – residents of several different psychiatric institutions were transported to Fort VII in Poznań (Posen) in autumn 1939 and murdered with carbon monoxide in a gas chamber erected in one of the large casemates. The first victims were patients from the mental hospital in the village of Owińska (Treskau), who were gassed there in October and November. This was the first example of such a form of killing and provides the beginnings of a methodological red thread running through to the industrialised mass murder of Jews in the extermination camps on Polish territory. Reichsführer SS and Chief of the German Police Heinrich Himmler personally attended a demonstration of this new method during a visit to Fort VII in December. Starting on 7 December, the clearance of the psychiatric institution in Dziekanka (Tiegenhof) near Gniezno (Gnesen) began; there, the ethnic German director, Victor Ratka, colluded with the occupiers. By Christmas 1939, at least 595 patients from Dziekanka had also been gassed at Fort VII. The man responsible for the killings at the fort, SS Second Lieutenant Herbert Lange, also murdered psychiatric patients by asphyxiating them in mobile gas vans using chemically pure carbon monoxide in steel cylinders. During the first months of 1940, patients from several institutions in the Wartheland were killed in this way: 532 patients in Kościan (Kosten), 499 in Warta, 107 in Gostynin and 600 in Kochanówka near Łódź. The institutions cleared in this way were then used for various purposes. For instance, an infantry battalion was billeted in Kościan, Warta received ethnic Germans from Romania and Gostynin was placed at the disposal of the Wehrmacht. Lange's gas vans were also used to murder 1,558 patients from various East Prussian institutions and around 300 Polish patients from the annexed territory of Ciechanów (Zichenau), who were deported to the transit camp in Działdowo (Soldau) in the second half of May 1940, where Lange and his special commando were stationed for nineteen days.[15]

Barbara Stimler, a Jewish girl from the small Polish town of Aleksandrów Kujawski, had been sent to the Kutno Ghetto in 1940 and then to the larger Łódź Ghetto the following year, where she initially worked in the children's hospital. There, aged fourteen, she witnessed the abduction of children from the hospital, who were then gassed in lorries:

> I was still working in this hospital for another month or six weeks, when two lorries came and they start[ed] loading up the children into the lorries, and we were wearing like long overalls, and these poor children, like they had a feeling that something [was] going to happen to them, they were hiding behind the overalls [and] didn't want to go into the lorries. But we were afraid also they shouldn't take us, and I mostly was

afraid if they take me who's going to look after my mother. It was terrible. Afterwards, we found out they gassed the children in the lorries.[16]

A total of at least 7,700 Polish and German mental patients were killed in the eastern borderlands of West Prussia, Pomerania, the Wartheland and East Prussia between September 1939 and spring 1940. However, the murder of Polish psychiatric patients was not limited to those Polish territories annexed to the German Reich. Killings also took place in the remaining German-held territory, the so-called Government General. For instance, on 12 January 1940, all 441 patients of the psychiatric hospital in the city of Chełm near Lublin, 17 children among them, were shot in front of the hospital entrance by SS forces using machine guns:

> At dusk, the soldiers drove the sick out of Building 2. At the exit, a machine gun was set up and the firing started, so that the sick people herded out of the hall were shot on the spot and fell on to a constantly growing heap of corpses. The unruly German [sic] patients were herded through the rooms and thrown out of first- or second-storey windows. One young girl suffering from a depressive disorder was chased by the Germans through the entire building, from one floor to the next, finally caught and thrown out of a second-storey window and then shot. [...] The most difficult task for the Germans was catching the children, patients of the children's ward, who dispersed on every floor and hid in cupboards, under beds, and so on. All the children were sought out and shot. The Germans guarded the heaps of corpses during the night. The groaning of the dying could be heard, as not all of the victims had been killed; some of them had only been seriously wounded.

The hospital buildings were subsequently used by the SS as barracks. Chełm also served as a fictitious place of death for those Jewish psychiatric patients who were gassed as part of Operation T4 from June 1940 onwards (as well as some non-Jewish patients), at a time when the psychiatric hospital in Chełm had long since ceased to exist.[17]

Clearly, the murder of mentally and physically disabled Poles had nothing to do with any attempts to strengthen the racial health of the German nation. The killing of patients in occupied Poland aimed instead, in the context of the war, at emptying buildings for use by German soldiers and civilians alike, and at eradicating 'useless eaters' who were regarded, furthermore, as racially inferior. By November 1939 at the latest, the mental asylums vacated as a result of the murder of psychiatric patients were the preferred provisional accommodation for thousands of ethnic Germans from the Baltic region. The ongoing spatial requirements of the newly appointed Reich commissioner for the strengthening of German nationhood (*Reichskommissar für die Festigung deutschen Volkstums*), Heinrich Himmler, no doubt contributed decisively to the continuation into 1941 of the violence that had been unleashed at the start of the war, as well as the dimensions it assumed. The killing of the disabled in occupied Poland between 1939 and 1941 was only the prelude to the huge killing operations that commenced with the invasion of the Soviet Union on 22 June 1941. In total, at least 16,500 Polish psychiatric patients – not including the victims of starvation and neglect – were murdered.[18]

Operation T4

Following Hitler's authorisation of an expanded 'euthanasia' programme, irrespective of the age of the victims, under the auspices of the Chancellery of the Führer, the systematic registration of institutional patients in the Reich commenced in October 1939. The directors of the mental hospitals were instructed in writing to report certain patients to the central planning office at Tiergartenstraße 4 in Berlin – from which Operation T4 took its name – on the basis of enclosed questionnaires. The questions related to the patients' need for long-term institutional care, their responsiveness to therapy, their behaviour, their capacity for work, the heritability of their illness and their family connections. The completed questionnaires were forwarded to consultants – almost exclusively renowned university and institutional psychiatrists – who then decided alone on this basis whether the patients would live or die. The prognosis of curability, the expense of care and the behaviour of the patient in question were all relevant criteria for the selection, but the patients' ability to work assumed crucial importance. If a patient was described in the questionnaire as a productive worker, he or she had by far the best chance of surviving Operation T4.[19]

The foundation for the initiation of Operation T4, however, was a radical willingness to use violence against mentally ill and disabled people, which was based on the racial–ideological idea of a healthy, highly efficient and able-bodied racial corpus. The Nazi regime did not want to eradicate unproductive workers as such, but rather people they considered genetically inferior and, among them, first and foremost those who could not (or could no longer) be employed. No German worker who failed to meet demands in production was sent to their death for a lack of efficiency or considerations of food supply. Racial-hygiene motives and perceived usefulness in wartime were at all times closely interrelated. The discussions since the end of the First World War demonstrate that these two factors did not exclude but rather complemented each other and radicalised not only racial ideology but also the discourse on 'euthanasia'.[20]

This approach was summed up by Kurt Pohlisch, professor of psychiatry in Bonn and T4 consultant:

> The realisation that everything is at stake has also brought about a change in connection with National Socialist education with regard to the assessment of sickness. In contrast to the healthy and able-bodied person, the sick person is not considered fully capable. The previously exclusive sentiment of only sympathising with the sick – a sentiment that reflects the former humanitarian notion – has been joined by a new factor beyond the personal: the assessment of a person according to their productivity for society as a whole.[21]

The chronology of Operation T4 clearly demonstrates how heavily this 'euthanasia' programme, too, was dependent on the events of the war. The registration of the institutional patients was already temporally staggered; the psychiatric institutions in the southwest and the northeast of the Reich were the first to receive the questionnaires. From January 1940 onwards, it was in precisely these two regions that the first two killing centres commenced operations, namely Grafeneck Castle near the town of Gomadingen in Württemberg and the old prison in Brandenburg an der Havel. As hostilities had already taken place or were imminent in these two territories, a connection between the course of Operation T4 and the planning for the military campaign is clear. The T4 organisers evidently calculated that the murder of the psychiatric patients would make accommodation available for military hospitals for the Wehrmacht's impending campaign in the west.[22]

This is shown by the example of Bedburg-Hau, the largest German psychiatric hospital at the time, with more than 2,500 beds. It was located at the Dutch border and thus in the deployment zone for the Wehrmacht's planned invasion of the Netherlands and Belgium. As insufficient time remained for the scheduled registration and review process, a more flexible approach was taken: a team of consultants arrived in Bedburg on 26 February 1940 and, within a week, completed the questionnaires for all potential candidates for 'euthanasia' among the patients. In early March, those patients selected as 'unworthy of life' were deported to the killing centres at Grafeneck and Brandenburg, while those classified as 'worthy of life' were transferred to other institutions. Within the space of ten days, the largest psychiatric institution in Germany had been completely emptied.[23]

The T4 physicians used medication to kill disabled children in the 'special children's wards', but in order to kill the far larger number of disabled people resulting from the expansion of the 'euthanasia' programme to include adults – estimates of 70,000 victims were circulating as early as autumn 1939 – they had to devise a different, more efficient method. Brandt, Conti and Dr Albert Widmann, head of the chemistry section at the Forensic Institute of the Security Police, eventually decided to use gas, whereupon the T4 technicians set about establishing special killing centres. Although there were differences between the various killing centres, the killing process itself was the same in all of them, and the facilities were therefore roughly similar. During his post-war testimony at Nuremberg, Viktor Brack described the simple design of the actual gas chambers in all killing centres:

> No special gas chamber was built. A room suitable in the planning of the hospital was used, a room attached to the reception ward, and the room where the insane persons were taken, where they were kept. That was made into a gas chamber. It was sealed, it was given special doors and windows, and then a few metres of gas pipe were laid, some kind of pipe with holes in it. Outside of this room there was a bottle, a compressed bottle, with the necessary apparatus, necessary instruments, a pressure gauge, etc.

The T4 managers chose the old prison in Brandenburg an der Havel as the site for the testing of gas as a killing method, thus making it history's first operational killing centre. The gassing demonstration, carried out on eight male patients no later than January 1940, was attended by numerous high-ranking officials, including Karl Brandt, Philipp Bouhler, Viktor Brack, Leonardo Conti, Paul Nitsche and the subsequent head of the Brandenburg killing centre, Irmfried Eberl.[24]

On 3 April 1940, Brack instructed a gathering of the German Council of Municipalities (*Deutscher Gemeindetag*) on the rationale behind the expanded 'euthanasia' programme. According to the notes of one of the participants, the head mayor of the town of Plauen, Eugen Wörner, Brack's remarks provide a remarkable smorgasbord of justifications for the murder of the mentally ill:

> In the many mental hospitals in the Reich, an endless number of incurably sick people of all kinds are accommodated, who are of no use to humankind and, on the contrary, constitute a burden and create never-ending supply costs, and there is no prospect of these people ever becoming healthy again. They are vegetating there, like animals; they are antisocial people unworthy of life [. . .]. They only deprive others of food and often require double and triple forms of care. The rest of the people must be protected from these people. If we are faced already today with the need to make provision for the preservation of healthy people, however, then it is all the more necessary that we eradicate these creatures first of all, if only for the better care of the curably sick people accommodated in the mental asylums. The space made available is required for all sorts of things vital to the war effort: military hospitals, clinics, auxiliary hospitals. The operation furthermore greatly relieves the pressure on the municipalities, because in each and every case the future costs for accommodation and care cease to apply.

It is striking how ideological considerations and material motives are strung together here as a matter of course. Brack justifies the murder of psychiatric patients, on the one hand, in terms of hereditary health and racial policy as the swiftest possible form of applied racial hygiene. Second, he vilifies the victims as 'useless eaters', who are of no value to society and whose eradication saves money and foodstuffs. Third, Brack argues that the 'annihilation of worthless life' creates much-needed capacity for the treatment of psychiatric patients classified as curable, though especially for the treatment of soldiers and members of the civilian population. This third argument in particular illustrates once again the importance of the war in the initiation and justification of the 'euthanasia' killing programmes.[25]

After Grafeneck and Brandenburg, a third killing centre began operating in May 1940: Hartheim Castle near Linz in Upper Austria, close to Mauthausen concentration camp. A month later, killing started in a fourth institution: Sonnenstein Castle in Pirna near Dresden. Rumours about what was taking place at Grafeneck Castle spread during the second half of 1940 and unrest among the local population grew. On 25 November, the wife of Walter Buch, chief justice of the Supreme Party Court of the NSDAP, received a letter from an acquaintance, Else von Löwis. In her letter, Löwis revealed that events at Grafeneck were no longer secret and expressed shock at the manner and scope of the killings (though without questioning the 'euthanasia' programme as such). She requested Buch's wife to pass the letter on to her husband. On 7 December, Buch wrote to Heinrich Himmler, enclosing the letter. In his reply to Buch from 19 December, Himmler wrote:

> I can inform you in confidence that the events taking place there are carried out with the authorisation of the Führer by a panel of physicians. [...] When the matter becomes known to the public, as it evidently has there, then the process must be faulty. On the other hand, it is clear that the process will always be difficult. I will immediately contact the agency concerned and bring these defects to their attention and advise them to put Grafeneck to sleep.

It is unclear whether Himmler intentionally or involuntarily used the telling expression 'put to sleep'. He did exactly as he told Buch he would and wrote to Viktor Brack the very same day. He informed Brack of 'the great commotion' caused by events at Grafeneck, and advised him to 'discontinue the operation of the institution'. The public response to the rumours thus led directly to the closure of the Grafeneck site in December 1940, and indeed the Brandenburg site, too, in October. There, complaints from local residents about the smoke and stench from the crematorium had already led the authorities to move the incinerators to a location out of town that summer. Closing these sites, however, was merely a tactical ruse. The personnel of

Brandenburg and Grafeneck were transferred as a group to a new killing centre, the former to Bernburg on the Saale river and the latter to Hadamar near Limburg an der Lahn. In both cases, the replacement centre commenced operations a mere month after the closure of its predecessor: Bernburg in November 1940 and Hadamar, as the last killing centre to be set up, in January 1941. Six killing centres were thus established, though only four operated at any one time.[26]

Each killing centre was broadly responsible for murdering disabled patients from institutions in a limited geographical region. The territory assigned to the Brandenburg killing centre included the Prussian provinces of Brandenburg, Saxony and Schleswig-Holstein, the states of Brunswick, Mecklenburg, Anhalt and Hamburg, and the city of Berlin. Later, the replacement centre of Bernburg assumed this territory. The Grafeneck killing centre covered southern Germany, that is, the states of Bavaria, Württemberg and Baden, as well as some northern German institutions. Later, the replacement centre of Hadamar handled this territory, in addition to the state of Hesse and the Prussian province of Hanover. The Hartheim killing centre was responsible for institutions in Austria but also some institutions in southern Germany and Saxony. The Sonnenstein killing centre covered the states of Saxony and Thuringia and the Prussian province of Silesia but also some institutions in southern Germany.[27]

The public response that led to the closures of Brandenburg and Grafeneck forced the T4 organisers to re-evaluate the operation's procedures. Beginning in autumn 1940, patients were collected in transit institutions, whose own patients had been killed to make room, and after two or three weeks were transferred from there as a group to the killing centre in question. Thus, patients left the surrendering institution for the transit institution and, from there, were taken to the killing centre. This increase in movement ensured greater secrecy regarding the final destination. It also added an extra layer of disinformation given to the relatives, who received notice of the patient's arrival at and then departure from the transit institution, thus confusing the matter and making complaints less effective. Again, relatives were not permitted to visit during this hiatus. Transit institutions were established across Germany. Each transit institution served as a collection point for a specific killing centre and each killing centre received patients from several of these institutions.[28]

Just as institutionalised Jewish patients had not been exempted from the compulsory sterilisation law, the onset of the 'euthanasia' killings naturally affected disabled Jewish patients, too. The murder of disabled Jews is documented for the Grafeneck, Brandenburg and Bernburg killing centres during the period from January to December 1940. Jews were thus victims of the 'euthanasia' killings from the beginning. In fact, they were often among the first to be transferred to the killing centres. The decision systematically to murder all Jewish patients still in German hospitals was taken as early as spring 1940. On 15 April, the Reich Ministry of the Interior requested all local authorities to report within three weeks the numbers of Jewish patients in state hospitals and nursing homes. The patients in question were then transferred to assembly centres and, from there, to the killing centres. All 4,000 to 5,000 Jewish patients institutionalised in Germany were systematically murdered in the framework of the 'euthanasia' programme without allowing for any exceptions regarding the nature of their illness or their ability to work, in contrast to other groups of patients. The decision to murder disabled Jewish patients forms an important link between 'euthanasia' and the later genocide of the Jews because it reveals the accelerated efforts to draw more targeted groups into the killing enterprise. The systematic murder of Jews thus began in the T4 killing centres on German soil.[29]

On 24 August 1941, Hitler officially ended Operation T4, the expanded 'euthanasia' programme. He gave the order to Karl Brandt, who transmitted it to the Chancellery of the Führer. By summer 1941, the secret 'euthanasia' killings had become common knowledge and were even known in neutral countries, as well as in the nations fighting against Germany. As Victor Klemperer, a German literary scholar of Jewish origin, noted in his diary on 22 August: 'There is now general talk of the killing of the mentally sick in the asylums.' After the purpose of the questionnaires, the destinations of the grey deportation buses and the function of the killing centres had all become well known, considerable unrest emerged among the general public. This reaction, as well as the critical stance of several clergymen, should not be equated, however, with a general rejection of the murder of the mentally ill. It was rather the way in which Operation T4 was implemented and especially its clandestine nature and potentially unlimited scope that provoked such unease. The widespread knowledge of the killings and the general popular disquiet about the way in which 'euthanasia' was implemented were the principal reasons for Hitler's decision, just as these same factors had led Himmler to suggest the closure of Grafeneck in late autumn 1940.[30]

In a famous sermon on 3 August 1941, the bishop of Münster, Count Clemens August von Galen, channelled these anxieties and openly condemned the murder of the mentally ill. As courageous as Galen's words were, he was by no means the lone voice in the wilderness, as has sometimes been suggested. His speech was preceded by public denunciations of 'euthanasia' by German Protestants. Indeed, Galen's protest came over a year after he had first heard about what was taking place at asylums in his diocese. Perhaps most importantly, his sermon alone would hardly have had the impact it did had it not reflected widespread popular disquiet and, moreover, been fuelled by two significant war-related factors. First, the Blitzkrieg campaign against the Soviet Union had stalled. Second, the Royal Air Force had intensified its aerial bombardments, particularly against the major Catholic centres in northwestern Germany, including Münster itself. The Nazi regime feared as a result of these two developments that the public's confidence in a swift victory in the war might be tempered. It opted, therefore, to shield the people from any fuel for conflict that might distract from the real objective, namely winning the war.[31]

A statistician employed by T4 compiled a summary of the numbers of patients killed at each of the centres up to the end of August 1941, arriving at a total of 70,273 'disinfections', that is, people murdered – remarkably close to the number of victims anticipated in autumn 1939. Hartheim accounted for the largest share of the victims, with a total of 18,269 dead. The swiftest rate of killing, however, was reached at Hadamar, where 10,072 patients were murdered in just over seven months between January and August 1941. The staff there celebrated the burning of the 10,000th victim with a mock ceremony in the basement crematorium. The naked corpse was laid out on a stretcher, covered with flowers, and the office manager at Hadamar, Walter Bünger, made a speech; every member of staff received a bottle of beer. Of the overall figure of 70,273 T4 victims, 35,224 were killed in 1940 and 35,049 in 1941. Other sources, however, suggest a total number of 80,000 patients killed at the six sites during the period in question, though the actual figure might have been even higher. The report, found after the war at Hartheim, also provided an exact account of projected future expenditures saved by killing the disabled. The T4 statistician calculated that

70,273 'disinfections' saved the German Reich 885,439,800 marks over a period of ten years – a macabre utilitarianism designed to rationalise the eugenic and racial ideology that created the killing centres and fuelled the mass murder.[32]

Unlike the unrest that had led to the closure of Grafeneck and Brandenburg a year earlier, the official stop to the expanded 'euthanasia' programme in August 1941 did not in fact result in the termination of any of the four killing centres still in use: Hartheim, Sonnenstein, Bernburg and Hadamar. Operation T4 resumed with great intensity but out of public view, while child 'euthanasia' – which had never utilised the gassing facilities – not only continued without interruption but was indeed intensified; many of the 'special children's wards' were established only after the stop. In fact, more victims of 'euthanasia' perished after the stop order was issued than before. What did change, however, were the killing methods used in the expanded 'euthanasia' programme. During this second phase, it was no longer gas but rather intentional neglect, starvation rations or overdoses of medication that were employed to bring about the death of patients. In Hadamar, for example, the systematic killings were resumed in August 1942, after the gassing facilities had been demolished there at the end of July, and continued until March 1945. The gassing facilities at Sonnenstein were likewise dismantled in summer 1942, after which the castle was used as a Wehrmacht hospital. Bernburg was not terminated until April 1943. Hartheim was the last of the six killing centres to be shut down; it stayed in operation until December 1944.[33]

Parallel to the resumption of the murders in the remaining T4 killing centres, the 'annihilation of worthless life' was also carried out in a more decentralised fashion: physicians in designated institutions were empowered to kill selected patients through medication or starvation. Hospitals with 'special children's wards' used for child 'euthanasia', such as Eichberg, Kalmenhof (both in Hesse) and the aforementioned Eglfing-Haar (Bavaria), which had also functioned as transit institutions for the expanded 'euthanasia' programme, were deemed obvious places for also killing adults following Hitler's stop order. Two institutions, Meseritz-Obrawalde in Pomerania and the aforementioned Dziekanka in the Wartheland, whose location at the eastern border of the German Reich served to hide mass death from the German population, were converted into killing hospitals. Finally, a vast number of hospitals that were unable after 1941 to utilise the central killing centres simply murdered their disabled patients themselves.[34]

The murder of psychiatric patients in the German Reich and the annexed Polish territories between 1939 and 1941 was Nazi Germany's first mass-killing programme and had in a number of respects a pioneering function for the Nazis' subsequent mass-murder campaigns: for the first time, they murdered a group of people defined by them in ideological terms; no distinction was made between age groups – indeed, children were among the earliest victims; the six T4 killing centres were the first institutions in history to be set up exclusively for the purpose of murdering their inmates, thus anticipating the extermination camps used to carry out the mass murder of Europe's Jews on an industrial scale. More than just a prologue, the 'euthanasia' killings were the first chapter of Nazi genocide.

Perhaps not surprisingly then, the programme for the systematic murder of psychiatric patients exhibits remarkable parallels to the murder of Europe's Jews from 1941 onwards. Not only were a large number of people murdered using gas in special killing centres, but a complex process based on a division of labour was developed, by means of which the victims were to be deceived until the last moment, the perpetrators seemingly freed from all responsibility and the secrecy of the entire programme ensured. The repeated transfer of the victims, the deployment of medical doctors for performing examinations or selections and the introduction of the criterion of 'unfitness for work' are all elements that illustrate the direct links between the two murder programmes.[35]

CHAPTER 2
DECAPITATION OF POLISH SOCIETY

More than a century after the three partitions of the Polish–Lithuanian Commonwealth in 1772, 1793 and 1795, Poland had re-emerged as a nation-state in 1918 in the aftermath of the First World War. It comprised territory that had previously belonged to the German, Russian and Austro-Hungarian empires, all of which had now ceased to exist in their previous forms. In June 1919, the Versailles peace treaty had granted an area of 51,800 km^2 to Poland at the expense of Germany. For the latter, then, Poland was an ever-present physical reminder of the defeat of 1918 and the substantial territorial losses Germany had incurred. The German invasion of Poland in 1939 and its subsequent occupation policy were designed to reverse these developments and literally erase Poland from the map, just as the Third Partition had done in 1795.

During the conquest of Poland in September and early October 1939, the German occupiers began with the systematic ethnic cleansing of the Polish ruling classes and elites. This took place parallel to and sometimes in conjunction with the killing of Polish psychiatric patients in the territories annexed to Germany. Politicians, landowners, teachers, lawyers, physicians, clerics, senior civil servants and intellectuals were arrested and murdered as pillars of Polish national identity and potential focal points for resistance to German rule. The dual aim of this decapitation was to obliterate the Polish nation and any sense of Polish national identity, on the one hand, and then reduce the leaderless Polish people to the status of slave labourers for the German Reich, on the other.

Operation Tannenberg

The seeds of this campaign had been sown on 31 July 1939 with the conclusion of a formal agreement between SS Major General Reinhard Heydrich, who was the chief of both the Security Police (*Sicherheitspolizei*, or Sipo) – which comprised the Secret State Police (*Geheime Staatspolizei*, or Gestapo) and the

Criminal Police (*Kriminalpolizei*, or Kripo) – and the Nazi Party's own Security Service (*Sicherheitsdienst*, or SD), and Colonel Eduard Wagner, the chief of staff to the quartermaster general of the German army. According to this agreement, Einsatzgruppen, special mobile detachments of SS security policemen and SD agents, would be responsible during the Polish campaign for 'the suppression of all anti-Reich and anti-German elements in enemy territory behind the fighting troops' and their transfer to concentration camps. However, the agreement explicitly prohibited the Einsatzgruppen from mistreating or killing detained individuals; the reality on the ground would look very different. The Army General Staff's knowledge of the intended deployment of Einsatzgruppen in Poland – though probably not of their precise mission – in fact dated back at least to the early spring, as shown by a speech delivered by the chief of the General Staff, Franz Halder, to generals and other staff officers in April 1939, whom he informed that 'the occupation of the country' would be 'carried out to a large extent by paramilitary formations of the party'.[1]

On 25 August, Reichsführer SS Heinrich Himmler instructed Heydrich to set up a special section within the Sipo Main Office in Berlin for organising Einsatzgruppen operations in Poland; it was codenamed 'Tannenberg' after the iconic First World War victory over the Russians in East Prussia. One such task force was subsequently assigned to each of the five German armies that would participate in the invasion of Poland. During the first week of hostilities, they were reinforced by two further Einsatzgruppen and three regiments of SS Death's Head units temporarily freed from concentration-camp duty. Though the Einsatzgruppen – in accordance with the Heydrich–Wagner agreement – were fundamentally subordinated to the Wehrmacht in the area of operations, that is, when it came to their march route, supplies or accommodation, they received orders relating to their specific tasks from the chief of the Security Police and the SD in Berlin.[2]

Events during the first week of September made it clear to all concerned the exact nature of the remit given to the Einsatzgruppen, in spite of the restrictions nominally imposed on them by the Heydrich–Wagner agreement. Two days into the military campaign, on 3 September, Himmler ordered all Einsatzgruppen 'to shoot on the spot [. . .] Polish insurgents who are caught in the act or with a weapon in their hands'. Four days later, Heydrich informed senior officials from Sipo and SD: 'The leading social classes in Poland are to be rendered harmless as far as possible.' Assisted by Wehrmacht formations, the Einsatzgruppen proceeded to decimate the ranks of the Polish leadership. By order of Himmler, they were then joined in mid-September by the newly founded *Volksdeutscher Selbstschutz*; within a matter of weeks, these 'self-defence' units had recruited at least 100,000 men among ethnic Germans native to Poland. On 21 September, Heydrich was able to announce to the same audience of Sipo and SD officials, this time joined from Poland by the Einsatzgruppen commanders, that 3 per cent of the Polish leadership at most was still in the occupied territories. This 3 per cent, he ordered, also had to be rendered harmless. As Hitler put it, 'only a nation whose upper levels are destroyed can be pushed into the ranks of slavery'.[3]

Up to 26 October 1939, that is, during the first fifty-five days of German military rule in Poland, around 20,000 Polish civilians were murdered. This figure does not include those who died as a result of air raids and artillery bombardments. It furthermore does not include Polish prisoners of war, 3,000 of whom were killed away from the battlefield in September alone. This violence was applied not only by the SS and police forces but also by regular units of the Wehrmacht. Indeed, German army formations were responsible for the deaths of more than half of all Polish non-combatants murdered during the period in question. Alleged guerrillas were shot, as were civilians selected at random following attacks on German troops. In individual cases, German soldiers massacred Polish prisoners of war whom they took for irregulars for no better reason than their lingering in wooded areas. The German troops suspected the inhabitants of Polish towns and villages collectively of partisan activity, although a genuine partisan move-ment, in which substantial sections of the population participated, did not exist in Poland in autumn 1939. This approach was reminiscent of the German advance through Belgium and northern France in 1914, when regular troops had killed thousands of civilians for largely imagined irreg-ular attacks. Twenty-five years later, the experiences of the First World War still served as a reference point for the German military.[4]

Polish civilians were murdered from the very outset of the military campaign. After a shooting incident during the night of 1–2 September in the small village of Torzeniec, 10km east of the border town of Ostrzeszów (Schildberg), the cause of which remained unknown but which left three German soldiers dead, the commander of Infantry Regiment 41 had all male inhabitants of Torzeniec sentenced to death the following morning and the sentence immediately enforced against every second man. On the afternoon of 4 September, an exchange of gunfire also took place under unexplained circumstances in the courtyard of a vocational school in Częstochowa (Tschenstochau), resulting in the death of eight German soldiers. The prompt search of neighbouring properties and buildings yielded neither suspects nor firearms. Retributive action was nonetheless launched immediately by Infantry Regiment 42, to which the dead soldiers had belonged, and cost the lives of 227 men, women and children from Częstochowa, including many Jews.[5]

On 5 September, the first members of the German Fourth Army entered Bydgoszcz (Bromberg), which had been situated in the Polish Corridor since 1920 and where, on 3 and 4 September, Polish reprisals following attacks by German saboteurs and paramilitaries within the city had resulted in the deaths of several hundred Germans. The Nazis used the German deaths as a pretext for lethal retaliatory measures and coined the propaganda term 'Bloody Sunday' (*Blutsonntag*). Wehrmacht and police units promptly commenced with so-called pacification operations within the city. After assuming control in Bydgoszcz on 8 September, the commander of the Fourth Army's rear area, Brigadier Walter Braemer, took stock:

> Pacification operations so far, set in motion by the individual troop formations, have resulted in the following: 200–300 Polish civilians shot. Report from the local headquarters in Bromberg. Provisional Lord Mayor Kampe estimates the number of those shot at no fewer than 400. Exact figures cannot be established. Carried out by police, SD Einsatzgruppe [IV] and troops, primarily the 1st Aerial Signals Regiment.

Braemer, however, was determined to escalate the measures of his predecessor.[6]

On 11 September, at which point the city had been under his command for only three days, Braemer summarised: 'An assessment of those shot and killed since my arrival in Bromberg yields a figure of around 370.' In stark contrast to this number, the only German casualties during the same period were one dead policeman, one dead member of the Luftwaffe, both killed during the night of 7–8 September, and two wounded soldiers. Victims of the shootings carried out by German units included clerics, Jews, women and adolescents. When Roland Freisler – who would later achieve infamy as the president of the

People's Court (*Volksgerichtshof*) – arrived in the city on 9 September in order to learn whether the special tribunal appointed the day before to try the Polish culprits of Bloody Sunday had already delivered any verdicts, Einsatzgruppe IV made it known that 'no more perpetrators were available to pass judgement on'. Nonetheless, by the end of the year, this special tribunal alone had managed to find 168 people to put on trial, of whom it sentenced 100 to death.[7]

An excerpt from the personal war diary of a member of a regiment of the German 29th Motorised Infantry Division describes the execution of 300 Polish POWs from a battalion of the 7th Infantry Division on 8 September near Ciepielów. The massacre was preceded by heavy fighting in a wooded area, during which a German captain had been killed by a shot to the head:

> An hour later, everyone gathers on the road. The company counts fourteen dead, including Captain von Lewinski. The regimental commander, Colonel Wessel ([from] Kassel), is furious: 'What insolence to attempt to hold us up, and they've shot my Lewinski.' The squaddies don't count for anything with him. He concludes that they're partisans, although every one of the 300 captive Poles is wearing a uniform. They have to remove their tunics. Now they look more like partisans. [...] Five minutes later, I hear the roar of a dozen German sub-machine guns. I hurry in the same direction and see [...] the 300 Polish prisoners lying in the roadside ditch, shot dead. I risk taking two photos.[8]

There are also documented instances during the military campaign of entire groups of Polish prisoners being burned to death in barns or other buildings, for example in Urycz in late September, where members of an unidentified Wehrmacht unit killed around a hundred Polish soldiers in this way. A similar incident took place on 12 September in Szczucin. A Polish lieutenant managed to shoot and kill a German during the former's interrogation. VIII Army Corps succinctly described its response in a cable: 'It is currently unclear how the Pole obtained the weapon. All prisoners, including the lieutenant, have been shot; the prison camp has been torched.' Polish eyewitnesses described the incident in more detail after the war:

> The German reaction was as instantaneous as it was ruthless. Hand grenades were thrown into the building and heavy fire opened through

the windows and doors. The building started to burn. The Polish soldiers trapped in it were being burned alive. [...] Some soldiers tried to jump from the upper storey and the roof of the building, but the Germans shot at them and killed them on the spot. The groaning of dying people could be heard until late at night.

Around 40 Polish soldiers and approximately 30 Polish refugees died in the course of this massacre. A group of Jews were forced to bury the corpses, after which 25 of them were killed on the spot and interred with the other dead.[9]

On 11 September, following fighting against the German XIX Panzer Corps, 4,000 soldiers of the Polish 18th Infantry Division were assembled in a camp on open ground. The guards informed them that anyone who stood up from his encampment during the night would be shot on the spot. The entire field was lit up with floodlights and motor vehicles mounted with machine guns were placed at each corner of the camp. In circumstances that remain unclear, a herd of Polish army horses accommodated next to the camp escaped and stormed the field, endangering the lives of the sleeping soldiers. Panic broke out among the Polish prisoners, at which point the German guards opened fire into the crowd and did not stop firing for fully ten minutes, when it was discovered that German soldiers had also been wounded by mistake. When the shooting stopped, the surviving Polish prisoners were once more told that no movement was allowed. No one came to the aid of the wounded and dying. In the morning, 200 dead and 100 wounded Polish soldiers were counted. The incidents described above were by no means isolated acts of excess but a mass phenomenon that manifested itself in all operational areas of the Wehrmacht in September 1939. Clearly, even at the outset of the war, the threshold for resorting to excessive violence was exceedingly low among German officers and enlisted men.[10]

The largest of more than 700 massacres carried out by German forces against local civilians during the German–Polish war was committed in Przemyśl on the San river, the eastern frontier of German-occupied Poland and the new German–Soviet border. Between 16 and 19 September, Einsatzgruppe z.b.V. (*zur besonderen Verwendung* = for special assignment) under SS Lieutenant General Udo von Woyrsch killed as many as 600 Polish Jews, though regular Wehrmacht soldiers – members of the Fourteenth

Army – also participated in the shooting operations. Evidently, this particular Einsatzgruppe had been systematically targeting Jews since the start of the second week of the war during its advance from East Upper Silesia to Galicia. Before its arrival in Przemyśl, it had already shot several hundred Jews in Będzin (Bendsburg) a week earlier and murdered more than 30 Jews in a wooded area close to Wieliczka near Cracow and then 170 Jews in Dynów; in both Będzin and Dynów, Woyrsch's Einsatzgruppe also burned down the synagogue. Not all German police, SS and army units that killed civilians in Poland in September and October 1939 targeted Jews in this way, however, and Jews remained a minority among the victims of the massacres carried out during these first eight weeks of the Second World War.[11]

Hitler's decree of 4 October, stipulating that those responsible for the deeds committed in the occupied Polish territories since 1 September 'out of bitterness over the atrocities perpetrated by the Poles' would not be prosecuted, signalled his explicit support for the killings and effectively nipped in the bud the isolated protests of what was in reality but a few Wehrmacht officers against the actions of SS and police units. Himmler's appointment as Reich commissioner for the strengthening of German nationhood on 7 October also acted as a catalyst. Accordingly, from early October onwards, a dramatic increase in the number of killings carried out by the Einsatzgruppen and the ethnic German Selbstschutz is apparent. Larger numbers of women and children were now also among the victims. The 83 Poles and Jews shot by the Selbstschutz in Świecie (Schwetz) on 7 and 8 October, for instance, included 28 women and 10 children aged between two and eight.[12]

On 14 October, nine days after the surrender of the last Polish troops, Heydrich openly stipulated in person to his senior officials from Sipo and SD that the 'liquidation of the Polish leadership' already under way had to be completed by 1 November. Significantly, this was the date on which Hitler's annexation order regarding the incorporation of the northern and western Polish territories into the German Reich was scheduled to take effect. As it turned out, Hitler decided to accelerate the transfer of German rule in Poland to senior Nazi Party officials. At a meeting in the Reich Chancellery on 17 October, he told the chief of the Wehrmacht High Command (*Oberkommando der Wehrmacht*, or OKW), Wilhelm Keitel, that the military should be pleased to be rid of the burden of responsibility in Poland. The hard struggle between two nations necessitated, in Hitler's view, that the occupation regime be freed from any legal obligations. Clearly, Hitler was keen to remove any potential obstacles to a continuation of the killings he had explicitly endorsed in his amnesty decree of 4 October. As a result, the annexation order came into force on 26 October, six days earlier than planned; the military government in Poland was dissolved and replaced by a civil administration. Heydrich's stipulation at the meeting of 14 October reveals his evident concern that the civil administrations due to replace the departing military might somehow limit his freedom of action. Although Heydrich did not attend the meeting of 17 October, his boss – Himmler – did; Heydrich's unease regarding the future of his mass-murder campaign against Polish civilians can, therefore, only have been short-lived.[13]

Intelligentsia Operation

Heydrich need not have worried about the attitude of the new administrative chieftains in the annexed Polish territories to the murder of local elites there. After the end of the German–Polish war, the terror was systematised in the so-called Intelligentsia Operation (*Intelligenzaktion*), and SS commandos now implemented their tasks with increased energy and brutality. As the Polish government-in-exile subsequently recognised in *The Black Book of Poland*, published in 1942: 'It appeared that the Germans had determined to exterminate entirely the leading elements in the Western provinces of Poland.' The new regional governors in occupied Poland collaborated closely with the SS here. Shortly before his appointment as NSDAP Gauleiter and Reich governor in the newly created Wartheland, Arthur Greiser had attended the aforementioned meeting with Heydrich on 14 October. He also maintained close contact with Heydrich's boss, Heinrich Himmler. In August 1940, he was even named Himmler's regional deputy in the latter's function as Reich commissioner for the strengthening of German nationhood. In his endeavours to 'Germanise' the Wartheland, Greiser did not shy away from ordering the deportation and murder of hundreds of thousands of Poles and Jews. In neighbouring Danzig–West Prussia, there was a similar willingness to wipe out the Polish ruling classes and elites. The head of Einsatzkommando 16, stationed in Bydgoszcz, reported that Hitler's desire for a transformation of Polish Pomerania into German West Prussia 'in a minimum of time' required, 'in the unanimous opinion of all relevant authorities', the 'physical liquidation of all those Polish elements that a) have come to the fore in any way as leaders on the Polish side in the past or b) could be bearers of Polish resistance in the future'. In those territories of Poland not annexed to the German Reich, Governor General Hans Frank issued a new Regulation for Combating Acts of Violence on 31 October that threatened any form of non-compliance with the death penalty.[14]

The express desire to kill all Poles who 'could be bearers of Polish resistance in the future' meant that not even Polish schoolchildren were safe, especially when German retaliation for even the most trivial of incidents was often barbaric. On one occasion in the village of Obłuże, near Gdynia (Gdingen) in what had now become Danzig–West Prussia, the German authorities arrested some fifty Polish schoolboys in response to the alleged smashing of a windowpane in the local police station on the night of 11 November 1939. The Germans demanded that the schoolboys name the culprit. Unable to learn who was responsible, they ordered the boys' parents to thrash them publicly in front of the church. When the parents refused, SS men brutally beat the schoolboys, shot ten of them and forbade the removal of the bodies, which lay for twenty-four hours in front of the church.[15]

One of the most infamous mass-murder sites of the Intelligentsia Operation was Piaśnica Wielka (Groß Piasnitz) near Wejherowo in Danzig–West Prussia. From the second half of October 1939 until April 1940, between 10,000 and 12,000 inhabitants of Danzig, Gdynia, Wejherowo and Kartuzy (Karthaus), as well as 1,400 German psychiatric patients from several Pomeranian institutions, were killed in the woods around Piaśnica. One of the victims of the Piaśnica massacres was the head of the convent at Wejherowo, Sister Alicja Kotowska. She had been arrested by the Gestapo on 24 October 1939 during prayer. The nuns knew that one of the workers at the convent was an ethnic German. Before she left the convent, Sister Alicja declared: 'I forgive Franciszek for everything.' On 11 November, National Independence Day in Poland, Sister Alicja was among 314 Poles and Jews murdered at Piaśnica. The killings that day lasted from early morning until three in the afternoon. Men and women were led in groups of five to the previously dug graves and shot. Some of the victims were buried alive. Witnesses report that, as she was being transported from the prison to the execution site, Sister Alicja huddled with and comforted Jewish children who were also going to their deaths in Piaśnica. Though the post-war exhumation failed to identify her corpse, it did uncover a grave containing a rosary of the kind worn by the sisters of her order.[16]

Even the official dissolution of the Einsatzgruppen on 20 November 1939 and the allocation of their personnel to other newly created offices in the annexed Polish territories did not signal an end to the killing. In the areas of Poland allocated to East Prussia, the Einsatzgruppe operating there at the end of the military campaign had initially transferred its prisoners, predominantly members of the Polish elites, to the State Police regional headquarters in Königsberg. When SS Brigadier Otto Rasch took up his duties there as inspector of the Security Police and the SD in early November, however, he arranged for those prisoners whom he considered to 'comprise political activists from Polish movements' to be shot'. The mass shooting took place in a forested area in January 1940. Heydrich then tasked Rasch with the establishment of a transit camp in Działdowo, with the purpose of continuing the massacres in East Prussia without attracting attention. It was here that Herbert Lange's special commando used its gas vans to murder 1,558 psychiatric patients from various East Prussian institutions.[17]

Rasch was not alone in preferring to kill Poles rather than detain them for an indefinite period. One Selbstschutz commander, SS Colonel Wilhelm Richardt, told the men in the Karolewo (Karlshof) internment camp that he did not want to have to build big camps and feed Poles, and added cynically that it was an honour for Poles to fertilise German soil with their corpses. SS Senior Colonel Ludolf von Alvensleben, district commander of the Selbstschutz in West Prussia, toured the province, encouraging his SS officers from the Reich to shoot more Poles. Selbstschutz units operated in the Wartheland, Upper Silesia and West Prussia, but they were particularly active in the latter, where at least two-thirds of their estimated overall total of 20,000 to 30,000 victims were killed. Alvensleben and his subordinates were encouraged by the newly appointed NSDAP Gauleiter and Reich governor of Danzig–West Prussia, Albert Forster, who announced that all Poles in his province would have to be expelled. In February 1940, Forster reported that 87,000 people had been evacuated from Danzig–West Prussia. From autumn 1939 through to spring 1940, German forces murdered around 40,000 local people in Forster's province.[18]

By the end of 1939, the Einsatzgruppen, the Wehrmacht and the ethnic German Selbstschutz had murdered more than 60,000 real or supposed members of Polish elites alone in the regions of western and central Poland annexed by Germany. The epicentre of the killings here were the territories of Danzig–West Prussia and the Wartheland. Five thousand more people were murdered in the central Polish areas of the Government General. The vast majority of those killed during these four months were Polish Christians noted for their education, nationalism or social status. Across Poland, at least 7,000 Jews fell victim to the German invaders during the period in question. Unlike the campaign against the Polish elites, however, the murder of Jews was not yet being implemented systematically or according to a clear plan. A more common fate for Polish Jews in the autumn of 1939 was deportation further east. For example, the 88,000 Poles deported by Nazi officials from the Wartheland to the Government General between 1 and 17 December in a total of eighty trainloads included around 10,000 Jews. The Wehrmacht and the Einsatzgruppen worked together in late September in forcing 18,000 Jews across the San river between Jarosław (Jaroslau) and Sandomierz into Soviet-controlled territory. Many of the Jews drowned while attempting to cross. These deportees nonetheless comprised a minority; most Jews remained where they were for the time being. When Hitler talked with one of his advisors on Eastern Europe, Alfred Rosenberg, on 29 September, he indicated that all remaining Jews, including those from the Reich, would be settled in the newly acquired territory between the Vistula and Bug rivers.[19]

Three Nazi mass-killing programmes converged in Poland in late 1939 and early 1940, targeting the Polish elites, Jews and psychiatric patients. Two of these programmes – the murder of the disabled in the annexed Polish territories and the eradication of the Polish intelligentsia – were already being applied systematically at this point in time, while the third – killings of (Polish) Jews – possessed as yet a more spontaneous and improvised character. These latter actions emerged from a long process of repressive measures against Jews in the German Reich between 1933 and 1939, including their disenfranchisement, segregation and impoverishment. The outbreak of the Second World War provided the trigger for mass murder, though not yet genocide. Although the systematic murder of Jews began in spring 1940 in the T4 killing centres on German soil, it was in Poland in late summer 1939 that Jews were victims of large-scale massacres for the first time.

Operation AB

In May 1940, at a time when attention was focused on Germany's invasion of France and the Low Countries, Heydrich's Security Police commenced its next major killing programme in the Government General. Hitler had decided that a pre-emptive measure was necessary in order to keep potential resistance scattered and prevent a Polish revolt during the military campaign in the west. Acting on Hitler's instructions, Governor General Hans Frank drew up a list of groups to be destroyed that was very similar to that of Operation Tannenberg the previous year: academics, clergy, political activists. Those already in German hands would be killed and those regarded as dangerous who were still at large would be arrested and then killed. Frank tasked SS Lieutenant General Friedrich-Wilhelm Krüger, who, as higher SS and police leader in the Government General, was Reichsführer SS Himmler's direct representative there, and SS Brigadier Bruno Streckenbach, the former chief of Einsatzgruppe I and now senior commander of the Security Police and the SD in Cracow, with the coordination and implementation of the operation. After it had begun, Frank declared: 'I openly admit that this will cost several thousand lives.'[20]

Initial planning for the 'Extraordinary Pacification Operation' (*Außerordentliche Befriedungsaktion*, or AB), as it was known, began in early March 1940. The Security Police had precise information about forty-four underground organisations and the names of around 2,000 alleged members of these organisations. On 30 March, in a preliminary strike, 1,000 people were arrested across the Government General, of whom 700 were regarded as leading underground activists. The second wave of arrests began shortly after the start of the military offensive against France. Frank arranged for Operation AB to commence officially on 16 May. It was originally scheduled to end on 15 June, but it continued through July and into August.[21]

Operation AB was carried out in all districts of the Government General. In the Radom District, a pretext for massive repression was provided by the activities of the Special Detachment of the Polish Army (*Oddział Wydzielony Wojska Polskiego*) under Major Henryk Dobrzański, the first Polish partisan group to be set up after the German invasion of September 1939. During the 'pacification operation' to capture the unit in March and April 1940, SS, police and Selbstschutz units attacked a total of thirty-one villages in the region, killing around 700 Polish civilians and burning down about 600 homes in the process. The Germans also conducted typical operations to liquidate members of the Polish intelligentsia. In Kielce, on 12 June 1940, the Gestapo transported 63 people to the Leśny Stadium and shot them. Other executions of inmates at the Kielce prison followed in June and July. In Sandomierz, 117 prisoners were selected, loaded on to lorries, taken to the woods near the village of Góry Wysokie and executed on 17 June. From 16 May to 10 July, about 250 people were killed in a dozen executions in Firlej near Radom. Around 760 members of two underground organisations were killed on 29 June in the Brzask Forest near Skarżysko-Kamienna. The inmates of the prison in Częstochowa were murdered near Olsztyn (28 and 29 June, and 1 July) and then near Apolonka (3 and 4 July, and 13 August). The preserved personal files reveal that executions were carried out without formal legal proceedings.[22]

In the territory of the Cracow District, executions were carried out in secluded forest areas, not too far from prisons. On 27 June 1940, 36 prisoners were executed in the woods near Rzeszów. On 28 June, 93 individuals were shot and killed with grenades in the Trzetrzewina Forest near Nowy Sącz (Neu Sandez). On 5 July, 111 prisoners were executed at Gruszka Hill near Tarnawa Dolna, close to the border with Soviet-occupied territory on the San river; for all the victims here, the cause of death was recorded as 'suicide'. On 6 July, approximately 90 people were murdered in the woods between the villages of Sieklówka and Warzyce. On 29 June and 2 and 4 July, about 150 prisoners were killed at Krzesławice, near Cracow, and more than a dozen at Przegorzały. As in other areas, Operation AB in the Warsaw District commenced with a wave of arrests; hundreds of people were detained on 30 March 1940. Some prisoners were soon shot. The others were held at the Pawiak prison in Warsaw, the biggest political prison on the territory of occupied Poland. During the months of May, June and July, large transports of people arrested during round-ups in the city arrived at Pawiak, sometimes more than 1,000 at a time. The largest mass executions took place in the Kampinos Forest near the village of Palmiry, northwest of Warsaw, where the Germans had used forced labourers to dig several long ditches. At least 1,700 people were murdered there, around half of them before Operation AB had even begun. The bloodiest night was 20–21 June 1940, when 358 individuals were shot. The victims included national activists, local government officials, cultural figures and famous sportsmen.[23]

Operation AB in the Lublin District began with the imprisonment in the Zamość Rotunda of about 200 representatives of the local intelligentsia on 20–22 June 1940. On 24 June 1940, 814 men were arrested in Lublin and imprisoned at the castle. On the same day in the city of Biała Podlaska, the Germans arrested 40 teachers of local secondary schools, who had previously been summoned to appear at the local district offices. On 26 June, a similar operation took place in Lubartów, where 400 people were arrested. In Chełm, the first arrests took place on 10 and 11 June and during the night of 3–4 July 1940. Similar operations were also carried out in Puławy, Janów Lubelski, Kraśnik and other towns. Some of those imprisoned were tried before ad hoc courts. In accordance with the recommendation of the governor of the Lublin District, Ernst Zörner, the courts passed only death sentences. Mass executions of the prisoners in Lublin Castle took place at Rury Jezuickie near Lublin on 29 June, 3 and 4 July, and 15 August 1940. The exact number of people shot there is unknown. According to estimates made during the exhumation, 450 to 500 were killed. All executions took place at night in the light of headlamps.[24]

By the end of summer 1940, some 3,500 Poles regarded as politically dangerous – teachers, priests, political and social activists – had been shot as part of Operation AB. It had also cost the lives of about 3,000 common criminals. Ten thousand more were interned in concentration camps, including Sachsenhausen and Auschwitz, which had been specially built for this purpose. Taken together, Operation Tannenberg, the Intelligentsia Operation and Operation AB claimed the lives of up to 100,000 Polish civilians in the space of a year. On 2 October 1940, during a discussion with Governor General Hans Frank, Gauleiter of Vienna Baldur von Schirach, Gauleiter of East Prussia Erich Koch and the chief of staff of the Party Chancellery, Martin Bormann, Hitler justified the murder of the Polish intellectual elites as follows: 'There can only be *one* master for the Poles, and that is the German; [...] therefore, all representatives of the Polish intelligentsia are to be killed. This sounds harsh, but it is simply the law of life.' During a speech in the town of Śrem (Schrimm) on 15 November, Arthur Greiser even invoked the Almighty to justify Germany's treatment of the Poles: 'When God introduced justice into the world, he also created hatred. And that is how we have learned to hate the Poles.' In June 1941, when Germany invaded the Soviet Union, the killings of Polish elites were extended to the eastern part of Poland, which had been annexed by the USSR in September 1939.[25]

Part II
SUMMER 1941 – SPRING 1942

CHAPTER 3
HOLOCAUST BY BULLETS

The German invasion of neutrals Norway and Denmark on 9 April 1940 brought an end to months of military inactivity. In May and June 1940, while Operation AB was in full flow in the Government General and the murder of psychiatric patients continued in the Reich and in Poland, Germany also attacked and occupied its four western neighbours: France, Belgium, the Netherlands and Luxembourg. Unlike in Poland, the invasion of these six states was not accompanied or immediately followed by mass killing operations, though the Wehrmacht did massacre several thousand black prisoners of war belonging to units drafted in France's West African colonies following a massive Nazi propaganda campaign approved by Hitler. As a rule, however, National Socialist ideology did not regard the Nordic and Western European countries and their peoples with the same contempt and sense of racial superiority as it did the Slavic nations of Eastern Europe.[1]

German attention turned (south)eastwards once more in April 1941. That month, German and Italian forces attacked Greece, following up on Italy's stalled invasion of the previous October, while German, Italian and Hungarian troops simultaneously invaded Yugoslavia. Although it had not participated in the attacks in April, German ally Bulgaria occupied parts of both Yugoslavia and Greece shortly after hostilities had ended. Like Poland a year and a half earlier, the Balkan Peninsula now became a testing ground for Nazi racial policy. Developments differed depending on the individual territory. It was the southern Slavic nation of Serbia, regarding which memories of 1914 and the assassination of Austrian Archduke Franz Ferdinand were still strong, that bore the brunt of German violence. While the fascist Ustasha movement seized power in Croatia under German and Italian aegis, Serbia was subjected to ruthless military rule.

Serbian Jews

While military operations against Yugoslavia were still in progress, the commander-in-chief of the German Second Army, General Maximilian von Weichs, ordered that 'ruthless measures' be adopted at the first sign of resistance, using 'the most draconian means possible'. The day after Weichs had accepted the unconditional surrender of Yugoslavian forces on 17 April, the Waffen SS division Das Reich executed 36 Serbs – 18 by shooting and 18 by hanging – in retaliation for the killing of one of its own men in the city of Pančevo. As a deterrent, the corpses of the dead were put on public display for three days. On 19 May, Weichs stipulated that in the future 100 Serbs should be shot for every German soldier who 'came to harm' in any Serb attack. As yet, German units in the field chose not to go that far, but Weichs's order contrasted sharply with the conduct of the military administration in occupied France, which had rejected in September 1940 a reprisals ratio of 100:1 envisaged by Hitler. It was a sign of things to come.[2]

Political, economic and terror measures directed against the civilian population were designed to consolidate the occupation and renew economic life in the interests of the German war economy in the run-up to the invasion of the Soviet Union, planning for which was already at an advanced stage. In order to ensure law and order in Serbia, martial law, obligatory military service and curfews were imposed, and communists were arrested. Inspections of existing German concentration camps were carried out, as similar camps modelled on them were to be set up in Serbia. Furthermore, the German occupiers shot hostages from the beginning. The brutal murder of civilians had a demonstrative character and pursued the aim – by virtue of its deterrent effect – of nipping in the bud any and all resistance against the occupiers.[3]

One group in particular was targeted and systematically persecuted from the outset: Jews. On 15 April, two days after the surrender of Belgrade, the commander of the SS Einsatzgruppe in Serbia, Wilhelm Fuchs, ordered that all Jews in the city report for registration. Jews who did not comply, the placards stated, would be shot. Similar to the approach in Poland and France, the German military commander in Serbia, Lieutenant General Ludwig von Schröder, promptly enacted anti-Jewish legislation: the marking of Jews with a yellow armband, their dismissal from public office and private enterprises, and the introduction of forced labour. Between late April and mid-June 1941, all male Jews fit for work and aged between fourteen and sixty, as well as all female Jews aged between sixteen and sixty, were deployed for forced labour. In Belgrade, around 3,500 Jews were put to work clearing bombed-out houses. Initially, the anti-Jewish legislation enacted by the military was also directed against Serbian Roma: 'Gypsies are to be treated like Jews.' In late July 1941, however, another regulation issued by the military commander in Serbia differentiated between sedentary and nomadic Roma, whereby the former – who comprised the vast majority of Serbian Roma – were for the time being exempted from this treatment.[4]

In fact, four days before the German invasion of Greece and Yugoslavia on 6 April 1941, the chief of the Army General Staff, Franz Halder, had issued an order in which the 'particularly important individuals' that the two envisaged Einsatzgruppen – one each in Serbia and Greece – were to 'seize' were explicitly identified as emigrants, saboteurs, terrorists, communists and Jews. It was on this occasion that the last two groups, communists and Jews, featured for the first time in such an order. Halder's instructions of 2 April were issued in the context of preparations for the invasion of the Soviet Union. They were heavily influenced by these preparations and constituted a qualitative leap in the combating of real and imagined enemies. For the first time, communists and Jews were singled out in advance of the invasion itself. Halder's order thus went further than the agreement reached between Reinhard Heydrich and Eduard Wagner – now quartermaster general of the German army – a week earlier, on 26 March, which had laid down the rules governing the relationship between the Einsatzgruppen and the Wehrmacht during the Soviet campaign (just as their agreement of July 1939 had done for the Polish campaign) and did not explicitly include communists and Jews as target groups. Thus, not the Soviet campaign but the Balkan campaign before it was the first to be conceived as a war of ideologies.[5]

As we saw in the previous two chapters, the outbreak of the Second World War provided the trigger for the mass murder of Jewish psychiatric patients in German hospitals and, less systematically, of Polish Jews. The turning point in the campaign against Jews and communists in occupied Serbia was no doubt the German invasion of the Soviet Union on 22 June 1941. The rump state of Serbia, with its 60,000 km^2 and 3.8 million inhabitants, was occupied by barely 25,000 German military and police personnel – one man, in other words, for every 2.4 km^2 and 152 inhabitants: a state of affairs that presaged the overstretched German security and personnel situation in the far vaster Soviet Union. The invasion of 22 June was followed almost immediately by a call from Soviet premier, Joseph Stalin, for the Europe-wide communist movement to take up arms in the anti-fascist struggle. The Serbian uprising duly erupted in July. By far its greatest boost came not, however, from the communists but from the hundreds of thousands of ethnic Serbs expelled from or fleeing the Ustasha savagery descending on the newly founded Independent State of Croatia (*Nezavisna Država Hrvatska*, or NDH).[6]

Though the communists had not started the Serbian revolt, they seized its reins as best they could. Reporting at the end of June, the SD perceived a strong communist propaganda drive across Serbia: 'well over half the population, particularly in Belgrade, has a Soviet-friendly attitude'. Field Marshal Wilhelm List, the Athens-based Wehrmacht commander southeast, observed that the revolt was rapidly developing into a full-scale national uprising. Against this backdrop, the German military – for fear of being overwhelmed – exacted fierce reprisals. One thousand Serbian citizens had already fallen victim to reprisals by the end of August. Initially, the bulk of the executions were carried out by Einsatzgruppe Yugoslavia (later renamed Einsatzgruppe Serbia). The principal victims were communists and male Jews, corresponding to the stipulations contained in Franz Halder's order of 2 April. Thus, the groundwork for this campaign had been laid on the eve of the Balkan campaign by the army leadership and, especially, the chief of the General Staff.[7]

The mass murder of Serbian Jews, carried out under the guise of reprisals, began shortly after the invasion of the Soviet Union and indeed took place parallel to the slaughter of Soviet Jews. As acts of resistance were anticipated following the invasion, occupation authorities in Serbia created a pool of hostages as a deterrent. Not surprisingly, given that the campaign against the Soviet Union was conceived as a war of ideologies against 'Judeo-Bolshevism', the hostages comprised Jews and communists. The order for the first mass shooting of these hostages was issued on 28 June, after the German police in Belgrade had discovered 423 packets of explosives. On 5 July, as 'atonement' for this, thirteen Jews and communists were shot. The same day, the first concentration camp on Serbian territory was set up in a former barracks in Belgrade. From now on, 'atonement measures' in the form of hostage shootings and arson attacks were implemented on an almost daily basis. On 25 July, the sixteen-year-old Jew Haim Almuzlino attempted to set fire to several German military vehicles in Belgrade using bottles of petrol. Although he turned himself in after the attack, 100 Jews and 22 communists were executed on 29 July as 'atonement' for this act of sabotage. Here, the reprisals ratio of 100:1 stipulated by General Weichs two months earlier was now being not only applied in practice but significantly exceeded.[8]

Second Lieutenant Peter Geissler of the 714th Infantry Division recounted developments in 'combating partisans' in letters he sent home at regular intervals:

> 26 July '41: Entire hordes of communists are now being shot and hanged on an almost daily basis. Aside from that, the situation is relatively peaceful. [...]
>
> 29 July '41: Can you receive [Radio] Belgrade on your [wireless] set? They also broadcast German news in the evening at 8 and 10 p.m. Perhaps you'll have the opportunity to listen. Don't be shocked if they happen to announce the figures of communists and Jews shot; they're cited on a daily basis straight after the news. Today, there was a new record! This morning, 122 communists and Jews were shot in Belgrade. You might by chance hear about [...] my location, too. It's often mentioned. [...] Yesterday, more than thirty people were shot.

With great candour and pride, Second Lieutenant Geissler thus relayed the shooting of communists and Jews to his family back in Germany. Furthermore, these operations were also publicly disseminated in radio broadcasts.[9]

In July and August, more than 1,000 communists and Jews were shot or publicly hanged. This did nothing to quell partisan activities, however, which continued to expand with increasing rapidity. The Wehrmacht was complicit from the start in seizing and killing Jews and communists, not to mention considerable numbers of Serbian Roma, and it became ever more complicit over time. On 9 August, Hitler officially entrusted the Wehrmacht with combating partisans in Serbia: 'Due to the increase in riots and acts of sabotage, the Führer now expects that the troops be deployed for restoring peace and order by means of swift and draconian intervention.' The following month, irregular forces under Draza Mihailović, known as Chetniks, temporarily joined forces with the communist partisans, and the Serbian national uprising mushroomed. The towns of Užice, Požega, Gornji Milanovac and Čačak all fell within the space of ten days, thus effectively placing all of Serbia west of the Belgrade–Kraljevo line in the hands of the insurgents.[10]

At this critical juncture, a new military commander in Serbia was appointed at the request of Field Marshal List. All military and civilian authorities were now placed under the command of Franz Böhme, a former Austrian officer who had served in the Imperial and Royal Army during the First World War. He arrived in Belgrade on 18 September, two days after the chief of the Wehrmacht High Command, Wilhelm Keitel, had issued a general directive stipulating that 50 to 100 communists be executed in retaliation for the death of every German soldier in the occupied territories. A week after his arrival, Böhme gave a clear signal of his intent in an order issued to his men:

> Your objective is to be achieved in a land where, in 1914, streams of German blood flowed because of the treachery of the Serbs, men and women. You are the avengers of those dead. A deterring example must be established for all of Serbia, one that will have the heaviest impact on the entire population. Anyone who carries out his duty in a lenient manner will be called to account, regardless of rank or position, and tried by a military court.[11]

Invoking the outbreak of the war that ultimately led to Germany's collective national trauma – the defeat of 1918 – was a sure way of motivating the troops to adopt a radical approach. It may particularly have galvanised Wehrmacht personnel of Austrian birth, of whom Böhme himself was one.

Böhme gave an example of how this stance might look in practice by releasing a directive on 4 October for the execution of 2,200 prisoners selected from 'the concentration camps in Šabac and Belgrade (predominantly Jews and communists)' in response to Serbian partisans gunning down twenty-two members of a Wehrmacht communications unit who had surrendered near Topola two days earlier. He followed this up with a general reprisal policy, communicated to all units on 10 October:

> In Serbia, it is necessary on account of the 'Balkan mentality' and the great expansion of the [...] insurgency movements to carry out the

orders of the OKW in the most draconian form. [...] At every location in Serbia, all communists, all male inhabitants suspected as such, all Jews [and] a certain number of nationalists and democratically inclined locals are to be seized immediately as hostages.

Of these hostages, 100 were to be shot for each German killed and 50 for each wounded. This reprisal policy did not constitute simply a minimal compliance with Keitel's guidelines: instead, it not only adopted the maximum suggested ratio of 100:1 (rather than the minimum of 50:1) but also explicitly included 'all Jews', a group Keitel had not mentioned.[12]

From October 1941, German reprisals were radically escalated not just in words but also in deeds. Divisional troops themselves became more extensively involved in seizing and killing increasingly large numbers of Jews and communists. As the combating of partisans with the forces available was proving to be militarily futile, the policy of murdering innocent hostages remained the keystone of operations conducted against the enemy. Predictably, the primary victims continued to comprise Jews and communists. In Serbia, as in the Soviet Union, German policy equated Jews with communists. Labelling Jews as communists was a convenient, indeed automatic way of justifying their liquidation. As radical as Böhme's reprisal policy was, however, it did not break new ground in the German occupation of Serbia: from the beginning of the uprising there, reprisals had been carried out against 'communists and Jews'. The German military in Serbia had long since accepted the identification or, at least, the natural combination of communist and Jew. What *was* new, however, was the pre-eminent role now assumed by the Wehrmacht under Böhme not only in dictating the shooting operations and the identity and number of the victims, but also in providing the shooters for the firing squads and carrying out the executions.[13]

As it turned out, the 2,200 reprisal shootings for the Topola ambush were enacted exclusively against Jews and – for the first time – Roma in Belgrade and Šabac, and not against communists, who were proving to be more elusive. On 9 and 11 October, a firing squad from the same communications unit that had suffered the casualties near Topola – Army Signals Regiment 521 – shot a total of 449 Jews. The executions were filmed and photographed by a propaganda company. Lieutenant Walter Liepe, commander of the 3rd Company of Army Signals Regiment 521, was in charge of the executions.

He noted that his men returned from these first shooting operations 'satisfied', but that 'unfortunately' they could not continue after the second day because of an assignment in the field. Instead, troops from the 2nd Company of Mountain Corps Signals Detachment 449 continued the executions in Belgrade thereafter. Further mass executions of Šabac Jews, as well as 200 Roma, were carried out on 12 and 13 October 1941.[14]

It is important to note that the soldiers here and elsewhere were not forced to participate in the shootings of Serbian Jews and Roma seized as hostages – entirely innocent victims who had nothing to do with the Topola ambush or any other form of resistance to the German occupation regime. Anyone who proved to be 'too weak' from the German point of view or was unable to overcome his scruples was permitted to absent himself from the firing squads. Mass executions by the Wehrmacht nonetheless functioned smoothly. No delays or obstructions occurred in the course of their implementation. Nowhere is there any mention of adverse effects on the internal discipline of the troops.[15]

Further massacres followed over the next days. After the 717th Infantry Division had suffered casualties during an attack on Kraljevo on 15 and 16 October, units of the division went on a house-to-house search through the city and, by the evening of the 17th, had shot 1,736 men and 19 'communist' women. This was followed by an even larger massacre in Kragujevac, when a German punitive expedition returning to the town suffered casualties and the commander of the 717th Infantry Division, Brigadier Paul Hoffmann, ordered immediate retaliation. However, the number of communist suspects, prison inmates, Jews and even men rounded up from the surrounding villages and shot on 20 October left the Germans far short of their quota of 2,300. Battalion commander Major Paul König thereupon had his troops seize numerous inhabitants of the city itself, including the pupils of the local secondary school, and continue the shootings on 21 October until their quota had been met.[16]

List and Böhme had reaped the whirlwind sown by their constant incitement to ruthless terror. Even for them, however, the massacres in Kraljevo and Kragujevac went too far, especially as the entire Serbian workforce of an aircraft factory in Kraljevo were among the victims. The mass-murder campaign was now so free from restraints that the perpetrators had succeeded in losing sight of whom they were actually murdering. Even collaborators got caught up in the killing machinery. Though Böhme expressly praised the troops, who had 'taken the measures necessary for crushing the insurgency in exemplary fashion and with due severity', he also suggested on 25 October that the arbitrary shooting of the population be replaced by an orderly regulation of the hostage shootings, as the executions of 'entire workforces of German arms factories' were 'irreparable blunders'.[17]

However, such economic considerations by no means meant an end to the killing operations. The selection of hostages just became more systematic. Not surprisingly, it was once more the Serbian Jews and Roma who bore the brunt of this realignment of policy. The chief of the German Military Administration in Serbia (and thus head of the administrative staff of the military commander), SS Major General Harald Turner, clarified matters in an order sent to all Wehrmacht district and field headquarters on 26 October:

As a matter of principle, it must be said in general that Jews and Gypsies constitute an element of insecurity and thus pose a threat to public order and safety. Jewish brainpower brought about this war and must be annihilated. As a result of his internal and external construction, the Gypsy cannot be a useful member of an ethnic community. It has been established that the Jewish element is substantially involved in the leadership of the bandits and it is precisely Gypsies who are responsible for particular cruelty and for intelligence. That is why it is a matter of principle in every instance to put all Jewish men and all male Gypsies at the disposal of the troops as hostages.

The next day, the third battalion of the 433rd Infantry Regiment – temporarily on loan from the 164th Infantry Division to support the 704th Infantry Division – commenced with the shooting of 2,200 hostages (250 Roma and the rest Jews) in retaliation for the death of ten German soldiers and the wounding of a further twenty-four after being surrounded in the town of Valjevo on 16 October. It had been Turner himself who, not wasting any time, had proposed on the very day of the Valjevo incident that '2,200 detained Serbs' be shot in atonement for the German losses.[18]

When Böhme was recalled as military commander in Serbia on 2 December 1941 after only two-and-a-half months in charge, his balance sheet of 160 Wehrmacht troops killed in action and 278 wounded contrasted sharply with the official figure of 3,562 partisans killed in battle and the unofficial figure of between 20,000 and 30,000 civilians shot as hostages and in other retaliatory massacres by Wehrmacht units under Böhme's command. Of these, more than 5,000 were male Jews and approximately 2,500 male Roma. Though the latter figure constituted a substantial proportion of the adult male Roma population of Serbia, the killing of male Serbian Roma in 1941 was not wholesale. The adult male Jewish population in Serbia, by contrast, had been wiped out in its entirety by the end of the year.[19]

Böhme's replacement, Lieutenant General Paul Bader, issued lower – but still vastly disproportionate – reprisal quotas on 22 December, stipulating ratios of 50:1 and 25:1 for German dead and wounded, respectively. A key consideration in this reduction was most likely the increasing difficulties faced by the Wehrmacht in preceding weeks when attempting to fulfil the old quotas. Still to be taken as reprisal prisoners, however, were those who 'because of their attitude and behaviour are earmarked to atone for German lives, for example communists seized without weapons, Gypsies, Jews, criminals and so forth'. Even after the male Jews in Serbia had all been murdered and the supply of readily accessible Roma had been largely exhausted, the Germans could not refrain from including them among the groups who, because of their alleged attitude and behaviour, could automatically be counted among the reprisal prisoners doomed to death.[20]

The mass murder of the male Jews of Serbia was not a conscious part of a Europe-wide 'final solution to the Jewish question'; that policy would soon be adopted, but it was not yet in place in summer and autumn 1941. The killing of Serbia's Jewish men emerged primarily out of local factors related to the partisan war and the German army's reprisals policy. The occupation authorities in Serbia resolved independently to commence (and subsequently radicalise) the programme of annihilation in the territory under their jurisdiction. Jews and Roma were convenient and supposedly expendable groups whose execution could satisfy the required reprisal quotas without producing undesired political repercussions and aggravating the anti-partisan struggle. Importantly, the German army did not operate with the avowed aim of exterminating the entire Jewish population, and thus the women, children and elderly were not yet killed. At the same time, however, the massacres in Serbia in autumn 1941 were an anticipation of the 'final solution', for ultimately the Jews were killed because they were Jews and, to quote Harald Turner, had 'to disappear'. The mass murder was the culmination of a process in which the German occupation authorities had first singled out the Jews for special persecution in spring 1941 and then subjected them to disproportionate reprisals and internment in the summer. Once partisan resistance led the Germans to impose upon themselves the obligation to fulfil the maximum reprisal quotas, all Serbs were at risk but the male Jews were doomed. The German military could conceive of innocent Serbs but not of innocent Jews, hence the totality of the destruction of Jewish men.[21]

By the end of 1941, the entire adult male Jewish population of Serbia had been put to death. This gender-selective mass killing was largely a crime committed by the Wehrmacht. The Jewish women and children were interned at the end of 1941 on the initiative of SS Major General Turner and then exterminated the following year in SS-run camps, as the Reich Security Main Office (*Reichssicherheitshauptamt*, or RSHA) finally relieved the Wehrmacht of overall responsibility for the campaign against the Serbian Jews. After Estonia, Serbia would be the first country occupied by Germany to be declared 'free of Jews'.

Soviet Jews: The First Wave

The Balkan campaign of spring 1941 had been conceived as a war of ideologies. For the first time, communists and Jews had featured explicitly in pre-invasion orders issued to the Einsatzgruppen for the seizure of particularly important individuals. The invasion of the Soviet Union – codenamed Operation Barbarossa – was the first campaign, however, in which the systematic mass murder of Jews and other racial opponents was the order of the day from the very outset. Since the mid-1920s, Hitler had yearned for a war against the Soviet Union, and with it the destruction of Bolshevism. In his autobiographical manifesto, *Mein Kampf*, he had written: 'In Russian Bolshevism we see Jewry's attempt in the twentieth century to acquire global hegemony.' 'Soviet Russia' was associated in Hitler's mind with the worst form of Jewish rule: it was the only country he believed to be completely controlled by Jews. The invasion of the Soviet Union in June 1941 was thus the culmination of Hitler's political and ideological programme, his defining work, the climax of his 'struggle against the Jewish Bolshevisation of the world'.[22]

Although the Einsatzgruppen had been deployed in previous military campaigns, they operated during the invasion of the Soviet Union in June

1941 for the first time officially under the title 'Einsatzgruppen of the Security Police and the SD'. Three of the Einsatzgruppen, A to C, were assigned to each of the three German army groups, North (for the Baltic), Centre (for Belarus) and South (for northern and central Ukraine), while the fourth – Einsatzgruppe D – was assigned to the German Eleventh Army, which was set to advance together with two Romanian armies through southern Ukraine, Crimea and the Caucasus. On 17 June, five days before the start of the invasion, Reinhard Heydrich hosted the heads of the Einsatzgruppen and their sub-units – the Einsatzkommandos and the Sonderkommandos – at his headquarters in Prinz-Albrecht-Palais in Berlin. It was most likely here that the group and commando chiefs were expressly informed that their commission in the area of operations would involve the decimation of Soviet Jewry. A written communication Heydrich sent on 2 July to Heinrich Himmler's most senior representatives in the occupied Soviet territories, the higher SS and police leaders (*Höhere SS- und Polizeiführer*, or HSSPF), claimed to summarise the instructions Heydrich had issued verbally to the Einsatzgruppen at the 17 June meeting and called specifically for the execution of 'Jews in party and state positions', among other groups.[23]

At the same time, the wording of Heydrich's written instructions from 2 July left the group and commando chiefs considerable discretion of interpretation. Since Communist Party functionaries had already been mentioned at the top of Heydrich's list of those to be executed, the additional reference to 'Jews in party and state positions' placed particular emphasis on Jews. Furthermore, the list also included 'all [...] other radical elements (saboteurs, propagandists, snipers, assassins, agitators, etc.)'. Thus, it appears that Heydrich expected, and indeed intended, that his instructions be interpreted broadly: how, for example, were the terms 'propagandists' and 'agitators' to be defined? Even the last word on the list, 'etc.', demonstrates that those who came under the heading 'other radical elements' were by no means clearly defined. Although Heydrich stipulated in writing only that Jews in party and state positions were to be killed, by emphasising Jews at all here (when such Jews were already subsumed under Communist Party functionaries), and by making other entries in the list very vague, he was – between the lines – leaving significant leeway for his subordinates to go beyond his written instructions.[24]

In fact, there is good reason to believe that Heydrich's verbal directives to the Einsatzgruppen of 17 June went even further than his consciously open-ended written instructions of 2 July. During the planning phase for the German invasion of the Soviet Union, Hitler, Himmler and Heydrich could not have been certain how the Wehrmacht would react to large-scale massacres of Soviet Jews – that is, non-combatants – within its own area of operations. It is likely, therefore, that the pre-invasion orders issued in writing to the Einsatzgruppen were roughly compatible with the instructions issued by the High Command of the Wehrmacht to the regular troops. These instructions, now known as 'the criminal orders', called for the execution of political functionaries (Red Army commissars), as well as a 'ruthless and energetic clampdown on *Bolshevik agitators, irregulars, saboteurs, Jews*, and the complete elimination of all active or passive resistance'.[25]

The evidence of the first five weeks of the campaign allows us to draw conclusions regarding the nature and scope of the pre-invasion orders, namely that Heydrich had specified on 17 June that the Jewish intelligentsia and as many male Jews of military-service age as possible be killed, since these target groups were regarded by the German leadership as likely communist activists and potential partisans or at least partisan supporters. The initial five-week period thus witnessed a dual-track approach on the part of the SS: officially, that is, according to written orders known also to the Wehrmacht, the Einsatzgruppen were instructed to kill leading communist functionaries (though they were not explicitly told to limit their operations to this group); unofficially, however, the Einsatzgruppen had evidently been supplied with verbal orders to include all male Jews of military-service age – or as many as possible – in the shooting operations. By the same token, the approach during the first five weeks of the campaign also demonstrates that the Einsatzgruppen had not received pre-invasion orders to kill *all* Soviet Jews, regardless of age or gender. Otherwise, the course of action taken by the SS commandos during these first five weeks would have amounted to insubordination.[26]

A further indication that the Wehrmacht's compliance was initially not taken for granted is to be found in the regular reports the Einsatzgruppen chiefs sent to Berlin. These contain repeated references to the effective cooperation between the two organisations and to the positive attitude of the Wehrmacht towards the activities of the Einsatzgruppen, that is, the massacre of Jewish non-combatants. In a report dated 6 July, for instance, Einsatzgruppe B remarked on the Wehrmacht's 'gratifyingly good attitude regarding the Jews'. Two weeks later, on 19 July, the same Einsatzgruppe reported that 'complete agreement regarding our further activity' had been reached following a discussion with the commander of the rear area for Army Group Centre (Max von Schenckendorff) and the relevant higher SS and police leader (Erich von dem Bach-Zelewski). The Wehrmacht's security divisions, furthermore, attached 'the greatest importance to cooperation with the Security Police'. One of Einsatzgruppe B's sub-units, Einsatzkommando 8, which was stationed in the Belarusian town of Baranovichi, was able to report that it collaborated 'particularly successfully with the relevant departments of the Wehrmacht'. The relationship between SS Brigadier Dr Walter Stahlecker, chief of Einsatzgruppe A, and his contacts in the Wehrmacht, was considered 'so good that [his proposed] removal would definitely bring about setbacks'. Not surprisingly, Stahlecker remained head of Einsatzgruppe A. According to a report dated 26 July, the Wehrmacht's security divisions made 'urgent requests' for the systematic capture by the Einsatzkommandos of partisans, saboteurs and communist functionaries in the rear areas, and 'appreciate[d] exceptionally' the presence of the Security Police there. In the estimation of SS Brigadier Arthur Nebe, chief of Einsatzgruppe B, cooperation in the rear areas – where, for Nebe, 'the most important executive Security Police task' was located – between the Einsatzkommandos and the security divisions, field headquarters and local headquarters of the Wehrmacht had been 'excellent' during the first three weeks of the campaign. During the same period, cooperation with the Wehrmacht's Secret Field Police and the Wehrmacht's counterintelligence troops in the operations area of Army Group Centre had been 'the best imaginable'. Nebe wrote: 'The activity of my Einsatzgruppe is acknowledged and promoted by all Wehrmacht departments in every way.' His 'measures' had been met with 'the most complete understanding' by the leadership of Army Group Centre. The Secret Field Police had even provided troops to support the 'liquidations'. Indeed, after less than four weeks of the campaign, the response of the Wehrmacht to the mass shootings was considered so favourable that concrete written instructions were issued by Heydrich on 17 July for the killing not only of all captured Jewish soldiers, but of all male Jews interned in camps. In fact, it was the Wehrmacht itself that had interned these male

Jews in the first place: in many Soviet cities, civilian internment camps were set up shortly after the arrival of the Wehrmacht and all men of military-service age (between fifteen and forty-five or sixty) were interned in them.[27]

From the very first week of the campaign onwards, mass-murder operations were carried out on a gigantic scale, dwarfing all previous Nazi atrocities. Large-scale executions of Jewish men are documented for all the Einsatzgruppen and their respective sub-units during the initial weeks of the war: Sonderkommandos (SK) 1a and 1b and Einsatzkommandos (EK) 2 and 3 of Einsatzgruppe A; Sonderkommandos 7a and 7b and Einsatzkommandos 8 and 9 of Einsatzgruppe B; Sonderkommandos 4a and 4b and Einsatzkommandos 5 and 6 of Einsatzgruppe C; Sonderkommandos 10a, 10b, 11a and 11b and Einsatzkommando 12 of Einsatzgruppe D, as well as Einsatzkommando Tilsit, which was subordinated to Einsatzgruppe A and operated in the German–Lithuanian borderlands, and Einsatzgruppe z.b.V., which was recruited from members of the Security Police in the Government General and dispatched to the formerly eastern Polish territories in support of Einsatzgruppe C.[28]

A handful of examples will suffice to illustrate the approach of the Einsatzgruppen during the opening stage of operations: On 24, 25 and 27 June, Einsatzkommando Tilsit murdered 201, 214 and 111 civilians, predominantly Jewish men, in the Lithuanian towns of Gargždai (Garsden), Kretinga (Krottingen) and Palanga (Polangen), respectively. In early July, SS Colonel Karl Jäger of EK 3 reported that a total of 7,800 Jews had been killed so far in Kaunas, 'partly by pogrom, partly by firing squad'. In early July, EKs 5 and 6 joined forces to murder as many as 3,000 Jews in Lvov (Lemberg). By the time it left the Lithuanian capital Vilnius on 23 July, EK 9 under SS Lieutenant Colonel Dr Alfred Filbert had shot more than 5,000 Jews there and in the nearby Paneriai Forest, all of them men. Following its departure from Vilnius, the unit killed no fewer than 527 male Jews in the Belarusian town of Oshmyany. This may have been the first time that EK 9 had killed the entire male Jewish population in a given locality. During the last ten days of July, Einsatzgruppe z.b.V. 'liquidated' a total of 3,947 people in Lvov, Brest and Białystok. Following its arrival on 6 July in Chernovtsy in northern Bukovina, which had been annexed from Romania by the Soviet Union in June 1940, SK 10b under Alois Persterer two days later shot and killed around 100 male members of the city's Jewish intelligentsia – doctors, lawyers, teachers, but also photographers – after brutal interrogations during which many had been tortured.[29]

The Einsatzgruppen did not act in isolation. The Wehrmacht was involved in every aspect of the persecution and annihilation of the Soviet Jews, from their identification, registration and marking, their incarceration in ghettos and their deployment for forced labour, via the seizure of property, the provision of transportation and the allocation of ammunition and cordons, to the detonation of pits, the obliteration of traces and the actual participation of soldiers themselves in shooting operations. Cooperation between the Wehrmacht and the SS and police apparatus developed in the process into a murderous everyday routine. In some cases, the initiative for killing the Jews as swiftly as possible came from the military. The murder of the Jews was not an official task of the Wehrmacht, but rather one that it voluntarily assumed.[30]

As in Serbia, active participation in mass shootings of Jews in the Soviet Union, either by providing shooters to the SS commandos or by carrying out killings on their own initiative, is documented for numerous regular German army units, including – though by no means limited to – the following formations: Signals Detachment 537 of the 286th Security Division; the 12th Company of Infantry Regiment 354 of the 286th Security Division; Infantry Regiment 691, also subordinated to the 286th Security Division; units of the 339th Infantry Division; the 707th Infantry Division; the 62nd Infantry Division; the 454th Security Division; the 25th Infantry Division; and the 72nd Infantry Division. In many other cases, military units expressly requested the SD to shoot Jews, as did the second battalion of Infantry Regiment 350 of the 221st Security Division in mid-August 1941. On 22 September, the staff of the Seventeenth Army requested SK 4b to 'exterminate' all Jews in the central Ukrainian city of Kremenchug because three instances of sabotage of power lines had occurred there. As its chief of staff had made clear in an order issued on 7 September, those in command of the Seventeenth Army equated Jews with resistance and regarded 'Jews of both sexes' and 'also all ages' as fundamentally 'suspect'. In July, SK 4a of Einsatzgruppe C killed 17 non-Jewish civilians, 117 'communist agents of the NKVD' and 183 'Jewish communists' in the Ukrainian town of Sokal following a request from the Sixth Army. In other instances, the military intervened to get executions sped up, as in the case of the Eleventh Army in Simferopol later in the year.[31]

In addition to the multifaceted support provided by the Wehrmacht, the Einsatzgruppen were also assisted by regular German police units. When the invasion was launched, a total of twelve uniformed police battalions were formed into regiments comprising three battalions each. On 27 June, a mere five days into the campaign, members of Order Police Battalion 309 and other units subordinated to the Wehrmacht's 221st Security Division killed at least 2,000 Jews in the formerly Polish city of Białystok, since 1939 part of the Belarusian Soviet Socialist Republic. More than 500 people, including women and children, were herded into a synagogue and burned alive. Those who tried to escape were shot. Wehrmacht units blew up adjacent buildings to ensure that the fire did not spread across the city. Few of the early killings demonstrate as obvious a link to Jew-hatred as this one. In another western Belarusian city, Brest, men of Police Battalion 307 arrested and shot around 5,000 male Jews. The motorised detachment of the 162nd Infantry Division provided lorries for transporting the victims to the execution site. In mid-July, Police Battalions 316 and 322, both part of Police Regiment Centre, massacred a total of around 3,000 Jewish men in Białystok.[32]

By the end of July 1941, at the close of this first stage of unprecedented destruction, a total of 63,000 people had been murdered by the Einsatzgruppen alone. More than 90 per cent of the victims of the massacres carried out by the Einsatzgruppen and the police regiments during these first five weeks of the campaign were Jews. In numerous instances, the murder of dozens or hundreds of Jewish men was carried out on the pretext of reprisals for one or more German soldiers having been shot from behind. Such absurd ratios were thus commonplace on the eastern front long before the OKW issued its general directive of 16 September 1941 stipulating that 50 to 100 hostages be executed in retaliation for the death of every German soldier in the occupied territories.[33]

The precise conduct of the different SS, police and Wehrmacht units depended on the initiative of the individual commanders and on regional conditions. For example, the local populace in Lithuania, Latvia and western Ukraine – all territories annexed by the Soviet Union between autumn 1939 and summer 1940 – proved more amenable to SS attempts to incite pogroms against Jewish citizens during the opening weeks of the campaign than the local populace in Belarus, not only in the eastern half but also in the formerly Polish western part. The marked disinclination among Belarusians to launch pogroms against Jews prompted Arthur Nebe to report the phenomenon to Berlin repeatedly during the months of July and August 1941. The murderous activities of the group and commando chiefs in the field were endorsed and encouraged by Himmler, Heydrich and other senior SS leaders during the frequent tours of inspection they conducted in these critical weeks and months.[34]

After five weeks of the military campaign against the Soviet Union, the SS leadership evidently felt ready to begin directing their commando chiefs to extend the killing to include Jewish women and children. The harmonious cooperation between the Wehrmacht and the SS Einsatzgruppen described above was a key factor in the decision to expand the murder of Soviet Jewry to entire communities – thereby shifting to a policy of wholesale and indiscriminate slaughter – and thus in the transition to genocide. This cooperation was certainly very encouraging for the German leadership. While the Wehrmacht was making considerable headway in its advance into Soviet territory, however, the military campaign was in fact already beginning to lose momentum by early July, not least for Army Group Centre's area of operations, which constituted the largest section of the front.[35]

Less than three weeks after the launch of Operation Barbarossa, leading figures in the military command, both in Berlin and in the field, were expressing concerns regarding unexpectedly tough enemy resistance, high casualty rates and, especially, the security of the rear areas and their 'pacification'. They went so far as to contemplate the possibility of leaving combat units in the rear areas to support the insufficient security divisions there. On 10 July, Army Group Centre was forced to go on the defensive. Army Group North was experiencing similar difficulties in its area of operations. Its commander-in-chief, Wilhelm von Leeb, had the impression on 12 July that losses were so high in Panzer Group 4 that 'a state of exhaustion will soon be reached'. The chief of the Army General Staff, Franz Halder, had written in his diary on 3 July: 'It is thus not saying too much when I claim that the campaign against Russia has been won within fourteen days.' A mere two days later, however, Chief of the OKW, Wilhelm Keitel, wrote to Chief of Army Armaments and Commander of the Reserve Army, Fritz Fromm:

> The war waged behind the front by gangs and snipers is a very considerable strain on the lines at the rear and for the pacification of the conquered

territory. If very brutal measures must be taken this time, the Führer sees in the vast expanses of the enormous occupied territory with its huge forests considerable dangers in the hinterland as a result of the completely hate-filled Bolshevist populace. The Führer has now once more obliged me to arrange for the equipping of the occupation troops, territorial defence formations and police, who must pacify and secure the territory *in the long run* (that could last the whole winter), with *captured combat vehicles.*

If any part of the Soviet population was regarded by the German high command as particularly 'Bolshevist', it was certainly its Jewish members.[36]

Concerns were growing within the political leadership as well. In a diary entry dated 12 July, Propaganda Minister Joseph Goebbels noted that things had come to 'something of a standstill' on all fronts. On 24 July, Goebbels's assessment of the situation only a month into the campaign was downright pessimistic: 'The mood in the Reich has become somewhat graver. It is gradually becoming clear that the eastern campaign is no stroll to Moscow.' With Directive No. 34, issued on 30 July, Hitler officially acknowledged what had been the case in practice for almost three weeks by instructing Army Group Centre to go on the defensive. By mid-July, the Blitzkrieg had failed; the commanders in the field knew this and so did the leadership in Berlin. The German high command was not, as often claimed, 'euphoric' over what it saw as an impending military victory. Instead, fear of failure seems to be a more appropriate description of the mood prevailing among Germany's military and political elites at this time. The weakness of the security forces deployed between the main transit routes left supply lines and economic infrastructure vulnerable in the rear areas and created a power vacuum in which irregular Soviet resistance could potentially jeopardise the ultimate success of the military campaign. The army leaders considered the Einsatzgruppen to be 'worth their weight in gold' precisely because they secured the troops' rear lines of communication.[37]

Once the Soviet campaign was no longer proceeding according to plan, Germany's defeat in the First World War loomed increasingly large and the willingness of the political and military elites to demonstrate whatever degree of ruthlessness was deemed necessary in order to avoid a repetition became correspondingly greater. Perceived necessity established itself as the central theme of military legitimation for the radical treatment of Soviet Jews and other enemies, real or imagined. The German leadership attempted to remedy weaknesses in the rear areas by resorting to pure terror, and a further escalation of the violence was not long in coming. Chief of the Party Chancellery Martin Bormann recorded Hitler stating during a high-level meeting at his headquarters on 16 July: 'The vast region must of course be pacified as quickly as possible; this is best done by "shooting anyone who even looks askance".' A week later, a presentation to Hitler by Commander-in-Chief of the Army Walther von Brauchitsch resulted in the issuing of a supplement to an OKW directive that stipulated:

> The troops available for securing the conquered eastern territories are only sufficient, given the vastness of this area, [. . .] if the occupying power spreads that terror which alone is capable of eliminating any appetite for defiance on the part of the population. [. . .] The commanders must find the means for keeping their rear areas in order by applying corresponding draconian measures and not by demanding more security forces.[38]

Precisely what form this terror would take was spelled out two days later, on 25 July, in a directive issued by the Army High Command (*Oberkommando des Heeres*, or OKH) and signed by Brauchitsch's general for special assignment, Eugen Müller. The directive drew attention to the 'intended deployment of partisan sections in our own rear area' as well as to 'the inflammatory impact in general of the pillars of the Jewish–Bolshevik system'. It then stated that 'attacks and acts of violence of every description' against German personnel and property, as well as any attempts to carry out such attacks, were to be 'ruthlessly put down by force of arms to the point of annihilating the enemy'. In the event that German personnel met passive resistance, or were unable to apprehend the perpetrator(s) of acts of sabotage, 'collective violent measures' were to be carried out immediately against towns and villages. 'Suspicious elements', the OKH directive continued, were to be handed over to the Einsatzgruppen purely on the basis of their 'disposition and attitude', even where it could not be established that a serious offence had been committed. Fleeing POWs were to be shot immediately; it was not necessary first to call to them to stop. All forms of actual or supposed defiance were to be put down brutally and without hesitation. At around the time when the OKH issued this new directive, Arthur Nebe reported back to Berlin that partisan squads were causing 'systematic destruction' behind German lines. He therefore emphasised that one of Einsatzgruppe B's main tasks was: 'The seizure of partisans, saboteurs [and] communist function-aries in the army rear areas, as they dare to emerge and become active only after the frontline troops have marched through. The Einsatzkommandos must remain deployed for the systematic seizure of the enemy.'[39]

This radicalisation of occupation and security policy during the second half of July was accompanied by an increase in SS and police manpower. Although Himmler did not attend the aforementioned meeting of 16 July, his presence at Führer Headquarters in East Prussia from 15 to 20 July made it possible for him to lunch with two of its participants the following day, and he subsequently received a copy of the minutes of the 16 July meeting. More importantly, the 17 July Decree of the Führer regarding the Securing by the Police of the Newly Occupied Eastern Territories made it clear that any and all 'policing measures' in the occupied east were 'a matter for the Reichsführer SS and Chief of the German Police', that is, Himmler. This offi-cial confirmation of his jurisdiction in the occupied Soviet territories – combined with appeals by Keitel – prompted Himmler to carry out the deployment of further SS and police forces. While the deployment had been planned for many weeks, the timing of its implementation is important here. On 19 and 22 July, respectively, two SS brigades (the SS Cavalry Brigade, consisting of SS Cavalry Regiments 1 and 2, and the 1st SS Infantry Brigade), with a combined force of more than 11,000 men, were attached to the HSSPF for central and southern Russia. Around 23 July, a further eleven battalions of Order Police, each of approximately 500 men, were reassigned from various military commanders in the rear areas to the HSSPF in the north, centre and south of the occupied Soviet territories. By the final week of July, 5,500 to 6,000 members of the Order Police and 11,000 SS men had within a matter of days reinforced the 3,000 members of the Einsatzgruppen to provide a total of almost 20,000 troops.[40]

Thus, it is likely that in mid-July 1941 the decision was taken to expand the scope of the killing operations to encompass the whole of Soviet Jewry, and that approval was granted for the deployment of the increased manpower necessary to achieve this goal. The imminent escalation in killing could only occur after Himmler had massively increased the number of SS troops and policemen operating behind the advancing German army. According to the original plans, the designated limit for the German military advance was a theoretical line connecting Arkhangelsk on the White Sea in the north with Astrakhan on the Caspian Sea in the south – a line some 480km east of Moscow. According to this projection, the Einsatzgruppen, with around 3,000 men, would have been expected to kill, at a minimum, all Jewish men of military–service age in an area three times the size of the territory that was actually conquered by the German army in 1941. The timetable for this mass murder was to cover twelve weeks, at which point the German planners expected the war to have been won. Due to the unforeseen military setbacks, SS troops, policemen and regular soldiers were thus called upon from the second half of July 1941 to expand and intensify the killing in the occupied east, first and foremost in the vulnerable rear areas. Soviet Jews, as the 'pillars of the Jewish–Bolshevik system' – in the words of Eugen Müller – and thus the main enemy, would be first in line in this frenzy of destruction.[41]

The first SS unit to make the transition to a policy of killing Jews indiscriminately, regardless of age or gender, was Einsatzkommando 9 of Einsatzgruppe B. Under the command of Alfred Filbert, EK 9 arrived no later than 25 July in the Belarusian town of Vileyka, where it remained for several days. Like the other commandos of the four Einsatzgruppen, EK 9 had targeted primarily Jewish men of military-service age during the first five weeks of Germany's campaign against the Soviet Union. This would change dramatically from Vileyka onwards. According to post-war testimony by two former officers in the commando, Gerhard Schneider and Wilhelm Greiffenberger, it was here, on 29 July, that Filbert gave a talk to his officers during which he explained that – on the orders of higher authorities – Jewish women and children were to be included in future shooting operations. As the reason for these new orders, Filbert cited criticism of the unit's execution figures for being too low. Schneider testified after the war:

Coming from Vilnius, we had just arrived in Vileyka when Dr Filbert, returning from a meeting of commando heads at another location, called a meeting of the officers. One could sense that he was himself agitated, bitter and very serious. He informed us that he was returning from a meeting of commando heads, at which either Heydrich himself must have been present or new orders of Heydrich's were announced. In any case, he was given a dressing down. EK 9 had attracted the negative attention of Heydrich in particular because its activity in fulfilling the shooting order had been far too limited. Furthermore, as the inclusion of women and children in the shooting operations had been ordered, he could now simply no longer avoid mandating the intensified deployment of his commando. Pointing at me, he then ruled: 'You assume command tomorrow.' He likewise ordered one or two other officers to participate.

Although Schneider and Greiffenberger were at odds both in their conduct in the field in 1941 and in their approach to testifying in court, Greiffenberger's post-war testimony corroborated Schneider's statement regarding the timing, context and nature of the new orders and the commando's location when it received them:

We had been in Vileyka only a few days when Filbert held a staff meeting with a small group of officers. I believe that, aside from Filbert and me, Schneider and [Friedrich] Klein were present at this meeting. During the course of this staff meeting, Filbert disclosed to us that he had received the order from a higher authority to shoot Jewish women and children as well in the future. Furthermore, Filbert took this opportunity to point out that the reported shooting figures had been criticised in high places as too low.

It is very doubtful that an allegedly sluggish fulfilment of execution quotas was the real reason for the issuing of new orders to include women and children in the shooting operations. After all, at this point in time, EK 9 had shot and killed more people than any of the other commandos belonging to Einsatzgruppe B. One member of the staff of Einsatzgruppe B, SS Second Lieutenant Andreas von Amburger, testified after the war that 'in Einsatzgruppe B it was common knowledge that EK 9 was particularly rigorous in its approach to the liquidation of the Jewish population'. We must also keep in mind that neither Schneider nor Greiffenberger had been present when the new orders were issued to Filbert. In their post-war testimony, they were simply relaying what Filbert had told them in Vileyka. Perhaps anticipating misgivings on the part of some of his officers regarding the murder of women and children – misgivings that were indeed voiced, as we shall see – Filbert may have presented the new orders less as a conscious expansion of an ideological or racial programme of mass murder and more as an inescapable chastisement for EK 9's (supposed) tardiness hitherto.[42]

Concerning Filbert's own receipt of the new commission, Schneider spoke after the war of an 'issuing of orders', 'at which either Heydrich himself was present or at which a direct order of Heydrich's was conveyed'. According to Greiffenberger's post-war testimony:

> We had radio contact with Einsatzgruppe B. On several occasions Filbert was ordered to attend meetings with the group staff. [...] To my knowledge, the RSHA [in] Berlin intervened in the matter of the shootings of Jews at a later date, when we were situated in Vileyka, on one single occasion, regarding the matter of also shooting women and children in the future.

As Heydrich was the head of the Reich Security Main Office and, in this capacity, in charge of the Einsatzgruppen, it is highly likely that the new orders had indeed come from him. If Heydrich had issued the order directly, as Schneider indicated, then Filbert must have travelled to Berlin to receive it. On 20 July, the same day as EK 9's departure from Vilnius, Heydrich had begun a three-day trip to the southern part of the Soviet front near Yampol in Ukraine. There he rejoined Fighter Squadron 77, with which he had already flown in air raids over Norway the previous year. He then returned to Berlin. His next trip to the occupied Soviet territories does not appear to have taken place until the beginning of September, when he visited Himmler's eastern headquarters at Hegewald near Zhytomyr. It was not unusual for members of a commando to travel back to the Reich during the course of their deployment in the occupied Soviet territories. Greiffenberger, for example, had travelled back to Germany in mid-July in order to send parcels with furs to the families of commando personnel. It thus appears that Heydrich issued the new orders to Filbert in person in Berlin during the week between 23 July, when Heydrich returned to the German capital, and 29 July, when Filbert communicated these orders to his officers.[43]

In order to combat the misgivings voiced in the wake of the meeting on 29 July by some of the officers, including Schneider and Heinrich Tunnat, to the effect that those members of the commando who were fathers or particularly young could not be expected to kill women and children, Filbert announced that he himself would lead the first shooting operation in Vileyka. He accordingly selected those men who appeared most suitable from the Order Police platoon assigned to EK 9. The following day, 30 July, at least 350 Jewish victims who had been arrested two days earlier during a combing of the town, including – for the first time – women, were driven out of the city and shot under Filbert's command. Filbert also made the preparations for the next shooting operation, but transferred command to Greiffenberger, as the next-highest-ranking officer. During the course of this operation, which lasted approximately three hours, at least 100 Jewish men, women and – again for the first time – children aged fifteen and above were killed. A member of the police platoon later estimated the total number of victims of the two shooting operations in Vileyka at between 300 and 500. Greiffenberger also subsequently put the number of Jews murdered in Vileyka at 500 and believed that 'all Jews who had resided in Vileyka' had thus been shot by EK 9. Einsatzgruppe B felt sufficiently certain of this at the time to report back to Berlin: 'In Vileyka, the Jews had to be liquidated in their entirety.' The report did not elaborate on why this 'had to be' done.[44]

According to testimony given by one member of the police platoon of EK 9:

> I can only say that the situation in Commando 9 was a different one as of Vileyka than previously. From our stay in Vileyka onwards, small sub-commandos under the command of different SS and SD officers were pulled off Filbert's main commando with increasing frequency for special tasks unknown to me, so that [the size of] the regular commando diminished ever further.

In the next RSHA incident report on the activities of the Einsatzgruppen, dated 5 August, Nebe made reference to the Jewish population and also noted 'the Security Police sweeps, which have become more comprehensive of late'. This was an understatement: the Vileyka massacres at the end of July in fact marked the transition to genocide against Soviet Jewry. As such, EK 9 was not only the first commando within Einsatzgruppe B to begin systematically killing Jewish women and children, but in fact the first commando of any of the Einsatzgruppen to do so.[45]

Although EK 3 of Einsatzgruppe A had killed Jewish women in small but increasing numbers from the first half of July onwards (reaching triple figures for the first time on 13 August), the commando did not include any children in their massacres until 15–16 August in Rokiškis, at a time when EK 9 had already carried out no fewer than two shooting operations targeting children. The second of these operations was the murder by EK 9 of all Jewish inhabitants – between 500 and 600 people, one-third of them men and two-thirds women and children of all ages – of the Russian town of Surazh on 12 August. The first commando in Lithuania to commence the systematic murder of children was not EK 3 but in fact EK 2 of Einsatzgruppe A in Biržai on 8 August. The first commando in Einsatzgruppe C to murder women and children was SK 4a, which began the large-scale killing of women at the start of August and, soon thereafter, children as well. All other commandos of the four Einsatzgruppen began killing women and children only at a later stage, some of them not until the beginning of October. This delay may have resulted from the time required for the new orders to be passed on verbally down the chain of command, from Himmler and Heydrich, sometimes directly (as in the case of EK 9) but often via the HSSPF and/or the Einsatzgruppen chiefs, to the individual commandos in the field. Another factor in the divergent timing of the transition to genocide was the varying zeal and interpretative will of the individual commanders. Jewish communities, furthermore, were distributed unevenly across the occupied territories; their presence and size – and, by extension, the 'accessibility' of Jews for the German killers – differed from place to place.[46]

Other SS formations deployed in the Soviet Union also began their systematic slaughter of Jewish women and children in August. The first such massacre carried out by the aforementioned SS Cavalry Regiment 1 took place on 3 August in the southwestern Belarusian town of Chomsk, which had a Jewish population of about 2,000. The unit shot as many of them as they could lay their hands on – men, women and children. Only a very few members of the Jewish population of Chomsk managed to flee or otherwise survive the massacre. On 6 August in the southern Belarusian city of Pinsk, SS Cavalry Regiment 2 shot at least 6,500 Jewish men aged between sixteen and sixty and, the next day, around 2,400 more Pinsk Jews, this time including men aged over sixty and boys of six and older. Women and girls were spared, at least temporarily. Beginning on 7 August and ending on 9 August, the

10th Regiment of the 1st SS Infantry Brigade murdered all the Jews living in the Ukrainian town of Chernyakhov – a total of more than 300 men, women and children. By the second half of August, the SS Cavalry Brigade had shot more than 25,000 Jews in the wetland area known as the Pripet Marshes. Over the course of three days at the end of the same month, the 1st SS Infantry Brigade murdered 23,600 Jews – men, women and children – in the western Ukrainian city of Kamenets-Podolsky. It was the largest single massacre of Soviet Jews up to that date. More than half the victims were Jews who had earlier been expelled from the region of Carpatho-Ukraine, Czechoslovak territory occupied and annexed by Hungary in March 1939.[47]

The Einsatzgruppen and regular army units continued to carry out mass-shooting operations alongside the massacres committed by the SS Cavalry Brigade and the 1st SS Infantry Brigade. Nowhere was the close cooperation between Wehrmacht and Security Police from the first days of the campaign better than during the advance of the Sixth Army through Ukraine. The division of labour between the Sixth Army and Einsatzgruppe C found its clearest expression in the murder of around 90 Jewish children in the city of Belaya Tserkov, located 80km south of Kiev, in late August 1941. The children's parents had been murdered earlier that month in a joint operation by the local military commander and SK 4a, led by Paul Blobel. For days the children, some only months old, were left without any food, until two Wehrmacht chaplains attached to the 295th Infantry Division – one Protestant, the other Catholic – approached their superiors to plead on their behalf. This is the only documented example of clergy attempting to prevent the murder of Jews during the Holocaust. The protest of the chaplains prompted a staff officer to raise the question of what should be done with the children. The Wehrmacht field commander, Josef Riedl, was convinced that 'this scum has to be exterminated'. The issue was then brought to the attention of the commander of the Sixth Army, Field Marshal Walther von Reichenau, who decided that the 'action had to be executed in an appropriate manner'. The children were shot by SK 4a.[48]

The exceptional barbarity, pleasure and cynicism with which many German perpetrators murdered children – Jewish and non-Jewish alike – in the occupied Soviet territories is particularly disturbing. On one occasion, the head of the SS guard in the Minsk Ghetto, Adolf Rübe, led a child by the hand to the cemetery with the words 'Now we're going to join papa and mama', where he then shot the child. He had indeed killed the parents a few days earlier. In the Lesnaya POW camp near Baranovichi, a German female doctor murdered an eight-month-old baby by lethal injection, only then to pose for a photograph with the child and its mother, who was present. In the village of Kovali in the district of Oktyabrsky, Belarus, German forces chased after fleeing children, caught them and threw them all into a fire. In nearby Dyomenka, little girls had their necks broken like chickens. Sometimes, during shooting operations, children were held over the pit by their hair and then shot; this resulted on at least one occasion in the shooter being left holding the child's skullcap with some hair still attached after the child had fallen into the pit. One could cite many other such examples.[49]

The thirty-six-year-old police official Walter Mattner from Vienna wrote to his wife on 5 October 1941 regarding the massacres of Jews in the Belarusian city of Mogilev:

> I was in fact present at the mass killings the day before yesterday. When the first truckloads [of victims] arrived my hand slightly trembled when shooting, but one gets used to this. When the tenth truck arrived, I already aimed calmly and shot assuredly at the many women, children and infants. Bearing in mind that I also have two infants at home, with whom these hordes would do the same, if not ten times worse. The death we gave them was a nice, quick death compared with the hellish torture of thousands upon thousands in the dungeons of the GPU [Soviet secret police]. Infants flew in a wide arc through the air and we shot them down still in flight, before they fell into the pit and into the water. Let's get rid of this brood that has plunged all of Europe into war and is still stirring things up in America. [...] Hitler's words are coming true, when he once said before the war: if the Jews believe they can again provoke a war in Europe, it will not mean victory for Jewry but the end of the Jews in Europe. [...] I am actually already looking ahead, and many say here that [after] we return home, then it will be the turn of our own Jews.

We certainly cannot generalise from such a source, but Mattner's grotesque letter is revealing in several ways. First, he blamed Jewish infants for the war, then justified their pre-emptive murder – which was anything but 'a nice, quick death' – with reference to his own children and to real or imagined crimes of the Soviet secret police. Second, according to Mattner, during one of the first large-scale massacres of Jews in eastern Belarus, 'many' of the murderers were already thinking about the annihilation of *German* Jews at a time when no corresponding order had yet been issued. Third, Mattner immediately thought of the infamous threat to exterminate the Jews made by Hitler during a speech in the Reichstag on 30 January 1939; he was even able to recite it accurately in terms of its meaning and syntax – in other words, he had *internalised* the message.[50]

Nonna Lisowskaja, a teenage Russian girl who ended up in a labour camp on Reich territory with her mother, recalled in her memoirs – based on handwritten diaries – an incident that occurred during the train journey to Germany. Passing through occupied Poland on 11 August 1942, their train encountered a transport loaded with Jews heading in the opposite direction; its destination was one of the extermination camps. The train carrying Nonna and her mother had stopped to allow the passengers to relieve themselves in the woods. As the train slowly moved off again, a young woman from the Jewish transport succeeded in somehow passing her baby to Nonna's mother, who was positioned at the open door of their train carriage. A dispute ensued among the women in the carriage regarding what to do with the baby girl. When the train next stopped, a German soldier heard the baby cry and – after one of the women told him that it was a Jewish baby thrown into the carriage at the previous stop – took it:

> The soldier handed the baby to an SS man who carried the baby away – holding her body in his one hand, and letting it hang down by his side. Mama broke into tears, and with terror in my heart, I watched the SS man carry the infant to the truck. He raised up one of his knees and with a swift motion brought the baby's body down against his knee.
>
> I no longer heard the baby cry, and when I tried to move, I could not. I felt the blood leaving my head, and I was feeling sick and dizzy. When I came to, I was standing by the door of the rail car, throwing up violently.[51]

A German court that tried six members of Police Battalion 306 documented gruesome scenes that had occurred during the dissolution of the ghetto in Stolin, a small town in Belarus, in September 1942. An infant seen kicking under its dead mother was pulled out of the pit, thrown into the air and blown apart by a volley from a sub-machine gun. In another instance, a German engineer who had served in Ukraine described how a gendarme officer seized a small child from the arms of its mother, spun it around a few times and then smashed the child's head against the doorpost. The officer then told his comrades: 'That is the best method; one just has to learn it.' The method of murdering children by smashing their heads appears by no means to have been uncommon.[52]

Back to SK 4a and its operations in central Ukraine: on 29 and 30 September 1941, the largest single massacre of Jews in the Soviet Union up to that date – later surpassed only by the so-called Operation Harvest Festival in the Lublin District of the Government General in November 1943 – occurred on the western outskirts of Kiev in a large ravine known as Babi Yar. On Sunday, 28 September, the newly installed Ukrainian police had posted 2,000 copies of an unsigned order in Russian, Ukrainian and German to the Jews of Kiev and the surrounding area, instructing them to appear the next day before 8 a.m. at a certain intersection between the Jewish and Orthodox cemeteries and to bring along 'documents, money and valuables, and also warm clothing, underwear, etc.' The largest of the texts on the trilingual placard, the Russian one, stated that 'Yids' who disobeyed would be shot. Tens of thousands of Jews, most of them expecting deportation, showed up at the appointed place. Instead of being deported, however, they were marched to Babi Yar and shot by SK 4a, the same unit that had murdered the Jewish children of Belaya Tserkov. Reserve Police Battalion 45 and Police Battalion 303 of the regular German police assisted in the operation. Ukrainian auxiliary policemen were also present. According to a report they compiled and sent to Berlin, the German forces on hand shot 33,771 Jews.[53]

News of this and other shooting operations soon came to the attention of many civilians in Germany, communicated either in letters sent home from the front (such as the one written by Walter Mattner, quoted above) or by soldiers and policemen on home leave. One of these civilians was Victor Klemperer, a German literary scholar of Jewish origin, who had converted to Protestantism in his youth and lived in Dresden. His non-Jewish wife, Eva, was informed of these events by a carpenter of their acquaintance, 'over a glass of beer'. Klemperer wrote in his diary: 'He spent several winter months (until Christmas) in Russia as a driver for the police troops. Horrific mass murders of Jews in Kiev. Small children's heads smashed against walls; men, women, adolescents shot down in their thousands at one blow; a hill detonated and the pile of corpses buried beneath the exploded earth.' The carpenter was clearly referring to the massacre at Babi Yar. This was not the first time, however, that Klemperer had heard about mass shootings of Jews. He had previously been told 'by various parties' that 'evacuated Jews have been *shot dead* by the dozen near Riga, as they left the train'. Willy Cohn, a Jewish schoolteacher in Breslau (now Wrocław), likewise heard about a 'big bloodbath' of Jews in Kiev less than two weeks after the massacre there had taken place.[54]

By early October 1941, all the Einsatzgruppen and their respective subunits, as well as both SS brigades, had commenced killing Jews indiscriminately, regardless of age or gender. Josef Perl, an adolescent Jew from Bychkiv in the region of Carpatho-Ukraine, witnessed the shooting of his mother and four sisters in late 1941. He was able to escape the shooting site during an air raid:

They used to take out people during the day. Very early in the morning. They used to dig their own graves. And they used to kill them, at dawn. Or in the evening, before evening came in. And by the time the morning came they were covered over, there was no trace that anybody was there. There was – as if anything happened [*sic*]. It was like – like the – the earth opened up and the people disappeared. The people disappeared. They used to come in, they used to say – 'Strip, you're going to de-lousing', – this is how they called it – 'And we'll go round and then you come back.' And you were stripped naked. There was no – that camp was already dehumanised. You know what I mean? This year which I am talking about, '40 to '41, beginning of 1942 – life was – life was nothing. They become zombies. You could see it in their faces. And it's – I will not try to dwell on this thing, to be quite honest, because you will say to me, 'You were such a child, how the hell do you know the difference between – between shining eyes, dim eyes and sad eyes?' And this, you know, you grew up so quickly. You grew up so quickly. That instinctively you become an animal. And instinctively you feel danger. You feel threatened. You feel it in the air. You – you – you pull yourself in. And – that is the only thing I can explain to you. And that particular morning, I saw my mother and my two sisters being marched out. It was very, very early in the morning. And there was another barracks being stripped and marched out. And my area was, me included, stripped and marched out. But it was in sections. This was the first line and we all lined up in a sort of a line. And a line was like that. Fired, in they fell. A line lined up. But what I noticed, it was a terrible smell of – of earth. Terrible smell of earth, and like painters – I can't explain. And what it was, it was this – this – huge grave was dug and it was – half filled – with – with – it looked like boiling lime, boiling – white – it was boiling. To me it reminded me – as a child I used to go to cheder, I used to have carbide, carbide. You remember there used to be lamps where you used to have – put a little bit of water in and it used to burn. And we used to have a sort of a little pump and we used to pump it up in order for it to burn. And I saw my mother and my four sisters being shot, and fell in. Now I don't know whether you would call this a miracle or you would call this God intervention or what you may call it, I don't know. There was another line taken, and there was about seven or eight people in front of me. Which we would have been the next line. Having said this – and that line went forward. Having said this – you also notice I dismissed the whole question of my mother and four sisters, that they were shot and the next line was taken. It's very hard to explain the feeling. A – a son to see his mother and four sisters being shot. But you know there was no tears in my eyes. There was no breakdown of – of – of the mechanical works of your body. Because you knew you were going to be next. It wasn't a question that they got killed and you are – you are – you somehow will be – will survive. There were – it was – it was no feeling, it was no – no pain, no – no – reaction. And the line was – things were happening so fast, the line went forward and before they were all shot, there was an air raid. There was somehow planes, foreign planes penetrated and there was an air raid. The sirens went. And everybody had to lay down face downwards. And in those – in those – probably must have been minutes, seconds – the whole people, those who were not shot yet, started running higgledy-piggledy. Including myself. So that we are all naked. We are all naked. And we all somehow think that we are going to survive. And some of us survived because we run and run and run – this was all in a forest, don't forget. This has all taken part in a forest. Till I saw a farm. I went into the farm. The people were at work, and whoever was at – was at – at the farm, was in the house, I took a sack, put a sack over me, upside down, made a hole in the bottom part and just put my arms out. And really, truthfully, I walked in and I said, 'You know I'm – I've just run away from – from the killing'. Didn't say I was a Jew. Just said I'd run away from the killings and would they – could they please – you know, I am naked – could they please give me something to put on and something to eat. They said yes. They gave me to eat. It was all women there; the men were in the field. And they gave me something to eat. For my age, although I was ten, I was – I was well built and a big fella. And when the men came home in the evening. Obviously, they were told that – I came in and I ran away from – from the killings and so forth. He said: 'Well, you can stay here until the Germans come. And when the Germans come, we'll let you know.' 'We'll let you know so it will give you a chance to – to – to run away.' Because they didn't want me there because they would have killed them in any case. So, they didn't want to have the responsibility to have somebody there which would threaten their lives. Which I quite understood.[55]

The most striking aspect of Josef Perl's remarkable testimony is perhaps his recollection – almost fifty years after the events in question – of his sensory experiences when confronted with imminent death: the instinctive feeling of danger, the smell of earth, the sight of 'boiling lime', the absence of pain when his mother and four sisters were shot, and the 'mechanical' functioning of his body.

Another memory Perl emphasises in his account is that of being naked. Forcing Jews to strip naked before murdering them was a frequent occurrence. All the victims of a public shooting by EK 9 in the Belarusian city of Vitebsk in early August 1941 – 27 male and female Jews – were forced to remove their clothing in its entirety before being shot. That same month, EK 9 made the entire Jewish population of the Russian town of Surazh – more than 500 men, women and children of all ages – strip naked at the assembly point before shooting them. The same thing happened during the Babi Yar massacre in late September. Many more examples could be cited. Forcing the victims to undress before killing them allowed the perpetrators, first of all, to steal the clothes instead of them landing in the mass graves or being burned on the pyres along with the bodies of their owners. The theft of

Jewish property had always been an integral feature of Nazi anti-Jewish policy, and the plunder of Jewish belongings likewise accompanied the murder operations. In the case of the Vitebsk shooting, however, the victims' clothing was burned where it had been left. This suggests that other motivations were in play, too, such as the deterrence of escape attempts or the deindividualisation of the victims through the creation of a seemingly homogeneous mass, but also voyeurism and a wish to maximise the humiliation of the victims before their death.[56]

Enforced nudity was frequently a constitutive element in the mass murder of Jews, not only during shooting operations but also in the extermination camps, where the Jews were required to undress under the pretext of showering before being killed by poison gas. Coercive nudity was not the only form of sexual and sexualised violence exercised during the process of mass murder. Many cases are documented of Jewish women being raped directly before or even during shooting operations. Members of a subcommando of EK 9 first raped some of the girls among the 1,025 Jews they shot when dissolving the ghetto in the Belarusian village of Yanavichy in September 1941. During the dissolution of the Brest Ghetto in October 1942, German policemen raped young girls before shooting them. In a number of occupied cities, such as Eishishki and Kaunas in Lithuania, lists were prepared of all the unmarried Jewish women, whom the Germans then rounded up, raped and shot. Jewish men were also the victims of sexual violence: in the Latvian town of Bauska, for instance, the local Wehrmacht commander, Lieutenant Nepil, a native of Vienna, and the town's police chief, Druveskalns, arranged for 56 male Jews – including 10 boys between the ages of eight and fifteen – to be castrated in July 1941. A Latvian physician, Steinharts, carried out the sickening procedure.[57]

By the end of 1941, more than 900,000 Soviet Jews had been killed by German forces. Around 460,000 of them – that is, half – were direct victims of Einsatzgruppen A to D, Einsatzkommando Tilsit and Einsatzgruppe z.b.V. Almost as lethal as Einsatzgruppen A to D in terms of total number of Jews murdered were the twelve police battalions that made up the four police regiments north, centre, south and z.b.V., the latter of which was placed at the disposal of higher SS and police leader Russia South and, later, HSSPF z.b.V. Overall, these twelve police battalions are responsible for the second largest share of murders after the Einsatzgruppen. Then there were the SS formations active in the army group or army rear areas during 1941: the 1st SS Infantry Brigade, the 2nd SS Infantry Brigade and the SS Cavalry Brigade. These forces killed at least 57,000 Soviet Jews in 1941. Finally, there were the Wehrmacht units deployed at the front and in the rear areas. The 707th Infantry Division alone murdered more than 10,000 Jews in Belarus in autumn 1941 (placing it on a par with some of the Wehrmacht units operating under Böhme in Serbia at the same time). The 707th Infantry Division may have been an extreme case among Wehrmacht formations in the occupied Soviet territories, but – as we have seen – it was by no means exceptional. Late December 1941 marked the end of the first wave of German killing operations against the Soviet Union's Jewish population. The onset of winter weather caused the ground to freeze and made it too hard to allow for the digging of pits for the victims of the shootings. However, this proved to be only a brief respite for the Soviet Jews. The killing would continue in a second wave the following spring.[58]

Soviet Jews: The Second Wave

In the occupied territories of the Soviet Union, the second sweep of the German killing units was launched, on an even larger scale than the first, in early 1942. It lasted throughout that year, though its scale and timing varied from region to region. The context in which this second wave of shooting operations against Soviet Jews began was very different to that of the first wave the previous summer and autumn. The Wannsee Conference of 20 January 1942 had cleared the way for the mass murder of Jews in the different German-occupied territories to be placed on a centralised, pan-European footing. Technical modifications in the 'euthanasia' gas vans had opened up new possibilities for the killers, and such vans had already been deployed for murdering Jews in the occupied Soviet territories since November 1941. Meanwhile, the first death camp at Chełmno (Kulmhof) in the Wartheland had gone into operation in early December 1941, while the mass murder of the Jews of the Government General had commenced in mid-March 1942 at Bełżec extermination centre, the first to be fitted with stationary gas chambers.[59]

The Germans and their allies in the occupied Soviet territories established a total of 822 Jewish ghettos, more than half of which (442) were located in

Ukraine. In Lithuania, Belarus and Ukraine, many of the ghettos were liqui-dated over the course of 1942 and operations carried out to obliterate any remaining Jewish communities. At the same time, the occupation forces intensified their efforts to root out Jews in rural areas, often killing them under the pretext of anti-partisan warfare. According to a report by the Wehrmacht Armaments Inspectorate, in some areas, such as Reich Commissariat Ukraine – established on 1 September 1941 under civil admin-istration – mass executions had never stopped and continued without inter-ruption, apart from brief organisational hold-ups, from mid-1941 to mid-1942. The units involved belonged mainly to the Order Police: they were assisted by Ukrainian auxiliaries and 'often, unfortunately, by the voluntary participation of members of the Wehrmacht', according to the report by the Armaments Inspectorate.[60]

By the time German killing operations against Jews recommenced across occupied Soviet territory in spring 1942, many of the mobile killing units had been converted into stationary posts, some of them as early as autumn 1941. This reflected, on the one hand, the appointment of civil administra-tions in some of the occupied territories and, on the other hand, the stagna-tion of the German advance and the military setbacks experienced by the Wehrmacht. As with other developments involving the Einsatzgruppen in the occupied Soviet territories, the partial conversion to stationary posts did not occur at the same time for all units. The establishment of stationary posts took place later in the case of Einsatzgruppe C than it did in Einsatzgruppen A and B, for instance. Not all sub-commandos of Einsatzgruppe C, further-more, became stationary units: though EK 5 and SK 4b were converted into stationary posts – now referred to as commanders of the Security Police – based in Kiev and Stalino (now Donetsk), respectively, EK 6 and SK 4a remained unchanged in their function as mobile units. In the case of Einsatzgruppe D, only a single stationary unit was formed. The Einsatzgruppen were also reinforced for the second wave by members of the gendarmerie – policemen from rural communities in Germany – and locally recruited police. These formations assisted in the deportation of Jews from the ghettos to the extermination camps and engaged in operations to hunt down Jews who had escaped the first wave of mass killings and gone into hiding.[61]

Of the approximately 75,000 Jews who were living in Latvia at the time of the German invasion, fewer than 6,500 were still alive by early 1942. No

Jews remained alive in Estonia. On 20 January 1942, it was noted at the Wannsee Conference that Estonia was the first country under German occupation to be rendered 'free of Jews'. The mass murder of Jews in General Commissariat Belarus – one of the sub-divisions of Reich Commissariat Ostland, which comprised the Baltic countries and parts of Belarus and had been established on 25 July 1941 under civil administration – was resumed in March 1942. Unlike in other parts of Ostland, most of the Jewish population of General Commissariat Belarus had remained alive in ghettos beyond the winter of 1941–42. During the first days of March, more than 5,000 Jews from the Minsk Ghetto – the largest in Belarus, with a population of about 49,000 – were shot, as well as more than 2,300 from the Baranovichi Ghetto and over 300 from the Vileyka Ghetto. Killing operations were conducted in other places, too, including the villages of Ilya and Rakov and the town of Cherven. On 8 May, 5,670 Jews were removed from the Lida Ghetto and murdered in the forest about 2km out of town. Only 1,500 working people and their families remained in the ghetto. A further 10,000 Jews were murdered between 8 and 12 May in townships in the Lida area. All of the area's remaining 2,000 Jews were subsequently brought to Lida. The transfer of Jews from smaller ghettos to a few larger ones and their concentration there facilitated their subsequent deportation to the extermination camps in occupied Poland: for instance, the transportation of thousands of Belarusian Jews from Grodno to Treblinka in January and February 1943 and from Lida and Minsk to Sobibór in September 1943.[62]

The annihilation of Jews in the Slonim Ghetto, which housed between 10,000 and 12,000 Jews, including several thousand from neighbouring villages, took place during the period from 29 June to 15 July 1942. Forces of the Baranovichi branch office of the Security Police, the office of the commander of the Security Police and the SD (*Kommandeur der Sicherheitspolizei und des SD*, or KdS) in Minsk under the personal command of KdS Eduard Strauch himself, a Waffen SS platoon, which was also subordinated to Strauch, and the 7th Company of SS Police Regiment 2 murdered between 8,000 and 10,000 Jews in Slonim. When the operation was over, fewer than 1,000 Jews remained; most of these were artisans. In May 1942, massacres took place in the Minsk Ghetto. On some nights, the number of those murdered reached 500. On one occasion, Germans surrounded two houses on Zavalna Street and set them on fire. The inhabitants were burned alive. These night-time massacres, in which an estimated 4,000 to 6,000 people were killed, kept the ghetto Jews in a state of constant terror. On 28 July, the ghetto inhabitants were ordered to report to Yubilee Square, ostensibly to receive new identity badges. Groups of workers left the ghetto as usual. A woman from the ghetto described what happened that morning:

> I rushed up to the attic. From there, I could see the pogrom continue. [...] At noon, everyone left within the boundaries of the ghetto was herded into Yubilee Square. In the square, enormous tables were decorated as if for a holiday. [...] In the centre sat Adolf Richter, the [Security Police] head of the ghetto. [...] The fascists forced the chairman of the Jewish council, the composer Ioffe, to speak from a platform. Deceived by Richter, Ioffe began to calm the frantic crowd, saying that today the Germans would only conduct a registration and exchange identity badges. He had hardly finished talking when covered trucks with gassing equipment drove into the square. Ioffe realised what this meant and shouted: 'Gassing trucks!' The terrible phrase passed like lightning through the frantic crowd: 'Comrades, I was deceived. They are going to kill you!' The insane crowd scattered, seeking salvation from the terrible death. [...] The fascists opened a steady stream of fire. [...] The entire square was littered with bodies and reddened with blood. This continued until late evening. [...] On 1 August, after the massacre was over, the Gestapo sent out an order to the factories where the Jewish workers had been kept during the four-day pogrom, directing that they return to their homes in the ghetto. [...] The people ran to their apartments, hoping to find their relatives safe in their hiding places. But the hiding places in the stoves, under the floor, between the walls had been ripped open by grenades. All the workers found there were the remains of their families, who had been ripped to pieces by the grenades. The majority, however, did not even find remains. Their loved ones had been taken in the gassing vans to Trostinets and Tuchinka.

This massacre lasted until 31 July and cost the lives of at least 10,000 Jews. They were murdered in Yubilee Square, in hiding places in the ghetto, in gas vans and at murder sites outside the city. Twenty or thirty trucks were used to transport people to the sites at Maly Trostinets and the village of Petrashevichi, west of Minsk. It was a joint operation in which German

Security Police and Order Police, local Belarusian police, Wehrmacht soldiers from an anti-aircraft artillery unit and German railroad workers joined forces. After the killing was over, 12,000 Jewish labourers remained in the ghetto. On the final day of the Minsk massacre, 31 July, General Commissioner in Belarus Wilhelm Kube reported to his boss, Reich Commissioner in Ostland Hinrich Lohse, that 'detailed discussions' with the SS and police leader in Minsk, SS Brigadier Carl Zenner, and 'the outstandingly capable head of the SD', SS Lieutenant Colonel Eduard Strauch, had established that 'we have liquidated around 55,000 Jews in Belarus in the last ten weeks'.[63]

In Rovno, designated instead of Kiev as the capital of Reich Commissariat Ukraine, some 18,000 Jews had been murdered during the second half of 1941, leaving around 5,000 still in the ghetto. On 13 July 1942, these were transported by train to a forest near Kostopol and shot. In the early spring of 1942, the Lutsk Ghetto still had a population of between 17,000 and 18,000 Jews. Several hundred men were sent to the city of Vinnitsa on 18 March 1942 to work on building Hitler's forward headquarters, which was to be transferred there from East Prussia. With the exception of three who managed to escape to Transnistria, they were all murdered in the course of 1942. The fate of the Jews originally living in the Vinnitsa area had already been sealed once Hitler decided to move his forward headquarters there. In the first days of 1942, 227 Jews who lived in the immediate neighbourhood of the planned headquarters were delivered by the Organisation Todt construction agency to the Wehrmacht's Secret Field Police and shot by the latter on 10 January. A second batch of approximately 8,000 Jews who lived in nearby Khmelnik were shot around the same time. Then came the turn of the Jews of Vinnitsa themselves. Here, the operation was delayed by a few weeks, but in mid-April the Wehrmacht's Secret Field Police reported that the 4,800 Jews of the town had been 'knocked off'. Finally, approximately 1,000 Jewish artisans who worked for the Germans in the same area were murdered in July on the orders of the local commander of the Security Police.[64]

The Reich commissioners in Ostland and Ukraine, Hinrich Lohse and Erich Koch, respectively, enthusiastically supported mass-murder operations. Koch in particular requested that in Ukraine *all* Jews be annihilated in order to reduce local food consumption and fulfil the growing food demands from the Reich. As a result, at a meeting in August 1942, the district commissioners agreed with the head of the Security Police, Karl Pütz, that all the Jews of Reich Commissariat Ukraine, with the exception of 500 special- ised craftsmen, would be exterminated: this was defined as the '100 per cent solution'. In the Baltic countries – Lohse's domain – particularly in Lithuania, the aforementioned Karl Jäger could always be relied on as far as mass murder was concerned. On 6 February 1942, Walter Stahlecker, chief of Einsatzgruppe A, asked Jäger urgently to report the total number of execu- tions by his Einsatzkommando 3, according to the following categories: Jews, communists, partisans, mentally ill, others; furthermore, Jager had to indi- cate the number of women and children. According to the report, sent three days later, EK 3 alone had killed 136,421 Jews, 1,064 communists, 56 parti- sans, 653 mentally ill and 78 others as of 1 February 1942. Added together, these figures amounted to a total of 138,272 victims (of whom 55,556 were women and 34,464 were children). Not unlike the Wehrmacht's slaughter of the entire Serbian workforce of an aircraft factory in Kraljevo in October 1941, Jäger, too, at times, exceeded the remit given to him by his superiors. In a letter written on 18 May 1942, following an army complaint about the liquidation of 630 Jewish craftsmen in Minsk, contrary to prior agreements, Gestapo chief Heinrich Müller had to remind Jäger of orders issued by Himmler: 'Jews and Jewesses capable of working, between ages 16 and 32, should be exempt from special measures, for the time being.' Throughout 1942, the extermination in the Baltic countries was carried out on a smaller scale than in General Commissariat Belarus, as the majority of Baltic Jews had already been murdered the previous year, including all Jews in Estonia. The killing in Lithuania and Latvia in 1942 nonetheless claimed the lives of several thousand Jews whom the Germans deemed unsuited to joining the workforce: women, children and the elderly.[65]

At times, technical difficulties hampered the killings. On 15 June 1942, for example, the senior commander of the Security Police and the SD (*Befehlshaber der Sicherheitspolizei und des SD*, or BdS) in Ostland, Heinz Jost, urgently requested an additional gas van, as the three vans operating in Belarus – two Diamond models and one (Swiss-made) Saurer – did not suffice to deal with all the Jews arriving at an accelerated rate. Furthermore, he demanded twenty new gas hoses, used for carrying the carbon monoxide from the engines back into the vans, as those in use were no longer airtight. In fact, the functioning of the vans had already occasioned a series of complaints that, in turn, had led to a spirited response from the head of Group II D (Technical Affairs) in the RSHA, SS Lieutenant Colonel Walther Rauff, ten days earlier, on 5 June 1942. Rauff reminded his critics that the three vans in Chełmno extermination camp had 'processed 97,000' since December 1941, when operations there had commenced, 'without any visible defects'. Nonetheless, he suggested seven technical improvements to deal more efficiently with the 'number of items' usually loaded into each van. When referring to the '97,000', the official had probably deemed it safer to avoid any further identification. In the second section of the report he alluded to 'items', and in the sixth section he changed the identification once more: 'It has been ascertained that when the back door [of the van] is shut and everything is enveloped in darkness, the load presses against the door. This stems from the fact that once darkness sets in, the load pushes itself towards the light.' BdS Jost got his fourth gas van: a large Saurer used to asphyxiate the last of the Serbian Jews from Sajmište concentration camp was subsequently returned to Berlin to be technically overhauled before being sent on to Minsk.[66]

One of the largest single massacres of Jews on Belarusian soil during this period took place in Brest. On 15–16 October 1942, members of the Brest branch office of the Security Police, Reserve Police Company 'Nuremberg' and Police Battalion 310, as well as Polish auxiliary police forces, cordoned off the ghetto and herded together its inhabitants. The old and weak, as well as mothers with their children, were shot on the spot. The great majority of the ghettoised Jews, at least 15,000, were taken on freight trains to a secluded location near the village of Bronnaya Gora, around 110km to the east, and murdered there. During the weeks that followed, many hundreds of hidden Jews were discovered during repeated searches of the ghetto. They were brought to a pit in the middle of the ghetto, forced to undress completely and shot. A total of around 19,000 Jews were murdered during the dissolution of the Brest Ghetto.[67]

The dissolution of the Jewish ghettos in the occupied Soviet territories and the murder of their inhabitants continued throughout 1942. As of the end of that year, an estimated 15,000 to 16,000 'legal' Jews remained in General Commissariat Belarus in ghettos and labour camps in the region's large towns and cities. A further 6,000 to 7,000 'illegal' Jews had managed to survive by going into hiding, and some thousands escaped into the forests and joined the partisans. As of early 1943, no ghettos remained in Reich Commissariat Ukraine. Here and there, small groups of Jewish artisans were kept alive in order to serve the local civilian administrations. The last of these Jews were murdered in 1943, on the eve of the German withdrawal from the region. By March 1943, only 30,000 Jews were left in the whole of the Białystok District, all of them in the ghetto in the city of Białystok itself. In total, around 2.6 million Jews living on the territory of the Soviet Union within the borders of 22 June 1941 were killed, that is, almost half of all Jews murdered in the Holocaust. Of these 2.6 million, all but 50,000 or so had lost their lives by the end of October 1943. At least half of all Jews killed on Soviet territory were citizens of Ukraine.[68]

The Holocaust by bullets against the Serbian and Soviet Jews, especially the transition from the end of July 1941 to the wholesale slaughter of all Soviet Jews, was the decisive precursor to a Europe-wide 'final solution to the Jewish question', and then, from 1942 onwards, an integral and ongoing part of it. The decision to exterminate Soviet Jewry in its entirety – the biggest Jewish population in Europe after Poland – constituted a metaphorical crossing of the Rubicon. Once this decision had been made and its implementation begun, it became much easier, both for the leadership in Berlin and for the frontline perpetrators on the ground, to extend this genocidal policy to other parts of German-occupied Europe. In the context of a war of extermination, the identification – however spurious – of Serbian and, especially, Soviet Jews as partisans, fifth columnists, saboteurs and agitators, in short, as the enemy within, and of Jewish children as not only potential partisans but also likely avengers of their parents, lowered any remaining barriers to their physical eradication. As we shall see, once these labels had been employed to justify the slaughter of the Soviet Jews, it was but a small step to apply these same labels to Central and Western European Jews and exterminate them, too, not least because National Socialist propaganda had long promoted the idea of a *global* Jewish conspiracy.[69]

CHAPTER 4
MURDER OF PSYCHIATRIC PATIENTS AND ROMA IN THE SOVIET UNION

Soviet Jews were the principal victims of the mass-murder campaign waged in the USSR between summer 1941 and spring 1942 by SS and police forces with the active support of the Wehrmacht, but they were not the only population groups murdered there for racial–biological reasons. Soviet psychiatric patients and Roma – both regarded by the Nazis as racially inferior and thus as posing a biological threat, and both targeted in an attempt to 'purify' the newly occupied territories – were also murdered in large numbers during this period. Roma had been persecuted in the German Reich since the mid-1930s, and in some cases deported and incarcerated in concentration camps, but – much like Jews in the Reich – they had not been murdered on a mass scale. This changed during Operation Barbarossa. Given that psychiatric patients in the German Reich and the annexed Polish territories had already been killed since the second half of 1939 in the context of Nazi Germany's first mass-killing programme, the 'euthanasia' campaign, it is not surprising that patients in Soviet psychiatric clinics fell victim to German forces from the first days of military operations.

Soviet Psychiatric Patients

The approach taken by the German occupying forces towards mentally ill people in the occupied Soviet territories can be compared to the killings in the Polish psychiatric institutions. However, on the territory of the Soviet Union, there was much greater involvement of Wehrmacht troops and departments. In contrast to the German Reich and the annexed Polish territories, neither a central programme nor corresponding orders can be identified for the Soviet territories. Instead, Wehrmacht and police units began to contemplate the fate of psychiatric patients after the conquest of individual cities and towns. The German occupiers regarded the mentally ill as uncontrollable, dangerous, a source of epidemics and 'useless eaters'. They were among those sections of the Soviet population who could not be exploited economically for the purposes of the occupation regime. This view was widespread, not only among the SS but also within the Wehrmacht. Given the central importance of 'racial health' in Nazi ideology, there could be no place for the mentally handicapped in a German-occupied Europe.[1]

A recurrent, though by no means ubiquitous, pattern in dealing with psychiatric patients emerged. It was not uncommon for military physicians to declare that they required the buildings of mental hospitals for the establishment of German sickbays. In one case, an enquiry of this nature even reached the Army High Command. In a second step, the Wehrmacht departments approached the Einsatzgruppen of the Security Police with the request to take care of the 'evacuation'. The civil administration later acted in a similar way, sometimes calling on the Security Police to take action against the patients. The Security Police murdered the patients either on its own initiative or at the behest of the occupation authorities. Some Wehrmacht physicians admittedly spoke out against such operations, but they appear to have been the exception. It was not uncommon for local medical personnel to be forced to carry out the killings themselves, for instance by means of lethal injection. Some took part in the murders of their own free will, however, as happened in the mental hospital in the Belarusian city of Mogilev.[2]

As with the murder of Soviet Jews, the measures carried out by the Wehrmacht and the SS Einsatzgruppen against mentally ill patients in Soviet institutions reveal a gradual radicalisation. First, the military administration reduced the patients' meals to below what was needed for subsistence. Thus, for example, the doctors at the psychiatric hospital in the city of Vinnitsa, Ukraine, were instructed by the German military administration to hand out only 100g of bread per patient per day. The food supplies of the hospital were confiscated by the Wehrmacht. In response to the doctors' protests, the regional commissioner in charge announced: 'For the mentally ill, even 70g of bread is too much.' In autumn 1941, 800 patients in Vinnitsa were shot and 700 more killed by lethal injection. The institution's premises were eventually used as a sanatorium and mess by the Wehrmacht. This clearly demonstrates a three-stage approach, from the reduction in food rations, via the extermination of patients unfit for work, to the final dissolution of the entire facility in order to vacate the buildings for the Wehrmacht.[3]

While the German military on Soviet territory does not appear to have paid particular attention to the psychiatric clinics during the first weeks of the campaign, this began to change at precisely the moment when Hitler ended Operation T4 and temporarily halted the centrally coordinated 'euthanasia' killings in the German Reich on 24 August 1941. This official stop to the programme did not result, however, in the termination of any of the four killing centres still in use: Hartheim, Sonnenstein, Bernburg and Hadamar. Operation T4 subsequently resumed with great intensity but out of public view, while child 'euthanasia' not only continued without interruption but was indeed intensified. Around the same time, the Wehrmacht and the SS began to target psychiatric patients in the occupied Soviet territories, and indeed in northern, central and southern areas alike. As early as 20 August, the command of XXIX Army Corps, subordinated to the Sixth Army in the southern section of the front, discussed the elimination of a group of 'lunatics running around freely'. Sonderkommando 4b of Einsatzgruppe C thereupon shot 60 mental patients. On 28 August, SS units shot 448 patients in the Latvian city of Daugavpils; the mental hospital in question was already being used by the Wehrmacht at the time of the killings. Also in late August 1941, on the initiative of the medical department of the Wehrmacht field headquarters in Choroszcz in the Białystok District, Wehrmacht troops themselves machine-gunned all 464 patients left in the psychiatric hospital there, after the majority had been evacuated to various Soviet institutions prior to the German invasion.[4]

These first mass-killing operations against Soviet psychiatric patients may have been triggered by a tour of inspection made by Reichsführer SS Heinrich Himmler. During his tour of Baranovichi, Minsk and the surrounding area in mid-August 1941, which included the attendance of a mass shooting of Jews and alleged partisans by Einsatzkommando 8 on the 15th, Himmler also visited the mental hospital in nearby Novinki the same day. Following the visit, Himmler – still under the immediate impression of the mass shooting that morning – requested Arthur Nebe to murder the psychiatric patients, but by other means than shooting, which was 'not the most humane way'. Instead, he instructed Nebe to experiment with new methods of killing that would be less burdensome for the perpetrators: Himmler and Heydrich feared that the mass shootings of people of all ages would have psychologically negative effects on the shooters and generate a group of brutalised men unable to reintegrate into post-war society. It was no coincidence that Himmler assigned to Nebe the task of finding an alternative to shooting: not only was he head of Einsatzgruppe B; as director of the Reich Criminal Police Office, he was also in charge of the Forensic Institute of the Security Police, which had played a key role in developing gassing facilities for Operation T4 in the Reich. Himmler's instructions were understood by several witnesses as a general authorisation for Nebe to kill all mentally ill people in his area of operations.[5]

Alternatives to Shooting

Gas vans had already been used two years earlier in the annexed Polish territories for murdering psychiatric patients as part of the 'euthanasia' campaign: carbon monoxide was released from bottles into stationary gas chambers or into vans. As the transport of canisters of carbon monoxide to the occupied Soviet territories was deemed impracticable and indeed dangerous, a new method was required. After experimenting with explosives, Nebe hit upon the idea of exhaust fumes. With the assistance of Dr Albert Widmann, head of the chemistry section at the Forensic Institute of the Security Police, Nebe then applied this method to asphyxiate 120 chronically sick patients at the aforementioned mental hospital in Novinki on 18 September 1941: the exhaust fumes from a truck belonging to the Order Police were directed via metal hoses into a sealed bathhouse in which the patients had been assembled.[6]

A corresponding technical modification in the 'euthanasia' gas vans, developed from September 1941 at the Forensic Institute under the auspices of Dr Widmann, opened up new possibilities for the killers. The redesigned vans would become mobile suffocating machines for batches of around 40 people per van and per operation: a metal pipe connected to the exhaust gas hose would be inserted into a hermetically sealed van. Running the powerful engine sufficed to asphyxiate its human cargo. From January 1942, larger Saurer models, which could carry up to 100 people, were also deployed in the Soviet territories under German occupation.[7]

On 26 September 1941, the chief of the Army General Staff, Franz Halder, tersely wrote in his diary following a presentation by his quartermaster general, Brigadier Eduard Wagner: 'Lunatic asylums in [the area of Army Group] North. Russians regard mental deficiency as sacred. Nonetheless, killing [is] necessary.' The OKH thereupon requested Wilhelm Koppe, higher SS and police leader in Poznań, to arrange for Herbert Lange to be flown to the northern Russian city of Novgorod in order to murder the residents of three local 'lunatic asylums', because Wehrmacht troops 'urgently' required the institutions as lodgings. Lange and his special commando were, after all, familiar with the killing of mentally ill people. Contacted by Koppe on 3 October, Himmler granted his permission the following day for Lange to be 'immediately' dispatched to Novgorod. It is unclear whether Lange used a mobile gas van in Novgorod, as he had in the Wartheland and East Prussia; there is instead evidence to suggest that lethal injection was the preferred method of killing in this case. In November, however, Sonderkommando 4a under Paul Blobel did use one of the redesigned gas vans to murder Jews in the Ukrainian city of Poltava. The Poltava operation appears to have been the first time a gas van was deployed for murdering Jews in the occupied Soviet territories. Once again, the 'euthanasia' campaign had acted as a precursor to the genocide of the Jews – Soviet Jews were being murdered using gas vans originally modified for killing Soviet psychiatric patients.[8]

In the meantime, mass shootings of psychiatric patients, as of Jews, continued across the occupied Soviet territories. In September 1941, a commando of Einsatzgruppe A was dispatched to the village of Mogutovo, 'where eighty-seven mental patients had armed themselves and roamed over the land, plundering', as a German report claimed. These mental patients, the report continued, had been 'stirred up' by eleven communists, some of whom 'presumably' belonged to a partisan group. The response of the commando was predictable: 'The eleven agitators, who included six Jews, as well as the mental patients were liquidated.' The German report succeeded in amalgamating multiple bogeymen in this one group of murdered civilians: the mentally sick, plunderers, communists, partisans and, for good measure, Jews. At the end of September 1941, the commander of Army Group Rear Area (Korück) 553 requested that measures be taken against the desolate state of the mental institution in the southern Ukrainian city of Kherson. Three weeks later, the 1,000 patients were murdered. Members of a Luftwaffe unit had participated in the killing operation. One of the largest massacres of psychiatric patients was carried out by Einsatzkommando 6 of Einsatzgruppe C in the Ukrainian city of Dnepropetrovsk, shortly before it was placed under civil administration. Eight hundred patients from the Igrin asylum had fallen victim to the unit by 12 November. By February 1942, EK 6 had killed another 760 patients there. As in occupied Poland, the murder operations were not limited to the mentally ill but occasionally also extended to other people who were considered to pose a 'medical threat'. Thus, the Security Police shot and killed 50 women suffering from venereal diseases in the southern Ukrainian city of Mariupol under the pretext that they might infect German soldiers. Individual cases are also recorded where, according to German documents, 'beggars' or 'vagrants' were shot.[9]

In November, Sonderkommando 4b of Einsatzgruppe C, which was stationed in Poltava at the time, prior to being relieved by its sister unit SK 4a, reported the 'liquidation of 565 incurable mental patients' from the city's psychiatric institution. This shooting operation took place following consultation with the leadership of the Sixth Army and local Wehrmacht headquarters. Reporting back to Berlin following the killings, SK 4a justified them in view of 'the exceptionally critical food situation in the city' and commented on a now familiar pattern: 'The cooperation with the Wehrmacht, as well as the Ukrainian Order Service, went smoothly.'[10]

On 26 December 1941, the Eighteenth Army under General Georg von Küchler, deployed in the northern section of the front, agreed to a request made by XXVIII Army Corps to have Sonderkommando 1b murder 240 women from the asylum in the former monastery of Makarevskaya Pustin. The women, who were suffering from mental illnesses, syphilis and epilepsy, were running low on food, and the request was made on the grounds that they might break out and then pose a risk of disease for civilians in the surroundings villages but 'above all for the German soldiers'. According to the army corps: 'What is more, the inmates of the institution, from a German point of view, too, represent objects of life no longer worth living.' A sub-commando led by SS Captain Hermann Hubig shot the women shortly thereafter. While the liquidation of the Makarevskaya institution was justified with the alleged threat of epidemics facing German soldiers, utilitarian considerations played the decisive role in the elimination of the roughly 1,300 patients of Kashchenko Psychiatric Hospital in the village of Nikolskoye by a task force of Einsatzgruppe A at the request of the leadership of the Eighteenth Army: the Wehrmacht was not prepared to feed the inhabitants of the institution, and the buildings were earmarked for use as a hospital. EK 3, another sub-unit of Einsatzgruppe A, counted 653 'mentally ill' among the total of 138,272 people it had murdered as of 1 February 1942.[11]

As in Germany and Poland, mentally handicapped children were also among those murdered in the Soviet Union. On 27 August 1941, the commander of the local Wehrmacht headquarters proposed the killing of the inhabitants of an asylum for disabled children in the Belarusian town of Cherven, near Minsk. He justified this measure with practical arguments, though his complete disregard for human life – or at least that of Soviet children – is clearly evident from the contents of his report:

> The retention of this nuthouse is causing major difficulties, as the institu-
> tion possesses no agricultural holdings of its own and is being fed by the
> municipal authorities. [...] Of the 144 children, only sixty are partly
> capable of work; the rest are veritable idiots. Three of the children have
> contracted dysentery. [...] The costs for this institution were estimated
> by the Cherven municipality at around 236,000 roubles for half a year.
>
> On the basis of the above information, the local headquarters in
> Cherven take the view that it would perhaps be better to dissolve this
> institution, as:
> 1.) it is a completely unproductive establishment,
> 2.) the maintenance of this institution constitutes a very significant
>   burden on the finances of the municipal authorities,
> 3.) there is no prospect of even one of the children regaining its
>   mental health,
> 4.) [it] creates considerable difficulties for the food supply,
> 5.) the shortage of clothing, footwear and undergarments, and the
>   poor heating facilities in winter in view of the poor state of the
>   buildings will have an unfavourable impact on health conditions.

Two days later, Field Headquarters 812 – noting that the SS had 'liquidated' the patients of a mental institution in a prior case – suggested to Einsatzgruppe B in Minsk that such an 'arrangement' would also be 'appropriate in the present case'. In spite of support from the German civil administration in the person of Hans Wolfgang Weber, head of the Department of Health and Public Welfare in General Commissariat Belarus, and repeated requests to murder the children, the SD eventually responded on 10 December that it was unable to comply with the request due to 'work overload', which presum- ably meant that it was too busy killing other unarmed civilians. However, this proved to be only a temporary respite for the children: SS Brigadier Carl Zenner, SS and police leader in Minsk, complied with the wishes of the Wehrmacht and the civil administration in May 1942 by killing the inhabitants of the asylum.[12]

Handicapped children also fell victim to the gas vans now operating across the occupied Soviet territories. In October 1942, the disabled boys and girls of an orphanage in Yeysk, on the east coast of the Azov Sea, were loaded into a gas van – which the children christened the 'Black Raven' – by a sub-commando of SK 10a of Einsatzgruppe D and asphyxiated. Across two successive days, at least 260 children were murdered in this way; only 7 managed to survive. One of these survivors later recalled:

> They quickly finished off some of the children, particularly babies. Then the Germans proceeded to the residential building and looked there and around the house for the remaining children. I can no longer exactly describe how the loading of the children [into the gas van] took place, as I didn't see anything because I was scared stiff. I can only remember that one of the Germans came to the toilet, knocked on the door and said in German: 'Children, children, come out.' But we didn't open up, so he said in broken Russian: 'Quick, quick.' As we assumed that he wanted to use the toilet, we opened up. Instead of going in, he herded us to the truck. [...] I didn't get in but seized a favourable opportunity to run into the house and hide on the upper floor. I was still able to hear the interpreter ask a female carer or nurse whether all the children had been loaded on to the truck. She answered: 'No, no, not all of them.' Then the interpreter said: 'Okay, we'll come back tomorrow.'

The tentative results of research carried out so far yield a total of at least 17,000 psychiatric patients murdered by German forces in the occupied territories of the Soviet Union.[13]

Soviet Roma

German forces marched into the Soviet Union without precise orders regarding the Roma minority but with radicalised prejudices and under the influence of experiences gathered during years of persecution. In the German Reich, Roma had already been one of the groups to fall victim to the Nazis' tendency to treat what they considered antisocial behaviour as a racial–biological threat. East of the Bug river, nomadic Roma in particular were regarded by both the Wehrmacht and the police leaderships as 'work-shy' and, even more ominously for the victims, as potential spies. In the climate of the siege mentality prevalent in the undermanned rear areas of the occupied Soviet territories, this translated into a blanket identification of Roma with partisans. These stereotypes prepared the ground for a murderous approach to this demographic group.[14]

Wehrmacht units began killing Soviet Roma on a small scale in August 1941. Six were shot and killed by the staff of Local Headquarters II/939 in the southern Ukrainian town of Berezovka. The first documented killing of Soviet Roma by one of the Einsatzgruppen was reported on 22 August: EK 3 of Einsatzgruppe A murdered four adult Roma, including a woman, and one child. The next documented operation against Soviet Roma was carried out by Einsatzgruppe B in September. In this case, Field Headquarters 181 of the Wehrmacht handed over twenty-three Roma (thirteen males and ten females) near the town of Lepel in Belarus to EK 9 'because they had terrorised the rural populace and committed numerous acts of theft'. These twenty-three 'Gypsies' were then shot by EK 9. Their murder does not, however, appear – at least at this stage – to have been part of a systematic programme to annihilate all Soviet Roma. In his post-war testimony, the commander of EK 9, Alfred Filbert, stated that he had not been issued with such an order parallel to the order to kill Soviet Jews. This seems likely, as Roma were neither among those earmarked for execution according to Reinhard Heydrich's written instruc-tions of 2 July to the higher SS and police leaders, nor were they mentioned in Heydrich's guidelines of 17 July for sifting Soviet POW camps.[15]

In Mogilev, 50 Roma were murdered on 10 October 1941 by police forces and EK 8; a further 33 were killed there in March 1942. In the Belarusian town of Marina Gorka, 200 Roma were interned for weeks in unspeakable conditions in December 1941, so that above all women and children perished, before the survivors were shot. Further Roma were killed there in spring 1942. Nowhere in the operations area of Army Group Centre was a differentiation made in practice between itinerant and sedentary Roma; ultimately, they were all systematically annihilated. Their wholesale murder took place at the same time as the second wave of killing operations against the Soviet Jews. In fact, from spring 1942, the Roma living in Bryansk province in western Russia were placed on the same level as the Jews there and in many cases murdered with them, as happened during several mass-shooting operations carried out by SK 7a in the area of Klintsy between February and April 1942.[16]

Events in Smolensk province are particularly important for understanding the German extermination of Roma in the Soviet territories under military administration. Here, the transition to a systematic and (at least intended) total extermination of Roma took place in spring 1942. Several thousand were murdered by Einsatzgruppe B in Smolensk province, where the local Roma population was comparatively dense. This made them far easier to find than in most other parts of the occupied Soviet territories. Illustrative of the German approach is a mass shooting of Roma from the village of Aleksandrovka near Smolensk on 24 April 1942. After two German officers had drawn up lists of the residents according to family and nationality the previous day, SS troops shot all Roma inhabitants of the village – men, women and children. One eyewitness recalled:

> Each family was led to the pit individually, and if someone did not approach the pit they [the Germans] grabbed them and dragged them to the pit. The shooting was carried out by a German soldier with his pistol. First, the children aged ten to twelve were shot before the eyes of their mother; then they snatched infants from the arms of their mothers and threw them alive into the pit. Only then, after all this, were the mothers shot. Some could not bear this torment and jumped in after their infants. [...] But not only were the children thrown alive into the pit. I saw with my own eyes how they threw the sick old woman Leonovič into the pit, who was unable to move by herself and had been wrapped in a blanket by her daughters and carried [to the pit] by hand.

The male Roma then had to fill the mass grave with earth, before they were shot into a second pit. A second selection of victims that had taken place at the edge of the trenches directly before the shooting commenced, namely a physical examination, underscores the racial–ideological motivation of the perpetrators. Those the Germans concluded were not, after all, Roma (but rather ethnic Russians) were sent home and, in this way, spared. A total of 176 Roma from Aleksandrovka were shot.[17]

In October 1941, Wehrmacht units deployed in Serbia had begun mass executions of Roma there. In a similar vein, it was often military authorities that took the initiative in the persecution and murder of Soviet Roma. In Belarus, the commander of the 339th Infantry Division, Georg Hewelcke, openly called for their systematic genocide on 5 November 1941: 'all vermin and useless eaters to be eradicated (escaped and recaptured prisoners of war, vagrants, Jews and Gypsies)'. Baron Gustav von Bechtolsheim, his colleague from the 707th Infantry Division, which was stationed in the area under civil administration, issued his units with corresponding orders on 24 November ('the Jews must disappear from the countryside and the Gypsies must be annihilated, too'), though he had already demanded as early as 10 October that any 'Gypsies picked up are to be shot on the spot'. In doing so, the two Wehrmacht commanders went beyond even Himmler's basic directives. In summer 1942, the chief of the Army Field Police demanded that the Roma be 'ruthlessly exterminated'.[18]

Like its counterparts to the north, Einsatzgruppe C had also documented its first killings of Roma by the end of September 1941. It was members of the group staff, rather than one of the subordinated commandos, who 'dispatched' – along with four NKVD functionaries and fifty-five Jews – 'six antisocial elements (Gypsies)' near the town of Novoukrainka in Ukraine, where the staff was headquartered for several days in mid-September. While travelling from Vyrva to Dederev the same month, SK 4a under SS Colonel Paul Blobel 'apprehended a Gypsy gang of thirty-two people. During the search of their wagons, German equipment was found. As the gang had no papers and could provide no information regarding the origin of the items they had with them, they were executed.' This example illustrates the thoroughly arbitrary and flimsy nature of 'justifications' given for murdering Soviet Roma: the general suspicion to which they were subjected by German forces meant that any one of a whole host of allegations – spying, partisan activity, antisocial behaviour, theft, itinerancy – was enough to get them killed. Later, no justification at all was needed; the term 'Gypsy' was reason enough for the Germans to murder Roma.[19]

In the northern section of the front, the commanding general of the rear area for Army Group North, Franz von Roques, issued an order on 21 November 1941 stipulating that 'itinerant Gypsies' were to be handed over to the nearest Einsatzkommando of the SD, which amounted to a death sentence. Sedentary Roma, on the other hand, who had already lived in their residence for two years and were classified as 'politically and criminally free from suspicion' were permitted to remain where they were. Some individual shootings of Roma are documented for 1941 for the area of Army Group North, such as the aforementioned murder of four adult Roma and one child by EK 3 in August, though large-scale massacres do not appear to have generally taken place in this region until early 1942. One exception is a mass shooting of Roma from the western Latvian city of Liepāja (Libau) by members of the regular German urban police (*Schutzpolizei*). On 13 December 1941, the SS and police garrison commander in Liepāja, Fritz Dietrich, reported that the entire Roma population of that city, almost half of them children, had been murdered in the nearby town of Saldus (Frauenburg): 'On 5 December, the Gypsies of the city of Liepāja, 100 people in total, were evacuated and executed in the vicinity of Saldus.'[20]

Shortly thereafter, and on the initiative of the commander of the Order Police in Ostland, Georg Jedicke, Reich Commissioner in Ostland Hinrich Lohse composed a letter in which he stigmatised the 'Gypsies roaming about the country' as 'carriers of contagious diseases, especially typhus' and as 'unreliable elements'. He furthermore expressed the 'justified suspicion' that they harmed the German cause 'by transmitting information in the interests of the enemy'. Lohse concluded: 'I therefore stipulate that they are to be equated with Jews in their treatment.' At the time this letter was composed, early December 1941, Jews were of course being physically exterminated root and branch across the occupied Soviet territories. Though Lohse, as chief of the civil administration, did not have access to the police apparatus, the letter – backdated to 4 December and addressed to the higher SS and police leader in Ostland, Friedrich Jeckeln – signaled his approval of the murder of the Liepāja Roma. Jedicke forwarded Lohse's text to his commanders on 12 January 1942, who in turn informed their subordinated units of urban police and gendarmerie. In Latvia, which had the largest Roma population in the Baltic, the commander of the Order Police understood Lohse's instructions to apply to all Roma, regardless of whether they were itinerant or sedentary. During the first months of 1942, therefore, the German Order Police handed over all Roma to the commandos of the Security Police and the SD to be shot.[21]

Indeed, the transition to the systematic genocide of the Soviet Roma took place across the northern section of the front in February and March

1942. In terms of scope and intensity, the annihilation process reached its climax there in May–June 1942. Among other killings, Einsatzgruppe A shot 71 'Gypsies' in the vicinity of Leningrad in April, and troops from the local Wehrmacht headquarters in the Russian town of Novorzhev in Pskov province shot 128 Roma in late May. During the first half of 1942, then, Wehrmacht, SS and police forces murdered the majority of the Roma living in this area, including all the Roma that the Germans could lay their hands on in the region of Novgorod. This fact explains why the intensity of the killing decreased in the second half of 1942. In spite of Franz von Roques's aforementioned order of 21 November 1941 to the contrary, no differentiation was made in practice between itinerant and sedentary Roma: they were all annihilated.[22]

The Novorzhev shooting in late May 1942 took place in the area of the 281st Security Division and was carried out by troops from the local Wehrmacht headquarters at the suggestion of Secret Field Police Group 714. Though their involvement in partisan activity was 'not fully established', there existed 'serious suspicions' against the Roma, so that 'their removal seemed necessary'. The local headquarters were acting here on an earlier order issued by Field Headquarters 822 on 12 May to the effect that Roma were 'always to be treated like partisans', that is, shot. Though the 281st Security Division subsequently instructed Field Headquarters 822 to rescind the order of 12 May, as it apparently ran counter to an order issued by the commander of Army Group North's rear area the previous November, the division defended the Novorzhev shooting in retrospect in a report to the rear area commander, noting that 'since the shooting of the Gypsies was carried out, no more raids have taken place in this region'. Although the Novorzhev shooting triggered an administrative enquiry, another mass shooting took place at exactly the same time in the adjoining region of Pushkinskie Gory, to the west. Here, as in Novorzhev, the Roma were victims of the local Wehrmacht headquarters; seventy Roma, including twenty-three children, were shot. In nearby Porkhov, another twenty-five Roma were also murdered as whole families. The extermination of Roma in the area of the 281st Security Division was evidently systematic in character, and the military administration carried it out on its own authority. The forces of the local Wehrmacht headquarters in the southeastern part of Pskov province killed all Roma they could get hold of. The Germans' blanket equation of 'Gypsies' with 'partisans' apparent from the cases cited above, and the root-and-branch extermination of all Roma, irrespective of age or gender, are reminiscent of the treatment of Soviet Jews.[23]

As can be seen, the approach taken to the Soviet Roma by the occupation authorities in terms of scope and timing initially differed from region to region. The most radical approach was taken by Einsatzgruppe D on the northern shore of the Black Sea, where Roma were systematically shot and killed from the outset. Two mass shootings in the region of Nikolayev in southern Ukraine date already from September–October 1941. In the first of these operations, between 100 and 150 *sedentary* Roma, including women and children, were murdered. Unlike the other regions discussed above, the systematic annihilation of all Roma living on the Crimean Peninsula began in late 1941 and ran parallel to the mass murder of the Jews. Alone in the period from 16 November to 15 December, Einsatzgruppe D shot 824 'Gypsies' there, most of whom fell victim to the large-scale massacre in the city of Simferopol. All Roma families in the Crimean city of Kerch were arrested and imprisoned on 29 December. The next day, they were loaded on to trucks, driven to the outskirts of town near the suburb of Bagerov and shot into a ditch by German troops with sub-machine guns. A Roma blacksmith survived the massacre:

My father and I were in the second group to be shot [...]. When the second round of sub-machine [gun] shots rang out, my father and I fell on corpses and I pulled a dead man over me [...]. After it was all over the Germans fired on the people who were still moving. That was when they wounded me in the left shoulder and I lost consciousness, but I later came to and saw that my father was alive next to me. That night my father helped me climb over the corpses and toward morning we reached Churbash village.

Between mid-January and mid-February 1942, the commandos of Einsatzgruppe D murdered 91 'plunderers, saboteurs, antisocial elements', in the second half of February 421 'Gypsies, antisocial elements and saboteurs', up to mid-March a further 810 'anti-social elements, Gypsies, lunatics and saboteurs', and by the end of that month another 261 'anti-social elements, incl. Gypsies'. Individual local and field headquarters of the Wehrmacht provided assistance, as in the case of Local Headquarters 882, which in early April 1942 handed over '40 Gypsies' to the SD in the southern Ukrainian city of Melitopol, which then murdered them all. A report sent back to Berlin and dated 8 April 1942 concluded for Crimea that, with a few exceptions in the north, 'Jews, [Turkic-speaking Jews known as] Krymchaks and Gypsies no longer exist'. Only in spring 1942 did the other Einsatzgruppen adopt the same general policy of annihilation.[24]

The aforementioned Simferopol, the second largest city on the Crimean Peninsula, had a Roma quarter. In November and December 1941, German occupation forces registered by name the people living there. In early December, the Eleventh Army, in particular Senior Quartermaster Friedrich Wilhelm Hauck, urged Einsatzgruppe D to murder the Jews and the Roma of Simferopol as soon as possible, preferably before Christmas, and undertook to supply trucks and men for the task. The Roma were then taken from their homes on 9 December and driven to a pre-selected site outside the city. As promised, the Wehrmacht provided trucks, drivers and armed guards. Otto Ohlendorf's adjutant in the staff of Einsatzgruppe D, Heinz Schubert, oversaw the shooting operation. The shooters were members of SK 11a and 11b, as well as the Wehrmacht's own Field Gendarmerie Section 683 and Secret Field Police Group 647. The victims – at least 600 Roma – were shot into anti-tank ditches, which were subsequently covered up with earth. Schubert then reported back to Ohlendorf, who was 'pleased', as his adjutant later recalled. The Russian dentist Khrisanf Lashkevich, a resident of Simferopol, cited in his diary a conversation with one of the Roma who survived the December shooting operation:

My first [conversation partner] (I don't know his name) told me: 'I was already in the truck with my daughter and we were waiting to be sent off. When I saw a Tatar acquaintance of mine talking to the Germans, I shouted at him: "Save me, tell the Germans that I'm not a Gypsy, but a Tatar, after all we're friends." And that Tatar began to tell the Germans that I wasn't a Gypsy, but a Turkmen, and they let me and my daughter out. Then I began to plead for them to release my wife and my other children and grandchildren, who were sitting in the other trucks. But the other Roma, seeing that I had been let out, began to shout all at once that they weren't Roma, but also Turkmen like me, and begged to be released.

113

Then my friend, the Tatar, said to me: "better to save yourself. You won't save your family anyway, and they'll take you back into the truck, and I'll catch hell for protecting you." So I ran away with my daughter, and my wife and all my children and grandchildren perished.

On the same day as the massacre of the Roma, 1,500 Krymchaks from Simferopol were murdered, while more than 10,000 Jews from the city were killed during the days that followed.[25]

During his post-war trial in Nuremberg for the murder of 90,000 people, the former head of Einsatzgruppe D, Otto Ohlendorf, attempted to justify the mass murder of Soviet Jews and Roma with military 'security considerations', pointing to the task of the Einsatzgruppen in keeping the Wehrmacht's rear free and murdering anyone who might put its safety at risk. He claimed that he had made no differentiation in the treatment of Jews and 'Gypsies' because both had always acted as spies 'in all wars' and therefore had to be regarded collectively as dangerous elements. Ohlendorf applied a general suspicion of espionage against the Roma – 'these nomadic people' – although the vast majority of Crimean Roma were in fact sedentary town dwellers. He furthermore considered the inclusion of children in the annihilation as a 'prerequisite' for establishing 'lasting security' in the conquered territories and for preventing them from taking revenge for their murdered parents. As the children of parents who had been killed, Ohlendorf continued, they had posed 'no lesser threat' to the Germans 'than the parents themselves'.[26]

Einsatzgruppe D in fact assumed a pioneer role among the Einsatzgruppen (and indeed the German occupation forces per se) when it came to the mass murder of Soviet Roma, for it was Ohlendorf's sub-commandos that were the first to make the transition to a systematic annihilation of the Roma population as a whole. The root-and-branch approach taken by Ohlendorf during the autumn of 1941 in comparison with the other commando chiefs illustrates the undeniable freedom of action enjoyed by the individual commanders on the ground. Ohlendorf was clearly acting on his own authority here, yet – far from being reprimanded or hindered by his superiors – he went on to become the longest serving of the four original Einsatzgruppen commanders. The fact that the intensity of the measures against the Roma in the different areas of operation then escalated almost simultaneously to complete annihilation in spring 1942 suggests, by contrast, that this particular radicalisation was coordinated at a higher level among the German occupation authorities. By the same token, it was Ohlendorf who had led the way and provided the impetus for a complete eradication of the Roma from the occupied Soviet territories.[27]

A total of around 30,000 Roma were murdered in individual operations across the whole of the Soviet territories under German occupation, comprising half of those living there at the time of the invasion of June 1941. Some 6,000 Roma were killed in Belarus alone. Though the Einsatzgruppen did not systematically hunt down Roma in the way they did Jews, they shot them whenever and wherever they found them. The victims were generally shot in small groups by the Security Police, though often after having been handed over by units of the Wehrmacht. It was not uncommon, furthermore, for Wehrmacht commanders to seize the initiative by expressly demanding the murder of Roma or for Wehrmacht units to conduct shooting operations themselves. After months of investigating German crimes against the Soviet Union, the latter's Extraordinary State Commission concluded that the physical annihilation of the Soviet Roma was to be placed on a par with the murder of the Soviet Jews in terms of its totality and intentionality (though the respective dimensions are not comparable). Indeed, from spring 1942, Roma living in the rear areas of all three army groups – north, centre and south – were treated de facto like Jews. As with the Jews, the motives for the annihilation can be found in a fatal combination of National Socialist racial ideology, which manifested itself not only in the blanket identification of Roma with partisans but also in the lack of differentiation in practice between itinerant and sedentary Roma, and a warped concept of military necessity that saw threats everywhere and envisaged the single option of further radicalisation as a response to any and all setbacks. Ultimately, Roma – like Jews and psychiatric patients – were regarded as racially inferior and as a threat to Germany's capacity to consolidate its territorial gains and eventually win a war in the east.[28]

CHAPTER 5
STARVATION POLICY AGAINST THE SOVIET URBAN POPULATION

The inadequate supply of foodstuffs to the German people during the First World War was regarded by the Nazi regime as one of the central reasons for the crumbling of the 'spirit of 1914' and the purported 'stab in the back' of 1918, and the growing food deficit in the areas under German control in 1940–41 threatened one of the basic requirements for a continuation of the new global conflict. As early as 11 August 1939, Hitler himself announced to an astonished Carl J. Burckhardt, the League of Nations high commissioner in the Free City of Danzig: 'I need Ukraine, in order that no one is able to starve us again, like in the last war.' In response to these considerations, over the course of six months between the end of 1940 and June 1941, German planning staffs developed a concept that envisaged the seizure of substantial amounts of grain from the occupied Soviet territories at the cost of tens of millions of Soviet lives. This concept – conceived even before other criminal policies vis-à-vis the Soviet civilian population, such as the Wehrmacht's so-called Criminal Orders or the deployment of the Einsatzgruppen of the Security Police and the SD – was the brainchild of the number two in the Reich Ministry of Food and Agriculture (*Reichsministerium für Ernährung und Landwirtschaft*, or RMEL), Permanent Secretary Herbert Backe. What began in the RMEL ultimately became state policy advocated by Germany's political elites, military leadership and ministerial bureaucracy.[1]

The Politics of Starvation

Proposals for a military campaign against the USSR could be heard in the corridors of power as early as July 1940, and Permanent Secretary Backe was informed of Hitler's intentions towards the Soviet Union no later than 6 November. The official order to commence preparations for an invasion of the Soviet Union – Directive No. 21: Case Barbarossa – was issued a month and a half later, on 18 December 1940. The directive placed emphasis on an early occupation of the Donets Basin, a major source of coal, and identified the capture of 'the important transport and armaments centre' of Moscow as constituting 'politically and economically a decisive success'. Beyond this, however, there was little reference to the economic gain to be had from the Soviet territories, and no reference at all to agricultural produce.[2]

Even before the war, Germany – in spite of the Nazi regime's efforts – had not been autarkic; it had been necessary to import from overseas as much as 17 per cent of its annual food requirements. The whole of continental Europe required imports of 12 to 13 million tons of grain a year, which was equivalent to the food requirements of over 25 million people. This was bound to increase in wartime due to loss of efficiency and Germany's inability to import from the Western Hemisphere as a result of the British naval blockade. Indeed, by the end of 1940, the grain deficit for continental Europe – much of which was by this time under German occupation – had already risen significantly. In Belgium, for instance, imports accounted for 49 per cent of total food consumption, while Norway relied on imports of 57 per cent of its foodstuffs. Thus, the need, in the eyes of the German leadership, to take decisive action to combat Germany's and German-occupied Europe's lack of self-sufficiency was becoming ever more pressing.[3]

During the Christmas holidays, just a few days after the issuing of Directive No. 21, Backe redrafted the annual report of the RMEL on the food situation in Germany. This was the third draft of the memorandum, as Backe felt that neither the first nor the second version, drawn up in November and December 1940, respectively, had sufficiently reflected 'the severity of the food situation'. On 9 January 1941, he passed the revised report to his immediate superior, Reich Minister Richard Walther Darré, for the latter's signature. That same day, Darré forwarded the report, just as he did every year, to Hitler via the head of the Reich Chancellery, Dr Hans-Heinrich Lammers. In addition to the report on the food situation for the economic year 1940–41, Backe – without the assistance of other members of the ministry – also produced a separate description of the likely food situation in the coming third year of the war; these deliberations had provided the basis for his revisions to the annual report. Backe then presented his findings to a combined session of the RMEL and the Reich Food Estate, which was responsible for the supervision of all aspects of rural life in Germany, from production to distribution. According to Backe, all those present voiced their full agreement with the findings of his account.[4]

On 13 January, four days after his submission of the RMEL's annual report on the food situation, Backe presented on the same subject together with Erich Neumann, permanent secretary in the Office of the Four-Year Plan (*Vierjahresplanbehörde*, or VJPB), which had been established in autumn 1936 to prepare the German economy for waging war. Their audience was Neumann's boss, Plenipotentiary for the Four-Year Plan Hermann Göring. In their presentation, Backe and Neumann recommended that meat rations in Germany be reduced. Neumann had already prepared a corresponding decree, which was then approved by Göring and circulated the same day among all Reich ministers, all NSDAP Gauleiters and various other state and party representatives. Pointing to the disappointing harvest in the second year of the war and uncertainty as to how long the war might last, the decree announced that certain combative measures would have to be taken, including the reduction of meat rations in the summer.[5]

Elsewhere, during a presentation on 22 January, Lieutenant General Georg Thomas, chief of the War Economy and Armaments Office (*Wehrwirtschafts- und Rüstungsamt*, or Wi Rü Amt) in the Wehrmacht High Command, informed Chief of the OKW Field Marshal Wilhelm Keitel that his office was in the process of preparing a study addressing its misgivings with regard to the planned operations against the Soviet Union. It was this very pessimism, however, that led to the realisation on Thomas's part that only a more radical approach could enable Germany to achieve its economic objectives. A two-and-a-half-hour meeting on 29 January between Göring and ministerial representatives, including Backe and Thomas, addressing eastern questions would have given Thomas the opportunity to explore other perspectives within the field of civilian economic planning and, if he did not know already, learn about Backe's proposals. In any case, a day after the 29 January meeting, Thomas was in a position to inform members of his staff:

Permanent Secretary Neumann has an expert for Russia, with whom we ought to work. Permanent Secretary Backe supposedly told the Führer that the occupation of Ukraine would liberate us from all economic concerns. In reality, however, Backe is believed to have said that if any territory can be of use to us then it could only be Ukraine. Ukraine alone is a surplus territory; the whole of European Russia, however, is not.

These new developments were reflected in calculations made by the Reich Food Estate in early February: 'Reich Food Estate estimates the shortfall of Germany and the territories controlled by Germany to be 5 million tons [of grain]. By means of a 10 per cent reduction in Russian consumption, around 4 million tons can be obtained from Russia.' Four million tons compared very favourably with the normal Soviet grain surplus of 1 million tons and even with the amount of 2.5 million tons promised by the Soviets in accordance with the German–Soviet trade agreement of 10 January 1941. According to the Soviets, however, it was only possible to achieve a grain surplus of 2.5 million tons by falling back on the national grain reserves.[6]

The study Thomas had mentioned to Keitel in January was sent to the latter on 20 February; Keitel in turn submitted it to Hitler. Göring received a second copy. In perhaps the most important section of his study, which was entitled 'The Effects on the War Economy of an Operation in the East', Thomas suggested that the German grain deficit could be offset at the expense of the Soviet population:

Even if it appears uncertain as to whether M.T.S. [Machine and Tractor Stations] and supplies can be protected from destruction in large amounts; if, moreover, as a result of the effects of war, a harvest of 70 per cent at the most can be expected, it must be considered that the Russian is accustomed to adapting his needs to poor harvests and that, with a population of 160 million, even a *small reduction* of the consumption per head would free up considerable quantities of grain. Under these circumstances, it could be possible to meet the German *shortfall* for 1941 and 1942.

On 26 February, Thomas presented his paper to Göring in person, who gave it his approval. Göring himself had already received Hitler's backing for his assumption of control over the entire economic administration in the Soviet territories to be occupied. Evidently impressed with Thomas's paper, Göring in turn transferred responsibility to him for preparing an economic organisation to exploit the territories in question and emphasised that Thomas would have a 'completely free hand' in the matter. This transfer of responsibility had been authorised by Hitler in advance. Thomas must have had some prior notice of this new commission, as he was already able to respond at the meeting itself by informing Göring that the relevant preparations were under way and that he would shortly be able to submit an organisational draft.[7]

By February, the quartermaster general of the army, Brigadier Eduard Wagner, was also privy to the planning under way, as demonstrated by the results of a war game that month in Saint-Germain-en-Laye outside Paris. A paper drawn up on the basis of the war game stipulated: 'The supplies must be limited through extensive exploitation of the land, [and] the acquisition must be tightly controlled. The country's stocks are not to be utilised through indiscriminate pillaging, but rather through seizure and collection in accordance with [the] well-thought-out plan.' Wagner's reference here to a 'well-thought-out plan' indicates his knowledge of Backe's starvation strategy. Indeed, by the end of February, Backe had received a 'special commission' in the food sector, as Thomas informed some of his military colleagues at a meeting on 28 February. One of the appendices to the paper on the February war game formed the basis of the 'Special Instructions for Provisioning, Part C', issued on 3 April in the name of the commander-in-chief of the army, Field Marshal Walther von Brauchitsch, and signed by the chief of the Army General Staff, General Franz Halder. Halder and Wagner had discussed the results of the February war game on 4 March and the forthcoming 'Special Instructions' ten days later. The latter made clear: 'Securing the major transport routes and exploiting the land for the requirements of the troops in order to relieve the supply is of decisive importance for the operations. It is therefore a question of all army forces in the rear areas being deployed exclusively for these tasks.'[8]

On 12 March, Thomas visited Backe and obtained his support for the incorporation of agriculture into the economic organisation that Thomas was in the process of setting up. A week later, Göring declared himself 'fully in agreement' with Thomas's organisational draft. The War Economy and Armaments Office would be responsible for the executive. Permanent Secretary Paul Körner from the Office of the Four-Year Plan, Permanent Secretary Backe, Deputy Secretary Major General Hermann von Hanneken from the Reich Economics Ministry, Permanent Secretary Friedrich Alpers from the Reich Forestry Office and Thomas himself would be on the organisation's command staff. On 25 March, a Wehrmacht colleague of Thomas's, Major General Dr Wilhelm Schubert of the Luftwaffe, assumed the leadership of the organisation, which was provisionally called the Planning Staff Oldenburg, but later became the Economic Staff East (*Wirtschaftsstab Ost*, or Wi Stab Ost).[9]

Three days later, on 28 March, the Staff Office of the Reich Farming Leader completed a study entitled 'Production and Consumption of Foodstuffs and Fodder in the USSR'. The study concluded that in the event of a reduction in the Soviet consumption of foodstuffs from 250kg to 220kg per head annually, that is, a reduction of 12 per cent, a grain surplus of 8.7 million tons could be achieved. This study constituted without doubt a limited but clear radicalisation of German food policy vis-à-vis the Soviet territories. The 10 per cent reduction in Soviet consumption proposed by the Reich Food Estate in early February had now been increased to 12 per cent. Like the Reich Ministry of Food and Agriculture and the Reich Food Estate, the Staff Office of the Reich Farming Leader was clearly operating under the aegis of Backe during this planning phase. Richard Walther Darré, the nominal head of all three organisations and Backe's superior, knew nothing of the planning, as documented by a series of letters exchanged between Backe, Darré and Göring after the start of the military campaign.[10]

A further meeting between Thomas and Backe took place on 31 March and was attended, among others, by Schubert, Hanneken, Head of Department Dr Hans-Joachim Riecke from the RMEL and Ministerial Counsellor Dr Friedrich Gramsch from the Office of the Four-Year Plan. The following day, Körner had lunch with Reichsführer SS Heinrich Himmler, giving the two of them the opportunity to discuss the starvation plans in which Körner was deeply involved. On 12 April, Körner signed a 'secret decree' conferring additional powers on Backe. These powers related to the implementation of the 'special task' concerning Barbarossa assigned to Göring by Hitler. The task resulting from this authorisation and all related organisational preparations were, 'on the order of the Führer', to remain strictly secret under all circumstances. The total bypassing of Backe's nominal superior, Darré, and the appointment of Backe to oversee the implementation of these tasks fostered a radicalisation of food policy towards the Soviet civilian population.[11]

The implications of the proposals developed over the course of the previous few months were stated with unmistakeable clarity at a crucial meeting on 2 May between Thomas, Schubert and the permanent secretaries of the various ministries involved in the economic planning for Barbarossa.

This meeting was in all likelihood an official session of the executive body of the Wi Stab Ost, the Economic Command Staff East (*Wirtschaftsführungsstab Ost*, or Wi Fü Stab Ost). A memorandum recorded the results of the discussion:

> 1. The war can only continue to be waged if the entire Wehrmacht is fed from Russia during the third year of the war.
> 2. As a result, if what is necessary for us is extracted from the land, tens of millions of people will doubtlessly starve to death.

In an astonishingly matter-of-fact way, the participants spelled out the human cost of German food policy in the soon-to-be-occupied territories of the Soviet Union by declaring that tens of millions of people would perish, and that starvation on this huge scale was inevitable if Germany were to win the war.[12]

The men involved envisaged a surplus of foodstuffs in the occupied east that would be used first and foremost to feed Germany's armed forces during the third year of the war (that is, September 1941 to August 1942), above all those 3 million soldiers serving on the eastern front. The Wehrmacht would thus be the main beneficiary of the starvation policy. Eliminating the necessity of supplying 3 million men with particularly high rations directly from the Reich would considerably ease the pressure placed on the existing transport routes between Germany and the Soviet territories for the (anticipated) duration of the war in the east, as well as on food stocks in Germany and German-occupied Europe as a whole, thereby simultaneously bolstering the home front and contributing to Germany's economic capacity to fight the expected war of attrition against the Anglo-Saxon powers. From the point of view of those who conceived of it, the importance of this ruthless approach in the occupied east cannot be overestimated. Three days later, on 5 May, in notes pertaining to issues still requiring a decision from Hitler or Göring, Thomas stressed the urgent need to provide for the fighting troops, agriculturally exploit the Soviet territories and strengthen the transport system. These were all integral components of the starvation policy.[13]

By early May at the latest, rumours were circulating – even among those not directly involved in the planning – to the effect that Hitler had resolved on the destruction of Soviet cities during the forthcoming hostilities. The

Austrian military diplomat Major General Edmund Glaise von Horstenau recorded the following information received during a meeting with SS Senior Colonel Dr Walter Stahlecker on 5 May: 'In Russia, all cities and cultural sites including the Kremlin are to be razed to the ground; Russia is to be reduced to the level of a nation of peasants, from which there is no return.' Stahlecker, as designated chief of Einsatzgruppe A for operations against the Soviet Union, is likely to have been well informed. On the same day as Glaise's conversation with Stahlecker, Backe gave a presentation at a gathering of the leading representatives of the Nazi Party – the Reichsleiters and Gauleiters – after which Reich Minister for Public Enlightenment and Propaganda Dr Joseph Goebbels recorded in his diary: 'If only this year's harvest is good. And then we want to line our pockets in the east.' Goebbels had been treated to a private presentation by Backe five days earlier, on 30 April, on which occasion Backe had informed Goebbels that meat rations in Germany would be reduced by 100g per week from 2 June. Goebbels demonstrated his faith in Backe by noting in his diary: 'Backe presides over his department, by the way, in masterly fashion. He'll do whatever is at all possible.' Two days after his presentation for the Reichsleiters and Gauleiters, on 7 May, Backe met with the designated head of a future civil administration in the occupied Soviet territories, Alfred Rosenberg, who in turn conferred with Permanent Secretary Körner a day later. A letter from Chief of the Wi Stab Ost Schubert to his superior in the Wi Fü Stab Ost, Thomas, on a meeting that had taken place between Schubert and Army Quartermaster General Wagner on 12 May, shows that the two men explicitly discussed the starvation policy. They agreed on the 'phenomenal importance of the area of operations' for their economic work and the necessity of beginning with this work as soon as the military campaign commenced. The fact that Schubert's request for an office next to Wagner's was immediately granted is testament to the close working relationship between their respective organisations.[14]

Liaison between the different departments involved in developing the starvation policy also took place at a lower level. On 14 May, two days after Schubert and Wagner had met, a discussion was held in Berlin between Section Head Dr Julius Claussen from the RMEL and an official in the Wi Rü Amt. Claussen described the food situation as 'strained and difficult'. The reduction in meat rations planned for the beginning of June would hit not only normal consumers but also all other sections of the German population, including the troops, 3 million of whom would be deployed in the Soviet Union as of 22 June. In the event of a longer-lasting war, a substantial reduction in fat rations from 270g to 200g (almost 26 per cent) was also foreseen by the RMEL. As almost all European countries had a significant grain deficit, most of those territories under German occupation had to be supplied by Germany. One European state that could be of greater assistance in terms of food supplies, continued Claussen, was the Soviet Union, more specifically Ukraine, 'the granary of Russia [sic]'. According to Claussen, Ukraine produced 40 million tons of grain annually, 40 per cent of the entire Soviet harvest of 100 million tons. Germany, on the other hand, without the newly annexed Polish territories, had produced 23.5 million tons the previous year. Claussen then claimed that the Ukrainian population could make do with 10 to 15 million tons of grain, so that Ukraine constituted a major surplus territory. He did not need to spell out what would happen to the remaining 25 to 30 million tons produced by Ukraine.[15]

Ukraine may have produced 40 per cent of the Soviet Union's grain, but its population constituted only around a fifth of the entire Soviet population, which meant that the territory also supplied other parts of the Soviet Union. Thus, the Germans would be removing grain that was intended for Soviet citizens, not for export. It was not a surplus, as Claussen claimed: it was required in order to feed part of the Soviet population. The figure of 25 to 30 million tons of grain per year to be plundered by the invaders appears to be the largest amount mentioned by anyone involved in these preparations, dwarfing as it did the earlier figures of 4 and 8.7 million tons calculated by the Reich Food Estate and the Staff Office of the Reich Farming Leader, respectively. It was admittedly uncommon for the economic planners to set the target quite so high, indicating that, even in their inflated view of what was possible, Claussen's colleagues were aware that such an expectation was completely unrealistic. By this stage in the preparations, the figure cited was more often than not around a third of that given by Claussen.[16]

In a letter dated 14 May, Backe reminded Chief of the OKW Keitel of the importance for the economy of the 'complete feeding of the army from [the] occupied territories' and added that he would be 'exceedingly grateful' to be granted as soon as possible the opportunity to speak to Keitel in person on a matter that was 'very important' for the food sector: 'It is regarding the balancing of provisioning for the troops.' Only five days later, Keitel issued

Special Instructions to Directive No. 21 (Case Barbarossa), in which it was stated: 'The exceptional conditions in the area "Barbarossa" necessitate the *comprehensive and tightly conducted exploitation of the land* for supplying the troops, especially in the food area. The troops must realise that *every reduction in supplies*, particularly in food, increases the scope of the operations.'[17]

On 23 May, the notorious Economic Policy Guidelines for Economic Organisation East, produced by the agricultural section of the Economic Staff East, were issued. Exactly who penned the guidelines is unknown. The man in charge of the agricultural section of the Economic Staff East was Dr Hans-Joachim Riecke, head of department in the RMEL and Backe's right-hand man. The guidelines constituted not only the most explicit elucidation of the starvation policy known but also the blueprint for a programme of mass murder unprecedented in modern history:

As Germany and Europe require [grain] surpluses under all circumstances, consumption [in the Soviet Union] must be reduced accordingly. [...] In contrast to the territories occupied so far, this reduction in consumption can indeed be implemented because the main surplus territory is spatially starkly separated from the main deficit territory. [...] The surplus territories are located in the black-earth territory (i.e. in the south and the southeast) and in the Caucasus. The deficit territories are located predominantly in the wooded zone of the north (Podsol soils). Thus, sealing off the black-earth territories must make more or less large surpluses in these territories available to us at all costs. The consequence is the non-delivery of the entire wooded zone, including the important industrial centres of Moscow and [St] Petersburg. [...] The population of these territories, in particular the population of the cities, will have to face the most terrible famine. [...] Many tens of millions of people in this territory will become superfluous and will have to die or migrate to Siberia. Attempts to rescue the population there from death through starvation by obtaining surpluses from the black-earth zone can only be at the expense of the provisioning of Europe. They prevent the possibility of Germany holding out until the end of the war; they prevent Germany and Europe from resisting the blockade. With regard to this, absolute clarity must reign.

If the participants of the 2 May meeting had established that the death by starvation of tens of millions of Soviets was inevitable if Germany were to win the war, the author(s) of the 23 May guidelines proposed that starvation be actively used as a weapon of warfare by describing how this 'most terrible famine' could be brought about. Among other things, the guidelines also confirmed the accuracy of rumours circulating since the beginning of May to the effect that Russian cities were to be destroyed and their inhabitants starved to death. They also contained the explicit endorsement of Hitler and the rest of the German leadership: the strategy had received 'the approval of the highest authorities'.[18]

As part of the Folder for District Agricultural Leaders, Backe issued his 'Twelve Commandments' on 1 June. The eleventh commandment served as a reminder, if one were needed, of the intention to starve large sections of the Soviet population: 'The Russian has already endured poverty, hunger and frugality for centuries. His stomach is elastic, hence no false sympathy. Do not attempt to apply the German standard of living as your yardstick and to alter the Russian way of life.' These words were very similar to the terminology used by Thomas in his study of February 1941, quoted earlier. This should come as no surprise, particularly in light of the close cooperation between these two men during the planning phase and their shared points of view, as expressed at the beginning of May. Indeed, alongside Backe, Thomas was the chief exponent of the starvation strategy.[19]

At the beginning of June, the reduction of meat rations announced in January came into effect into Germany. Just over a week later, on 10 June, Backe visited Reichsführer SS Himmler to discuss agriculture in the Soviet territories. A post-war statement by the designated higher SS and police leader for central Russia, SS Major General Erich von dem Bach-Zelewski, indicates that the two men may have discussed the starvation policy. In any case, Himmler was aware of it by this time at the latest, as demonstrated by comments he made at a gathering of a dozen senior SS leaders he hosted at his Westphalian castle, the Wewelsburg, between 12 and 15 June. Bach-Zelewski, who was among those present, recalled Himmler saying that 'the purpose of the Russian campaign' was 'the decimation of the Slavic popula-tion by 30 million'. Coincidence or not, 30 million was the amount by which the Soviet population – indeed, exclusively the urban population – had grown between the beginning of the First World War in 1914 and the beginning of the Second World War in 1939. We may recall that, according to the economic policy guidelines of 23 May, it was 'in particular the population of the cities' that would 'have to face the most terrible famine'. The references to the death from starvation of 'tens of millions' at the 2 May meeting and to 'many tens of millions' in the economic policy guidelines of 23 May had by mid-June at the latest been concretised: German plans envisaged the murder of 30 million Soviet citizens.[20]

The explicit reference to the decimation of the Slavic population during the campaign against the USSR demonstrates that, although economic motivations lay at the core of proposals to starve millions of Soviet citizens to death, racial considerations shaped the discourse when it came to what was deemed possible or not. It is barely imaginable that the starvation policy would have achieved such a consensus among Germany's military and political elites had it been directed, for instance, against the people of France or Norway. Thus, supremacist ideology became the means by which allegedly superfluous human beings were identified. It was racial considerations that convinced the German leadership that the Soviet state would 'fall apart like tinder', in the words of Joseph Goebbels, and that this collapse could be accelerated by the mass murder of the so-called Jewish–Bolshevik intelligentsia, which was supposedly the core of Soviet power and the supporting pillar holding the Soviet Union together by means of terror. The accelerated collapse of Soviet state structures would, in turn, hasten an end to the war, thus enabling Germany to get to grips with the dreaded problems of food supply and transport. The regime thus combined ideological assumptions regarding the way in which Soviet rule functioned and short-term calculations about the plundering of the Soviet harvest.[21]

According to post-war testimony by the designated higher SS and police leader for southern Russia, SS Lieutenant General Friedrich Jeckeln, it was Bach-Zelewski, as higher SS and police leader for central Russia, whom Himmler had tasked with the 'annihilation of 20 million Soviet citizens' in Belarus and the territories further east, a fact Bach-Zelewski had neglected to mention in his statement at Nuremberg. This was confirmed by comments made by the chief of Advance Commando Moscow of Einsatzgruppe B, Professor Dr Franz Alfred Six, during a visit to the headquarters of Army Group Centre in July 1941:

Hitler intends to extend the eastern border of the Reich as far as the Baku–Stalingrad–Moscow–Leningrad line. East of this line as far as the Urals, a 'blazing strip' will emerge in which all life is to be erased. It is intended to decimate the around 30 million Russians living in this strip through starvation, by removing all foodstuffs from this enormous territory. All those involved in this operation are to be forbidden on pain of death to give a Russian even a piece of bread. The large cities from Leningrad to Moscow are to be razed to the ground; the SS commander von dem Bach-Zelewski will be responsible for the implementation of these measures.

Clearly, the SS aimed to play a central role in the fulfilment of the starvation policy.[22]

On 16 June, less than a week before the launch of military operations against the Soviet Union, the Guidelines for the Management of the Economy in the Newly Occupied Eastern Territories were issued in Göring's name. These instructions, known as the Green Folder because of the colour of their binding, constituted the official economic handbook for the occupation troops. They served first and foremost to orientate those in the highest leadership and command positions down as far as divisional level. The first print run of 1,000 copies was issued in June, followed in July by a second print run of 2,000 copies. In his preamble to the guidelines, Chief of the OKW Keitel stated that it was of exceptional importance for the continuation of the war that the economic exploitation of the Soviet territories be carried out 'immediately and to the greatest extent possible'. The Green Folder itself then stated that the first task in the area of food and agriculture was to ensure as soon as possible that the German troops were completely fed from the occupied territory in order to relieve Europe's food situation and unburden the transportation routes. The outflow of the most important foodstuffs – oil crops and grain – from the southern territories into the agricultural deficit territories of central and northern Russia was to be ruthlessly suppressed.[23]

These instructions constituted the explicit endorsement of the strategy set out in the economic policy guidelines of 23 May. It is thus no wonder that the Green Folder described Leningrad, Moscow and the territory east of them as constituting a 'difficult problem' with regard to the treatment of the population, as the million-strong cities required substantial food subsidies. The guidelines of 23 May had already made clear what fate awaited the inhabitants of these cities. The Green Folder had been compiled by Colonel Hans Nagel of the Wi Rü Amt, who was Thomas's liaison officer with Göring, and it was approved by Alfred Rosenberg's staff prior to its release. Its contents confirm that the state policy of mass starvation was communicated in written form to the troops themselves down as far as divisional level. Corresponding instructions would conceivably have been passed further down the chain of command in oral form, just as they were for the Einsatzgruppen regarding shooting operations against Soviet Jews.[24]

Two days before the launch of the military campaign, Rosenberg gave a speech in which he signalled his approval of the starvation policy:

> During these years, the feeding of the German people stands without doubt at the top of German demands in the east, and here the southern territories and northern Caucasus will have to balance out German food requirements. By no means do we acknowledge the obligation to feed the Russian people as well [as ourselves] from these surplus territories. We know that it is a harsh necessity that is beyond any emotion. A very extensive evacuation will no doubt be necessary, and very difficult years will certainly be in store for the Russian people.[25]

By the time Wehrmacht troops crossed the border on 22 June 1941, Germany's leading military and political institutions had either contributed to formulating the starvation strategy or signalled their explicit endorsement of it. It had become state policy.

There was no serious attempt within the corridors of power to engage in a critical analysis of the economic implications of an invasion and occupation of the European USSR or, crucially, of the existence of potential alternative scenarios should the military campaign – and, with it, the programme of economic exploitation – not go according to plan. Not only was confidence in victory high but the mindset of Hitler and those around him was also such that potential difficulties were expected to be worked around, particularly in the case of the Soviet Union, where ideological motives combined with what were perceived as strategic and economic necessities. As defeat could not be countenanced, it was up to the planning staffs to find a solution, whatever that might be, to the problem in question. This insistence effectively removed any potential uncertainty among the economic planners and assisted in paving the way for the acceptance and advancement of the concept of starving millions of Soviet citizens for agricultural gain, though this concept was in no way based on economic certainties.[26]

In referring during his testimony at Nuremberg to the decimation of the Slavic population by 30 million, Bach-Zelewski stated: 'I am of the opinion that these methods really would have led to the annihilation of 30 million if they had in this way been pursued further and if the situation had not been completely altered due to changes in circumstances.' The consultant for eastern questions in the Office of the Four-Year Plan, Second Lieutenant Dr Friedrich Richter, was of the same opinion. In a letter from the front written in the spring of 1943, Richter commented on some of the reasons for invading the Soviet Union two years earlier:

> Economic interests and the predicament, as a result of the isolation of Europe, of having to obtain yet more grain and oil crops and oil from our own sphere of influence also brought about for many an affirmation of the campaign on economic grounds, although experts at the time pointed out that Russia already in peacetime could only fulfil German treaty demands at the greatest cost to itself, much less so after disruption of the transportation routes and the economic cycle there. [Senior Government Counsellor Dr Otto] Donner and my department also pointed at the time to this expected deterioration. Out of this situation, the Backesian thesis developed [that] one must separate the western and southern Russian territories, as main producers, from their consumer territories in central Russia and incorporate them once more into the European supply zone; a real possibility if one is militarily in a position to keep the central Russians from their fields for a long period of time and if one wins over the inhabitants of the occupied territory.[27]

In the event, by mid-July 1941, entirely contrary to expectations, the German advance had stagnated, the encirclement of Soviet soldiers had not taken place on the scale anticipated, the Soviet Union had not collapsed and the Red Army remained resilient and fully capable of fighting. In short, the Blitzkrieg had failed. In the weeks and months after the start of the invasion, it became clear that it would not be possible to cordon off entire regions and thereby exclude the victim group originally envisaged – the inhabitants of the agricultural 'deficit territories' in central and northern Russia – from access to food on the scale and in the space of time deemed necessary to ensure the supply of the German Reich and German-occupied Europe in 1941–42. In other words, as the military campaign was not going to plan, the National Socialist starvation policy could not be implemented as intended.[28]

The objective of eliminating rivals for foodstuffs nonetheless remained in force and in fact became more urgent in view of the critical turn taken by the war from the German point of view. The occupation authorities on the spot knew how they were expected to treat the indigenous population. In a speech given in 1942, Plenipotentiary for Labour Deployment Fritz Sauckel recalled that, during a visit to Ukraine in late autumn 1941, all German authorities there were convinced that in the winter of 1941–42 'at least 10 to 20 million of these people will simply starve to death'. During a discussion in Berlin in late November 1941, Göring told the Italian foreign minister, Count Galeazzo Ciano, that between 20 and 30 million inhabitants of the Soviet Union would 'starve to death this year'. Göring added that it was perhaps a good thing that this was so, 'because certain peoples must be decimated'. For Göring, then, the death of tens of millions of Slavs was a welcome side effect of ensuring that the Wehrmacht and the German home front could eat their fill.[29]

Adapting to the new military and strategic situation, the Reich leadership modified its food policy in late July 1941: instead of huge swathes of interconnected territory being cordoned off, individual groups of people were to be isolated in camps and smaller territories systematically neglected. The German occupiers now selected victim groups to which they had ready access. Thus, it was ultimately the Soviet POWs who constituted the largest group among the victims of the adapted starvation policy. In fact, captured Red Army soldiers comprised the largest single victim group of National Socialist annihilation policies after the European Jews. Their treatment and fate will be discussed in the next chapter. Among Soviet civilians, it was primarily the urban population that succumbed to the effects of the deliberate policy of starvation. Most Soviet Jews – almost 85 per cent – lived in towns and cities. Moreover, German agencies were well aware of this fact. The ghettoisation of those Soviet Jews who had not yet been shot by the

Germans facilitated in some cases their starvation, for example in the Belarusian city of Vitebsk. Security concerns and, above all, ideological motivations were more decisive, however, in shaping German policies against Soviet Jews and most of the victims were murdered by bullets rather than starvation. Though Leningrad was ultimately besieged instead of conquered and razed to the ground, as had been the pre-invasion intention, at least 1 million civilians starved to death during the almost 900-day siege. Urban centres that German forces did conquer and occupy, such as the Ukrainian cities of Kiev and Kharkov, also suffered a horrendous loss of human life.[30]

Leningrad

As a result of the stagnation of the Wehrmacht's military advance by mid-July 1941, Germany's operational war aims were reassessed. Arguments in favour of a concentration of the available forces and a reduction of the scale of the original plans gained ground. This decision-making process ultimately led the German political and military leaderships to settle on an encirclement and siege of Leningrad in place of the original plan first to conquer the city and then raze it to the ground. Thus, military considerations for saving troops merged here with the economic objectives of the adapted starvation policy. The consequences of this modified approach for the residents of Leningrad would be their immediate starvation within the city itself rather than their expulsion and gradual starvation in adjoining territories divested of all their foodstuffs.[31]

As early as 8 July, Chief of the Army General Staff Franz Halder had indicated a shift in approach when he noted in his war diary: 'It is the Führer's fixed decision that Moscow and Leningrad be razed to the ground in order to prevent people remaining there, whom we would then have to feed in the winter. The cities should be destroyed by the Luftwaffe. Tanks are not to be employed for this purpose.' Though the destruction of Leningrad was still intended, as per the pre-invasion plans, it would now be carried out from outside the city, without the deployment of tanks or ground troops. The reason Hitler gave for this approach is striking: from his point of view, it was not the industrial potential of the city or its symbolic status as the scene of the October Revolution in 1917 but rather German food policy that necessitated the destruction of Leningrad and, by extension, its inhabitants. As it turned out, however, Air Fleet 1, assigned to Army Group North, was too weak to transform this intention into reality. Instead, the German leadership resolved to trap the city in a siege ring and starve it out.[32]

On 28 August 1941, a few days before the German attack on Leningrad commenced, the Army High Command issued an order to Army Group North 'to surround [the city] by means of a [siege] ring, which is to be pushed as close as possible to the city and will in this way save manpower'. The fact that Army Group North was then supposed to cede its armoured formations and aviation corps to Army Group Centre made it clear that the encirclement of Leningrad was not intended as a temporary measure or a prelude to the capture and occupation of the city but as an end in itself for the purpose of starving out its inhabitants. Leningrad had now been relegated to little more than a sideshow in the military campaign, but over the next 900 days it would become the setting for human suffering on a huge scale.[33]

Hitler was not the only one with no intention of feeding the residents of Leningrad. On 9 September, Army Quartermaster General Wagner wrote to his wife: 'For the time being, Petersburg [sic] will have to sweat it out; what are we supposed to do with a city of 3½ million, which just rests itself on our supply pouch? There are no sentimentalities here.' He accordingly rejected all preparatory measures for feeding the civilian population: 'It is better that our soldiers have something to eat and the Russians starve.' On 18 September, Army Group North informed the Eighteenth Army that there was no need to make any preparations for feeding the population of Leningrad. The fact that this line of thinking also extended to German field commanders and was not limited to Leningrad but applied rather to Soviet cities in general is illustrated by an order issued on 20 November by Lieutenant General Erich von Manstein, commander of the Eleventh Army in the southernmost section of the front: 'The food situation on the home front necessitates that the troops live off the land as far as possible [...]. Especially in the enemy cities, a large part of the population will have to starve.'[34]

On 19 September, Goebbels wrote in his diary: 'An urban drama is currently being played out in Petersburg [sic], the likes of which history has never before seen. The effects of the siege will only then become visible to the eyes of the world when Leningrad has fallen.' On 7 October, Chief of the OKW Operations Staff Alfred Jodl conveyed an unequivocal order to Army

Commander-in-Chief Walther von Brauchitsch: 'The Führer has again decided that a surrender by Leningrad or, later, by Moscow will not be accepted, even in the event that it is offered by the enemy. [...] No German soldier, therefore, is to set foot in these cities.' This decision made no sense from a military point of view and thus cannot be explained in terms of the military situation in front of Leningrad in autumn 1941. It was instead directly linked to Hitler's decision to destroy the city completely – and the city's inhabitants along with it.[35]

After the Wehrmacht had closed the siege line around Leningrad on 8 September 1941, the only access route to the besieged city was via Lake Ladoga, Europe's largest lake. During the initial weeks of the blockade, however, the Soviet Union possessed neither sufficient transport capacity nor the necessary logistics to organise the delivery via Lake Ladoga of the foodstuffs required by the inhabitants of Leningrad. Thus, from September to mid-November, only 172 tons of foodstuffs arrived in the city each day, though Leningrad's daily food demands came to 2,000 tons. During the winter, the only route into the city was across the ice that typically covered Lake Ladoga from December to April. The influx of food via this 'ice road' rescued many residents from death by starvation, but it was not enough to feed all inhabitants during the winter of 1941–42.[36]

The winter months of 1941–42 were the bitterest of the entire blockade for the residents of Leningrad. During this period, dogs and cats largely disappeared from the city. Some residents saw no alternative but to kill and eat their beloved pets. Others did not stop at eating dead animals: in December 1941, 26 people were held criminally responsible for cannibalism or the sale of human flesh. In January 1942, this number increased to 366 people, and during the first half of February it rose again to 494 people. During the blockade, a total of around 1,500 people were prosecuted for this offence. The figures are nonetheless difficult to interpret, as these are only the cases that were uncovered. On the other hand, in most instances it was the corpses of persons already deceased that were processed into meat. What the figures certainly do illustrate, however, is the desperation of the people of Leningrad.[37]

Yura Ryabinkin, a sixteen-year-old boy who lived with his mother, Antonina, and younger sister, Ira, in the besieged city, noted on 9 December 1941 in his diary:

I've eaten a tomcat, pilfered food out of Anfisa Nikolayevna's pots, stolen every spare breadcrumb from Mother and Ira — cheated both of them — frozen standing in line, cursed and fought at the entrances to shops to get in and buy 100g of butter. I've been dirty, had lice by the score, no strength from exhaustion and undernourishment. I could not even rise from my chair; it was incredibly difficult.

Continual bombing raids and artillery fire, keeping watch in the attic at school, squabbling and scenes at home when it was time to share out the food. I've learned to appreciate the breadcrumbs; I've collected the crumbs on the table with my finger. In the process, I've come to know a little of my coarse and selfish character. There is a saying that only a grave can straighten a hunchback. Will I not be able to improve my character?

Yura's heartbreaking struggle between hunger and conscience pervades his uncommonly candid diary entries throughout December 1941. The following day he wrote:

The wisdom of the people says: 'What doesn't kill us makes us stronger.' 'Adversity doesn't build character, it reveals it.' That's me. Adversity hasn't made me harder; it's made me weaker. And my character has revealed itself as selfish. I feel that it's beyond my power to change my character right now. All the same, I have to make a start!

This morning, I should have brought the cakes home, but I can't resist – I eat at least a quarter of a cake on the way. This is a manifestation of my selfishness. But tomorrow I'll try to bring all the cakes home. All of them! All of them!!! Fine, perhaps I will die of starvation, swell up, get dropsy, but I'll know that I acted honestly and demonstrated a strong will. Tomorrow, I want to give evidence of this will. I won't take a single crumb of what I buy. Not a single crumb! [...] Everything has become bitter, sombre, hungry and cold. All our thoughts revolve around food and warmth. There is heavy frost outside and it's 20–25 degrees below zero. In the room, although we heated it, it is so cold that my feet begin to freeze; shivers run down my spine. If someone had only given me a loaf of bread, I would liven up and laugh again, I would sing, I ... Oh, what's the point.

He ended his entry of 10 December with the prescient words: 'The pages of my notebook are almost at an end. It seems that my diary itself has limited the amount of time I have for writing.' After secretly stealing bread and sweets from the share intended for his mother and sister, Yura wrote on 15 December:

> I have plunged into the abyss characterised by indiscipline, unscrupu-lousness, dishonour and disgrace. I am an unworthy son to my mother and an unworthy brother to my sister. I am selfish, a person who in a grave hour forgets all his relatives and friends. And I do such a thing at a time when Mother is completely exhausted. With her swollen feet, her sick heart, in light shoes in frosty conditions, without having eaten a crumb of bread, she visits the authorities, makes pitiful efforts, because she wants to get us out of Leningrad. I've lost all hope of being evacuated. It's over, as far as I'm concerned. Food is my whole world. Everything else is only there as a way of finding food. What lies ahead is no life for me. I want only two things: I want to die, and that my mother should read this diary after my death. Let her curse me, a dirty, heartless and duplicitous beast; let her disown me, so low have I sunk, so low. [. . .]
>
> It is so sad, I am ashamed, I cannot look at Ira . . . Will I take my own life?
>
> Food! I want to eat!

Yura's final diary entry is dated 6 January 1942:

> I can hardly walk or do anything. I have almost no strength left. Mother, too, can barely walk – I can't imagine how she manages it. Nowadays she hits me often, scolds and shouts. She has wild nervous fits because she can't stand my wretched appearance – that of a weak, hungry, tormented person who can barely move from one spot to another, is always in the way and 'pretends' to be ill and helpless. But I'm not pretending. Oh Lord, what's happening to me?

Yura's mother eventually succeeded in getting evacuation slots for the whole family, but when the time came to leave, she found that she could not carry her son downstairs. Faced with the agonising choice of remaining with Yura to await almost certain death or attempting to save at least her daughter, she opted for the latter. Leaving Yura lying on the sofa, mother and daughter set off, towing the sled loaded with necessaries and tradeable silver cutlery. From spring 1942, the food situation in Leningrad continually improved, but it was too late for Yura, who died that year. Having escaped the blockade, his mother perished during the evacuation journey, on a bench at Vologda railway station. Only Ira survived the war. The siege of Leningrad was not lifted until 27 January 1944. By that time, between 1 and 1.3 million people trapped within the siege line had starved to death.[38]

The well-known fate of Leningrad and the tremendous suffering of its people have perhaps overshadowed the crisis faced by the residents of those towns, such as Pushkin and Pavlovsk, that fell within the German siege line. German units seized and occupied these suburbs in October 1941, and their inhabitants almost immediately faced the spectre of widespread starvation. In the town of Pushkin, L Army Corps notified the Eighteenth Army in early October that '20,000 people, most of whom are factory workers, are without food. Starvation is expected.' The Eighteenth Army's quartermaster noted in response that 'the provision of food for the civilian population by the troops is out of the question'. This attitude towards the civilian population mirrored that of other commands in Army Group North. In late October, the Sixteenth Army told XXVIII Corps that there could be no question of feeding the civilian population in its area of operations and instead ordered the establishment of evacuated zones behind the front lines, with the civilians sent to labour camps. This, of course, did nothing to help starving civilians; it merely shifted responsibility for their fate to other German units in the rear areas.[39]

The organised plunder of Pavlovsk, for instance, received official sanction. Soon after their arrival in the town, soldiers and other German officials confiscated all food stocks in warehouses and markets as well as those held by individuals in their homes. This resulted in the death of more than 6,000 inhabitants from starvation and the various diseases that accompany hunger; the overwhelming majority died during the winter of 1941–42. In one of the most tragic cases of organised starvation, 387 children between the ages of three and thirteen died during the winter while staying in an orphanage established by the Germans. According to witnesses, the death from starvation of ten to fifteen children on a single day occurred more than once.[40]

In an attempt to survive, many civilians resorted to crimes of desperation. In Pushkin, an ethnic German killed his aunt in order to trade her jewellery for food; he was arrested and shot. The disappearance of a dozen children and adolescents in the same town led to the arrest of a man whose home contained various female body parts. He had been selling human flesh as pork at the local market. In Pavlovsk, a married couple were hanged for cannibalism in February 1942. Apparently, they had killed one of their grandfathers and, after using part of his remains at home, sold the rest at market as rabbit meat. The couple then murdered three children and disposed of their bodies in the same manner as that of the elderly man. They were finally apprehended while in the process of dismembering a fifth victim – a nine-year-old girl. An investigation into the disappearance of several children led German police units to the apartment of yet another woman in April 1942. Finding human flesh there, they arrested her and brought her in for questioning. While admitting to having eaten five children, she claimed to have killed no one; rather, she maintained that she had disinterred them from the town's cemetery. Neither members of the collaborationist Russian auxiliary police nor the German Security Police believed the woman, and she was executed. Such acts illustrate the desperation felt by Soviet citizens and the harrowing depths to which some of them plunged under the inhumane German occupation.[41]

Kiev and Kharkov

Tens of thousands of people living in other large Soviet cities also lost their lives as a result of the German starvation policy. In the two largest cities in Ukraine, Kiev and Kharkov, 10,000 and at least 30,000, respectively, starved to death. The fact that the inhabitants of urban centres in Ukraine – a grain 'surplus territory', according to the German planners – also suffered such loss of life as a result of starvation is illustrative of the adaptation of the original starvation policy to the unexpected circumstances created by the Wehrmacht's change in military fortunes. Indeed, in the area of operations of Army Group South, swathes of territory emerged that were entirely stripped bare of all foodstuffs. The German armies resembled a swarm of locusts. As of January 1942, according to information provided by Hans-Joachim Riecke following a trip to Ukraine, this territory reached to a depth of 150km behind the front, and by May 1942 to a depth of 300km.[42]

As of mid-August 1941, a month before the Germans captured the city, the High Commands of the Wehrmacht and the Army intended to destroy Kiev by means of incendiary bombs and artillery fire. As in the case of Leningrad, this plan ultimately could not be realised because of the weakness of German airborne units and a shortage of the necessary ammunition required for the envisaged five-day bombardment. Though the pre-invasion intention to raze Kiev to the ground – like all major Soviet urban centres – could not be realised, the starvation of substantial parts of the civilian population of the city went ahead as planned during the 778-day German occupation from 19 September 1941 to 7 November 1943.[43]

By October 1941, Kiev's pre-invasion population of 900,000 had drastically shrunk to around 400,000 as a result of the evacuation and flight of civilians, enlistments in the Red Army and the aforementioned massacre of 33,771 Jews at the ravine of Babi Yar. On 24 September, the Economic Inspectorate South estimated that existing stocks of food would last the city's inhabitants for eight to fourteen days. Shortly before the end of this period, on the second day of the Babi Yar massacre, the inspectorate abruptly discontinued the supply of the population with foodstuffs. From this point on, German police forces endeavoured to prevent people from entering Kiev and to confiscate any food imports, including milk from farmers attempting to sell their produce in the city.[44]

A Soviet intelligence report from spring 1942 emphasised: 'As a result of the systematic robbery of Kiev's inhabitants, a substantial share of the residents are starving to death and begging. Many children and elderly people are collapsing in the streets. There is no corner of the city where beggars do not ask for alms. Everywhere, one sees dirty, unattended children in rags.' In February, the head of the German Southern Armaments Headquarters declared: 'Something has to be done to supply the civilian population if we do not want to deny ourselves all workers and services.' Such appeals, though scarcely made out of humanitarian motives, went unheard. The same month, the SD reported on 'a famine, for which no end is in sight'.[45]

In no other European city occupied by the Wehrmacht did so many (non-Jewish) people suffer and die from starvation as in the eastern Ukrainian city of Kharkov. The Germans ruled there from 24 October 1941 to 22 August 1943, with the exception of a four-week period in February and March 1943. Unlike Kiev, Kharkov was never transferred from military to civil administration. At the time of the German arrival in Kharkov, around 450,000 people remained in the city. The first reports of starvation there were already circulating after only a few days of the German occupation. Shortly thereafter, hunger claimed its first victims. At a meeting of leading representatives of the Economic Staff East and other military departments in mid-November 1941, those present stated with indifference that because they were 'unable' (read: unwilling) to provide the local population with anything from either the Wehrmacht's existing supplies or stocks seized from the enemy, those 'people not working in the interests of the Wehrmacht' would 'just have to starve to death'. Those in attendance interpreted the absence of hunger riots as evidence of a sort of childish trust in the occupiers on the part of the civilian population.[46]

On Christmas Eve 1941, Hitler personally forbade Kharkov's inhabitants to leave the city in search of food; all roads leading into and out of Kharkov became no-go areas until spring 1942. The civilian population of Kharkov was thus cordoned off by the local German military commander. On top of that, some German officials not only plundered canteens and markets but also seized food from the private households that had been forced to shelter them. While substantial parts of the population were suffering starvation, the Sixth Army fed its horses with precious grain. As of January 1942, the Germans were supplying only 24,000 of the approximately 420,000 people still in the city with minimal starvation rations, that is, little more than 6 per cent of the total population. The Wehrmacht's policy of living off the land functioned so well for LI Army Corps, which was stationed in Kharkov from January 1942 onwards, that the standard rations of its soldiers were *increased* in March 1942 – at a time when starvation among the civilian population was very severe – for fear that the ample stocks might spoil. These measures resulted in the death from starvation of many thousands of the city's inhabitants, 1,202 alone in the first half of May 1942.[47]

In times of food shortages and famine, babies and toddlers tend to be the first victims. Under German occupation, infant mortality in Kharkov rose from 12 to 50 per cent. At particular risk from starvation were, furthermore, members of the professional elites, the sick and the elderly. One inhabitant of Kharkov recalled:

> In offices and other organisations, people worked side by side with
> dying human beings, who slowly drained away before the eyes of their

colleagues. The deadly symptoms of starvation could be clearly seen from the swollen faces – or, in extreme cases, from the hollow cheeks and sharpened facial features, grey complexion, blue lips, bleary eyes (which gazed at the world with endless apathy and exhaustion), as well as the badly swollen legs and hands, the sluggish gait and the tired, slow movements. They were only shadows of those human beings who had once been professors, lawyers, doctors, important figures in society.

Some went mad from hunger and many killed themselves, while others seriously considered doing the same. Burials in temperatures as low as minus 30 degrees were difficult and costly. According to official figures, in March 1942 not even half of those inhabitants of Kharkov who had died the previous month (from starvation or other causes) had been buried.[48]

The noose around Kiev was not quite as tight as that around Kharkov. For residents of Kiev, it was easier to take to the country roads in search of food, trade on the black market, beg, steal or visit markets in small towns. In addition to begging, barter and smuggling, there were also other, less socially accepted or even criminal ways of obtaining food. One female medical student from Kiev caught and ate cats, while some residents of Kharkov ate the elephant from the city zoo. At least one person from Kharkov was publicly hanged for selling human flesh as pork. In early 1943, rumours circulated of cannibalism in Kiev. Some people related how a gang had been arrested for murdering people and selling their flesh. There were other tales about a man who had sold sausages for a year and was then arrested after part of a finger had been found in a sausage – or because a neighbour had discovered human body parts in his house. The only such report in the official press concerned a man in his early fifties who had eaten at least one sixteen-year-old girl. He was publicly hanged.[49]

Many thousands of people from Kiev and Kharkov died in artificially engineered famines that were foreseeable and resulted from conscious actions taken by the German occupiers. The very perceptive among the inhabitants of Kiev and Kharkov recognised this. The anatomist Professor Lev Nikolaev, for instance, who spoke fluent German, concluded in his diary on 1 November 1941 that the Germans were indifferent to the needs of the local population. Four days later, he was (rightly) convinced that the Germans had brought about the famine themselves, with the aim – as he wrote in January 1942 – of eliminating superfluous people. He knew that potatoes in abundance were awaiting harvest in the countryside around Kharkov. In late December 1941, at least one German division confirmed this when it reported on easy access to potatoes and vegetables. Two years after the occupation ended, Nikolaev summarised the events as follows:

> [The Germans] consciously pursued a policy of annihilation against part of the Ukrainian population, in order to facilitate the colonisation of Ukraine. To this end, they created an artificial famine and obstructed the supply of the cities. Transportation was in their hands. They could easily have brought foodstuffs from the countryside into the cities, but they intentionally chose not to. Tens of thousands of people starved to death in Ukraine, though conditions for the elites were particularly bad.

On 25 April 1942, the Kiev schoolteacher L. Nartova wrote in her diary: 'What ought to be done; how can we stay alive? They probably want to let us die slowly. It's evidently too impractical to shoot everyone.'[50]

Alongside the cases already discussed – Leningrad and surroundings, Kharkov and Kiev – other regions especially affected by famine were Kramatorsk and Slavyansk (Donets Basin), Poltava and Sumy (northeastern Ukraine), Stalino (eastern Ukraine), Simferopol, Kerch, Sevastopol and Yalta (Crimea). Ukraine was thus the region of the Soviet Union ultimately most affected by the German starvation policy. In the central regions of western Russia, too, reports of imminent famines in Kaluga, Bryansk and Oryol, among other places, accumulated from late autumn 1941 onwards. In the historic town of Rzhev, 9,000 residents died from starvation and epidemics under German occupation. During the month of January 1943, for instance, around 10 people starved to death every day.[51]

Ivan Steblin-Kamenskii, a Russian interpreter serving with the German 206th Infantry Division, part of the Ninth Army, was stationed in the area of Rzhev. On 21 December 1941, he noted in his diary regarding the Wehrmacht soldiers: 'Along with cordiality one also encounters cruelty – they take the last cow, the last potato or even things like sheepskin coats and felt boots. As for how the population are going to live, they are indifferent – they have the same attitude toward them as toward flies, they'll die, and that's how it should be.' Six days later, the commander of the Ninth Army, General Adolf Strauß, demanded that everything necessary be undertaken to protect German soldiers against the Russian winter. He ordered: 'Ensuring that this is done by ruthlessly utilising whatever the country and the civilian population possess is at present one of the most important tasks for the [troop] leaders at all levels.' On 30 March 1942, Steblin-Kamenskii wrote: 'All in all, it is very painful for me to see this new, unknown face of the German soldier, without any human feelings. Having more than is needed to sustain himself, he then takes away the last essentials from women and children. I'm completely overwhelmed, shocked, insulted, and yet I can do nothing and have to serve alongside them.'[52]

The diary of Nina Semyonova, a young woman living in Rzhev, gives an idea of what life was like for the inhabitants of the occupied town, and clearly illustrates the direct link between the actions of the German soldiers and the death by starvation of Soviet civilians:

25 October [1941]. One cannot get milk anywhere. But we can still get hold of something for Marinka somewhere. Soon that will be over, too. How will we feed the child then?

1 November. They've occupied our entire house. For a senior officer. Now we're all crammed into one small room. [...] In the kitchen, there are mountains of provisions, bars of butter, meat, white bread. All stolen from us, of course. From our stores, from our collective farms. And we must go hungry and perhaps even starve to death.

[...]

22 November. Mama weeps. The last sack of grain, which we had saved for Marinka, and two bowls of potatoes, everything we have, have been taken by the soldiers. Mama complained to the officer. He drew himself up and stonily said: 'A German soldier does not steal!' [...]

2 February [1942]. Hunger torments us more and more. Marinka cries, pleads for something to eat. I give her the breast. But there is no milk in the breast. [...] Our famished little nipper. Sasha would not recognise her. Her overlarge eyes.

5 February. [...] Mama said that, if we economise, we would still have enough for a few more days. She looked at me pleadingly. I said nothing and turned away.

10 February. We are very hungry. Two days without eating. I asked the neighbours for a little grain for Marinka. Buckwheat. I cooked porridge with water. She pounced on the food. [...]

15 February. No light, no water, no bread. We fetch water from the Volga. The soldiers shoot at us. Yesterday evening, Father returned with empty buckets: bullet holes in the buckets. [...]

20 May. I have already forgotten what bread tastes like. And the feeling of being full. I can no longer imagine it.

12 June. I went to the neighbours and asked for something for Marinka. Nothing, nothing.

15 July. What luck! I got some chaff for Marinka.

[...]

20 October. They chase us from the house. [...]

15 November. We are living in a dirty, dark cellar. They also took our last little corner upstairs. We saw with our own eyes how they burned down our house, in which Mama, me and Marinka were born and grew up. The flames rose up to the sky. I thought of Sasha. Will he ever learn of what we are going through here? [...]

25 December. Last night – Papa is no more. These bandits did him in. He had been spitting blood of late, as a result of those beatings [by an SD officer]. Mama almost lost her mind. [...]

10 January 1943. Life has become unbearable. I can no longer hear the two-year-old nipper scream from hunger. I will try to go to a village. Perhaps I will succeed in getting something there, after all.

[...]

25 January. Today, I found it hard to get up. A strong pain in the side; my head hurts. I am nonetheless determined to go to a village and find something for Marinka and Mama.

27 January. The German controls took everything away. I had found a few potatoes and some rye. I lost my composure and screamed that this is for the child. But they beat me and threw me into the barn, where I lay all night. When I got home, Mama almost didn't recognise me. I have no strength left. I'm in a very bad state. – My Sasha – I know, we will never see each other again. What will become of Marinka?

This was Nina Semyonova's final diary entry. She died of starvation and from the beating she had taken. Rzhev was liberated five weeks later.[53]

Around half of all Soviet civilians living under German military administration suffered from starvation, many of them on a constant basis from autumn 1941 until the Wehrmacht's withdrawal from those particular territories in autumn 1943. These famines were at least as devastating as the more well-known famines in Nazi-occupied Europe: in Athens from autumn 1941 to mid-1942 (mitigated by Canadian deliveries of wheat), in the west of the Netherlands during the so-called starvation winter (*Hongerwinter*) of 1944–45 or in the large Jewish ghettos in East-Central Europe. Furthermore, the famines in Greece and the Netherlands, unlike those in the Soviet territories, were not the result of a deliberate and premeditated German policy of starvation.[54]

The acquisition of agricultural surpluses to the detriment of the indigenous population remained the primary aim of German occupation policy in the Soviet territories right through to 1944. The view taken by the political and military elites that the war against the Soviet Union could be won only with the utmost ruthlessness, and that this ruthlessness was therefore legitimate, had already hardened into a fixed doctrine before the military campaign even began. All problems that emerged during both the planning phase and the war were thus met with a radicalisation of methods; alternative suggestions for solutions were regarded as defeatist and excluded from the discourse. In this way, the decision not to feed substantial parts of the Soviet civilian population was predetermined by a discourse of radicalism. The dogma of German inability to feed substantial parts of the Soviet civilian population was accepted by the occupation authorities as something that was incontrovertibly and self-evidently true.[55]

CHAPTER 6
EXTERMINATION OF CAPTIVE RED ARMY SOLDIERS

The fact that the number of dead among certain groups of Soviet civilians would have been much greater if the extent of German control had allowed for it is demonstrated by the far higher mortality from starvation of those groups who were most closely controlled by the German occupiers. It was the Soviet prisoners of war who constituted the largest group among the victims of the starvation policy. It was clear to the Wehrmacht on exactly what scale they could expect to capture Soviet troops and yet they neglected to make the requisite preparations for feeding and sheltering the captured soldiers, who were viewed by the economic planners and the military leadership alike as German troops' direct competitors when it came to food. The number of extra mouths to feed was simply not compatible with German war aims. The obvious limitations on their freedom of movement and the relative ease with which large numbers could be segregated and their rations controlled were crucial factors in the death of over 3 million Soviet POWs, the vast majority directly or indirectly as a result of starvation and undernourishment.

Before the onset of Operation Barbarossa, Germany's military leadership was convinced of the inferiority of its opponent on the battlefield. Chief of the OKW Operations Staff Alfred Jodl declared that 'the Russian colossus' would prove to be 'a pig's bladder; prick it and it will burst'. Instead of the bitter resistance that the Red Army actually offered, the OKH expected fierce border battles for the duration of four weeks and thereafter only minor resistance. This would allow the Wehrmacht to surround and capture the bulk of Soviet soldiers. Indeed, the success of the Blitzkrieg was dependent on the encirclement and seizure of entire Soviet armies during the opening weeks of the military campaign. Thus, the deputy chief of the OKW Operations Staff, Brigadier Walter Warlimont, noted in a communication to the Section for Wehrmacht Propaganda the day before the invasion began: 'In accordance with the information available to us so far, the *opponent* has deployed the bulk of his forces in the border areas, thereby accommodating German expectations.' Accordingly, the planning staffs reckoned on capturing at least 2 to 3 million Soviet prisoners, 1 to 2 million of them within the first six to eight weeks of the fighting.[1]

It was the Wehrmacht – the main beneficiary of a policy that envisaged the elimination of millions of 'useless eaters' – that was responsible for the Soviet POWs. Institutional jurisdiction was divided between the OKW and the OKH. The Prisoners of War Section within the Wehrmacht General Office of the OKW, headed by Major General Hermann Reinecke, was responsible for POW camps on the territory of the German Reich, the Government General and the occupied areas under civil administration. Subordinated to the Prisoners of War Section were the commanders of the POWs in the seventeen military districts in the Reich itself and those attached to the Wehrmacht commanders in the Reich commissariats. These commanders were in charge of the POW district commandants in the occupied territories, who were in turn responsible for the regular camps for enlisted men (*Stammlager*, or Stalags) and the camps for officers (*Offizierslager*, or Oflags), as well as the guard detachments. In the occupied territories under military administration, it was Quartermaster General Wagner of the OKH who bore responsibility for the camps for officers, the camps for enlisted men, the transit camps (*Durchgangslager*, or Dulags) and the army prisoner collection points. In this area administered by the military, the security divisions and the other troops subordinated to the commanders of the rear areas of each of the army groups were responsible for guard duty, forced labour deployment and return transportation at those times when the prisoners were not in the camps themselves.[2]

Mass Starvation

Within three weeks of the start of the military campaign, on 11 July 1941, the number of Soviet prisoners captured by the Wehrmacht already totalled 360,000. By 20 August, Army Group Centre alone had captured more than 800,000 Red Army troops. However, as discussed above, and as Lieutenant General Georg Thomas, chief of the OKW's War Economy and Armaments

Office, wrote on 29 July, these figures remained far lower than the Wehrmacht's pre-invasion expectations. By 19 July, the whole of Army Group North had taken only a little more than 45,000 prisoners. The Sixteenth Army alone had expected 27,000 prisoners after twelve days, but as of 5 July the number was only around 8,000. Not only that, but the Wehrmacht had captured, accommodated and fed 1.9 million prisoners the previous year in the campaign against France, and in a shorter space of time. Clearly, then, neither supply nor logistics problems were the cause of the impending mass starvation of Soviet POWs. Their starvation on a massive scale began locally and in phases. In the first two months of the campaign, rations for POWs were very low. In some cases, the prisoners received no food at all. During this time, death rates in the camps varied depending on locality. In some Belarusian camps, such as Dokshytsy, Orsha and, intermittently, Vitebsk, they were comparatively low, with one to two prisoners dying each day. In other camps, however, the figures were very different: 100 a day in Baranovichi or even up to 250 a day in Lida.[3]

On 8 July, Ministerial Counsellor Xaver Dorsch, head of the central office of the Organisation Todt construction agency, visited Dulag 127 in Drosdy near Minsk. It was subordinated to the 286th Security Division. The transit camp had been set up in an open field on the Svisloch river; there were no buildings. Two days after his visit, Dorsch reported on what he had seen in a letter to Reich Minister for the Occupied Eastern Territories Alfred Rosenberg:

The prisoner camp in Minsk accommodates in an area roughly the size of Wilhelmplatz around 100,000 prisoners of war and 40,000 civilian prisoners. Squeezed into this confined space, the prisoners can hardly move and are forced to relieve themselves where they stand. [...] The prisoners of war, for whom the food problem cannot be solved, have gone in some cases six to eight days without food and know only one obsession in their state of bestial apathy brought on by starvation: to find something edible. [...] During the night, the starving civilians fall upon those with supplies and beat each other to death in order to obtain a piece of bread. The only possible language of the weak guard detachment, which carries out its duty day and night without being relieved, is firearms, of which it ruthlessly avails itself.

Despite the extreme heat, some of the German guards forbade the prisoners to drink from the river; hundreds were shot while attempting to do so.[4]

In the first two months of the military campaign, in spite of their drastic undernourishment, most prisoners still possessed a remnant of physical resilience, and weather conditions were favourable. Around this time, however, the first hunger-related epidemics broke out. Already in September 1941, death rates increased considerably. During that month, between 5,000 and 9,000 Soviet prisoners died in Army Group Centre's rear area alone, and 9,000 in the POW camps of the Government General. In Stalag 342 (Molodechno) in General Commissariat Belarus, 200 prisoners a day were evidently dying with a terrible constancy – perhaps 6,000 per month in a single camp. There, prisoners tormented by hunger even requested the Wehrmacht guards *in writing* to end their suffering by shooting them. Cases of cannibalism occurred in the Molodechno camp in early September and in Borisov no later than the end of the month. Cannibalism is also documented for other camps in Belarus, namely those in Bobruisk, Mogilev, Minsk and Glubokoye. Instances of cannibalism were also reported for the camp in Shepetovka and for a transit camp in the vicinity of Krivoy Rog, both in Ukraine, in late September and October 1941, respectively. In all POW camps, the death penalty was imposed for cannibalism.[5]

In September 1941, the overcrowded Stalag 359 B (Kaliłów, near Biała Podlaska), where the prisoners had to live in large burrows, was suffering from the worst epidemic in the whole of the Government General. As of 19 September, 2,500 prisoners had already died of dysentery. On the orders of Odilo Globocnik, the SS and police leader in the Lublin District, the 2nd Company of Police Battalion 306 thereupon shot at least 6,000 POWs between 21 and 28 September 1941 – 3,261 of them on the first day alone – in order to dissolve the camp. When the orders were issued, the policemen were told that the food situation for Soviet prisoners was 'causing some problems' and that it was no longer possible 'to feed the majority of the prisoners'. In their report on the operation – codenamed 'Chicken Farm' – the perpetrators referred to the prisoners they had murdered as 'laid eggs'. The incident, though an extreme case in this particular form, demonstrates the growing concern over the potential consequences, particularly in the form of epidemics, of the incipient mass mortality caused by the German policy of undernourishment and neglect.[6]

The mass mortality of the Soviet prisoners increased significantly in autumn 1941. The decision to switch from a regional undernourishment and neglect of the prisoners to a systematic, selective murder of most of them through starvation was taken already in mid-October, that is, *before* the end of the twin encirclement battles of Bryansk and Vyazma, at which 662,000 prisoners fell into German hands. The drastic reduction in official rations on the basis of decisions made at senior level in October accelerated an intentional and sharp increase in the mortality rates in the POW camps. As early as 16 September, Göring – with reference to the German military collapse in 1918 – had pointed to the vital importance of avoiding a further reduction of food rations, especially meat, in the German Reich and issued a corresponding directive stating:

> As a basic principle, in the occupied territories only those who work for us ought to be fed adequately. Even if we *wanted* to feed all other inhabitants, we *could not* do so in the newly occupied eastern territories. When it comes to feeding the Bolshevik *prisoners*, in contrast to other prisoners, we are not bound by any international obligations. Their rations, therefore, can only be determined by their work performance.

As a signatory of both the 1907 Hague Convention on Land Warfare and the 1929 Geneva Convention, Germany was in fact obliged to treat *all* POWs humanely. On 13 October, Hans-Joachim Riecke from the Reich Ministry of Food and Agriculture met with Army Quartermaster General Wagner and agreed that a 'strict distinction' would be made 'between working and not working prisoners of war' in the food guidelines that were shortly to be issued. Accordingly, on 21 October, Wagner reduced rations for prisoners not working by 27 per cent to 1,490 calories (and by 46 per cent in the case of protein), whereas the rations of those working for the Germans remained almost unaltered. In doing so, he issued the categorical instruction: 'The unit commanders must understand that any foodstuffs that are administered to the prisoners unjustly or in too great a quantity must be deducted from our relatives back home or from German soldiers.' As those prisoners who were not working were not doing so because their already poor physical condition did not allow them to, it was clear that a reduction in their rations must have devastating effects, especially as rations would normally be *increased* in the autumn, as the human body customarily uses more energy during the winter.[7]

From October 1941, mass mortality in all Wehrmacht camps holding Soviet POWs assumed monstrous proportions: in October, November and December, between 300,000 and 500,000 prisoners died each month; in January 1942, it was 155,000; in February, 80,000; and in March, 85,000. During November 1941, 83,000 prisoners died in the Government General alone: 38.2 per cent of the prisoners present at the start of the month. In the rear area of Army Group Centre, the death toll for November came to around 80,000. During a discussion in Berlin in late November 1941, Göring informed the Italian foreign minister, Count Galeazzo Ciano, of conditions in the POW camps (including cases of cannibalism) and disparagingly compared the Soviet prisoners to 'a herd of ravenous animals'. The clearest and most direct instruction for the murder of a substantial share of the Soviet POWs was issued by Army Quartermaster General Wagner during a meeting of the chiefs of staff of all armies and army groups deployed on the eastern front with the chief of the Army General Staff, Franz Halder, on 13 November in Orsha. Wagner declared unequivocally: 'Prisoners of war in the POW camps who are not working have to starve to death.' This was a death sentence for 55 per cent of the prisoners.[8]

A rare letter sent by a captive soldier to his family illustrates the suffering of Soviet prisoners in Kaunas's Sixth Fort, which had been converted into a POW camp. Captured north of Novgorod on 14 September 1941, F.J. Koshedub was transferred from one camp to another before making the journey on foot from Gomel to Kaunas, 'where a ready-made mass grave is awaiting me'. On 19 October, he wrote:

> Since the first day of captivity, I've been starving and I expect every day to be my last. [...] We are incarcerated in the Sixth Fort. [...] We are sleeping in a pit under open skies. We receive 200g of bread a day, half a litre of boiled cabbage and half a litre of tea with mint. Everything is unsalted, so that we don't swell up. With sticks and steel rods, we are driven to work, though we don't receive any extra food. We have millions of lice. For two months, I haven't shaved, washed or changed my clothes. I have underwear, overgarments, a military coat, a field cap and shoes with putties. It is cold, muddy and dirty. Between 200 and 300 men die

every day. That is the situation I'm in, and my days are numbered. Only a miracle can save me. So farewell, my darlings; farewell, my loved ones, friends and acquaintances. If a good person can be found to pass on my letter, at least you'll know where I met my inglorious and bitter death.[9]

A basic decision to deploy Soviet POWs in the Reich for the benefit of the German war industry taken at the highest level at the end of October 1941 temporarily opened up the prospect of an increase in the life span of a substantial number of prisoners by virtue of their access to higher rations. Within a week, however, Göring announced that Soviet civilians ought to be sent in large numbers to work in the Reich, too. After all, Soviet civilians appeared to be a preferable alternative to the exhausted and undernourished POWs. Indeed, during 1942 around 1.4 million Soviet civilians were sent to Germany; this was three times as many as the number of Soviet POWs sent there during the same period (456,000). Even those prisoners who *were* capable of working were fatally weakened by the cold and the hard labour. In many territories, the number of prisoners 'fit for work' sank to record lows. Brutal treatment by the German guard detachments also played its part; they often made little distinction between the 'useful' and the 'useless'. Characteristic of this was the conduct of the personnel of Dulag 220 (Gomel), who not only shot between 15 and 50 prisoners a day from the work squads during their outward and return marches, but also staged a so-called marathon race to the railway station for selecting the labour force for the first transport to Germany: the guards shot the 200 men who collapsed from exhaustion along the way and herded the rest into the carriages. As the German war economy did not require all Soviet POWs, it was possible for the state and private industry to select those deemed 'fit for work' from among the mass of prisoners, while the rest – in the words of Quartermaster General Wagner – would be left to 'starve to death': deliberate and organised mass starvation on the one hand was thus compatible with an expansion of forced labour deployment on the other hand.[10]

The parallel developments during autumn and winter 1941–42 in completely different territories under German control – the Government General, the rear area of Army Group Centre, the rear area of Army Group South, Reich Commissariat Ukraine and Reich Commissariat Ostland – point towards a common cause for the mass mortality of the Soviet POWs.

It is worth noting here that neither in the Government General, nor in the rear area of Army Group Centre, nor in Reich Commissariat Ukraine were the numbers of prisoners previously envisaged reached. Even at the two major battles in September and October 1941 – Kiev and Bryansk/Vyazma – German troops took fewer prisoners than the 1.9 million that had been taken in 1940 in France during a similar time period and whom they had by no means allowed to starve to death. It was a similar story in the Reich itself: the number of Red Army prisoners transported to Germany by the end of 1941 came to 500,000; this figure was well below the total anticipated during the planning phase in the spring.[11]

By the beginning of February 1942, that is, over the space of little more than seven months, 2 million Soviet prisoners of war had died or been murdered in German custody. This was almost 60 per cent of the 3.35 million Red Army soldiers captured during this period, most of them by the end of October 1941. On Reich territory, at least 265,000 Soviet POWs died during these months; this constituted a death rate of around 53 per cent. (By contrast, death rates among Polish and Soviet *civilian* forced labourers inside Germany were well below 10 per cent.) The fact that this rate of mortality was scarcely lower than the death rate in the POW camps east of the Reich's borders not only sheds an unmistakeably clear light on living conditions for captive Soviet soldiers in Germany. It also throws into stark relief the common fate of Soviet POWs in German captivity regardless of their whereabouts, and gives the lie to the claim that long transportation routes and the associated supply problems were to blame for the mass mortality. Over an extended period between October 1941 and February 1942, as many people died in a single large POW camp in the occupied Soviet territories as could be murdered during the same time span by an entire Einsatzgruppe. Indeed, as of winter 1941–42, captured Soviet troops constituted the largest single victim group of Nazi mass-killing policies.[12]

The fate of Soviet POWs during winter 1941–42 even prompted Reich Minister for the Occupied Eastern Territories Alfred Rosenberg, mentioned earlier, to send a letter of protest to Chief of the OKW Wilhelm Keitel at the end of February 1942:

The fate of the Soviet prisoners of war in Germany is [...] a tragedy of the greatest magnitude. From 3.6 million prisoners of war, today only several hundred thousand are fully capable of working. A large proportion of them have starved or perished as a result of the adverse weather conditions. Thousands have succumbed to typhus. It is clear that feeding such masses of POWs gives rise to difficulties. All the same, [...] death and ruin on the scale described could have been avoided. [...] In the majority of cases, however, the camp commandants prohibited the civilian population from giving the POWs food, and instead preferred them to starve to death. Indeed, in many cases in which POWs could no longer go on during marches due to starvation and exhaustion, they were shot before the eyes of the horrified civilian population and their corpses left behind. In numerous camps, no shelter whatsoever was provided for the POWs. By rain and by snow, they lay under the open sky. They were not even given the tools necessary to dig burrows or holes. A systematic delousing of the POWs in the camps and of the camps themselves was evidently not carried out. Remarks were heard such as: 'The more of these prisoners die, the better it is for us.'

It is clear from Rosenberg's letter that the woefully inadequate accommodation in the camps and starvation resulting from the refusal to allow the civilian population to give prisoners food were the main causes of the mass mortality among Soviet POWs. Rosenberg was a senior party official and a member of the Nazi old guard. He was himself guilty of war crimes and crimes against humanity, for which he would be executed in Nuremberg after the war. At the beginning of September 1941, he had expressly declared that the provisions of the 1907 Hague Convention on Land Warfare, which stipulated that prisoners of war 'must be humanely treated' and had been signed by Germany and Russia, were not valid in the occupied Soviet territories. Even he, however, was appalled at the Wehrmacht's inhuman treatment of captive Soviet soldiers. Rosenberg had known about what was happening in the POW camps since the first half of July 1941, when he had received a detailed report about conditions in a transit camp in Drosdy near Minsk. At the time, however, he was not willing to openly condemn this treatment. Only at the end of February 1942, in a radically different situation following the deaths of 2 million Soviet POWs, did he support appeals for an improvement in conditions made by a senior member of his staff, Dr Otto Bräutigam – the real author of Rosenberg's letter – and protest.[13]

At a meeting of the senior quartermasters of the army groups and the armies on 17–18 April 1942, it was noted that as of the beginning of that month 47 per cent of Soviet prisoners of war lodged in the German Reich had perished from starvation and typhus – a disease commonly linked to chronic malnutrition. By mid-April 1942, the proportion of Soviet POWs in camps in the Government General who had died or been killed was a staggering 85 per cent. The prisoners died overwhelmingly from starvation and exhaustion. Epidemics, above all typhus, claimed far fewer lives. Of the POWs in the rear area of Army Group Centre, there were between 3,700 and 4,900 new cases of typhus each month during the winter of 1941–42, which constituted 2 to 5 per cent of all prisoners there; this resulted, however, in less than 10 per cent of the fatalities. In Reich Commissariat Ukraine, 14 per cent of the deceased prisoners in February 1942 died of typhus. This means that the vast majority of deaths among Soviet prisoners during these months resulted directly – and the rest indirectly – from undernourishment.[14]

The Ukrainian Grigoriy Pavlovich Donskoy managed to survive the ordeal and later described an all-too-common experience:

> My captivity began on 17 May 1942. We were held for several days in encampments in Crimea (Dzhankoy, Feodosia). We weren't given any food; we kept ourselves alive with grass or whatever God sent us. My body began to devour itself, and I quickly lost weight. Some aspects of our behaviour were already reminiscent of animals. We had but one thought in our minds: finding food. On top of this, the eternal companions of starvation and filthy bodies had emerged – lice. The merciless insects sucked the little blood left in us. After all, these parasites didn't care that we were humans – the pinnacle of Creation.[15]

Forced Marches and Lack of Shelter

Until November 1941, a significant proportion of captive Red Army soldiers were forced on debilitating marches westwards to the rear areas. During October, most prisoners in the rear area of Army Group Centre were transferred westwards on foot. They were escorted above all by Wehrmacht security divisions and, in some cases, infantry divisions. In that month, more than half of the 320,000 prisoners taken to the regular POW camps in Reich

Commissariat Ukraine following the battle of Kiev were brought there on foot: this was a distance of more than 400km. During this march, soldiers of the 24th Infantry Division shot more than 1,000 of the approximately 200,000 prisoners entrusted to them. The victims were evidently not limited to those who attempted to flee; the divisional commander, Major General Hans von Tettau, felt compelled to take action against the shootings and order that 'defenceless and truly exhausted prisoners of war' were not to be shot. On the other hand, he continued, the 'most draconian measures' were to be adopted in order to maintain discipline among the prisoners. Other troop commanders escorting prisoner convoys issued explicit orders to shoot those sick and wounded who could not be carried by the other prisoners. The shootings carried out by the 24th Infantry Division, described above, were by no means exceptional. The 8th Infantry Division was charged with escorting 9,000 prisoners captured at the aforementioned encirclement battle of Vyazma to Smolensk and Dorogobuzh, but it arrived at its destination with only 3,480 prisoners. While there had admittedly been numerous escape attempts along the way, the main reason for this huge discrepancy was a massacre carried out by the German soldiers, resulting in the deaths of up to 4,000 Soviet POWs. Underlining their similarity to the more well-known evacuations of concentration-camp prisoners in 1944–45, the treks undergone by Soviet POWs in 1941 have been referred to as 'death marches'.[16]

Hunger and thirst contributed to the general state of exhaustion. One Red Army veteran captured in Ukraine, east of the Dnieper river, on 18 September 1941 later described the desperation of the prisoners and the response of their captors during the march westwards: 'At the sight of water, the column simply lost its mind. We were ready to drink from any dirty pool, but they did not allow us to drink, not even from a river.' (This example demonstrates that the aforementioned refusal of German guards to let prisoners drink from the river at the Drosdy transit camp was not an isolated case.) As if this were not enough, some Germans engaged in sadistic teasing. In one village that the prisoners passed through, a Wehrmacht unit was stationed:

Half-naked Germans were splashing each other with water from wells. An officer in ironed breeches with lowered suspenders was standing in the shadow with his arms behind his back. A soldier standing next to him had taken a bundle of concentrated buckwheat from an opened case, and was throwing the package in the air, like a ball. It was our army concentrate, very tasty, soft-boiled, with fat and fried onions. Whenever somebody leaped from the column to catch the packet, the officer whacked him with a stick.[17]

While searching for a relative who had been with the Red Army, Irina Khoroshunova from Kiev encountered some 35,000 POWs east of the Dnieper. In her diary entry of 28 September, she recorded what she saw:

They are sitting. They look so terrible that our blood turns cold. It is very clear that they don't get food. The women bring them food, but the Germans don't allow them to approach. The women are crying. There are heartbreaking scenes at every turn. The women throw themselves towards the prisoners. The prisoners throw themselves at the offered food like animals, they grab it and rip it apart. But the Germans beat them on the head with rifle butts. They beat them and the women too.

Other German guards subsequently allowed the women to approach. Khoroshunova was able to give her relative the food, and learned that the prisoners had not eaten for nine days. In her diary entry of 2 October, she noted that Jewish POWs were driven naked through the city. 'They are killed if they ask for water or bread.'[18]

Such scenes were witnessed not only in the countryside but also in major cities. Early in October 1941, Gerhard Kegel, a diplomat with the German Foreign Office, waited at a pontoon bridge in Kiev for two hours — this was the time it took for just one convoy of POWs to march across. Afterwards:

in the divided street, which had a green strip in the middle and along which the prisoners of war had been driven, lay dozens of dead Soviet soldiers. [...] The escorts shot with their submachine guns any prisoner who displayed signs of physical weakness or wanted to answer the call of nature on the green strip. I saw for myself how the Nazi escorts approached them from behind, murdered them, and moved on without deigning another glance at the victims.

The same month, a ten-year-old girl in Zhitomir was shot by a German guard while attempting to give Soviet prisoners a piece of bread.[19]

A decisive contributory factor in the mass mortality of the Soviet prisoners was the cold. In spite of bitter temperatures, the quartermaster general's ban on transporting the prisoners in anything other than open freight trains remained in force until 22 November 1941; this cost many thousands of prisoners their lives. Accommodation in the camps was completely inadequate. Even in the Reich or the Government General, where material scarcity was not a problem and the POWs were supposed to remain in the long term, often only the most primitive facilities were envisaged. In Stalag XI C (311) in Bergen-Belsen, for instance, prisoners lived in leaf hut shelters. It was not until November that work commenced on the systematic construction of barracks in the Reich and the Government General. It was hardly surprising, then, that only sluggish progress was made in building POW camps in the area of operations, where it was in any case not intended that the prisoners would remain for any length of time. In early September 1941, the head of POW administration in the OKW, Major General Hermann Reinecke, ordered that the erection of new buildings in the prisoner camps be avoided 'at all costs', as they might later prove to be superfluous. Thus, in mid-September, only 6,000 of the 12,365 prisoners at that time in Dulag 314 (Bobruisk) had a roof over their heads. While 8,000 of the 8,500 internees in Dulag 220 (Gomel) had shelter, only 3,000 of them could actually lie down, while the remaining 5,000 had to stand, resulting in them being denied sleep. In Dulag 240 (Orsha), the fact that 'buildings are not available' did not lead the camp administration to conclude that some should be built; instead, it arranged for huts to be made of earth.[20]

Many of the internees lived in burrows they had been forced to dig themselves with their bare hands. In late autumn 1941, this approach was elevated to the status of a general directive in the rear area of Army Group Centre. Other prisoners languished through the autumn or even over the entire winter under the open sky, as in Glubokoye, Borovukha, Vitebsk, Polotsk, Krichev and Orsha. They slept on the bare ground or in unheated rooms, as in Baranovichi and Minsk. The cold ensured that the physical resilience of the prisoners crumbled. Once the bad weather set in during the autumn, mortality rates rose rapidly, even before the devastating winter temperatures. This was by no means a natural or inevitable death, however. It was instead a direct consequence of the deliberate undernourishment of Soviet POWs combined with the German authorities' refusal to provide appropriate shelter against the freezing temperatures. The soldiers were systematically murdered by those who reduced the rations for non-working – that is, debilitated or sick – prisoners in the autumn, instead of increasing them, as would have been necessary to sustain them during this time of year. In some regions, such as Belarus, it would have been relatively easy for the camp personnel to obtain wood for barracks and heating, even without being officially allocated it.[21]

After death rates among Soviet prisoners had temporarily declined in summer 1942, starvation and mortality again increased significantly in autumn 1942. In Stalag 397 in Yasynovataya, north of Stalino, conditions similar to the previous winter set in; in October 1942, 80 to 90 prisoners died there on a daily basis. In Stalag 352 (Minsk), 70 to 80 people died every day during autumn 1942. The mass mortality of the previous year was repeated in the winter of 1942–43, if not on quite the same enormous scale. Although rations for Soviet prisoners were somewhat better than they had been during the period of the murderous cutbacks from October to December 1941, they remained inadequate. Furthermore, general living conditions for Soviet prisoners had not fundamentally changed. In many camps, therefore, typhus was again rife from early 1943 onwards. In Dulag 131 (Bobruisk), no fewer than 2,600 of the 3,500 prisoners contracted it.[22]

Mass Shootings

Alongside death by starvation – facilitated not only by deliberate undernourishment but also a lack of shelter and extreme exhaustion – there was a second method of annihilating Soviet POWs: mass shootings. Certain groups among the prisoners were targeted for selection and immediate execution. The so-called Commissar Order issued by the OKW on 6 June 1941 stipulated that, as a rule, political officers in the Red Army were to be shot on the spot should they fall into German hands. In accordance with this directive, a minimum number of almost 4,000 (and perhaps as many as 10,000) Soviet political officers were murdered at the front or in the rear areas between June 1941 and May 1942. For almost all German formations that fought on the eastern front, there is evidence of their adherence to the

Commissar Order. Reports of executions of captive Soviet political officers exist for all thirteen armies, all forty-four army corps and more than 80 per cent of the almost 150 German front divisions. Following the inclusion of additional cases where there are indications to this effect, the proportion at divisional level increases to over 90 per cent of units. The Commissar Order was a blatant breach of law, for hardly any contravention of international law was more obvious than the premeditated and systematic murder of regular, uniformed prisoners of war.[23]

Particularly zealous in its implementation of the Commissar Order was the 403rd Security Division. It was this security division to which SS Einsatzkommando 9 was assigned for logistical purposes. As discussed earlier, EK 9 was the first unit to make the transition to a policy of killing Soviet Jews indiscriminately, regardless of age or gender. This particular area of operations, then, contained two units – one Wehrmacht, the other SS – that were especially vigorous in their implementation of Nazi policies of mass killing. The 403rd Security Division reported for the month of July 1941 a total of 62 'dispatched' (*erledigt*) political commissars, divided into those who were disposed of by the troops themselves, civilian commissars 'liquidated' by the subordinated Secret Field Police for 'guerrilla activity' and civilian commissars who were handed over to the SD, that is, EK 9. In the month of August, 9 military commissars were killed by the troops and 27 were finished off in the subordinated transit camps for POWs, whilst 89 civilian commissars were murdered by the division and a further 2 delivered to the SD. In September, 1 military commissar was killed by the troops and 6 were disposed of in the transit camps, whereas 108 civilian commissars were murdered by the division and a further 3 handed over to the SD. In October, 51 military commissars were finished off in the transit camps, 12 civilian commissars were killed by the division and another 2 delivered to the SD.[24]

Two-thirds of all the *verifiable* shootings of Soviet commissars by regular German troops between June 1941 and May 1942 were committed by combat units at the front. The remaining third took place in the rear areas. Of these, more than half were killed by a single security division: the 403rd. This was in spite of the procedure prescribed by the Commissar Order, which required the Wehrmacht to kill Red Army commissars found in the operations area, whereas commissars 'seized in the army group rear areas due to dubious conduct' were instead to be handed over 'to the Einsatzgruppe or Einsatzkommandos of the Security Police (SD)'. As the statistics cited here demonstrate, the 403rd Security Division handed over only a handful of commissars to EK 9 during the four-month period in question; it preferred to take care of them itself. The radical approach of the unit in this matter was evidently a result of additional orders issued by its commanding officer, Major General Wolfgang von Ditfurth.[25]

In addition to Soviet political officers, Jewish troops in the Red Army were also targeted for systematic execution. On 17 July 1941, three-and-a-half weeks into the Soviet campaign, Reinhard Heydrich issued guidelines on POW camps, which had been drawn up in consultation with Hermann Reinecke's OKW department responsible for prisoners of war. The guidelines granted commandos of the Security Police and the SD access to the regular POW camps in order to identify for selection and execution numerous groups among the Soviet prisoners, including 'all Jews'. Significantly, this applied not only to Jewish soldiers but also, explicitly, to Jewish civilians interned in the POW camps. From early October 1941, the commandos of the Security Police and the SD were also allowed unrestricted access to the transit camps in the army group rear areas under the jurisdiction of the OKH 'for the elimination of intolerable elements'. Between 80,000 and 85,000 Jewish Red Army soldiers ended up in German POW camps. Many of them attempted to conceal their religion, but only a small minority succeeded. Little more than 5 per cent of Jewish soldiers returned from captivity. The rest were either shot or starved to death in the camps. Very few were murdered by regular troops immediately after their capture; most were only identified by Wehrmacht counterintelligence officers in the camps themselves. In his memoirs, Soviet army captain Vladimir Bondarets described one common method of identifying Jews from his own time in German captivity:

One day in early July [1942], the camp commandant [...] appeared at morning roll call. [...] He stood aside, holding on to a leashed, muscular German Shepherd dog. [...] The commandant walked slowly along the line of prisoners, examining each of the men's faces. [...] 'All Jews are to step out of the lines!' he ordered in Russian. 'You have two minutes to decide.' Two minutes passed. [...] 'Form a single line!' he ordered. 'Take off your trousers, quick!' Once again, accompanied by the corporal, he passed along the line of prisoners, who had lowered their heads in shame and humiliation. This time he did not look at their faces, but passed slowly from one to the other. [...] The commandant stopped for a longer time by one of the prisoners. 'Jew?' he asked. The young man paled and nodded his head. The dog, which felt itself freed from its leash, leapt forward. A wild cry filled the air. The trained dog sunk its teeth into the poor Jew, tore apart his thigh with its claws and dragged him down to the ground. The weakened young man tried to free himself from the animal, but fell after a few steps. [...] The show lasted for several minutes. Satisfied with the show, the [lieutenant] pulled the blood-smeared dog to him. The corporal shot the prisoner in the ear. [...] The commandant said, 'I advise the Jews to step out of the line.' Three stepped out. The commandant smiled and signalled to his soldiers. The Jews were taken away, and the roll call was over.

Shootings of Jewish prisoners were carried out by the Security Police and the Order Police but also, equally, by camp guards from the Wehrmacht. The murder of Jewish Red Army soldiers was illustrative of how certain groups simultaneously fell victim to more than one Nazi programme of mass killing, in this case the extermination of Soviet POWs and the genocide of European Jewry.[26]

Victims of shooting operations in the POW camps were not limited to Soviet political commissars and Jewish soldiers. During the first months of the invasion, Asian prisoners or those who had such an appearance in the eyes of their German captors were repeatedly separated out by the Wehrmacht and shot by the Security Police. The most primitive racist thinking was at play here, a traditional identification of Russia as an 'Asiatic menace' poised to engulf Europe or of the supposedly Mongol character of ethnic Russians. More than a month before the military campaign began, the OKW had issued Guidelines for the Conduct of the Troops in Russia, which stipulated: 'Especially the *Asiatic soldiers* in the Red Army are unfathomable, unpredictable, devious and cruel.' The guidelines were intended to be read out to the Wehrmacht soldiers at company level. For this reason, thousands of copies were printed and issued to the units shortly before the invasion began. Panzer Group 4, for example, sent 900 copies to XXXXI

Army Corps alone. The Commissar Order of 6 June 1941, mentioned earlier, identified political officers in the Red Army as the supposed originators of 'barbaric Asiatic fighting methods'. The Security Police began at an early stage with the murder of Asian-looking civilians who had been separated out in the transit camps. Even some regular Wehrmacht units, such as the 99th Light Infantry Division, emphasised ethnicity in their reports of having shot such prisoners. A disproportionately high number of these groups were killed in winter 1941–42; only around 20 per cent of the male members of the Turkic peoples survived the killings of this period.[27]

A further group of Red Army soldiers was targeted on the grounds of a perceived gender-specific abnormality, namely women in uniform. Although initial reports of encounters with so-called *Flintenweiber* (literally 'shotgun women') indicate that the confrontation with female soldiers came by no means unexpectedly for the Wehrmacht, the haphazard response to these encounters suggests that German troops were uncertain how to deal with them. Some senior commanders at the front, such as Field Marshal Günther von Kluge of the Fourth Army, reacted with particular radicalism. On 29 June, a week into the campaign, he ordered: 'Women in uniform are to be shot.' An intervention from the OKH, however, led to the retraction of this order two days later. The OKH stipulated that women in uniform, whether armed or not, were to be treated as prisoners of war; irregular female combatants, on the other hand, were expressly denied this protection. In spite of these superior orders to the contrary, however, some German units continued to issue orders calling for the murder of women in uniform. Major General Ernst Hammer, commander of the 75th Infantry Division in Ukraine, declared that 'female persons in Russian uniform' were to be 'categorically shot immediately', as they could 'not be regarded as members of the enemy armed forces'. Entries in unit war diaries indicate that such orders were sometimes passed on only orally in order to avoid a paper trail. The contravention of explicit orders from the OKH illustrates the dynamics of centre–periphery relations: units on the ground seized the initiative and proceeded more radically than their superiors in Berlin.[28]

Numerous regular Wehrmacht units summarily shot captured female soldiers. One NCO in the 167th Infantry Division noted laconically in his personal diary on 15 August 1941: 'Fourteen-year-old *Flintenweib* is shot.' However, there were likewise numerous female soldiers who survived capture at the front and were then transported with their male comrades to POW camps in the rear. Evidently, there was no standardised approach by German combat units in their treatment of captured female soldiers. Many of them clearly adhered to the OKH's instructions not to kill women in uniform. Once in captivity, so-called *Flintenweiber* – unlike Jews and Soviet political commissars – were not among the groups referred to in Heydrich's guidelines of 17 July 1941 as 'politically intolerable' and, therefore, not subjected to systematic selections and shootings. For those Wehrmacht units who shot female members of the Red Army, the decisive demarcation line was between those women who bore arms and took part in armed conflict and those who did not. Captured women serving in the Red Army as nurses, secretarial staff or in other auxiliary functions, though in uniform, were generally left alive. This explains why scarcely any female *combatants* in uniform reached the POW camps on Reich territory: it was these women who were meant when Wehrmacht soldiers disparagingly referred to *Flintenweiber*. When female members of the Red Army were captured at the front, then, their chances of surviving depended decisively on whether their captors regarded them as non-combatants or as combatants, that is, as *Flintenweiber*. Women who bore arms and took part in armed conflict were regarded by their German adversaries as the embodiment of a norm violation. The Wehrmacht's murder of female Soviet soldiers can be understood as a reaction to the destabilisation of traditional gender roles and hierarchies, not least as a result of the First World War, and what the Wehrmacht perceived as a challenge to male domination in what was seen as one of the last bastions of male identity – combat.[29]

In 1942, a new group of prisoners was targeted by the POW organisations and the Einsatzgruppen: so-called invalids. If they had not already succumbed to the mass starvation of 1941–42, the seriously wounded and maimed prisoners were subjected to various initiatives launched by camp functionaries. In many cases, the police and the Wehrmacht arranged for POWs unfit for work to be murdered. In transit camps in places such as Gomel, Bobruisk or Polotsk, the camp personnel regularly killed the sick by shooting them. In the same camps, the very weakest prisoners were simply abandoned to the extreme cold on winter days, so that they would freeze to death – a tactic also known from German concentration camps. Beginning in October 1942, many prisoners unable to work were removed in groups from Stalag 358 in

Berdichev and shot nearby by members of the Security Police. The last group was murdered on Christmas Eve. In a number of POW camps, sick prisoners were killed in regular cycles. In Stalag 324 (Lososna, near Grodno), for instance, the sick were shot once a week. In winter 1942–43, the inhabitants of entire barracks – many tens of thousands – suffering from typhus were shot in the camps in Daugavpils and Rēzekne in Latvia. Immediately before its withdrawal from Gomel in November 1943, one Wehrmacht unit transferred 600 sick prisoners to a hospital and blew them up along with the building. In camps on Belarusian soil, more killings were in fact based on the selection of the sick and the weak than on the elimination of political opponents. Even at a time when the manpower of Soviet POWs had become more valuable for the German war economy, by no means all Red Army prisoners were claimed by German industries. As noted above, three times as many Soviet civilians as Soviet POWs were sent to work in Germany during 1942. In particular, the chronically sick and seriously wounded among the POWs were never regarded as a valuable labour force; from the German perspective, they remained expendable.[30]

In fact, the similarities between the treatment of Soviet POWs, on the one hand, and (especially Jewish) concentration-camp inmates, on the other hand, go beyond their shared fate of being abandoned to the extreme cold on winter days to freeze to death. With Hitler's backing (and prior to his fundamental decision of 31 October 1941 to deploy Soviet POWs in the German war industry in the Reich), Reichsführer SS Heinrich Himmler moved to exploit captive Soviet soldiers as a labour force. On 2 October, the OKW accordingly ordered the military district commands to discharge a total of 25,000 Soviet prisoners of war into the hands of the SS. During the course of October, these POWs were transferred as slave labourers to SS-run concentration camps in the Reich, including Mauthausen, Flossenbürg, Auschwitz (which received 10,000), Buchenwald, Sachsenhausen and Neuengamme. An additional 2,000 were dispatched to Lublin-Majdanek in the Government General. Though more urgent demands from state and private industry ultimately sidelined SS claims, and the huge numbers envisaged by Himmler never reached the SS camps, a total of more than 100,000 Soviet POWs spent time in German concentration camps during the course of the war. Some were transferred directly from POW camps to concentration camps and were still classified as prisoners of war following their arrival;

others were sent to SS camps after they had escaped from a POW camp and been recaptured; still others had already been released from POW camps only then to be arrested for such offences as cultivating intimate relationships with German women, refusing to work or insubordination. While nearly all of the second group – recaptured escapees – were immediately shot or starved to death in the concentration camps, a substantial number of the first and third groups were initially subjected to labour deployment there. Indeed, the largest of these groups – those transferred as POWs – were handed over by the Wehrmacht for the express purpose of being exploited for work by the SS. They generally had an inferior status compared to the other concentration camp inmates and their rations were accordingly reduced well below those of other prisoners. Not surprisingly then, the most common cause of death among these 'labour Russians', as they were known, was starvation. Of those 27,000 Soviet soldiers who had arrived for forced labour in concentration camps in autumn 1941, for instance, no more than 5,000 were still alive the following spring. Thus, mortality among Soviet POWs in SS concentration camps far exceeded the death rate of other groups of inmates at this point in time.[31]

For some of the mass-shooting operations, it has proved impossible to ascertain the exact motives for the killing of a specific group of prisoners. These cases include the largest single shooting operation against Soviet POWs on Belarusian territory. During transportation to Krasnodar in late January 1943, the 3rd Battalion of Infantry Regiment 595 of the 327th Infantry Division detrained in Minsk for the task of shooting 10,000 people – mainly POWs – from a camp at the freight station a few kilometres away, over the course of three nights. The total number of those killed during shooting operations and in mobile gas vans came to 12,500. Among the victims was a small number of civilians, including women. One platoon alone murdered 1,500 men.[32]

Several tens of thousands of Soviet prisoners of war were shot while still on the battlefield, during transportation from the front or in the POW camps in the area of operations. In addition, at least 120,000 Soviet prisoners fell victim to mass shootings in the POW camps in the German Reich, the Government General and the occupied Soviet territories under civil administration. In Germany alone, for instance, no fewer than 33,000 Soviet prisoners had been shot by the end of July 1942. Though many of the killings were carried out by the SS and police, it was the Wehrmacht personnel in the camps who handed over the Red Army soldiers to be murdered. Furthermore, a substantial number of the victims were shot by Wehrmacht camp personnel themselves; quite a few camp commandants preferred not to wait for the SS and police commandos and instead had the selectees murdered by their own soldiers. Indeed, in some territories, such as Belarus, *most* prisoner shootings were carried out by Wehrmacht units. The total number of Soviet POWs shot as commissars, Jews, 'Asians', female soldiers or disabled prisoners is likely to have been far in excess of 140,000.[33]

In spite of the huge numbers involved, those Soviet prisoners of war shot by SS, police and Wehrmacht nonetheless comprise only a relatively small proportion of the total number of Red Army soldiers killed by their German captors. As discussed above, the vast majority perished directly or indirectly as a result of deliberate policies of neglect, undernourishment and starvation while in the 'care' of the Wehrmacht. The most reliable figures for the mortality of Soviet POWs in German captivity reveal that up to 3.3 million died from a total of just over 5.7 million captured between June 1941 and February 1945 – a proportion of almost 58 per cent. Of these, at least 845,000 died in camps in the area of operations according to the Wehrmacht's own statistics, though this figure almost certainly does not include those who perished on their way to the camps, so that a total number of 1 million deaths in areas under military administration is more likely. Around 1.2 million prisoners died in the Reich Commissariats Ukraine and Ostland under civil administration, approximately 500,000 in the Government General and up to 400,000 in the Reich. To these totals must be added those prisoners who were shot immediately after being captured and, therefore, not registered as prisoners. The Soviet prisoners of war were thus the largest single victim group of the German war of annihilation against the Soviet Union.[34]

All in all, the German starvation policy cost the lives of millions of Soviet citizens. The examples discussed in the previous chapter – between 1 and 1.3 million deaths in Leningrad, more than 6,000 in the nearby town of Pavlovsk, 10,000 in Kiev, at least 30,000 in Kharkov, 9,000 in the town of Rzhev – constitute particularly severe urban instances of a more widespread phenomenon. A conservative estimate of hunger-induced mortality in the zone of operations of Army Group Centre, for example, amounts to 200,000 deaths from starvation and related diseases. As discussed above, the people of Ukraine were even worse affected by the starvation policy. To the death toll from starvation among Soviet civilians must be added around 3 million Soviet prisoners of war who died directly or indirectly as a result of deliberate starvation and undernourishment. All in all, then, the German starvation policy cost the lives of at least 5 million Soviet civilians and other non-combatants.[35]

CHAPTER 7
PREVENTIVE TERROR AND REPRISALS AGAINST CIVILIANS

As we have seen in the preceding chapters, several major groups of non-combatants among the Soviet population in the territories invaded and occupied by German forces were targeted by Nazi mass-killing policies purely on the basis of their belonging to these groups (or being assigned to one or more of them by the perpetrators): Jews, psychiatric patients, Roma, urban dwellers in general (especially children, the sick and the elderly) and captive Red Army soldiers. In fact, the range of victim groups extended even further. Inhabitants of the countryside were likewise at serious risk of succumbing to so-called pacification operations; hundreds of thousands of residents of rural regions in Belarus, Ukraine and Russia fell victim to German terror and reprisals carried out during the campaign waged against Soviet partisans, real and imagined. In actual fact, then, regardless of one's ethnic background, religion, physical and mental state, place of residence or whether or not one wore a uniform, there was a very real chance of falling prey to the ubiquitous violence spread by German agencies in the occupied Soviet territories. It is perhaps hardly surprising, then, that the total number of Soviet dead in the conflict with Germany between 1941 and 1945 comes to a staggering 26.6 million people. Of these, Red Army dead account for 14.6 million, according to recent Russian figures. This leaves 12 million Soviet civilian deaths. If the 3.3 million troops who perished as POWs are deducted from the total of Red Army dead and added to the civilian toll, it becomes clear that the majority of Soviet war dead – more than 15 million people – comprised civilians and unarmed, captured soldiers.[1]

As Germany's political and military leadership expected a swift campaign and a substantial collapse of the Soviet state, it did not anticipate having to fight a guerrilla war of any real significance. It was clear, however, that, during the envisaged encirclement of entire Soviet armies, Red Army soldiers separated from their units would remain in the rear of the Wehrmacht and that the planned starvation of parts of the local population might well trigger unrest. The weakness of the German security forces deployed between the main transit routes left supply lines and economic infrastructure vulnerable in the rear areas and created a power vacuum in which irregular Soviet resistance could potentially jeopardise the ultimate success of the military campaign. For these and other reasons discussed above, the Wehrmacht was not only keen to work hand in hand with the SS and police but also to react to any stirring of resistance with its own draconian measures.[2]

Even with the German military advance soon stalling, many months still passed before the first real Soviet underground groups organised themselves. Furthermore, they were often poorly equipped and insufficiently armed well into 1942 and even 1943. Until mid-1942, armed resistance frequently emanated from groups of scattered Red Army soldiers acting on their own initiative. Though it would not be accurate to speak of a partisan war without partisans, the occupying forces relied from the outset on a 'preventive' approach to combating resistance and regarded mass arrests and murder as effective instruments to this end. Already six weeks before the German invasion, on 13 May 1941, the OKW had issued a Decree on the Exercise of Martial Jurisdiction in the Area Barbarossa and on Special Measures of the Troops, which set the scene for what was to come by allowing collective reprisals against whole villages and enabling each and every German officer to decide on matters of life and death regarding Soviet civilians without consulting superior authorities.[3]

The primary clause of the so-called Jurisdiction Decree Barbarossa stated that 'offences committed by enemy civilians' were to be removed from the 'responsibility of the courts-martial and military courts until further notice'. Any 'elements suspected of criminal action' taken prisoner should be summoned to the nearest officer, who was to decide promptly as to 'whether they are to be shot'. The capture and detainment of what were termed 'suspect perpetrators' was 'expressly forbidden'. In the event that following attacks on the troops no perpetrators could be seized, the Jurisdiction Decree furthermore granted all troop commanders from battalion commander upwards the right to initiate 'collective violent measures'. In discussing the order three days after it had been issued, the OKH recommended for the practical implementation of these reprisals immediately to 'shoot thirty men' in the

1. Smoke rises from the crematorium chimney at Hadamar Hospital, one of six facilities used to carry out the murder of disabled patients in the Operation T4 'euthanasia' programme, 1941.

2. Group portrait of the staff of Hartheim Castle near Linz – one of six facilities used to carry out the murder of disabled patients in the Operation T4 'euthanasia' programme – as they relax with an accordion; undated.

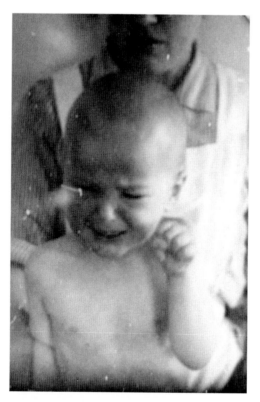

3. Four-year-old Richard Jenne, the last child murdered by Sister Mina Wörle, the head nurse in the 'special children's ward' at Irsee Monastery near Kaufbeuren, on 29 May 1945, three weeks *after* the German surrender.

4. SS personnel (note the eagle on the left sleeve) lead a group of blindfolded Polish prisoners to an execution site in the Kampinos Forest near the village of Palmiry, autumn 1939.

5. A German army firing squad shoots Polish civilians; undated.

6. Regular German policemen (note the distinctive brown collar and cuffs with two buttons worn by the man on the left) search through piles of clothing belonging to the 33,771 Jews shot in the Babi Yar ravine near Kiev on 29 and 30 September 1941.

7. A man kneeling at the edge of a grave filled with corpses is about to be shot by a member of the SD (note the empty collar tab) in Vinnitsa, Ukraine, 1942. The onlookers include Wehrmacht and German police personnel. Handwritten on the reverse of the photo in German are the words 'The last Jew in Vinnitsa'.

8. Yura Ryabinkin and his classmates, 1937. Yura is in the third row, on the far right. He died of starvation during the siege of Leningrad.

9. Two women cut meat from a dead horse on a Leningrad street in early 1942. A human corpse lies nearby.

10. Bread is distributed to captured Soviet soldiers in a prisoner-of-war camp in Vinnitsa, Ukraine, 28 July 1941.

11. In the absence of alternative shelter, two Soviet prisoners of war dig a burrow with their bare hands and metal bowls in Stalag XI D (321) Fallingbostel-Oerbke, in the province of Hanover, 1941.

12. Soviet prisoners of war often had to live in burrows they were forced to dig themselves, like this one in Stalag XI D (321) Fallingbostel-Oerbke, 1941. On the reverse of the photo, 'cave dwellings' is handwritten in German.

13. Corpses of countless Soviet prisoners of war in Dulag 184 in Vyazma, Russia, 19 November 1941. Two Wehrmacht guards (far left) look on while prisoners fetch the bodies of their dead comrades and bury them in mass graves.

14. Captured Soviet soldiers in a POW camp, 1942.

15. A soldier from a Wehrmacht security division secures the rope with which a man is hanged as a partisan, Vitebsk, Belarus, October 1941.

16. German paratroopers massacre the male inhabitants of the village of Kondomari on Crete, 2 June 1941. This is one of a series of photographs taken by a member of Wehrmacht Propaganda Company 690 documenting the whole operation.

17. Children from the Łódź Ghetto are deported to Chełmno death camp in September 1942.

18. Emaciated corpses in a mass grave at Bełżec extermination camp, 1942.

19. A rare photograph of Sobibór extermination camp taken from a watchtower in early summer 1943. The SS flag on the far right marks the main gate. The light roof of the railway station is visible behind it. A Trawniki auxiliary patrols the passageway between the inner and outer fences.

20. Hungarian Jews are selected for work or immediate death in the gas chambers after their arrival at Auschwitz-Birkenau, 19 May 1944. The Birkenau main gate can be seen in the background.

21. Women and children await selection following the arrival of Hungarian Jews at Auschwitz-Birkenau, late May 1944.

22. German policemen guard Roma at a collection point in Asperg, Germany, before their deportation to Radom in the Government General, 22 May 1940.

23. A still of Sinti girl Settela Steinbach departing Westerbork transit camp in the Netherlands on a freight train bound for Auschwitz, 19 May 1944, from a film made by Werner Rudolf Breslauer.

24. Members of the SS Storm Brigade Dirlewanger march up Chłodna Street in Warsaw, August 1944.

locality concerned. In the second section of the Jurisdiction Decree, the obligatory criminal prosecution of 'offences committed by members of the Wehrmacht' against the Soviet civilian population was annulled. Provided that it did not relate to actions resulting from 'sexual abandon' or 'a criminal disposition', the responsible judge, as a rule a divisional commander, could leave it at a disciplinary penalty instead of court-martial proceedings.[4]

The most consequential innovation of the Jurisdiction Decree was the introduction of executions without legal proceedings. According to the hitherto existing legal regulations, the sentencing of irregulars necessitated proceedings before a court-martial, of which there were only around a dozen in a typical Wehrmacht division, military courts of the regimental commanders included. By contrast, after the Jurisdiction Decree came into effect, all officers, the number of whom in a full-strength division amounted to over 500 men, could henceforth make decisions concerning life and death. This universalisation of executive power, the envisaged reprisals on the basis of mere suspicion and the creation of a lawless region through the abolition of obligatory criminal prosecution made the Jurisdiction Decree a deeply radical order that was to form the basis of German tyranny in the occupied Soviet Union.[5]

Another feature of the 'preventive' approach to combating resistance in the occupied Soviet territories was the internment of all men of military-service age. In many Soviet cities, civilian internment camps were set up shortly after the arrival of the Wehrmacht and all males aged between fifteen or eighteen and forty-five or sixty were interned in them. The largest and best documented of these camps was erected in Minsk on the orders of the garrison commander, Bernsdorf, within days of the conquest of the city on 28 June 1941. Posters called on all men between eighteen and forty-five to come to an assembly point at the opera house; anyone not complying, stated the posters, would be killed. The camp – part of the aforementioned Dulag 127 – contained for a time 100,000 captured soldiers and 40,000 civilian prisoners. It was relocated shortly thereafter to Drosdy, 5km north of Minsk. Most of the civilians were released after ten or twelve days, though the civilian internment camp was not completely closed until October or November 1941. During that time, the detainees – a small number of women and children among them – were left for days on end without any food or water in the searing summer heat. Such conditions drove some of the prisoners to cannibalism.[6]

On 7 or 8 July, Field Marshal Günther von Kluge, commander of the Fourth Army, gave Einsatzgruppe B and the Wehrmacht's Secret Field Police the task of 'sifting' the civilian internment camp at Drosdy. Einsatzgruppe B repeatedly drove into the camp with lorries and took groups of people to a nearby excavation pit, where they were shot. The chief of Einsatzgruppe B, Arthur Nebe, reported to Berlin:

> So far, only those people have been discharged who could provide posi-tive identification and are neither politically nor criminally incriminated. Those left in the camp will be subjected to careful examination and in each case dealt with according to the result of the investigation. One thousand and fifty Jews have been liquidated to begin with. More are sent for execution on a continual daily basis. With regard to the remaining non-Jews in the camp, the liquidation of the criminals, the functionaries, the Asians, etc., has commenced.

Due to concerns over the loss of a substantial proportion of the Minsk workforce as a result of starvation and epidemics, however, the time avail-able to Nebe for these killings was cut short and the majority of the civilian internees, including many Jews, were released between 10 and 12 July.[7]

An OKH directive issued on 25 July, just over a month after the campaign had commenced, further radicalised German 'pacification' measures. It drew attention to the 'intended deployment of partisan sections in our own rear area' as well as to 'the inflammatory impact in general of the pillars of the Jewish–Bolshevik system'. It then stated that 'attacks and acts of violence of every description' against German personnel and property, as well as any attempts to carry out such attacks, were to be 'ruthlessly put down by force of arms to the point of annihilating the enemy'. In the event that German personnel met passive resistance, or were unable to apprehend the perpetrator(s) of acts of sabotage, 'collective violent measures' were to be carried out immediately against towns and villages. (It is worth noting that the reference to 'passive resistance' had been absent from a similar passage on collective measures in the earlier Jurisdiction Decree.) 'Suspicious elements', the OKH directive continued, were to be handed over to the Einsatzgruppen purely on the basis of their 'disposition and attitude', even where it could not be established that a serious offence had been committed.

Fleeing prisoners of war were to be shot immediately; it was not necessary first to call to them to stop. All forms of actual or supposed defiance were to be put down brutally and without hesitation.[8]

Belarus

The geographical focal point of the crimes committed against the Soviet civilian population during the pursuit of partisans was Belarus. In spite of the orders issued by the OKW in May and the OKH in July 1941, discussed above, German occupation forces applied collective violent measures comparatively rarely in 1941. From a total of 5,295 Belarusian localities destroyed or affected by German massacres committed in the course of anti-partisan operations during the war (and in which more than 147,000 inhabitants were killed in the process), only 3 per cent of these cases occurred in 1941, that is, around 150, which is closely related to the limited partisan activity during that year. Of the 628 villages in which the Germans attempted to annihilate the entire population, and in which a total of around 83,000 people were murdered, only twelve villages (with 1,628 inhabitants) suffered this fate in 1941. The OKW's notorious general directive of 16 September 1941, stipulating that 50 to 100 hostages be executed in retaliation for the death of a German soldier in the occupied territories, changed little in this particular respect.[9]

Of course, each and every one of these massacres in 1941 caused immeasurable suffering. The first took place in Ablinga in neighbouring Lithuania on only the third day of the invasion. Soldiers of the 291st Infantry Division murdered a total of 42 civilians – 33 inhabitants of Ablinga and 6 from nearby Žvaginiai, as well as 2 other men and 1 woman. The massacre was a reprisal for the death of two German cyclists there on the previous day. Around 20 residents survived the massacre, including a woman with her injured five-month-old baby, who managed to crawl out of the pit of corpses after the Germans had left the site. The village was burned to the ground. The same fate befell the Lithuanian village of Švendūna, where Wehrmacht troops shot and killed 11 men as 'retribution'.[10]

In some Belarusian villages, the number of fatalities of German massacres in summer 1941 was substantial: 436 in Sviataya Volya, 123 in Velikaya Gat (both in Ivatsevichy district), 250 in Pridorovo (Brest district) and 300 in

Zapesoche (Zhitkovichi district). Although it was not reflected in a rising number of destroyed villages, in the combating of partisans an escalation of mass crimes was prepared in September and implemented in October. As we have already seen, this intensification also manifested itself in policies against Jews and POWs. This occurred once it had become clear to both the commanders in the field and the leadership in Berlin that the Blitzkrieg had failed and a definitive military victory over the Soviet Union could not be achieved in 1941, leading to the conclusion that the morale of the partisans and the resilience of the civilian population might be strengthened. It seemed all the more important, then, to destroy the *potential* danger posed by *potential* partisans before the spring. In the rear area of Army Group Centre, for instance, a total of 24,668 alleged partisans had been killed by the end of September 1941. In October alone, the figure was 14,265 and in November 14,037. In December, 6,063 alleged partisans were killed and in January and February 1942 a total of 4,224. As of 1 December 1941, there had been 52,970 fatalities overall, and as of 1 March 1942 a total of 63,257 – against German losses of 638 dead.[11]

These figures were all compiled by the German forces themselves. In the words of one of those submitting these reports, the commander of the rear area for Army Group Centre, Lieutenant General Max von Schenckendorff, '300–400 partisans *on average each day* were dispatched in battle' in 1941. In view of the figures cited above and, especially, the ratio of German to Soviet dead (1:99), however, there can of course be no talk of the victims having generally been killed 'in battle'. The military units operating in the rear area of Army Group Centre 'dispatched' 300 to 400 people a day during 1941 – almost as many as all murder victims of (the numerically far weaker) Einsatzgruppe B over the same period. SS and police units, by contrast, killed relatively few alleged guerrillas in autumn 1941, and their figures in fact decreased during the course of the autumn. The four police regiments and two SS brigades, for instance, reported fewer killed partisans and communists in October and November than in September. As with the victims of Wehrmacht anti-partisan operations, however, the majority of those that they did kill appear to have been unarmed civilians. For example, between 18 October and 18 November, the SS Cavalry Brigade shot '2,120 partisans and suspicious persons', but recorded a haul of only 5 machine guns and 116 rifles. Einsatzgruppe B reported a total of 1,300 slain 'partisans' by the end of November. Sonderkommando 7a, for instance, arrested 693 men aged between 15 and 55 during an operation near the town of Demidov in early October, of whom 438 (mainly peasants from collective farms) were released, 72 former Red Army soldiers brought to POW camps and the rest – no fewer than 183 – shot or hanged as 'partisans and communists'.[12]

The simultaneous escalation of violence against Soviet partisans and Jews in late summer and early autumn 1941 was reflected in the conflation of these two bogeymen. It was the aforementioned Max von Schenckendorff who initiated the infamous anti-partisan warfare seminar in Mogilev on 24–26 September, the result of which was the slogan: 'Where there is a partisan, there is a Jew, and where there is a Jew, there is a partisan.' Many of the key figures in the ruthless operations against Jews and partisans in Belarus attended the seminar, including Bach-Zelewski, Nebe and Hermann Fegelein, commander of the SS Cavalry Brigade, all three of whom gave speeches. The seminar was so successful that it was repeated in May 1942. As a result of equating Jews with partisans – and, by extension, of the extermination of Jews (and civilian non-combatants in general) during anti-partisan operations – military tasks increasingly blended with the eliminationist strategy of Nazi racial ideology, even if the identification of the two groups was in no way confirmed by reality. Thus, the war against the partisans was crucial for the involvement of the Wehrmacht in large-scale massacres of Jews and other civilians.[13]

Until spring 1942, the principal victims of German anti-partisan operations in the occupied Soviet territories were certainly not actual partisans. There were two main victim groups: on the one hand, Red Army soldiers who had been separated from their units and gone into hiding, and, on the other hand, refugees from the cities or those in search of food. As mentioned above, an average of around 8,000 so-called partisans were killed each month from July to September 1941 in the rear area of Army Group Centre. Groups of scattered Red Army troops comprised the majority of these victims during the first two months of the campaign. This means that captured enemy soldiers were often murdered without further ado. German persecution of 'non-locals' and 'travellers' – that is, refugees attempting to escape the devastation and unemployment in the towns and cities, trying to make their way to relatives or endeavouring to procure food from the countryside – also began in July. They were regarded as a destabilising factor. In late August, the commander of Army Group Rear Area (Korück) 580 was among those who ordered that refugees, 'as a matter of principle, be arrested or liquidated'. German troops killed members of both these groups preventively as *potential* partisans. This does not mean that Red Army fugitives and civilian refugees were always murdered in their entirety and in every instance. The aforementioned figure of 24,668 alleged partisans killed during the first three months of the campaign can be seen in the context of a total of 37,934 prisoners taken in the rear areas of Army Group Centre during the same period, as another German report from the end of September records. Thus, while a large proportion of Red Army fugitives and civilian refugees *were* killed during these months, many – especially Soviet soldiers who had previously been captured and then managed to flee columns marching westwards – were instead sent to prison camps (where their chances of survival, admittedly, were also slim).[14]

The failure of the German offensive against Moscow and the fruits of the Soviet counteroffensive significantly improved strategic and political conditions for the Soviet partisans, which in turn led to an intensification of partisan activities. In the first months of 1942, the Germans responded to this development with a new tactic. It was devised above all by the regional military leadership in the rear area of Army Group Centre at the request of the OKH. Starting in March, the Germans organised large-scale operations – so-called *Großunternehmen* – against the partisans and their alleged accomplices. Combined forces of Wehrmacht, SS and police encircled a given territory and then advanced inwards, gradually drawing the ring tighter and tighter, in the process confiscating cattle and foodstuffs, burning down entire villages and often massacring their inhabitants, including women and children. These operations were carried out mainly but not exclusively in Belarus and the region southwest of Moscow.[15]

The pilot project – Operation Bamberg – took place south of Bobruisk between 26 March and 6 April 1942. The strengthened 707th Infantry Division, with the support of the 102nd Slovak Infantry Regiment and the German Police Battalion 315, was tasked with its implementation. In the days before the operation began, the divisional commander, Brigadier Baron Gustav von Bechtolsheim, issued orders in which he pointed to the 'decidedly hostile' attitude of the civilian population to the Germans and demanded a 'most ruthless crackdown on men, women and children'. It was on this premise that 'Bamberg' commenced. Over the course of a week, the division surrounded the territory between Glusk, Parichi and Kopatkevichi and gradually tightened the envelopment. This was followed by the destruction of a series of villages within the pocket, the murder of their inhabitants and the plunder of all available foodstuffs. In their final report on the operation, the units involved recorded the shooting of 3,423 partisans and their accomplices (the actual figure was in the range of 5,000 to 6,000) at a cost of only 7 dead, 8 wounded and 3 sick on the German side. They furthermore reported the plunder of 2,454 head of cattle, 2,286 sheep, 312 pigs, 115 tons of grain and 120 tons of potatoes – livestock and food stolen from the civilian population at the end of a severe winter. By contrast, only 47 rifles and sub-machine guns were captured.[16]

In light of these figures and the fact that no major resistance was reported, it is clear that this operation had little or nothing to do with conventional anti-partisan warfare. Indeed, the way in which many of the Soviet fatalities came about can leave no doubt as to the true nature of Operation Bamberg. In Khvoinya, Police Battalion 315 murdered 1,350 people, some of whom were locked in their houses and then killed with hand grenades or burned to death. In Rudnia, 800 people were gathered together and shot in groups (the men first had to undress). In Oktyabrsky, 190 people were burned alive in the club house, while the inhabitants of Kurin were in some cases shot and in others burned to death. It was a similar story in Kovali, where the children were burned to death.[17]

The nature of the German response to the intensification of partisan activities during the first months of 1942 was also reflected in Hitler's appointment of Himmler in July of that year to take charge of combating partisans in the Soviet territories under civil administration. This decision was made at precisely the moment when the slaughter of Jews across Europe was being accelerated by Himmler and the SS, and it underscores once more the close link between the extermination of Jews and the war against partisans. The large-scale operations carried out over the course of the next two years were very much in the same vein as the pilot project 'Bamberg'. The bloodiest of these included 'Swamp Fever' in western Belarus in August and September 1942 (10,063 dead, including 8,350 Jews), 'Hamburg' north of Slonim in December 1942 (at least 6,100 dead, including 3,000 Jews, as compared with a mere 7 German dead), 'Hornung' (from the old German word for February) in February 1943 (13,000 dead, including at least 3,100 Jews, at a cost of 29 German dead), 'Cottbus' north of Borisov in May and June 1943 (9,796 dead, as compared with a death toll of 128 Germans), 'Seydlitz' in the Pripet Marshes in June and July 1943 (5,106 dead, at a cost of 34 German fatalities), 'Heinrich' north of Polotsk in November 1943 (5,452 dead, as compared with a death toll of 358 Germans, as the action transitioned into a frontline operation), 'Spring Festival' around Polotsk in April and May 1944 (7,011 dead, as compared with 300 German fatalities) and 'Cormorant' around Minsk in May and June 1944 (7,697 dead, at a cost of at least 110 German dead).[18]

Jacob Grigoriev, whose own village of Kuznetsovo in Pskov province, western Russia, was destroyed in one such killing spree, recalled the nightmare in his testimony at Nuremberg after the war:

On the memorable day of 28 October 1943, German soldiers suddenly raided our village and started murdering the peaceful citizens, shooting them, chasing them into the houses. On that day I was working on the threshing floor with my two sons, Alexei and Nikolai. Suddenly a German soldier came up to us and ordered us to follow him. [...] We were led through the village to the last house at the outskirts. There were nineteen of us, all told, in that house. [...] A little later three German machine gunners came in, accompanied by a fourth carrying a heavy revolver. We were ordered into another room. So, we went, all nineteen of us, and were lined up against a wall, including my two sons, and they began shooting at us from their machine guns. I stood right up to the wall, bending slightly. After the first volley I fell to the floor, where I lay, too frightened to move. When they had shot all of us, they left the house. When I came to, I looked round and saw my son Nikolai who had been shot and had fallen, face downwards. My second son I could not find anywhere. Then, when some time had passed, I began to think how I could escape. I straightened my legs out from under the man who had fallen on me and began to think how I could get away. And instead of that, instead of planning my escape, I lost my head and called out, at the top of my voice, 'Can I really go now?' At that moment my small son, who had remained alive, recognised me. [...] My little son called out, 'Daddy, are you still alive?' [...] He was wounded in the leg. I calmed him down: 'Do not fear, my small son. I shall not leave you here. Somehow or other, we shall get away from here. I shall carry you out.' A little later the house began to burn. Then I opened the window and threw myself out of it, carrying my little boy, who had been wounded in the leg.

The next day, a villager named Vitya, who had also somehow managed to escape the conflagration, told Grigoriev what had happened in the second hut, where his wife and son Petya had been taken. Grigoriev related:

> The German soldiers, having driven the people into the hut, opened the door into the passage and proceeded to shoot from their machine guns across the threshold. According to Vitya's words, people who were still half alive were burning, including my little boy, Petya, who was only nine years old. When he ran out of the hut, he saw that my Petya was still alive. He was sitting under a bench, having covered his ears with his little hands.

Grigoriev's wife (in her sixth month of pregnancy), his youngest son, Petya (aged nine), his eldest son, Nikolai (aged sixteen), his brother's wife and her two infants all perished. Grigoriev himself and his middle son, Alexei, were the only surviving members of the family. A total of 47 villagers were killed that day; the oldest victim was a woman of 108 years; the youngest was a baby of four months. Grigoriev did not know why the Germans had destroyed the village and murdered its inhabitants. One German told him that 'partisans were hiding in your village'. 'But his words were untruthful,' testified Grigoriev, 'because we had no partisans in the village; nobody indulged in any partisan activities, since there was nobody left. Only old people and small children were left in the village.' Kuznetsovo was only one of several villages attacked during this particular operation. There and in the neighbouring villages, a total of 400 people were killed, including 43 shot in Kurysheva, 47 shot in Vshivova and 23 burned to death in Pavlovo.[19]

The aforementioned figure of 9,796 dead reported by the Germans for Operation Cottbus in May and June 1943 did not include another 2,000 to 3,000 civilians 'blown up' – as newly appointed 'Chief of Anti-Gang Formations' Bach-Zelewski wrote to Himmler – during mine clearance. On the orders of Oskar Dirlewanger, commander of the SS Special Battalion Dirlewanger, locals were forced to cross minefields on the access routes to partisan camps. This not uncommon tactic had first been employed by the Wehrmacht; LIX Army Corps had issued a corresponding order on 2 March 1942. The 403rd Security Division used Jews and POWs for the task. From autumn 1942, civilians living in the area of the 286th Security Division had to plough, harrow or walk roads and lanes. Of the twenty-eight people who were blown up during one such mine clearance near Artishevo, eighteen were children. As of January 1944, the 78th Storm Division insisted that 'all local residents (incl. women and children)' perform mine clearances every morning at six o'clock on the routes frequented by German troops. The following month, Curt von Gottberg – SS and police leader in Belarus and, since the assassination of Wilhelm Kube in September 1943, acting general commissioner there – compelled the entire population of Belarus's towns and villages to perform mine clearances every day on roads and lanes. Anyone refusing to carry out these 'mine-clearance and road-supervision duties' was subject to death. It is difficult to imagine a more perverse piece of legislation.[20]

Looking at the paltry weapons haul from some of the aforementioned operations – 17 machine guns and 11 heavy weapons from Operation Hamburg; 133 weapons from Operation Hornung – compared with the huge death tolls, it is clear that the use of large-scale operations was not an effective way to fight the partisans. Describing an attack on a Soviet village in January 1943, Artur Wilke from the office of the commander of the Security Police in Minsk wrote: 'I have the inner conviction this evening that scarcely any real bandits were killed.' In fact, these operations were actually *designed* to kill Belarusian civilians rather than partisans as such. With their military fortunes in decline, the Germans resolved to wipe out those people who might conceivably provide aid to the partisan struggle behind German lines. Thus, German units stuck to the roads and targeted adjacent villages (especially those bordering forested areas) during the large-scale operations, and intentionally avoided forging deeper into wooded areas where actual partisans and their bases might be encountered. As the former driver of Einsatzkommando 8, Georg Frentzel, later stated: 'Our objective here was to deprive the partisans in the forests of any opportunity to supply themselves with food, clothing, etc. from the villages.' The large-scale operations were a complete failure not only when it came to eliminating partisans, however, but also in their aim of cutting the partisans off from potential support networks. On the contrary: the brutality of German tactics only contributed to the growth of the partisan movement from 30,000 partisans in Belarus at the end of 1941 to 57,700 there in January 1943 and 122,600 in November 1943, which in turn led to even more desperate measures on the part of the Germans. Surprised by the number of bicycles found in partisan camps, the commander of the 1st SS Infantry Brigade, Karl von Treuenfeld, issued orders stating: 'Anyone bicycling must be shot.'[21]

None of this is to say that the Wehrmacht completely abandoned any attempts to locate and destroy *actual* partisans. During 1942 and 1943, a number of smaller-scale operations, such as some of those carried out by the 221st Security Division, targeted partisans. Even here, however, the lack of success against well-equipped and highly trained partisan forces – many of them Red Army soldiers cut off from their units – frequently led German soldiers to resort to the slaughter of civilians to boost their kill counts and justify their own heavy losses. For instance, between March and June 1942, the 221st Security Division lost 278 men against the Yelnya-Dorogobuzh partisans operating east of Smolensk. This was a serious loss for an already over-stretched security division. The enemy death toll was admittedly more than three times that of German dead: 806 killed in combat and another 122 partisans shot following capture. This disparity in itself, however, suggests that a substantial proportion of the reported partisan dead were actually unarmed civilians. This suspicion is hardened by the fact that only 51 machine guns and 150 rifles were captured from more than 900 enemy dead.[22]

Returning to the large-scale operations: they clearly also possessed a strong economic dimension. A key objective of these operations was the acquisition of agricultural produce. As the aforementioned commander of the 707th Infantry Division, Gustav von Bechtolsheim, stated in his final report on Operation Bamberg: 'Our task was the complete encirclement and destruction of the partisan groups and the securing and pacification of the area, in order to be able to seize and extract the substantial agricultural stocks.' The aforementioned livestock and food plundered during Operation Bamberg was in fact considered a major disappointment, as at least 10,000 to 20,000 head of cattle had been expected. The Germans succeeded in steadily increasing their yield in subsequent large-scale operations, seizing 7,907 head of cattle and 1,678 tons of grain during Operation Hamburg,

16,122 head of cattle and 222.8 tons of grain during Operation Hornung, and 19,941 head of cattle during Operation Seydlitz.[23]

Orders issued in early 1943 to collect more potential labourers for the German war economy also gradually made themselves felt in anti-partisan operations. From mid-spring onwards, though the death tolls of the large-scale operations remained huge, there were comparatively more survivors; they were then either resettled or deported to Germany as forced labourers. Following Operation Cottbus in May–June 1943 and Operation Cormorant in May–June 1944, for instance, 6,053 (4,997 men and 1,056 women) and 5,973 labourers, respectively, were deported. The number of those deported as forced labourers after Operation Spring Festival in April–May 1944 was almost as high as the figures for Cottbus and Cormorant combined: 11,233. Following Operations Seydlitz in June–July 1943 and Heinrich in November of the same year, 9,166 and 7,894 people, respectively, were removed from the areas in question and resettled (as compared with only 1,217 people after the earlier Operation Swamp Fever in August and September 1942). The selection of labourers in the Belarusian forests in 1943–44 resembled the selections in Auschwitz: the criteria for being killed had shifted to those *least likely* to be partisans. This resulted in more women and children than men being murdered on the spot in Belarus in 1943 and 1944. Many victims were herded into large buildings and burned alive.[24]

The mass deportations of would-be forced labourers were closely related to another policy, namely the complete depopulation and destruction of whole swathes of Belarusian countryside, creating so-called dead zones. A typical example was Operation Hermann – named for Hermann Göring – in the Naliboki Forest area between 13 July and 11 August 1943. After the afore-mentioned Curt von Gottberg had declared the region to be 'infested with gangs' and 4,280 inhabitants had been killed there, all remaining civilians, livestock and anything else of value found were removed and what was left behind was burned – even the woods. Civilians who subsequently entered this 'dead zone' were declared fair game and shot. Operation Hermann yielded around 21,000 head of cattle, more than 100 farm machines and 20,954 deported forced labourers.[25]

In the course of these large-scale operations, but also during hundreds of smaller police actions, countless villages were razed to the ground and many of their inhabitants murdered. Thousands of localities met this fate in the areas where a partisan presence was suspected, while several hundred suffered total destruction. Thus, the type of thing that happened elsewhere in Lidice, Kalavryta or Oradour – places that have rightly gone down in history as symbols of barbarity – was an everyday occurrence in the occupied Soviet territories. Though the large-scale operations – of which between 80 and 100 took place – were generally restricted to Belarus and the territories southwest of Moscow, the occupation forces carried out devastating massacres elsewhere, too. After a partisan unit of 50 locals and former Red Army soldiers had destroyed the police station in the village of Kortelisy near Ratne in northwest Ukraine in September 1942, a German battalion murdered almost the entire population of the village. Nearly 2,900 people were shot with sub-machine guns and pistols, drowned or bayoneted to death. The next day, Kortelisy itself was burned to the ground and ceased to exist. In March 1943, the same thing happened in the towns of Kosary and Koryukovka in northeast Ukraine. In Koryukovka, the Germans killed 6,700 inhabitants and burned 1,290 homes in retribution for the death of 78 mainly Hungarian soldiers during a partisan attack on the local Axis garrison; only ten brick buildings and a church survived. In Kosary, around 4,000 inhabitants were killed, leaving virtually no survivors.[26]

The measures taken by German forces in the context of their 'pacification' campaign constituted an attack on a substantial section of the Soviet population and, simultaneously, on the national and ethnic fabric of the state. These so-called anti-partisan operations were in effect an attempt to depopulate the Soviet countryside. German forces massacred hundreds of thousands of Soviet civilians, destroying thousands of homes and, indeed, entire villages in the process, more than 600 in Belarus alone. The vast majority of the victims of these massacres had little or no connection to guerrilla resistance, and virtually all of these deaths had a racist component. This alleged anti-partisan war, waged in fact largely against Soviet peasants, cost the lives of 345,000 people in Belarus alone, its territorial focal point, of whom perhaps only 10 per cent were actually partisans. (By contrast, the Germans themselves lost 6,000 to 7,000 men in Belarus at the hands of Soviet partisans.) If we include all other Soviet territories affected – the Leningrad area, central Russia, northern Ukraine, Crimea and parts of the northern Caucasus – the death toll as a result of German preventive terror and reprisals across the whole of the Soviet Union comes to around 640,000 people.[27]

Yugoslavia

As in Belarus and elsewhere in the Soviet Union, the Germans also shot huge numbers of civilians in occupied Yugoslavia under the guise of combating partisans. Indeed, Yugoslavia was the first killing ground of German anti-partisan warfare. From the outset, the military administration in Serbia responded with extreme brutality and in accordance with racist criteria to the Serbian uprising that erupted in July 1941 in the wake of the German invasion of the Soviet Union. Unable to combat communist partisans and Serbian nationalist Chetniks effectively with the forces available, the central feature of German operations was the murder of easily accessible hostages and other civilians. Prominent among these victims were Jews and Roma, who were convenient and supposedly expendable groups whose execution could satisfy the stipulated reprisal quotas without producing undesired political repercussions. By the end of 1941 alone, Wehrmacht and subordinated police units had shot up to 30,000 Serbian civilians as hostages and in mass shootings.[28]

Indicative of the German approach to anti-partisan warfare in Serbia (and, for that matter, the Soviet Union) were the actions of the 342nd Infantry Division in late September 1941 in the Mačva region, a 600km^2 area west of Šabac between the Drina and Sava rivers, and a major centre of rebel strength. For this mobile operation – its first – the division was loaned the second battalion of the 750th Infantry Regiment and a company of Reserve Police Battalion 64. The SD reported that the entire area between Šabac and the town of Bogatic was to be evacuated. Its menfolk were to be sent to concentration camps, where they would be screened by the SD, while its women and children were to be driven from their homes 'on to Mount Cer, south-west of Šabac, there to be left to their fate'. Franz Böhme, the German military commander in Serbia, himself issued an order on 22 September claiming that the population 'between the Drina and Sava has attached itself to the uprising. Women and children are running messages and maintaining the bandits' basis of supply'. The enactment of 'ruthless measures will set a terrifying example which will, in a short space of time, resonate across all Serbia'.[29]

After German soldiers had 'incurred losses' in Šabac on 23 September, the 342nd Infantry Division, the second battalion of the 750th Infantry Regiment and the 3rd Company of Reserve Police Battalion 64 descended on the city the next day and began arresting all men and male adolescents there. By the end of the three-day operation, 4,459 male civilians had been seized, including 450 Jews interned on the outskirts of Šabac. During their search of the city, however, the German troops neither encountered any armed resistance nor discovered any weapons. In spite of this, 75 men from Šabac were shot during the operation. German losses were minimal: one man killed and one lightly wounded from enemy action. On the same day the sweep of Šabac was launched, a pioneer battalion of the 342nd Infantry Division commenced work on the erection of a concentration camp north of the town, in the village of Jarak. The men of Šabac were sent to the camp, though they did not remain there long before being sent back to Šabac. This back-and-forth was preceded by the 342nd's massacre of 80 prisoners for 'insubordination'.[30]

Following its sweep of Šabac, the 342nd Infantry Division turned its attention to the rest of the Mačva region. Its approach there was shaped by an order issued on 25 September by its commander, Walter Hinghofer, that went even further than Böhme's order of three days earlier: 'Anyone who raises a weapon against the occupier *or* supports corresponding resistance is an irregular. Accordingly, *every member* of a rebellious band against whom the division fights is to be treated as an *irregular*. The *juridical punishment* of a member of a rebellious band is to be carried out [...] *with execution in every case* [...].' The division followed up on this order four days later by declaring that, though the preceding night had passed quietly, 'no one should be fooled by this. Attacks must be reckoned with. Every man encountered in no-man's land is to be shot without delay'. On 27 September, the division shot 250 of its prisoners and ordered its subordinate 698th Infantry Regiment to obliterate the village of Metković and murder its male population in retaliation for unspecified 'hostile activities' that had taken place there at the beginning of September. Two days later, the division shot 84 prisoners, from whom only one machine gun and a handful of rifles were seized.[31]

Between 21 and 30 September 1941, the 342nd Infantry Division shot 830 of its 8,400 prisoners. The great majority of these victims were unarmed civilians, and the division accordingly seized only a handful of rifles and a couple of machine guns from them. For its part, the 342nd suffered a mere 3 dead and 20 wounded. By 9 October, the division had shot a further 1,130 civilians in the Mačva region. In applying reprisals – in the words of the division's intelligence officer – 'indiscriminately against the entire popula-tion', the 342nd was not merely following Lieutenant General Böhme's lead, but also acting on its own initiative. After all, it was not until the following day, 10 October, that Böhme issued to all units his notorious order for the shooting of 100 hostages for each German killed and 50 for each wounded. As it was, the reprisal ratios specified by Böhme were actually less severe than the ratio of Serbs to Germans killed at the division's hands up to that date. During subsequent operations against Mount Cer (10–15 October) and the town of Krupanj (19–20 October), the 342nd Infantry Division shot 1,081 and 1,800 civilians, respectively. By the time the division had relieved the town of Valjevo in late October 1941, it had lost 10 dead and had 39 wounded. It thereupon declared that it would shoot 1,000 hostages in retaliation for its dead and 3,950 hostages in retaliation for its wounded. This meant that it intended to shoot 100 hostages not only for every one of its own dead but also for every one of its wounded. This clearly exceeded the reprisal ratios stipulated by Böhme. As it turned out, by 11 November, the division had run out of prisoners with whom to meet its targets.[32]

Already by the end of 1941, Wehrmacht and subordinated police units had shot as many as 30,000 Serbian civilians (including around 8,000 adult male Jews and Roma) as hostages and during reprisals for partisan attacks. Though the focus of the partisan war in Yugoslavia gradually shifted in 1942 and 1943, alongside Slovenia, to Bosnia and Croatia – that is, into the sphere of influence of the fascist Ustasha state – thousands more Serbian civilians lost their lives as hostages at the hands of the German military during these years. The commander of the Second Panzer Army in Yugoslavia, Lothar Rendulic, who was in charge of anti-partisan operations in Croatia, Montenegro and Albania between August 1943 and June 1944, reported 30,000 dead 'communists' for the last four months of 1943 and another 19,000 for January 1944. For the entire period of the war, German forces may have killed as many as 200,000 people across Yugoslavia under the guise of anti-partisan warfare.[33]

Greece

Although Greece, like Yugoslavia, had been occupied in spring 1941, mas-sacres masquerading as reprisals initially played only a regional role there, as no comparable resistance movement existed. Nonetheless, German para-troopers killed as many as 2,000 residents of the island of Crete following the landing there with the argument that these murders were retaliation for shelling by civilians. On 2 June, for instance, an ad hoc firing squad shot the male inhabitants of Kondomari in cold blood in the olive groves outside their village. After the conquest of Crete, all of Greece was occupied in June 1941 and divided into Italian, German and Bulgarian occupation zones. In a similar way to Yugoslavia in autumn 1941, a massive wave of so-called paci-fication operations and reprisal massacres were then carried out in occupied Greece in summer and autumn 1943. Various Wehrmacht units proceeded to carry out mass shootings of locals in response to partisan attacks. The most notorious of these massacres were inflicted first on the village of Komeno and the town of Kalavryta in late summer and autumn 1943. In Komeno, 317 villagers, including 74 children below the age of ten and 20 entire families, were murdered by the 1st Mountain Division, an elite Wehrmacht unit that had previously been deployed in the Caucasus and Yugoslavia. In Kalavryta, all the men of the town, more than 500, were shot by the 117th Light Infantry Division, which had likewise gained practical experience of anti-partisan operations in Yugoslavia. In spring 1944, further massacres were carried out by the 7th Regiment of the 4th SS-Police Armoured Infantry Division at Klisura in Macedonia and then at Distomo, near Delphi. In each case, hundreds of men and, sometimes, women and children were slaughtered. A Red Cross team from Athens that arrived in Distomo a few days after the massacre even found bodies dangling from the tress that lined the road into the village.[34]

The case of Komeno is illuminating. After a Wehrmacht reconnaissance team had sighted a small group of guerrillas in the village square on 12 August 1943, the 1st Mountain Division decided to carry out a surprise attack on the village. The task was assigned to the 98th Regiment, whose commander, Colonel Josef Salminger, told his men that German soldiers had been killed and that they were going to wipe out a guerrilla lair. On the morning of 16 August, Komeno and its inhabitants were subjected to six hours of total destruction. Thirteen-year-old Alexandros Mallios had been instructed by his father to take the family's sheep and goats out of the village, so the Germans could not steal them. Hiding behind the churchyard wall, he watched the Germans leave:

I was probably the first person to enter the village once the Germans left. All the houses that I passed were burnt. I heard the crackling of the corn burning and thought at first the Germans were still shooting. I did not realise at first what it was. I took another path through the village, but everywhere I looked the houses had been burnt. I saw no one alive. There were many bodies in the street: men, women and children, and most of the bodies appeared to be burnt. I saw one old woman, who had apparently burnt to death in a sitting position. The houses were burning as I walked through.

He went on to his own house and on the road outside he found the bodies of his own family lying on the ground. 'I did not go into my house, because I fainted at this point. When I regained consciousness, I was by the river, and someone was bathing the blood off me.'[35]

Less well known but with comparably high numbers of victims are the massacres in Vianos on Crete (280 people killed), Pargos, Mesovuna and Chortiatis (146 residents killed, including 109 women and girls). From May to July 1944, the reprisal policies of the occupying forces escalated once more. An SS-run internment camp had existed in Haidari, near Athens, since September 1943; there, the SS regularly shot prisoners as hostages, over 2,000 in total, including 25 women. During the course of the occupation, a total of around 6,500 Greek towns and villages were destroyed by the Germans in their attempt to crush the partisan movement. Of that number, 1,600 towns and villages with between 2,000 and 3,000 civilians were wiped out on the island of Crete alone, which was part of the German occupation zone. All in all, German forces killed up to 100,000 people across Greece during reprisals and so-called pacification operations.[36]

Well before the escalation of these operations, plunder and requisitioning by the occupation regime during the months that followed the armistice of April 1941 had already led to a catastrophic breakdown in the Greek national food supply. Unlike the starvation of substantial sections of the Soviet urban population and Red Army prisoners, the famine that ensued in Greece had not been planned by the Germans. Once a famine became unavoidable, however, they – like the Italians, who controlled much of mainland Greece, and the Bulgarians – not only did little to stop it but actually continued confiscating foodstuffs. 'We cannot worry unduly about the Greeks,' commented

Göring. 'It is a misfortune which will strike many other people beside them.' The division of the country into three occupation zones with internal borders inhibited the free circulation of people and commodities. The Bulgarians, for example, prohibited any transport of grain out of Eastern Macedonia and Western Thrace, where 30 per cent of Greece's pre-war grain had been produced. The population of Athens could only be fed with imported food-stuffs. Italy sent around 10,000 tons of grain to the capital, Germany only 5,000 tons and Bulgaria none at all. The Red Cross, which commissioned its own study, estimated that about 250,000 people died directly or indirectly as a result of the famine between 1941 and 1944. Taking into account the shortfall in the number of births over the same period, it reckoned that the total popu-lation of Greece was at least 300,000 less by the end of the war as a result of food scarcity than it would otherwise have been. Of the 250,000 deaths from starvation, more than 40,000 occurred in the Athens–Piraeus area – like Crete, part of the German occupation zone – in the year following October 1941, in addition to several thousand deaths in the months before October.[37]

As partisan strongholds, Belarus, Yugoslavia and Greece each suffered six-figure totals of civilian deaths during reprisals and so-called pacification operations. Tens of thousands of civilians were also killed in other territories occupied by the Germans. At least 10,000 Italian civilians across genders and age groups – including 1,000 in Rome alone – were killed during massacres and hostage shootings between 1943 (when Mussolini was deposed and German troops entered Italy) and 1945, while a further 37,000 died following their deportation to German camps. Around 30,000 partisans were killed in combat or executed as prisoners, while on the German side at least 3,000 members of the Wehrmacht, police and SS died fighting the partisans. During punitive expeditions and so-called pacification operations in Poland, 20,000 people in the countryside were killed. Such acts of violence also resulted in the partial or complete destruction of around 800 Polish villages. In Slovakia, almost 25,000 people were killed during the suppression of the Slovak National Uprising in 1944 and as a result of German reprisals.[38]

While German troops in Eastern Europe acted with much more brutality than they had in the First World War, the German military in France wished to appear more restrained than it had during that conflict in order to avoid a repetition of the excesses of 1914, when thousands of civilians in Belgium and northern France had been shot as alleged irregulars in the opening weeks of the war. Accordingly, the military administration tried to keep down the number of hostages who were shot, so as not to alienate the French public. German terror in occupied France escalated, however, when communist guerrillas – who formed the core of France's weak resistance movement (until 1943, when the Gaullists began to engage in open resistance) – started to carry out attacks against the occupation regime. Genuine and alleged communists therefore comprised the majority of the 200 hostages killed by the end of 1941. Not until February 1944, however, did the types of measure that had long been commonplace in Eastern and Southeast Europe reach France against the backdrop of a looming Allied invasion and increased Résistance activity. Among the massacres that followed was the notorious murder by the Waffen SS division Das Reich of 642 residents – including women and children – of Oradour-sur-Glane on 10 June 1944 and the razing of the village. Unlike in the Soviet Union, Yugoslavia or Greece, however, the destruction of entire localities and the murder of all their inhabitants remained limited in France to this single case. The total number of people killed during anti-partisan operations in occupied France in 1943 and 1944 nonetheless came to between 13,000 and 16,000, of whom between 4,000 and 5,000 were civilians. A further 3,000 people were executed after being convicted by German military courts, and another 1,000 were shot as hostages between 1941 and 1943. Taken together, almost 20,000 people were killed in the context of anti-resistance measures in the territory administered by the German military commander in France during the years 1940 to 1944. A further 61,000 non-Jewish French people were deported to German camps and prisons for political reasons or resistance activities, of whom almost 25,000 perished there.[39]

Under the guise of anti-partisan warfare, the Germans shot and killed a total of around a million people – generally unarmed civilians and mostly non-Jews. It is no coincidence – and, still less, a contradiction – that the largest numbers of victims lived in those European territories that were partisan strongholds: the Germans mostly targeted precisely those people who might conceivably provide aid to the partisan struggle behind German lines, rather than the partisans themselves. Thus, in Belarus, the rest of the German-occupied Soviet territories, Yugoslavia and Greece the number of deaths reached six figures apiece. Tens of thousands of civilians, respectively, were also killed during reprisals and so-called pacification operations in

France, Italy, Slovakia and Poland (not including, in the latter case, those murdered during the campaign against the Polish elites in 1939–40 or the suppression of the Warsaw Uprising in 1944).[40]

The German invasion of the Soviet Union in June 1941 was the prelude to mass killing on an unprecedented scale. In the two years prior to summer 1941, the Nazi regime had murdered more than 70,000 mentally and physically disabled people in the German Reich and Poland, tens of thousands of Jewish and non-Jewish Poles and several thousand concentration-camp inmates on German soil. By the end of 1941, German programmes of mass murder had cost the lives of a further 3 million civilians and other non-combatants, including almost 2 million Soviet prisoners of war, around 900,000 Jews (90 per cent of them in the occupied Soviet territories), at least 100,000 civilians in the context of anti-partisan warfare (above all in Belarus, central Russia and Serbia) and hundreds of thousands of residents of besieged Leningrad. In the first six months of Operation Barbarossa, German forces wiped out 1 in every 500 people on the planet. As we have seen, the killing continued unabated into the following year. Only during the course of 1942 would Europe's Jews overtake Soviet POWs as the biggest group of victims of Nazi annihilation policies.[41]

Part III

SPRING 1942–SPRING 1945

CHAPTER 8
HOLOCAUST BY GAS
OPERATION REINHARDT

The year 1942 marked the peak of the murder of Europe's Jews. Under German command, in excess of 3 million Jews – more than half of all the victims of the Holocaust – were killed in that year alone. Yet Auschwitz, which is often used as symbolic shorthand for the Holocaust as a whole and is still regarded as the foremost site of the genocide, was not central to the murder of European Jews until 1943, the year *after* the greatest destruction. Instead, the focal points of the killing in 1942 were the central and eastern Polish territories of the Government General. It was here that during 1942 at least 1.37 million Jews – more than the total number of people who perished at Auschwitz in the years 1940 to 1945 – were murdered in the three Operation Reinhardt camps: Bełżec, Sobibór and Treblinka. Operation Reinhardt was indeed the largest single murder campaign of the Holocaust. Between March 1942 and November 1943, it cost the lives of at least 1.8 million Jews in total.[1]

The failure of the Blitzkrieg against the Soviet Union by mid-July 1941 and the subsequent radicalisation of German occupation and security policies there had repercussions not only for Soviet Jews but also for Polish Jews. It was now clear that a definitive German military victory over the Soviet Union could not be achieved in 1941 and, by extension, that the envisaged resettlement of Europe's Jews 'further east' after a victorious end to the war was now no longer a realistic possibility. On 13 October, Governor General Hans Frank was informed that the option of deporting Jews from the Government General to the occupied Soviet territories in the foreseeable future had been ruled out. That same evening, Heinrich Himmler tasked Odilo Globocnik, the SS and police leader in the Lublin District in the eastern Government General, with the murder of the Jews of his district. Before the end of the month, Globocnik arranged for work to start on the construction of Bełżec extermination camp, south of Lublin. This was followed by visits from Viktor Brack and Philipp Bouhler, two key figures in the 'euthanasia' killing operations in the Reich, and, at the end of November, the first specialists from the Operation T4 programme arrived at Bełżec. As the first commandant of the new camp, Globocnik appointed Christian Wirth, who had gathered valuable experience during his work in the T4 killing centres of Brandenburg, Grafeneck, Hartheim and Hadamar.[2]

The Chełmno Prototype

The first German extermination camp had in fact already been set up in the village of Chełmno near Łódź – renamed Litzmannstadt in April 1940 in honour of the German general Karl Litzmann, who had defeated Russian forces near the city during the First World War – in the Wartheland, a new Reich Gau created in the Polish territories annexed to Germany. While also related to the (self-inflicted) problems of deporting Jews further east, the background to the construction of Chełmno was somewhat different to that of the Operation Reinhardt camps: local circumstances were more to the fore here. In the Wartheland, there was special pressure to remove many of the resident Jews. About 150,000 Jews were crowded in adverse conditions in the Łódź Ghetto – the second largest ghetto in German-occupied Europe. Here, the number of deaths from starvation and disease had risen to more than 1,000 per month. Plans to evict Jews from the Wartheland and send them further east, into the Government General, had failed as a result of opposition from Hans Frank. On 18 September 1941, Himmler then informed Arthur Greiser, NSDAP Gauleiter and Reich governor in the Wartheland, that the commencement of deportations of Jews from the Old Reich (Germany within the borders of 1937) was imminent and that the first trainloads would be sent to the Łódź Ghetto (a destination personally selected by Hitler). In this situation, with nowhere to send the Jews of the Wartheland and deportations of more Jews from the Old Reich looming, Greiser obtained the agreement of Hitler and Himmler to kill the Wartheland Jews where they were. Herbert Lange, who – with his special commando – had gathered considerable experience murdering thousands of psychiatric patients with gas in Greiser's own Wartheland domain and in East Prussia, was hereupon tasked with finding a suitable killing site for the annihilation of the Wartheland Jews. On 1 October, he agreed to the lease of a plot of land in the village of Chełmno.[3]

In the course of October and November, the first members of Lange's special commando – fresh from murdering patients of three psychiatric hospitals in the northern Russian city of Novgorod – arrived in Chełmno. Three gas vans were delivered to the Chełmno camp by the Reich Security Main Office sometime in November, and by early December everything was ready for the first batch of victims. Mass murder at Chełmno began on 8 December 1941: the first victims were Jews from the villages and small towns of the Łódź area. They were brought to a manor house on a vacated estate that bordered the leased plot of land. Here, they were asked to undress, told that they had to shower and then led via the basement to one of the three closed gas vans. They were then crammed into the vans, whose exhaust fumes were piped into their airtight interiors, and driven to a nearby forest. Between 60 and 80 people could fit into each of the two smaller vans; the larger van had space for between 100 and 120 people. Within ten minutes of the engine being started, everyone trapped in the van was dead. Upon arrival in the forest, a team of captive Jews was forced to unload the vans and throw the corpses into mass graves, while other members of this work squad had to clean the van of blood and excrement.[4]

Just as Himmler had told Greiser in mid-September, 20,000 Jews from the German Reich were deported to the Łódź Ghetto between 15 October and 4 November; 5,000 Austrian Roma were likewise sent to Łódź between 4 and 8 November. The Roma were herded into a sealed area of the ghetto, where a typhus epidemic broke out in early December; the Germans decided to solve the problem they had created by murdering those infected with the disease: 4,400 Roma were sent on to Chełmno at the turn of the year and gassed. Between 16 January and 2 April 1942, more than 44,000 Polish Jews from the Łódź Ghetto were deported to Chełmno, followed by almost 11,000 mainly German, Austrian, Czech and Luxembourgian Jews the following month (more than half of the 20,000 deported to Łódź in October and November). During the first six months of mass murder at Chełmno, the three gas vans there 'processed 97,000' people, as an RSHA memorandum of 5 June 1942 put it. Large-scale transports to Chełmno ended with further deportations from Łódź in the first half of September 1942, though several smaller transports continued to arrive until the following spring. Between December 1941 and April 1943, when the camp was destroyed, approximately 145,000 Jews were gassed in Chełmno, as well as the aforementioned

Roma, an unknown number of Soviet POWs, Polish nuns and most likely the children of the eradicated Czech village of Lidice. The camp and its gas vans were briefly reactivated in June and July 1944 for the murder of 7,196 Jews from the Łódź Ghetto who had been exempted from the earlier deportations as forced labourers for the German war economy.[5]

The transition to killing Soviet Jews regardless of age or gender had commenced at the end of July 1941; construction of Bełżec extermination camp for gassing Jews from the Lublin District of the Government General was under way by the end of October; and the mass murder of the Wartheland Jews at Chełmno began on 8 December. As discussed above, however, each of these measures emerged out of specific local and regional developments. Hitler and the Nazi regime had not yet resolved to murder all Europe's Jews *during the war*. On 17 October, Heydrich vetoed plans of the Reich Foreign Office to expel 2,000 Jews of Spanish nationality from France to Morocco on the grounds that this would remove them from German control when it came to 'the measures to be taken after the end of the war for the fundamental solution of the Jewish question'. When the RSHA issued a general prohibition of Jewish emigration from German-occupied Europe six days later, on 23 October, the intended 'solution of the Jewish question' was still a territorial one that would take place after the war. Accordingly, when the first large-scale deportations of Jews from the German Reich took around 41,000 German, Austrian, Czech and Luxembourgian Jews on a total of forty-two transports to Łódź, Minsk, Kaunas and Riga during the months of October, November and December 1941, most of the deportees were sent to ghettos and not massacred on arrival.[6]

A total of almost 5,000 German and Austrian Jews on 5 transports *were* shot after arriving in Kaunas on 25 and 29 November, and just over 1,000 Berlin Jews met the same fate in Riga on 30 November on the orders of the higher SS and police leader in Ostland, Friedrich Jeckeln, following coordination with the chief of the civil administration there, Reich Commissioner Hinrich Lohse. These were local initiatives, however, and Himmler had even informed Heydrich during a telephone conversation at midday on the 30th that the Berlin Jews were not to be killed. Himmler's intervention came too late, however – the Jews had already been murdered that morning. The following day, in a radio telegram to Jeckeln, Himmler threatened to punish 'unauthorised acts', and even summoned Jeckeln to a personal meeting on

4 December. It was only after the Soviets had launched their counteroffensive outside Moscow on 5 December and, crucially, Germany had declared war on the USA on 11 December, shortly after the Japanese attack on Pearl Harbor, that Hitler signalised his determination to kill all European Jews *during the war*. Addressing the leading representatives of the party, the Reichsleiters and Gauleiters, Hitler concluded: 'The world war is here; the annihilation of the Jews must be the necessary consequence.' Hitler's announcement did not immediately lead to an acceleration of the killing or the erection of new extermination centres; a workable plan was needed for murdering Jews on a continental scale. This plan did not yet exist, and it would take several months for it to emerge.[7]

Stationary Gas Chambers

It was but a short step from the gas van to the stationary gas chamber, which functioned on the same technical principles: the use of carbon monoxide produced by attached engines. Unlike Chełmno, which used gas vans, Bełżec was ultimately fitted with multiple stationary gas chambers fuelled with engine exhaust fumes. The actual gas used, however, was the same in Chełmno and the three Operation Reinhardt camps: carbon monoxide. It had first been deployed in spring 1940 for gassing psychiatric patients in the annexed Polish territories as part of the 'euthanasia' campaign, and later to murder Soviet Jews. The staff at Bełżec did not immediately arrive at the idea of stationary gas chambers, however, but started instead by experimenting with existing technologies. In early 1942, camp commandant Wirth carried out several trial gassings, first on physically and mentally disabled people from the surrounding villages, then on political prisoners from the prison in Zamość, using a converted postal van. Wirth and his men decided, however, that the use of gas vans for the huge numbers of expected victims would be too time-consuming. They therefore continued experimenting with alternative methods, eventually concluding that stationary gas chambers would be more efficient, whereupon they constructed three gas chambers with a combined capacity of up to 500 people, and tested their functionality on Jewish forced labourers from the nearby town of Lubycza Królewska in late February or early March. The victims died anything but a quick and painless death; on the contrary, during their death throes they experienced severe headaches, dizziness, nausea, confusion, vomiting, respiratory distress, convulsions and coma.

As the length of time it took to die from the toxic gas varied depending on an individual's physical constitution, some of the victims consciously witnessed the agonising death of others before their own asphyxiation. Throughout this process of trial and error using human beings as test subjects, Wirth and his men responded to the decision-making powers bestowed on them by displaying a high level of personal initiative and a murderous creativity.[8]

The mass murder of the Jews of the Lublin District – disguised as 'resettlement to the east' – began on 17 March 1942 with the arrival of the first transports in Bełżec. During these days, several trainloads also arrived from the district of Galicia in southeastern Poland (which had been conquered from the Soviets the previous summer and officially incorporated into the Government General on 1 August 1941), first from Żółkiew and then from Lvov. The first ghetto to be dissolved in the Lublin District was that of Lublin itself, Globocnik's official place of work. SS and police units surrounded the ghetto and herded the Jews to the railway station, sometimes using whips and firearms, and into the waiting freight trains. Those too sick or weak to travel, the elderly and infants left behind were immediately shot by the Germans – often in the hospital where they lay. The Sobibór survivor Thomas Blatt, who was deported to the camp as a fifteen-year-old in April 1943, recalled just such a ghetto dissolution in the village of Izbica in the Lublin District in late October 1942:

> Since there were not enough boxcars, [the German commander of the ghetto, Kurt] Engels decided to make a selection. Everyone was screaming and crying, pushing to be chosen. There was chaos. Engels became furious. As he rested his machine gun on the shoulder of Judenrat [Jewish Council] chairman Abram Blatt, he mowed down a group of people and forced the others into the boxcars. They were packed so tightly that some suffocated to death before the train even left town. I went to the station. An open meadow by the tracks was strewn with about three hundred dead bodies. The setting sun was reflected in streams of fresh blood.

The railway stations were not always located in close proximity to the ghettos. Where this was not the case, the Germans simply massacred the Jews on the spot, in order to avoid the long walk to the nearest station. Such shooting operations before the trains had even arrived at the extermination camps claimed the lives of several hundred thousand Jews, including 70,000 in the Cracow District (around a quarter of the total Jewish population there) and 65,000 in the Lublin District. In total, up to 350,000 of the victims of Operation Reinhardt were murdered outside the extermination camps themselves.[9]

In February 1942, as soon as Bełżec had been completed, construction work began on the next killing centre, Sobibór, to the east of Lublin. Site selection and initial planning had already commenced the previous year. According to the stationmaster at Sobibór, Jan Piwonski, a group of SS officers had first arrived there in autumn 1941 to measure the platform and the sidings. Like Chełmno and Bełżec, then, Sobibór emerged out of specific local and regional developments before the decision to murder all Europe's Jews had been taken. Again, like Bełżec, the new camp possessed three gas chambers, but it was initially four times as big as its forerunner: 24 hectares as compared with 6. In April 1942, Globocnik appointed SS Captain Franz Stangl, a former Austrian police officer, as the first commandant of the camp. He brought twenty or thirty SS men with him who, like Stangl himself, had previously worked on the 'euthanasia' programme. As in Bełżec, a trial gassing was carried out in Sobibór in mid-April, when 250 Jews, mainly women, from the forced-labour camp in nearby Krychów were brought to Sobibór and gassed in the presence of all the SS staff. The first phase of killing operations then commenced in early May. Up to the end of July, between 90,000 and 100,000 people were murdered in Sobibór. Among the victims were many Jews from the Lublin District but also Jews deported from outside Poland; at least 10,000 German and Austrian Jews were killed in Sobibór during this period. At the end of July 1942, the railway line between Lublin and the town of Chełm had to be repaired, as the tracks were sinking into the marshy ground. The deportation trains were unable to reach Sobibór for several months and killing operations had to be suspended. The camp personnel used this hiatus to double the number of gas chambers from 3 – in which 500 people could be killed simultaneously – to 6.[10]

Developments in May and June 1942 reflected the decision-making process of the preceding months and allowed for an acceleration of killing operations and an expansion in their geographical scope. Construction work began on the third and final Operation Reinhardt camp – Treblinka – in May, the same month that Sobibór went into operation. Also in the same month, Friedrich-Wilhelm Krüger – who, as higher SS and police leader in the Government General, was Himmler's direct representative there – was appointed permanent secretary in Hans Frank's government in Cracow. Then, in early June 1942, the decision was taken to expand operations beyond the Lublin and Galicia Districts to incorporate the ghettos in the rest of the Government General. In mid-June, the three wooden gas chambers in Bełżec were torn down and replaced by 6 new, larger gas chambers, which could hold more than 2,000 people at a time. By 20 June 1942, a total of around 90,000 Jews had been sent to Bełżec and a further 70,000 to Sobibór. In the third week of July, Himmler personally visited Globocnik in Lublin and from there issued Krüger in writing with the central order for Operation Reinhardt, with the aim that 'the resettlement of the entire Jewish population of the Government General be carried out and ended by 31 December 1942. As of 31 December 1942, no more people of Jewish descent are permitted to reside in the Government General.' The operation was named in honour of Reinhard Heydrich, who had succumbed on 4 June 1942 to injuries sustained during an assassination attempt in Prague and whose first name Himmler – and even Heydrich himself for a time – generally wrote with 'dt'.[11]

Treblinka extermination camp was located in the Warsaw District, north-east of the city of Warsaw itself. Once completed in July 1942, it covered 19 hectares and, like Bełżec and Sobibór, was fitted with stationary gas chambers fuelled with engine exhaust fumes. The three gas chambers had a slightly larger capacity than those in Bełżec and Sobibór; at least 600 people could be killed simultaneously. Treblinka would serve first and foremost to murder the more than 400,000 Warsaw Jews. The first commandant of Treblinka was the thirty-one-year-old Austrian physician Irmfried Eberl. Like Wirth and Stangl, the first commandants in Bełżec and Sobibór, respectively, Eberl had gathered relevant experience of poison gas in Operation T4, where he had headed first the Brandenburg and then the Bernburg killing centres. Though fanatical, Eberl was not well suited to his assignment in Treblinka and he was soon overwhelmed with the task of disposing of so many corpses. Ambition, careerism and pride had led him to request ever more trainloads of Jews. Odilo Globocnik and Christian Wirth – the latter now promoted to inspector of the extermination camps of Operation Reinhardt – arrived in Treblinka to find thousands of dead bodies lying all over the camp, awaiting disposal. The Polish Jew Jankiel Wiernik, one of Treblinka's few survivors, later described the sight that met him on 24 August 1942: 'The camp yard was littered with corpses, some still in their clothes and others stark naked, their faces distorted with terror, black and swollen, the eyes wide open, with tongues protruding, skulls crushed, bodies mangled.' Outside the enclosed space of the camp itself, thousands more Jews died of thirst in the trains that were forced to wait in the sidings for days before unloading. This state of affairs resulted in extensive structural and personnel changes. Eberl was relieved of his command at the end of August 1942 and replaced by Franz Stangl, who, in turn, was succeeded in Sobibór by another Austrian T4 veteran, Franz Reichleitner. Eberl then returned to Bernburg, while Stangl remained commandant of Treblinka for the next twelve months. Transports to Treblinka were suspended for just under a week, from 28 August to 3 September, and Globocnik ordered the camp to be restructured and its capacity increased by means of the construction of new, larger gas chambers. This work was carried out between early September and early October 1942.[12]

The Deadliest Phase

Himmler's 19 July order to Krüger ushered in the second phase of Operation Reinhardt. At this point, the annihilation assumed a scarcely imaginable tempo. The emptying of the Warsaw Ghetto – the largest ghetto in German-occupied Europe, with 350,000 inhabitants – commenced on 22 July 1942. Even before the 'great deportation' started, 70,000 individuals had already died in the Warsaw Ghetto from the horrendous conditions in which they were forced to live. Between July and September, 265,000 Jews from Warsaw, including virtually all the children in the ghetto, were deported to their deaths in Treblinka. In addition, over 10,000 Jews were killed on the spot during the exceedingly violent deportation operations, and another 11,000 were sent to various labour camps. Chaim A. Kaplan, founder and headmaster of a Hebrew school in Warsaw, began his diary entry of 2 August with the words: 'Jewish Warsaw is in its death throes. A whole community is going to its death!' A few days after the beginning of the deportation of Warsaw's Jews, it was the turn of Radom, the last of the five districts of the Government General; the ghetto in the district capital was again the first to be emptied. Within a period of six weeks, 300,000 people were deported from the Radom District to Treblinka. Thousands of Jews were shot on the spot in the ghettos during the dissolution operations. The large Jewish communities of Kielce, Radom and Częstochowa, as well as numerous smaller ones, were obliterated; only forced labourers working directly for the SS or the Wehrmacht and their families were (for the time being) spared. By November 1942, the Germans had deported around a million people to the gas chambers of the three Operation Reinhardt camps.[13]

The Reich Railways (*Reichsbahn*) made freight trains available for these deportations. In summer and autumn 1942, a single carriage often contained up to 150 people. The carriages were so full that the deportees could scarcely move. Then the tortuous journey began. The expanded capacity of now three extermination camps allowed for trains with up to 6,000 'passengers'; as a result of the number of carriages, these trains could travel at only 50km per hour. The overcrowded trains stopped at further localities along the way to collect more Jews, before eventually reaching their final destination. Some of the trains from Warsaw carried as many as 7,000 people. Fully-loaded freight trains with fifty-eight carriages travelling from Częstochowa to Treblinka needed seventeen hours (including a two-and-a-half-hour stop in Warsaw) for the journey of around 375km. Deportees from the Wartheland were sent to Chełmno, those from Upper Silesia to Auschwitz and those from the Government General mainly to the camps of Operation Reinhardt and, in some cases, to Majdanek, located on the outskirts of the city of Lublin, where three gas chambers had been installed no later than October 1942.[14]

In the three Operation Reinhardt camps, the final hours of the victims passed uniformly. Part of the arriving freight train was uncoupled and shunted into the camp. There, the camp guards – for the most part Ukrainian auxiliaries from the SS training camp Trawniki – forcibly hauled the victims out of the carriages. Some of the deportees had not survived the tortuous journey, so that the trains were full of corpses. Unlike in Auschwitz and Majdanek, where a concentration camp existed alongside (and indeed predated) the extermination facilities, there was virtually no sorting of new arrivals in Bełżec, Sobibór and Treblinka; selections had already taken place at the transports' points of origin before the trains had departed. Instead, upon arrival in the extermination camps, the Jews had the last of their belongings taken from them and their hair shorn; they were then forced to undress, and the camp guards herded them into a building with several gas chambers, into which exhaust fumes from large engines were then pumped; the victims suffocated. The weak and the sick, who could not walk to the gas chambers on their own, were shot by the camp personnel where they were standing. The Polish Jew Berek Freiberg, one of the few survivors of Sobibór, testified after the war:

> On another occasion, after one such bathing operation [a gassing], we found a child of a year and a half among the rags. A Ukrainian told me to take the child and put it in a dung pit. He said: 'Oh, it would be a shame to use a bullet!', took the spade from the dung and sliced the child in pieces. The child only let out a pitiful squeal. Sometimes, mothers would give birth to children overnight on the [unloading] square. The children were generally thrown into the refuse; they were either torn in two pieces by the feet, or thrown into the air, and they smashed when they hit the ground. They didn't make a fuss about the children.

Only a few prisoners were initially left alive upon arrival at the camps to serve in one of the various labour squads. These 'work Jews' were forced to sort the clothing of the victims, cut their hair, prise out any gold teeth from the mouths of the dead and carry out the disposal of the bodies after the gassing had taken place. Their stay of execution was only temporary, however; they could be killed at any moment, and frequently were. Again, unlike Auschwitz, none of the Operation Reinhardt camps had crematoria for burning the bodies. Instead, the corpses were buried.[15]

As Irmfried Eberl had experienced at first hand in Treblinka, the capacity of the Operation Reinhardt camps for continued killing was primarily dependent on the disposal of the corpses. The Czech Jew Richard Glazar, one of the very few survivors of Treblinka, was selected for the corresponding labour squad. After the war, he described what happened after the doors to the gas chambers had been closed:

> In around twenty minutes, Treblinka's finished product emerges. And other slaves already reach for this naked, compressed, ashen, purple-dyed product. Some of them pull the corpses through the upturned openings in the exterior walls of the gas chambers; other specialists prise out the gold teeth of the dead. [...] Still others arrange them in the mass

graves. Then the final work sequences take place: the 'powdering' with chalk and the filling in with the sandy soil of Treblinka – a ceaselessly working digger takes care of this.

All these individual tasks – aside from the final filling in of the mass graves – had to be carried out by prisoners; the perpetrators considered such work beneath them. It should be expressly noted here, however, that the Jews forcibly assigned to these special labour squads on pain of death did not – unlike the T4-Reinhardt personnel and the Trawniki auxiliaries – kill any human beings.[16]

Following the enforced suspension of killing operations at Sobibór caused by repair work on the railway line leading to the camp, the second phase of mass murder began there in early October 1942. Alongside further deportees from the Lublin and Galicia Districts of the Government General, numerous non-Polish Jews were likewise sent to Sobibór during the next twelve months: 4,000 French Jews (March 1943), 34,131 Dutch Jews in nineteen transports (July–September 1943), 8,700 Belarusian Jews from the ghettos in Lida and Minsk (September 1943) and at least 4,000 Jews from Lithuania (September 1943). The situation in Treblinka during the same period was not dissimilar: 6,000 Greek and 7,100 Yugoslavian Jews arrived there in March and April 1943. Their arrival had been preceded by that of 5,000 German Jews and 20,000 Jews from the Protectorate of Bohemia and Moravia in September and October 1942. While Polish Jews from the Government General constituted by far the biggest single victim group of Operation Reinhardt – around 1.3 million reached the three camps – the identity of many of the deportees to Sobibór and Treblinka illustrates the truly pan-European dimensions of this largest single murder campaign of the Holocaust.[17]

The Operation Reinhardt camps even received transports from another camp with gassing facilities: Majdanek. The concentration camp there served as a selection site for some of those sent to Bełżec and Sobibór, including deportees from the German towns of Hanau, Kassel and Merseburg in May 1943. In July 1943, around 5,000 prisoners from Majdanek were deported to Sobibór. The new arrivals were wearing striped prison clothing and were extremely weak. Many had already died during the journey. Due to a technical problem with the killing installation, the prisoners were forced to wait for a day and a night in the open air, before they were murdered. Around 200 people died of exhaustion during the night, or were beaten or shot to death. The next morning, the stronger members of the group were forced to prop up the weaker ones on their way to the gas chamber. Several of Sobibór's 'work Jews' had to take away those people who had died overnight. One of those deployed for this task was the aforementioned Berek Freiberg. He later wrote:

> SS Private Frenzel selected twenty prisoners and told us that we should work naked, as the corpses were dirty and full of lice. We had to bring the dead to the trolleys, which were 200m away. Although we were used to this type of work, it is impossible for me to describe how we felt while we carried the dead on our naked bodies. The Germans drove us on with shouts and blows. While I carried the body of a man, I stopped and, as I couldn't see any Germans nearby, laid him on the ground. Then the man, whom I had taken for dead, sat upright, looked at me with wide eyes and asked: 'Is it far?' It required the greatest effort for him to speak these words, and then he collapsed. At that moment, I felt blows on my head and back. SS Private Frenzel was striking me with his whip. I took the living dead by the feet and dragged him to the trolley.[18]

Of the 3 million Jews who were murdered during the course of 1942, more than 2 million of them perished in gas chambers and mass-shooting operations during an 18-week period between late July and mid-November, almost exclusively on Poland's pre-war territory. These three-and-a-half months were the most intense, the deadliest of the entire Holocaust. Neither the mass shootings carried out by the Einsatzgruppen, the police battalions, the SS brigades and the Wehrmacht in the occupied Soviet territories during the second half of 1941 nor the extermination of the Hungarian Jews deported to Auschwitz-Birkenau between May and July 1944 resulted in the death of so many people within such a short space of time. Between July and November 1942, a massacre the size of Babi Yar was committed almost every day. Never before in history had people been killed on an assembly-line basis.[19]

In Bełżec, the final deportation trains arrived in December 1942. At this point, the gruesome task of exhuming and incinerating the bodies commenced. This (vain) attempt to eliminate all trace of the genocide – known as Operation 1005 (*Aktion 1005*) – was carried out across German-occupied Central and

Eastern Europe. In Bełżec, this process was completed in March 1943. The work of disinterment and cremation in Treblinka commenced immediately after Himmler visited the camp the same month. Though the killing continued in Sobibór and Treblinka into autumn 1943, there appears to have been no more room in Bełżec for new mass graves or ash fields. As the first and smallest of the three Operation Reinhardt camps, Bełżec had been used from the outset as a testing ground; it now once more assumed this function during the exhumation of mass graves and the burning of the victims' remains. In spite of this experimental status, 470,000 people were murdered there in the space of only nine months between March and December 1942.[20]

Crucial for the termination of the mass murder in Treblinka and Sobibór, by contrast, were the prisoner uprisings that took place there in August and October 1943, respectively, as well as those in the Warsaw and Białystok ghettos in April–May and August of the same year. Pursuing a different but related goal, up to 10,000 Jews succeeded in fleeing the Minsk Ghetto in the spring and summer of 1943 and joining armed partisan units in the surrounding forests. The courageous resistance of these prisoners refutes the common assumption of Jewish passivity during the Holocaust encapsulated in the phrase 'like sheep to the slaughter'. For the Germans, the revolts appeared to provide confirmation of what the Nazi regime had erroneously claimed all along: the Jews posed a threat, and the remaining occupants of the camps and ghettos had to be killed. The Treblinka and Sobibór extermination camps had in any case existed much longer than originally planned. The prisoners at Treblinka were encouraged – but also disheartened – by the uprising in the Warsaw Ghetto, of which they had learned from the deported Warsaw Jews. On 2 August, between 200 and 250 prisoners succeeded in fleeing Treblinka, though only about 100 were able to escape the immediate vicinity of the camp and live to see the next day. The insurrectionists did not manage to kill a single SS guard; only two Trawniki auxiliaries died during the revolt. As planned, however, the prisoners did set ablaze most of the wooden buildings and the workshops, so that large parts of the camp were destroyed.[21]

The uprising in Sobibór on 14 October pursued two objectives: to enable as many prisoners as possible to escape the camp, and to kill as many guards as possible. Unlike in Treblinka, the targeting of the guards took concrete shape. During the revolt, the insurrectionists were able to kill twelve SS guards and ten Trawniki auxiliaries. Around 380 prisoners succeeded in fleeing, of whom around 200 reached the nearby woods, which promised salvation. During the hunt for the escaped Jews, the remaining members of the camp personnel received support from units of the Security and Order Police. The Wehrmacht also supplied two companies of Security Battalion 689 from Chełm. It was as a result of the uprisings that many more prisoners survived Treblinka and Sobibór than Bełżec (only three); in the smallest of all the German extermination camps, surveillance of the prisoners was much more effective due not least to the limited surface area. Many of those who succeeded in escaping from Treblinka and Sobibór were subsequently caught and killed. From Treblinka, around 70 escapees were still alive when the war ended in 1945, while just 54 male and 8 female escapees from Sobibór – 49 Poles, 2 Netherlanders, 9 Soviets, 1 Czech and 1 French – are known to have survived the war.[22]

Shortly after the uprising in Treblinka in August 1943, Globocnik resolved to dissolve the camp completely, though the SS there still murdered around 10,000 Jews from Białystok in the second half of the month. The demolition of Treblinka commenced in early September and lasted two-and-a-half months. During this process, some of the T4–Reinhardt camp personnel were transferred to Sobibór. In Treblinka, the final victims, who had been forced to assist with the dismantling of the camp, were shot by the Germans on 17 November 1943. The day after the uprising in Sobibór, the remaining Jews in that camp were murdered. The camp personnel then commenced with the demolition of the complex, and brought in Jews from Treblinka to help. The demolition of Sobibór took only a month. The last prisoners there were killed on 23 November 1943 and their bodies burned. On 19 October, just five days after the Sobibór uprising, Globocnik declared Operation Reinhardt to be ended. In Treblinka, 870,000 Jews had been murdered in the space of little more than a year. The death toll at Auschwitz would not exceed that of Treblinka until 1944. In Sobibór, 180,000 Jews in total had been murdered. As Globocnik informed Himmler in his final report, Operation Reinhardt had made a financial profit of more than 178 million Reichsmarks. This was certainly no small amount, but it came from more than 1.8 million Jews, from whom the SS had even stolen hair and gold teeth. For each murdered Jew, the Reich pocketed less than 100 Reichsmarks. The perpetrators used the opportunity to enrich themselves at the expense of the Jews, but the purpose of Operation Reinhardt was to murder them. As the perpetrators themselves were fully aware, the murderous ideological objective of the 'final solution' always took precedence over economic aspects. In autumn 1942, the district governor in Warsaw, Ludwig Fischer, openly stated: 'These economic drawbacks must be accepted, however, as the eradication of Jewry is imperative for political reasons.'[23]

Operation Reinhardt might have been over, but the murder of the Jews in the eastern parts of the Government General was not. Parallel to the genocide in the three Operation Reinhardt camps, more than 100,000 had been left alive to be exploited as forced labourers for the German war economy. The revolts in Treblinka and Sobibór, however, had forced the Germans to close down these camps earlier than they would otherwise have done. With the dismantling of the two camps already under way, Himmler ordered the annihilation of the vast majority of the remaining Jewish forced labourers in the Lublin District. By this time, Globocnik had already been promoted to higher SS and police leader for the Adriatic coast and trans-ferred to Trieste. Himmler therefore entrusted the task to his successor as SS and police leader in Lublin, Jakob Sporrenberg. In order to carry out the operation, Sporrenberg requested reinforcements from the neighbouring districts. By 3 November 1943, almost 3,000 German policemen had gath-ered in Lublin. Over the next three days, in an operation idyllically code-named Harvest Festival, around 42,000 of the remaining 50,000 Jewish forced labourers from Majdanek, Trawniki, Poniatowa and other smaller camps in the vicinity were massacred. On the first day, the SS killed 18,400 prisoners in Madjanek over the course of nine hours while music was played over loudspeakers to drown out the sounds of shooting and the cries of dying Jews. It was the single largest massacre in any concentration camp. More people were murdered in Majdanek on 3 November 1943 than on any other day in any other concentration camp, including Auschwitz. Around 6,000 people were killed in Trawniki forced-labour camp the same day. On the second day of Operation Harvest Festival, 4 November, 15,000 people were murdered in Poniatowa. After the brutally efficient mass murder by gas, Operation Harvest Festival was a return to the shooting operations involving considerable numbers of perpetrators. As a whole, it was the largest mass shooting of Jews during the entire war, surpassing the death toll of 33,771 Jews shot at Babi Yar on 29 and 30 September 1941.[24]

The mass shootings of Operation Harvest Festival were not an anomaly for 1943, however. The existence of gas chambers and gas vans did not stop the mass shootings, which continued through 1942 and into 1943, claiming well over half a million victims in 1942 alone, including 300,000 in western Ukraine and more than 200,000 in Belarus. Indeed, the notion of 'industrial' German mass murder is somewhat misleading, given that half of the murdered Jews were not gassed, three of the five main extermination centres did not possess crematoria, some of these complexes consisted for the most part of wooden buildings and the crematoria in Auschwitz were often out of order due to their sloppy construction. New technologies or operational procedures for murder introduced at one of the killing centres did not necessarily lead to a change at the others. In Majdanek, another major site of mass killing, more people died from shooting than in the gas chambers there. Many years after the war, former SS sergeant Franz Suchomel, who had been stationed in Treblinka from August 1942 to October 1943, described the camp as 'admittedly a primitive but efficient production line of death'. Treblinka remained 'primitive' even though the experience gathered during the construction and initial operations of the first two Operation Reinhardt camps – Bełżec and Sobibór – was taken into account when building the camp. It was nonetheless the least primitive and the most efficient of the three Reinhardt camps. Indeed, in view of the number of people killed there, and measured against the short duration of its existence and its modest number of staff (25 to 30 Germans from Operation T4 and 100 to 120 auxiliaries from the Trawniki camp), Treblinka was the most efficient killing installation in human history.[25]

Even before the Operation Reinhardt camps of Sobibór and Treblinka were established, and before Bełżec had commenced operations, another – albeit improvised and temporary – site for the gassing of Jews had been set up by the Germans in the town of Zemun on the banks of the Sava river, opposite Belgrade, on the territory of the Independent State of Croatia, which was governed by the fascist Ustasha. The concentration camp on the former trade-fair grounds – the Sajmište – had been completed in early December 1941. In the autumn of the same year, virtually all adult male Jews and Roma in Serbia had been put to death by firing squads of the Security Police and, above all, the Wehrmacht. Beginning in December, the women, children and elderly Jews and Roma of Belgrade were then interned in the Sajmište camp. Internees from elsewhere in Serbia followed.[26]

Living in large, unheated exhibition pavilions, underfed and subjected to hard physical labour, the prisoners suffered grievously during the severe winter. As a result of these harsh conditions and executions in the camp, around 1,000 Jews perished. Even worse was to come, however. During this same period, the motor pool of the RSHA in Berlin was commissioning gas vans designed to lighten the burden on the perpetrators of shooting operations against women and children. In January 1942, Reinhard Heydrich appointed Emanuel Schäfer as senior commander of the Security Police in Serbia and sent him to Belgrade with a 'special assignment'. Shortly thereafter, in early March, a large Saurer gas van with two drivers – Wilhelm Götz and Erwin Meyer – arrived from Berlin. It was clear to Schäfer what was intended.[27]

It was at this point that the Roma women and children interned in Sajmište were released; their ultimate fate had not yet been determined. For a period of two months, from early March to early May 1942, the Saurer gas van took Serbian Jews day in, day out from the Sajmište camp to the Avala shooting range, southeast of Belgrade. In order to accelerate the clearance of the camp, trips were generally made twice a day. During the journey from Sajmište to Avala, which took the van through the middle of Belgrade, one of the drivers stopped and redirected the exhaust gas into the sealed interior. Upon arrival at the Avala shooting range, seven Serbian prisoners, guarded by four members of Reserve Police Battalion 64, emptied the dead Jews into a mass grave. By the time the operation was completed in early May, all the Jews in Sajmište concentration camp, overwhelmingly women and children, had been gassed; they numbered approximately 7,500 people. After the last Jews had been buried in mass graves, the seven Serbian prisoners who had emptied the dead Jews into the trenches were shot and killed with sub-machine guns.[28]

In June 1942, SS Colonel Schäfer reported 'with pride' to the RSHA that Serbia was now 'free of Jews'. After Estonia, Serbia was the first country occupied by Germany to be declared so. In a little over a year of military occupation, the Wehrmacht and the Security Police had murdered almost all of the approximately 17,000 Jews living on Serbian territory. The gas van used to asphyxiate the last of the Serbian Jews from Sajmište was subsequently returned to Berlin to be technically overhauled and then sent on to Belarus, where it was deployed to gas Soviet Jews in Minsk.[29]

CHAPTER 9
THE GATES OF HELL
AUSCHWITZ

Auschwitz was not only the largest but also the most lethal camp complex of all. From a total of at least 1.3 million people who were deported to Auschwitz between 1940 and 1945, 1.1 million perished, of whom approximately 900,000 – that is, over 80 per cent – were Jews. This means that around one in six Jews killed in the Holocaust died here. In view of Auschwitz's pre-eminence in Holocaust memory, it is worth noting that the camp was not created for the annihilation of Jews. Unlike the single-purpose death camps in the Government General, Auschwitz was always a site with multiple missions. This applies indeed to the concentration-camp system as a whole: as of early 1942, Jews made up fewer than 5,000 of the 80,000 concentration-camp inmates. Initially, what made Auschwitz – the seventh main camp in the National Socialist orbit, following Dachau, Sachsenhausen, Buchenwald, Flossenbürg, Mauthausen and Ravensbrück – different to its forerunners was the fact that it was the first concentration camp to be set up for overwhelmingly non-German-speaking prisoners. Aside from a few exceptions, such as German prisoner functionaries, only Polish prisoners were in Auschwitz in the years 1940 and 1941. Mass deportations of Jews began only in March 1942 with the admittance of German and Slovak female Jews to the newly created women's compound, located on the grounds of the main camp. From the second half of 1942 onwards, Jewish inmates accounted for around 50 per cent of all prisoners at Auschwitz, including the satellite camps. From 1943, Jews comprised the majority of prisoners. Ultimately, almost every country in Europe was represented in the inmate community of Auschwitz and its satellite camps.[1]

Auschwitz Concentration Camp

With planning for the German invasion of Western Europe already under way, as a result of which large-scale arrests were expected, Heinrich Himmler ordered Inspector of the Concentration Camps Richard Glücks on 1 February 1940 to search for suitable locations for the construction of new concentration camps. Since late 1939, Erich von dem Bach-Zelewski had been pushing for the construction of a new concentration camp in Silesia, where he was higher SS and police leader, as the local jails were overflowing with Polish political prisoners. On 21 February 1940, Glücks informed Himmler of the suitability of a site in the town of Oświęcim in East Upper Silesia. As the handover of the property was delayed, it was the second week of April before Glücks was able to send an inspection team to Oświęcim in order to survey the necessary renovation work. The team was headed by one Rudolf Höß, who was at this time in charge of 'protective custody' in Sachsenhausen concentration camp on the outskirts of Oranienburg, north of Berlin. On the basis of the report compiled by this inspection team, Himmler resolved to have a 'quarantine camp' – that is, a transit camp for prisoners on their way to concentration camps in the interior of the Reich – established in Oświęcim for around 10,000 prisoners. On 4 May, he appointed Höß as the commandant of the new camp of Auschwitz (the German name for Oświęcim). Like Chełmno, the first German extermination camp, Auschwitz was located in newly annexed German territory. At the time of the dissolution of the German military government in Poland and its replacement by a civil administration on 26 October 1939, East Upper Silesia had been incorporated into the already existing Gau Silesia, thereby becoming part of the German Reich.[2]

On 20 May 1940, the first thirty German 'criminals' from Sachsenhausen arrived at Auschwitz concentration camp. They received the prisoner numbers 1 to 30, and were utilised as prisoner functionaries, also known as 'kapos'. They were followed at the end of the month by thirty-nine Poles from Dachau concentration camp near Munich. The date of 14 June 1940, when the first transport with 728 Polish prisoners from Tarnów prison near Cracow arrived at Auschwitz, is regarded as the founding day of Auschwitz concentration camp. These victims of Operation AB in the Government General, mainly young men, were accused of a wide range of anti-German activities. Most of them had been arrested while attempting to cross the border from Poland to Slovakia. In August and September, larger transports with 1,666 and 1,705 prisoners from Warsaw reached Auschwitz. By this time, the concept of a 'quarantine camp' had been revised. Instead, it was decided that Auschwitz concentration camp would become a long-term detention and torture site for Poles, and the camp was expanded accordingly over the course of summer 1940.[3]

On 10 July, Auschwitz's first satellite camp was established in Gliwice-Sośnica (Gleiwitz-Öhringen). Thirty prisoners tore down a former POW camp there. The barbed wire acquired as a result was used to fence in Auschwitz. The Auschwitz camp complex eventually included forty-seven satellite camps, the majority of which were established in 1943 and 1944. Most of them were situated close to the main camp, either on occupied Polish soil or in the industrial area of Upper Silesia. Two satellite camps – Freudenthal and Lichtewerden – were located in the Reich Gau Sudetenland, which had been formed from the majority German-speaking border regions of Czechoslovakia annexed to Germany in October 1938. In Freudenthal, 300 female Jews worked in an SS-owned drinks factory, in textile firms, in arms production and in agriculture. In Lichtewerden, the same number of female Jews were put to work in a textile factory. Both satellite camps existed from summer 1944 until the end of the war. Far away, in the Protectorate of Bohemia and Moravia – as the formerly Czech lands were now known – there existed a further satellite camp, namely in Brno (Brünn), where prisoners from Auschwitz were deployed in construction work in the Technical SS and Police Academy. Typical for the Auschwitz satellite camps was the deployment of prisoners as forced labourers in the arms industry and in mining. In Monowitz, which, under the name Auschwitz III, was, from autumn 1943, the command centre for all satellite camps in which the prisoners were deployed in industry, the prisoners built the synthetic rubber works of I.G. Farben. Monowitz was at the same time the largest of all the Auschwitz satellite camps.[4]

Almost unbearable daily camp life began for the prisoners immediately after their arrival at Auschwitz. Totally inadequate accommodation – the inmates initially had to sleep tightly packed on dirty straw on the floor, and sanitary facilities were practically nonexistent – led to a permanent lack of sleep, which accelerated the prisoners' physical exhaustion. Even after the conversion of the buildings and the erection of three-storey bed frames, the accommodation remained overcrowded. To the very end, several prisoners had to share a bed. The prisoners were not permitted to leave their quarters at night. They were woken at 4 a.m. and then had to make their beds and attempt hurriedly to wash themselves a little in spite of the lack of sanitation facilities. After roll call, the work squads were formed and marched off, accompanied by the playing of the camp orchestra. A working day lasted eleven hours, and the prisoners often had to work at a run. They were continually driven on by the SS guards with cries of 'quick, quick'. The SS set dogs on the defenceless, and indiscriminately shot and beat prisoners to death. When returning to the camp in the evening, the dead or seriously injured had to be dragged along. Before food was served, the prisoners had to survive the evening roll call, which often lasted for hours. The roll call ended only when the number of registered inmates corresponded to the number of those present. If a prisoner had fled, a punitive roll call took place. This could last for up to nineteen hours, like the roll call of 6 July 1940 following the flight of Polish prisoner Tadeusz Wiejowski. 'It was a terrible night,' recalled the survivor Henryk Król, 'in the morning, everyone was shivering from the cold. The rays of the rising sun brought relief only for a brief time. Soon, it became swelteringly hot and our torment ever greater. One after another collapsed.'[5]

Sustenance in the camp was totally insufficient from the outset and led within a matter of weeks to complete emaciation. Diseases caused by undernourishment, such as diarrhoea and typhus, were the result. Bread equalled life, and the theft of bread was a serious crime and often punished by death. From autumn 1942, food parcels could be sent to Auschwitz by relatives of prisoners, and from 1943 also by the Red Cross. Jews and Soviet prisoners, however, were excluded from this. In contrast to other concentration camps, in which food parcels helped many of the inmates to supplement their starvation rations, theft by the SS and prisoner functionaries was so extensive in Auschwitz that the parcels did not provide any real improvement to the food situation. Only those who could organise additional food at their workplace or by means of illegal exchange had any chance of not falling victim to starvation.[6]

Second Lieutenant Witold Pilecki, a member of the Polish resistance, let himself be captured during a Warsaw street round-up in September 1940, in order to join the prisoner underground in the concentration camps and gather intelligence on Auschwitz from the inside. Pilecki is the only person known to have willingly entered Auschwitz. He subsequently composed a report of his experiences in the camp, including his arrival:

We were rushed towards a brightly lit area. On the way there, one of us was told to run towards a pole at the side of the road, only to be followed by a swift burst of fire from a submachine gun. Killed. Ten men were pulled out at random and shot as part of a collective punishment for the 'escape', which had been orchestrated by the SS men themselves. All eleven corpses were then dragged away, pulled by straps tied to one of their legs. The dogs were set loose on the bloodied corpses. All of that was accompanied by laughter and mockery. We were approaching a wire fence with a sign above it that read: *'Arbeit macht frei'* [Work sets you free]. It was not until later that we learned the meaning of that inscription. [...]

The bestiality of the German tormentors, which emphasised the degenerated instincts of the outcasts and former criminals – today, prisoners with several years of experience in German concentration camps – those who were our figures of authority in Auschwitz, was manifested in a number of ways. In the penal company the tormentors enjoyed themselves by smashing the testicles – usually of Jewish prisoners – with a wooden hammer on a stump. [...]

One time, through the upper floor window [of Block 3a], I saw a scene that etched itself in my memory for a long time. [...] It was raining, the day was grim. The penal company was working in the square, transporting the gravel that was dug out of a pit. Apart from that, some commando was freezing while carrying out 'exercises'. Next to the pit, three SS men, reluctant to leave the commandos for fear of [SS Reporting Officer Gerhard] Palitzsch or the commandant, who was roaming through the camp, came up with a game. They were making bets, with each of them putting a banknote on a brick. Then they would bury a prisoner alive, upside down, covering his upper body in the pit. They would look at their watches, and time how long the prisoner kicked his legs up in the air. Modern sweepstakes, I thought. The one able to most accurately predict how much time a prisoner buried alive would kick his legs before he died – was the one who collected the money. Thus ended the year 1940.

In April 1943, after 947 days in what he termed 'hell on earth', Pilecki managed to escape from Auschwitz. He would later fight in the doomed Warsaw Uprising of 1944.[7]

All told, between May 1940 and January 1945, approximately 405,000 men, women and children from every country in Europe and from many lands overseas arrived at the Auschwitz main camp – Auschwitz I – for registration, tattooing (after August 1942) and assignment to one of the other camps in the complex. Of those 405,000, approximately 200,000 perished. This 49 per cent mortality rate for registered inmates was much higher than that of the SS concentration camps at Dachau, Sachsenhausen or Buchenwald, and higher even than the death rate at Mauthausen, which by SS classification standards was a harsher concentration camp than either the Auschwitz main camp or Auschwitz II – Birkenau. As of March 1941, around 700 SS guards were deployed in Auschwitz. By June 1942, the number had risen to 2,000; in April 1944, the figure was 2,950, in August 1944, 3,342 and, finally, on 15 January 1945, 4,481 male SS guards and 71 female over-seers were deployed in Auschwitz. The SS guard formations experienced a continuous fluctuation of employees. A total of more than 7,000 SS men were deployed in Auschwitz at one time or another. Some of them were accommodated on the grounds of the main camp, others in confiscated resi-dential buildings in the town of Oświęcim and in the newly established SS settlement, where the good infrastructure persuaded many family members to follow their menfolk and relocate to Auschwitz.[8]

Prior to the construction of the first crematorium at Auschwitz, the dead were brought to the municipal crematorium in Gliwice. The first cremator-ium in Auschwitz was installed in the main camp by the Erfurt firm Topf & Sons. It was equipped with only one incinerator containing two combustion chambers, in which more than 100 corpses a day could be burned. It was ready for use on 15 August 1940. From summer 1941, tests were carried out in the main camp with prussic acid – more commonly known by its trade name, Zyklon B. This poison gas was regularly delivered to Auschwitz by the Hamburg firm Tesch & Stabenow for the fumigation of vermin-infested buildings. It had never before been used by the Nazis to kill people, but it was easier to deploy than the carbon monoxide used in the T4 killing centres, as there was no need to install pipes or gas cylinders – the murderers just had to drop Zyklon B pellets into a sealed chamber. The tests took place in the cellar of Block 11 (at the time Block 13), where all the windows had been filled with earth, and their first victims were a small number of Soviet pris-oners of war, who at this time were already dying in droves in the

Wehrmacht-run POW camps. Then, in early September, a more substantial test took place. This time the victims were 250 sick prisoners from the camp infirmary, 600 Soviet POWS just arrived from Stalag 308 in Neuhammer (now Świętoszow), Lower Silesia, and several prisoners from the Auschwitz penal company. Once the last of the prisoners had been crammed into the cellar, the SS threw Zyklon B crystals inside and sealed the doors. On contact with the warm air and the captives' bodies, highly toxic prussic acid was released and desperate screaming started, carrying all the way to the adjacent barracks. The gas quickly destroyed the victims' mucous membranes and entered their bloodstream, asphyxiating them from within. Some dying men stuffed bits of clothing into their mouths to block the gas. But in vain: none survived. It was both the largest single killing operation in Auschwitz to date and the first mass gassing inside a concentration camp.[9]

Three nights later, after the cellar had been sufficiently aired, a large number of inmates were deployed to clear the gas chambers and drag the dead across the camp to the crematorium, which led to these events soon becoming known within the wider Auschwitz prisoner community. The cellar of Block 11 did not serve for long as a mass-killing site: it was too far away from the Auschwitz crematorium and lacked a built-in ventilation system; the building had to be aired for a long time before the SS could force other inmates inside to recover the bodies. In autumn 1941, therefore, the morgue – which lay outside the camp compound – was repurposed to serve as a gas chamber with a capacity of between 700 and 1,000 people. Its doors were insulated and holes were hammered into the ceiling, so that Zyklon B could be dropped in from the flat roof above. Afterwards, the corpses would be burned in the adjacent crematorium ovens (by 1942, the crematorium had received two additional ovens, increasing the daily capacity to 340 corpses). Mass shootings also took place in the morgue of up to 200 people at a time. Its first lethal test came in mid-September 1941, when the SS gassed some 900 Soviet POWs there.[10]

The new gas chamber in the Auschwitz morgue, in turn, operated for only a year, serving thereafter as a back-up installation. The reason for this was the construction nearby from autumn 1941 of a new camp of gigantic proportions. On 17 July 1941, Heinrich Himmler – in his capacity as Reich commissioner for the strengthening of German nationhood – had appointed Odilo Globocnik, already SS and police leader in the Lublin District, as 'plenipotentiary for the establishment of SS and police outposts in the new eastern space'. Three days later, Himmler travelled to Lublin to meet with Globocnik in person and instruct him to build a huge concentration camp in Lublin for 25,000 to 50,000 prisoners, to help turn the region into a major outpost for German settlements. On 22 September, Hans Kammler, chief of the SS Main Office for Budgets and Building, formally ordered the erection of the camp on the edge of Lublin; it would become known as Majdanek. Four days later, on 26 September, Kammler issued another order verbally (and the following day in writing) for the construction in both Lublin and Auschwitz of POW camps for 50,000 inmates: 'In Lublin and Auschwitz, immediately on 1 October, prisoner-of-war camps are to be built with a capacity of 50,000 prisoners each in accordance with the directives issued in Berlin and the drawings provided. [...] The work is to be undertaken at once and carried out with maximum acceleration.'[11]

The background to these expansive plans was Himmler's intention to acquire Soviet POWs from the Wehrmacht, deport them to concentration camps and deploy them as forced labourers in SS construction and industrial enterprises. After Kammler had personally inspected potential sites to the west of the Auschwitz main camp, it was Rudolf Höß who proposed the exact location for the new camp; this site was fixed on 4 October: the village of Brzezinka (Birkenau), situated at a distance of approximately 3km from the main camp. Construction work on the new camp began on 15 October 1941, by which time its anticipated capacity had already been doubled to 100,000 prisoners. The Germans brought in 10,000 Soviet POWs to construct the camp, over 90 per cent of whom died in the first five months due mainly to the primitive conditions under which they had to live and work while building it. Birkenau would go on to become the largest of the camps and sub-camps within the Auschwitz complex, and eventually reach a surface area of 140 hectares.[12]

Birkenau

There were no signs yet that Birkenau would one day be central to the Holocaust. Contrary to some suggestions, Auschwitz did not become a death camp for European Jews as early as 1941. This function gradually emerged during 1942. Just as the experiments with prussic acid in the Auschwitz main camp in September 1941 – primarily on (non-Jewish) Soviet prisoners of war – had no direct connection with the start of the extermination of Jews, the new sub-camp at Birkenau was not built to murder the Jews of Europe but to exploit vast numbers of Soviet POWs. Between the commissioning of Birkenau in late September 1941 and the commencement of mass deportations of Jews to Auschwitz in March 1942, however, something changed in this respect. On 20 January 1942, Reinhard Heydrich chaired a meeting of senior party and state officials in the Berlin suburb of Wannsee. Those present envisaged that 'in the course of the final solution the Jews are now to be deployed for work in the east', whereby 'the bulk of them will no doubt be eliminated by natural causes'. Five days later, on the morning of 25 January 1942, Himmler met with Oswald Pohl, head of the SS Main Office for Administration and Economics, at Dachau concentration camp to discuss 'new economic tasks'. Later the same day, Himmler lunched with Hitler at Führer Headquarters in East Prussia, on which occasion Hitler stated:

The Jew must get out of Europe. Otherwise, there can be no European reconciliation. Everywhere, he's the one inciting the most. Ultimately: I don't know; I'm tremendously humane. [. . .] All I say is that he has to go. If he is destroyed in the process, there's nothing I can do about it. I see only one thing: complete annihilation if they do not leave voluntarily. Why should I see a Jew through different eyes than a Russian prisoner? Many are dying in the prison camps because we have been forced into this position by the Jews. But what can I do about it? Why did the Jews provoke the war?[13]

As the RSHA had officially prohibited Jews from leaving German-occupied Europe 'voluntarily' three months earlier, on 23 October, this left only 'complete annihilation'. On the evening of the same day that he had met with Pohl and Hitler, Himmler rang Reinhard Heydrich in Prague, noting in his appointment diary: 'Jews to the KLs [= concentration camps]'. The following day, 26 January, Himmler contacted Inspector of the Concentration Camps Glücks with the message:

Now that Russian prisoners of war are not to be expected in the near future, I will send to the camps a large number of the Jews and Jewesses who are to be expelled from Germany. Prepare to receive 100,000 male Jews and up to 50,000 Jewesses in the KL in the next four weeks. The concentration camps will be approached with major economic tasks and orders in the coming weeks. SS Major General Pohl will give you the details.

It was thus Jewish labour that was now to be exploited on a huge scale in abominable conditions in the concentration camps. Even this, however, was not the death knell for all Jews destined for Birkenau. The gassing of prisoners, among them Jews, started on a small scale in February 1942, but the first murder of Jews who had just arrived did not take place until July 1942.[14]

The new role assigned to Auschwitz prompted the SS to take two major initiatives in late February and early March 1942. First, it resolved to build a large crematorium in Birkenau, capable of disposing of 800 bodies in twenty-four hours. The plans for a big crematorium were not new. Back in autumn 1941, with an enormous new camp for Soviet POWs scheduled at the Auschwitz complex, SS planners had decided to erect a high-capacity crematorium in the main camp, in order to deal with the anticipated surge in prisoner deaths. This location was now changed to Birkenau during a local inspection by Hans Kammler on 27 February 1942. Large numbers of Jewish prisoners were expected to arrive soon in Birkenau and all of them would eventually perish by means of 'annihilation through labour'. Instead of going to the trouble of hauling their corpses all the way back to the main camp, it was resolved to burn them in Birkenau. Second, Auschwitz prepared for the mass influx of women. On 3 March 1942, Himmler visited Ravensbrück in the Province of Brandenburg, the largest concentration camp for women in the Old Reich. He then briefed Oswald Pohl the next day, in preparation for transferring the Inspectorate of the Concentration Camps to Pohl's newly created SS Economic Administration Main Office (SS-Wirtschafts-Verwaltungshauptamt, or WVHA) on 16 March. A week after Himmler's visit to Ravensbrück, Inspector of the Concentration Camps Glücks ordered two Auschwitz officers to go there in order to become acquainted with the running of a women's concentration camp. Shortly thereafter, Johanna Langefeld, the senior Ravensbrück camp supervisor, travelled in the opposite direction to oversee the new women's compound in Auschwitz; she was joined by more than a dozen female guards from Ravensbrück. At the end of March, 999 (non-Jewish) female German prisoners were transferred from

Ravensbrück to Auschwitz, where they would become block elders and camp functionaries in the women's compound.[15]

Systematic mass deportations of Jews to Auschwitz began in late March 1942. The first registered transport sent by Adolf Eichmann's Section IV B 4, which was responsible for 'Jew affairs' and 'evacuation affairs' within the RSHA, brought 999 women from Poprad in Slovakia and arrived on 26 March, the same day as the transport carrying the aforementioned 999 non-Jewish German women from Ravensbrück. Two days later, a further 798 women arrived from Slovakia, this time from Bratislava. On 13 April, 1,077 Jews – 634 men and 443 women – arrived on the next RSHA transport from Slovakia. On 30 March, 1,112 men arrived on the first mass transport carrying Jews from France. Eichmann had instructed his representative for Jewish affairs in Paris, Theodor Dannecker, to arrange for the deportation of 'around 5,000 Jews to the east'; the deportees were to be 'male Jews, fit for work, not over 55 years of age'. Five more transports from France fitting these criteria arrived at Auschwitz between 9 June and 19 July. Clearly, then, the orders issued by Eichmann were neither for a general deportation of Jews from France nor for their delivery to a death camp. Instead, Eichmann was looking for forced labourers for Auschwitz concentration camp. He also ordered that the individual transports should not include more than 5 per cent women. These instructions were indeed observed for the aforementioned six transports. For example, the third RSHA transport from France, which arrived on 24 June, contained 933 male and 66 female Jews. These transports of Jews to Auschwitz were interspersed with trains carrying non-Jews, including Polish political prisoners. From the middle of 1942, Jews comprised for the first time the largest group among the inmates of Auschwitz concentration camp. None of the new arrivals was subjected to selection, though many died from dire conditions, lethal violence and draining labour in Birkenau. It is likely that two-thirds or more of all Jewish prisoners newly registered in spring and summer 1942 were dead within eight weeks. Some RSHA transports were almost completely wiped out; three months after their arrival on 19 April, just 17 of the 464 male Jews sent from Žilina (Slovakia) were still alive. Among the dead were some boys, after the Slovak authorities had begun to include families in the deportations; the youngest victim was seven-year-old Ernest Schwarcz, who had survived for barely one month.[16]

Before Auschwitz became a site of mass extermination of the European Jews, it served as a regional death camp for the systematic slaughter of Silesian Jews. While non-working Jews from the Wartheland were being killed in Chełmno, and those from the Lublin District in Bełżec, Silesian Jews selected as unfit for work were killed in Auschwitz. This began on 5 May 1942. During that month, around 6,500 Jews selected as unfit for work arrived from forced-labour camps in several towns in Upper Silesia. The following month, another 16,000 Jews were deported from Silesia to Auschwitz, leading Nazi officials in several localities to declare themselves proudly 'free of Jews'. For logistical reasons, it was not Eichmann's Jewish desk in Berlin that was in charge of these operations but rather the Gestapo head office in the East Upper Silesian city of Katowice (Kattowitz), which was located at a distance of only 30km from Auschwitz. There, local Gestapo chief Rudolf Mildner assumed personal control of where and when the deportations departed. The deported Silesian Jews were murdered in new killing facilities in Birkenau: an empty farm-house converted into a gas chamber and renamed Bunker 1. Gassings in the main camp ceased a few months later.[17]

The first trainload of Jews to be subjected to selection upon their arrival in Auschwitz was an RSHA transport from Slovakia that arrived on 4 July 1942. During the selection, 264 male and 108 female Jews were classified as fit for work and registered in the camp, while the remaining 628 Jews were immediately sent to the gas chambers. From here on in, immediate death awaited the vast majority of the arriving Jews: out of a total of approximately 1.1 million Jews transported to Birkenau, perhaps 200,000 were temporarily saved when selected for labour. Those whom the Germans selected for work faced a slower but usually no less certain fate than those who went straight to the gas chambers. For most prisoners, the work was extremely hard and often dangerous. The guards drove the prisoners furiously and beat anyone who faltered, often to the point of death. Selections commonly took place immediately upon arrival of the trains at the Birkenau railway ramp. The exact sequence of events varied somewhat, but typically the Jews selected for death were marched to the extermination compound, ordered to undress (under the pretext of bathing and being disinfected before entering the camp proper) and herded into the gas chamber. Specially trained SS technicians then dumped hydrogen-cyanide tablets (Zyklon B) into the chamber. When the prisoners were dead, the chamber was ventilated and the so-called Special

Squad (*Sonderkommando*), made up of other Jewish prisoners, dragged out the bodies, cut off women's hair, removed any gold dental work, burned the corpses in the crematoria and scattered the remains. None of the Special Squad members volunteered for these tasks; they were selected by the SS and faced a stark choice: obedience or certain death. In the words of Auschwitz survivor Primo Levi, the creation of the Special Squad was 'National Socialism's most demonic crime'. Their work temporarily saved these inmates from extermination, though often not for long. While the SS did not murder all Special Squad members at regular intervals, selections took place just as they did elsewhere in the camp; weak and sick prisoners were killed with phenol injections in the infirmary. The SS furthermore occasionally killed a proportion of the prisoners in order to reduce the relative size of the Special Squad during periods when fewer deportation trains arrived. In the end, only a very few of them survived from 1942 through to 1945.[18]

One of the more than 2,200 men who were forced into the Auschwitz Special Squad during its existence was Shlomo Venezia, a Greek-born Italian Jew who arrived in Auschwitz in April 1944 after a seventeen-day journey from Thessaloniki. He recalled that his Special Squad needed between forty-eight and seventy-two hours to empty a gas chamber with 1,500 dead bodies and then cremate the corpses. On one occasion, while removing corpses from the gas chamber, a member of the Special Squad heard cries and discovered that they were coming from a baby girl, not even two months old, who had somehow survived the gassing and was still suckling, in vain, at her mother's breast. Alerted to the survival of the baby, a German guard, rubbing his hands, told the Special Squad prisoners to 'bring it here'. He thereupon pulled out his pistol and shot the baby. The little girl, who had miraculously survived the gas, was dead. Shlomo Venezia noted how 'very happy' the guard was to be able to kill her.[19]

At least 232,000 of the 1.3 million people deported to Auschwitz were children and adolescents up to the age of eighteen years, including approximately 216,000 Jews. Anyone younger than fourteen had little chance of being categorised during the selections as 'fit for work' and, in this way, of escaping immediate murder in the gas chambers. The vast majority of children and adolescents were murdered on arrival. Fewer than 2,500 Jewish children survived the initial selections. Those who did suffered many of the same hardships as adults – abuse, hunger, roll calls and hard labour. Nor were child prisoners exempt from SS beatings and official punishments like the penal companies. Like anywhere else, babies were born in Auschwitz. The Polish inmate Anna Palarczyk recalled: 'When an expectant woman came to the camp in 1942, neither she nor the child remained alive. I frequently saw newborn babies in the outpatient clinic. They continued to lie there until they died.' Other newborns were drowned or given a lethal injection.[20]

The systematic mass deportations of Jews to Auschwitz that began in late March 1942 were initially sporadic. From mid-July, they became routine. The transports, usually carrying around 1,000 people, arrived on a daily basis; occasionally, two trains came on the same day. In all, more than 60,000 Jews were sent to Auschwitz in July and August 1942; they came from France, Poland, the Netherlands, Belgium, Slovakia and Croatia. In 1942, a total of around 190,000 Jews died in Auschwitz, the great majority of them in the Birkenau gas chambers. By contrast, at least 1.37 million Jews were murdered in the three Operation Reinhardt camps that year, well over 700,000 in Treblinka alone. At the end of 1942, just 12,650 Jewish prisoners were registered in Auschwitz. By comparison, nearly 300,000 Jews were still alive in the Government General, most of them toiling in large ghettos such as Warsaw, with its 50,000 inmates. Ghettos in other parts of Nazi Europe, such as Łódź (87,000 inmates) and Theresienstadt (50,000), also held far more Jews than Auschwitz. It was only during 1943 that Auschwitz would become central to the genocide of the European Jews.[21]

On 17 July 1942, Himmler visited Auschwitz for the first time since 1 March 1941. He was joined by the Gauleiter of Upper Silesia, Fritz Bracht, the higher SS and police leader in Breslau, SS Lieutenant General Ernst-Heinrich Schmauser and SS Brigadier Hans Kammler. During his visit, Himmler witnessed the complete process of extermination from start to finish: the arrival in Birkenau of a transport of Dutch Jews, the selection of those deemed fit for work, the murder by gas in Bunker 2 – a second converted farmhouse, a few hundred yards away from the first – of those not selected and the emptying of the gas chamber. The following day, Himmler inspected the Auschwitz main camp. His itinerary included watching a demonstration of a flogging in the women's camp. During a final discussion with Höß, Himmler told the camp commandant to accelerate the expansion of Birkenau, exterminate those Jews considered unfit for work and get rid of the pits full of rotting corpses behind the bunkers – the old crematorium in Auschwitz I was out of commission, while the new one planned for Birkenau was not yet built. Höß then received a promotion to SS lieutenant colonel. (The next day, Himmler was in Lublin with Globocnik, ordering the deportation of 'the entire Jewish population of the Government General' by the end of 1942.) With more trainloads of Jews bound for the gas chambers on the way, the SS hurried to accelerate the completion of the new cremation facilities in Birkenau. By August 1942, the decision had been taken to build three additional crematoria for Birkenau; together, the four new buildings – Crematoria II, III, IV and V – would be able to burn 120,000 corpses each month. Furthermore, the morgues in the basement were converted into undressing rooms and gas chambers, so that the SS could murder and burn the victims in the same location.[22]

In the meantime, SS Colonel Paul Blobel, a former commando chief with the Einsatzgruppen in occupied Ukraine and an expert in open-air crema-tion, was sent to Auschwitz to teach the guards how to dig up and burn the rotting corpses in Birkenau. As head of Operation 1005, Blobel had already experimented in destroying dead bodies at Chełmno death camp. For several weeks in autumn 1942, the SS forced Special Squad prisoners to unearth all the corpses buried in Birkenau, working day and night with their bare hands. By the end, the prisoners had pulled out more than 100,000 bodies. One of the Special Squad prisoners, Erko Hejblum, later described the task: 'We waded in a mix of mud and decaying bodies. We would have needed gas masks. The corpses seemed to rise to the surface – it was as if the earth itself was rejecting them.' After a week, Hejblum felt like he was 'going mad' and wanted to kill himself; he was saved by a friend who engineered his transfer to a different work detail. Several prisoners who refused to carry on were shot point-blank. The others had to continue stacking the decomposing bodies for burning, first in huge pyres, later in long rectangular ditches. Meanwhile, the bodies of new victims deported to Auschwitz for extermina-tion were cremated in other pits, near the bunkers.[23]

After months of delays, the four huge crematoria with integral gas cham-bers finally became operational between March and June 1943. At the end of June, SS Major Karl Bischoff, head of the SS Central Construction Management at Auschwitz, reported in a letter to his superiors in Berlin that the four new crematoria could turn 4,416 corpses into ash within twenty-four hours; in addition, 340 corpses could still be incinerated in the old Crematorium I in the Auschwitz main camp. In April 1944, two escapees from Auschwitz-Birkenau described the new gassing and cremation facilities there:

> At the end of February 1943, a new modern crematorium and gassing plant was inaugurated at BIRKENAU. The gassing and burning of the bodies in the Birch Forest was discontinued, the whole job being taken over by the four specially built crematoria. The large ditch was filled in, the ground levelled, and the ashes used as before for fertilizer at the farm labour camp of HERMENSE, so that today it is almost impossible to find traces of the dreadful mass murder which took place here.
>
> At present there are four crematoria in operation at BIRKENAU, two large ones, I and II, and two smaller ones, III and IV. Those of type I and II consist of 3 parts, i.e.: (A) the furnace room; (B) the large hall; and (C) the gas chamber. A huge chimney rises from the furnace room around which are grouped nine furnaces, each having four openings. Each opening can take three normal corpses at once and after an hour and a half the bodies are completely burned. This corresponds to a daily capacity of about 2,000 bodies.

In their reference to 'nine furnaces', the escapees conflated the five furnaces each of Crematoria I and II (actually II and III, if we include the old crematorium in the Auschwitz main camp) and the four furnaces apiece in Crematoria III and IV (= IV and V). As it turned out, the furnaces were shoddily built and Crematorium III (hereafter referred to as IV) was already out of commission again by mid-May 1943, less than two months after going into operation. It thereafter ceased to be used. Crematorium IV (hereafter referred to as V) was likewise out of service between September 1943 and May 1944, when it was reactivated following the installation of a deaeration system. By mid-1943, with the new gassing and cremation facilities operational, all registered Jewish inmates had been moved from the Auschwitz main camp to Birkenau.[24]

Hungarian Jews

In early 1944, work began on the extension of the railway tracks to Birkenau. They were lengthened by a distance of 2km, so that they led directly to the crematoria. There, a new ramp was built. These modifications were designed to eliminate the need to transport victims from the old ramp to the crematoria in anticipation of the arrival of hundreds of thousands of people from the last major Jewish community in Europe – Hungary. The significance of these developments was not lost on the Jews already in Birkenau. Furthermore, SS guards had been overhead speaking about looking forward to the arrival of 'Hungarian salami'. According to one survivor: 'When a series of transports of Jews from the Netherlands arrived, cheese enriched the meagre rations. Sardines were the fare when a series of transports of French Jews arrived, and halva and olives when transports of Jews from Greece reached the camp. Now the SS were talking of "Hungarian salami".'[25]

After Hungary had distanced itself from its German partner, seeking a separate peace with the Allies, German forces occupied the country on 19 March 1944. The German occupation was a catastrophe for Hungarian Jewry, which had so far been spared from the Holocaust. The first two RSHA transports from Hungarian territory arrived at the Auschwitz main camp on 2 May, one from Budapest carrying around 1,800 male and female Jews aged between sixteen and fifty, and one from the town of Bačka Topola carrying 2,000 Jews. Both transports were classified as fit for work, but a combined total of 2,698 people – almost two-thirds – were nonetheless selected for death upon arrival and gassed. Large-scale deportations directly to Birkenau began on 14 May. Until 9 July, in the space of just eight weeks, around 425,000 Hungarian Jews from rural areas and the Budapest suburbs were deported to Birkenau in 141 transports. A week after that, another 4,000 Hungarian Jews from internment camps reached Birkenau on three trains, while several hundred more from various prisons and camps arrived between August and October. Thus, a total of around 430,000 Hungarian Jews reached Birkenau. The operation was personally coordinated by Adolf Eichmann. During the three-week period between 16 May and 8 June, three or four freight trains carrying around 12,000 Jews arrived at Birkenau *every day*. Each train comprised around forty-five carriages containing more than 70 people apiece. Most of the trains needed three days to reach their destination.[26]

Almost three-quarters of the Hungarian deportees – 320,000 people – were selected as unfit for work upon their arrival in Birkenau and immediately gassed. In accordance with instructions issued by Rudolf Höß

– returning to Auschwitz after an interim of six months, during which time he had occupied a senior position in Oswald Pohl's WVHA – the remnant of approximately 110,000 people were selected as fit for work and thereafter either formally registered in Auschwitz, transported to other concentration camps or sent on to the German Reich to be deployed as forced labourers in the armaments industry. The slaughter of the Hungarian arrivals in Birkenau was carried out with such speed that the SS murdered more Jews than they could burn in the three crematoria still operational (II, III and V), so that it was decided to use open-air pits for cremation as well, just as they had in 1942. Sometimes the killers bypassed the gas chambers altogether, shooting Hungarian Jews at the burning pits, beating them to death or throwing them into the flames alive. On 11 July, the Reich plenipotentiary for Hungary, Dr Edmund Veesenmayer, reported to Berlin the completion of the deportation of 437,402 Hungarian Jews. The figure submitted by Veesenmayer included some Jews who never reached Auschwitz, namely approximately 15,000 people on four transports sent from southern and western Hungary in June and rerouted to Strasshof, near Vienna, where the deportees were deployed as forced labourers.[27]

During the deportation and extermination of Hungarian Jewry, between 5,000 and 6,000 female Jews were sent *from* Auschwitz on 9 June 1944 to the slave-labour camp in Plaszów, a southern suburb of Cracow (taking the number of Jewish inmates there to over 20,000), only to be returned to Auschwitz two months later. Josef Perl, an adolescent Jew from Bychkiv in the region of Carpatho-Ukraine, Czechoslovak territory occupied and annexed by Hungary in March 1939, spent a year in the Plaszów camp before being sent on to Auschwitz (and, from there, to Dachau). He later recalled the commandant in Plaszów at the time, Amon Göth:

the head of this camp, he – he was a fanatical person. He – he used to like to sit in his – in his house, which he had built on top of the hill. And for fun he used to shoot people – just – for kicks. For kicks. That was only sitting on his balcony. If he used to go out on his white horse for a ride – he used to have two Dalmatians he had, which he would train to kill people at one jump. For him – for him to – to leave behind him forty, fifty, sixty people dead, was – was a day's outing. You know, like somebody goes out pheasant shooting or something like that.[28]

On 10 April 1944, two Slovak Jews, Rudolf Vrba (born Walter Rosenberg) and Alfréd Wetzler, managed to escape from Auschwitz-Birkenau after two years in the camp. They made their way on foot to Slovakia, crossing the border on 21 April. In the city of Žilina, they met with members of the Jewish Council, representing the 25,000 Jews still alive in Slovakia. During the first meeting, a Swiss journalist was present. Wetzler later recounted an exchange between Vrba and the incredulous newspaperman:

'Can you tell us anything about specific bestialities by the SS men?' the Swiss asks.

Val's [= Vrba's] face reflects boundless astonishment. They are all surprised, because nothing else has been talked about so far.

'That is,' Val replies embarrassedly, 'as if you wanted me to tell you of a specific day when there was water in the Danube. Maybe that's not a good example,' he continues pensively, 'but those bestialities are performed there non-stop, day and night. It was bestial that they drove us out of our native lands, out of our homes, the conditions in which people live there are bestial, the labour is inhuman and the dying there is inhuman too.'

'What I had in mind were specific instances about which you might recall names: this or that happened and it was done by so and so,' the journalist amplified his question.

Val lights a cigarette. Yes, now he understands the question, now he can answer it.

'Those who didn't catch typhus at the Buna plant [in Monowitz],' he continues calmly, 'had to paint skis for the German army in the camp. Cushy job, would you say? But SS man Henkel checked the numbers every day and finished off anyone who had not painted at least one hundred and twenty skis. Other men from Buna made boxes for shells. That's not heavy work either – for men with a full stomach. Some fifteen thousand crates didn't have the prescribed dimensions. For every one hundred crates they shot one prisoner. Want me to continue?'

The Swiss correspondent turns a page in his notebook and nods.

'The SS man Palitzsch throttled a prisoner, a weak asthmatic, because he had a coughing fit just as the command "Silence" was given. Another prisoner, also a new man who'd only arrived a few days before and didn't

231

yet know what was and what wasn't allowed, ran up to him and started shouting at us: "Help him, people, he's still moving, he's still alive!" Palitzsch seized that man by his throat and asked him "Is he really still alive?" "Yes, he is, can't you see his chest heaving?" shouted the young man. "You can see that?" Palitzsch asked him. "I can, I've got two eyes in my head," the prisoner answered back. "But quite needlessly," Palitzsch said and as he held him by the throat, he drew his revolver and shot both his eyes out.'

While in Žilina, Vrba and Wetzler spent three days writing and rewriting a detailed statement of their first-hand experiences in Auschwitz. It offered a thorough analysis of the Auschwitz complex, outlining its development, layout and administration, as well as conditions inside. Most critically, Vrba and Wetzler gave a meticulous account of the Birkenau death camp, detailing the arrivals of Jews from across Europe, and the selections, gassings and cremations. The sober tone and the mass of details made their account all the more devastating. The report was finished and the final version typed by 27 April 1944. Originally prepared in Slovak, the report was immediately translated into German and Hungarian, and later into English and French. One of the copies of the report found its way to Switzerland, where parts of it were published for the first time. This led to extensive press coverage in Switzerland, which caused an international chain reaction that finally induced Miklós Horthy, the regent of Hungary, to demand an end to the deportations during a session of the Crown Council on 26 June. It was not until 6 July, however, that he was able to force through his demand in the face of fear among Hungarian officials that this would trigger further military action by Germany. The final transport left Hungary on 9 July.[29]

Between May and July 1944, more Jews were deported to Auschwitz than during the entire preceding two years, and nearly all of them came from Hungary. As of late August 1944, 74 per cent of all the men, women and children held in Birkenau were Jewish. The murder of the Hungarian Jews marked the climax of the Holocaust in Auschwitz, at a time when most European Jews under German control had long since been killed. In addition to the 430,000 Jews who arrived from Hungary, substantial numbers of Polish, French, Dutch, Greek, Czech, Slovak, Belgian, German and Italian Jews were also deported to Auschwitz in 1944. That year indeed witnessed the phase of greatest destruction in the history of the Auschwitz camp: of more than 600,000 people who arrived there during 1944, up to 500,000 were murdered. Not even an uprising by members of the Special Squad could interrupt the mass extermination of Jews in Birkenau. On 7 October 1944, members of the Special Squad wielding hammers, axes and iron bars attacked a small group of SS men during a selection outside Crematorium IV. The revolt spread to Crematorium V, but SS reinforcements soon put down the uprising, leaving 250 prisoners dead. A second uprising broke out at Crematorium II and up to 100 prisoners succeeded in fleeing after cutting a hole in the fence surrounding their compound. However, the SS hunted them all down and, over the weeks that followed, executed most of the survivors of the uprising. In contrast to the revolts at Sobibór and Treblinka, not a single Special Squad prisoner escaped. Though the prisoners had managed to burn down Crematorium IV, it had in any case been out of commission since May 1943. Three SS guards were killed during the uprising and twelve others wounded. Gassings at Birkenau continued until the end of October 1944, during which time a further 40,000 men, women and children were murdered.[30]

At the end of October 1944, the ramp at Birkenau was for the last time the scene of a selection of passengers from an arriving transport. The following month, Himmler ordered the murder in the gas chambers to be halted and the extermination facilities to be destroyed. The gas chambers and furnace rooms in Crematoria II and III were demolished in November and December, and their structural remains blown up on 20 January 1945. Crematorium V continued to be used for burning corpses until mid-January; it was then detonated on 26 January. The SS did not succeed in obliterating all traces of mass killing before Auschwitz was liberated by the Red Army on 27 January. During the demolition process, the SS continued to kill prisoners by shooting them. The final roll call took place on 17 January. By the next day, the Red Army had advanced as far as Cracow, at which point the SS leadership ordered the final evacuation of Auschwitz. Over the course of the next four days, more than 58,000 prisoners from Auschwitz and its satellite camps were forced along the main routes to Gliwice, 55km away, and Wodzisław Śląski (Loslau), 63km away. From there, some of the emaciated prisoners were transported in open carriages to Mauthausen, Ravensbrück, Sachsenhausen and Bergen-Belsen concentration camps. Thousands of other prisoners were forced westwards on foot in the middle of winter. Those unable to go on were shot or beaten to death on the spot by the attendant SS personnel. Prisoners from Jaworzno satellite camp had to march 250km to Groß-Rosen concentration camp. Between 9,000 and 15,000 prisoners died during the Auschwitz death marches.[31]

These evacuations of prisoners from concentration camps across the disintegrating Nazi empire into the interior of the Reich had started in early summer 1944 in eastern Poland and the Baltic countries in the face of the Soviet advance and would continue until the German surrender in May 1945. For several reasons, the evacuations sit uneasily in a history of Nazi mass killing. First, the main purpose of the concentration-camp evacuations was not the murder of Jews or other prisoners. They began as an attempt to *preserve* the labour force of the camp inmates at any cost and thus keep the war effort going. Himmler himself, moreover, irrationally regarded prisoners – especially Jews – as valuable pawns in his pursuit of a separate peace with the Western Allies. It is these factors that explain why no explicit, comprehensive order for the murder of concentration-camp prisoners before their liberation is known to have been issued. As a result, the Allies found prisoners – still alive, albeit very emaciated – in well over 100 camps, including Buchenwald, Sachsenhausen, Flossenbürg, Dachau, Ravensbrück, Mauthausen and, most notably, Bergen-Belsen. In April and early May 1945 alone, approximately 90,000 inmates were liberated from satellite camps and around 155,000 from main camps.[32]

Second, although popular memory of these evacuations is dominated by death marches, much of the journey to camps further inside the Reich was covered by rail. The vast majority of prisoners evacuated from Western European camps from September 1944 were transported by train, making prisoners easier to guard and journey times much shorter. As a result, almost all those inmates survived the initial evacuations in the west. By the time of the evacuations of early 1945, by contrast, conditions on the trains were far worse. This was largely a consequence of the state of the crumbling German rail network: with rolling stock in short supply, the SS frequently used open freight trains, which offered no protection against the elements, while congestion and damaged tracks slowed down the transports, forced them to change direction or brought them to a complete standstill; this, in turn, prolonged the suffering of the transportees and vastly increased the number of dead among them.[33]

It is also worth keeping in mind that the camp prisoners during these months were a highly heterogeneous group; the Jews were only one – albeit large – component part, making up somewhere between a third and a half of the evacuated prisoners. For the reasons outlined above, the SS made no attempt systematically to kill all Jews during evacuations. It is not even clear that Jews were treated fundamentally worse than other prisoners. Ultimately, it was strength and luck, as much as anything else, that determined whether a prisoner would survive the transports and forced marches. Not only is it problematic, then, to place the forced marches in the wider framework of Nazi genocide as a whole but also to place them in the specific framework of the Holocaust.[34]

The death rates of the marches varied greatly, depending on factors such as available food supplies and distances covered. Where general conditions were better and prisoners healthier, a large proportion of the evacuees survived even lengthy marches. It was illness, exhaustion and exposure to the elements that were the main killers. The desperate physical state in which many of the prisoners embarked on the evacuations was a product of the camps; during the marches and transports, they often went for days with little food and no hope of respite. Shootings were endemic, too, particularly from early January 1945, when forced marches were increasingly conducted in chaotic circumstances; during this completely decentralised process, a huge number of indiscriminate killings were carried out by SS guards determined at any cost to keep ahead of the advancing Allies. Though there were some large-scale massacres, they were the exception rather than the rule and are not representative of the fate of prisoners during the forced marches. Nonetheless, the overall mortality rate of the evacuations was exceedingly high. Between early summer 1944 and the German surrender in May 1945, the evacuation of concentration camps may have led to the death of as many as 250,000 prisoners: 35 per cent of all inmates of the camp system as of January 1945.[35]

One of the last large-scale massacres of Jews during the war took place in late January 1945, when around 7,000 Jews, mostly women, were sent on a forced march from several satellite camps of the Stutthof main camp near Danzig to the East Prussian locality of Palmnicken (now Yantarny in the Russian semi-exclave of Kaliningrad) on the Baltic Sea coast. Directing the march were 25 SS guards and more than 120 members of the Organisation Todt construction agency. Only 3,000 prisoners reached Palmnicken; the rest perished along the way, including more than 2,000 who collapsed from sheer exhaustion and were then shot by the guards. The plan, it seems, was to murder the remaining Jews by forcing them into a disused shaft of the Palmnicken amber mine and walling it up. Instead, the SS were confronted with the unexpected resistance of the mine director, who – awoken in the night of 26–27 January – refused to open the mine shaft intended for the murder, arguing that the mine was needed for the Palmnicken water supply. The mine director was supported by the estate manager, Hans Feyerabend, who arrived the following morning, stated that no one would be killed and arranged for the Jews, who were temporarily lodged in a factory building, to be fed. Faced with this obstacle to their plans, the SS improvised a new way of killing the Jews. On the evening of 31 January 1945, the SS guards – assisted by a dozen local Hitler Youth members – forced the prisoners out on to the ice covering the Baltic Sea and then machine-gunned them down. One of the very few survivors was Pnina Kronisch, a Russian Jew. She testified after the war:

> Then they threw the murdered Jews into the water by kicking them. As the seacoast was covered with ice, the murderers pushed their victims into the icy water with their rifle butts. Since I was at the front of the column with my sister Sara, we were the last in line to be shot. I was also laid down on the seacoast together with my sister, though I was not killed by the shot that was aimed at me but only wounded in my left foot, and my face was soaked in the blood of the murdered Jews lying next to me. During this time my sister was killed. I did not wait until the Germans threw me into the sea — I threw myself in and remained lying next to the ice floe, which already was caught up in the water and hit by the waves. The Germans believed I was dead, and since I was alone, to my good luck, and last in line to be murdered, the Germans got into their sleds and drove off. Before dawn I scrambled out of the sea and hid in the coal store of a German farmer who did not live far from where these events occurred.

Of the original group of 7,000 individuals sent on the forced march to Palmnicken, only around 15 survived.[36]

Another infamous massacre during the period of the death marches, this time of non-Jewish prisoners, took place in Gardelegen, a small town to the north of Magdeburg, where German locals also participated in the murder of prisoners still under SS control. On 9 April 1945, a group of prisoners – mostly Polish forced labourers – travelling by freight train to concentration camps further north had to disembark in nearby Mieste, as the tracks ahead were damaged. The area was almost completely encircled by US troops. After two days and nights of indecision, the SS resolved to march the prisoners on foot to Gardelegen. Hundreds of prisoners died or were shot during the initial wait at Mieste and then during the forced march. In Gardelegen, the head of the NSDAP district branch, Gerhard Thiele, argued that the prisoners, who numbered more than 1,000, would pose a grave threat to the local population if liberated by the advancing Americans, and pushed for their murder. On the evening of 13 April, the prisoners were marched to a brick barn on the outskirts of the town and forced inside. The guards – SS men, paratroopers from a nearby army base and members of the local home guard – used machine guns, flamethrowers and hand grenades to set alight the petrol-soaked straw inside the barn. Most of the prisoners burned to death or were asphyxiated; those who attempted to escape by digging under the barn walls were shot. When US troops from the 102nd Infantry Division reached Gardelegen only twenty-four hours after the start of the massacre, they discovered 1,016 corpses. Only around 25 prisoners had managed to survive the slaughter.[37]

Between May 1940 and January 1945, a total of at least 1.3 million people were deported to Auschwitz. Jews comprised the largest group of deportees: almost 1.1 million. In terms of individual countries, 430,000 Jews came from Hungary, 300,000 from Poland, 69,000 from France, 60,000 from the Netherlands, 55,000 from Greece, 46,000 from Bohemia and Moravia (Theresienstadt), 27,000 from Slovakia, 25,000 from Belgium, 23,000 from Germany and Austria, 10,000 from Yugoslavia, 7,500 from Italy and 690 from Norway. A further 34,000 Jews were deported to Auschwitz from different concentration camps, satellite camps and other locations. Of these almost 1.1 million deported Jews, approximately 900,000 perished in Auschwitz. Altogether, well over 200,000 prisoners – Jews and non-Jews – left the camp alive between 1940 and 1945. However, most of these prisoners were transferred on to camps elsewhere, and many did not live to see the end of the war. As we have seen, some perished en route to other camps, and many lost their lives during the last phase of the war. This means that from a grand total of at least 1.3 million people transported to Auschwitz, 1.1 million prisoners were killed or died in the camp; four-fifths of them were Jews.[38]

Why has Auschwitz become the central symbol of the Holocaust; indeed, a synonym for the genocide? The fact that more Jews perished here than in any other single place certainly contributes significantly to Auschwitz's present-day status. However, it is arguably two other factors that have played the most decisive role in establishing Auschwitz as the central symbol of the Holocaust. First, it operated much longer than other killing sites (and was so lethal partly for this reason) and was at its murderous peak when the other main extermination camps had closed down; therefore, unlike Chełmno, Bełżec, Sobibór or Treblinka, it was liberated by the Allies rather than being dismantled, destroyed and concealed by the Germans themselves. As a result, substantial parts of the camp infrastructure remained intact. Second, its triple function as a concentration camp (Auschwitz I), an extermination camp (Auschwitz II – Birkenau) and a labour camp (Auschwitz III – Monowitz) meant that – again, unlike the single-purpose death camps – several tens of thousands of people survived Auschwitz, and many of them gave testimony on their experiences there after the war. Their memoirs constitute an important element of Holocaust survivor literature. It is true that another major site of mass killing with gassing facilities, Majdanek, shared these two distinctions with Auschwitz – its liberation by the Red Army while still largely intact and its possession of additional functions beyond pure extermination. The construction of Majdanek and Birkenau was furthermore commissioned simultaneously. However, when it comes to sheer scale, Auschwitz dwarfs Majdanek: at least ten times as many people were killed at Auschwitz.

CHAPTER 10
GENOCIDE OF THE EUROPEAN ROMA

During the Holocaust, Auschwitz developed first and foremost into a concentration camp for Jews, who replaced Poles as the largest inmate group. The third largest group in Auschwitz were Roma, known widely and pejoratively as 'Gypsies'. The first transport of Sinti – a Central European branch of the Roma living primarily in German-speaking areas – from Reich territory arrived in Auschwitz-Birkenau on 26 February 1943. Unlike other prisoners in Birkenau at the time, the Sinti were not separated according to gender and age. Instead, they were all sent to the 'Gypsy family camp' at the far end of the Birkenau complex. In fact, the 'family camp' did not yet exist; the new arrivals themselves had to build it from scratch on the bare earth, just as Soviet POWs had constructed Birkenau in autumn 1941. Here, sanitary conditions were even worse than elsewhere in Birkenau. In the early months, with the compound still under construction, there were no toilets or washrooms. Conditions barely improved after the SS added rudimentary facilities; the overflowing latrines were rarely emptied, and water was scarce and contaminated. From 7 March 1943, Roma and Sinti from German-occupied foreign territories also arrived. During March, 12,259 people were transported to the 'Gypsy camp'; by the end of July, the number had risen to around 23,000. They came from at least eleven different countries; more than half of them were from Germany and Austria.[1]

The trigger for these transports to Auschwitz-Birkenau was an order issued by Heinrich Himmler on 16 December 1942 for the deportation of those Sinti and Roma still living in Germany. The genesis of Himmler's deportation order, in turn, can be traced back to an agreement of 18 September 1942 reached by Himmler and Otto Georg Thierack, who had been appointed Reich minister of justice less than a month earlier. Their arrangement foresaw:

Delivery of antisocial elements from the penal system to the Reichsführer SS for annihilation through labour. Following a decision by the Reich minister of justice, those in preventive detention, Jews, Gypsies, Russians and Ukrainians, Poles serving more than three years, Czechs or Germans serving more than eight years will be delivered in their entirety. [...] There is a consensus that – in consideration of the intended objectives of the state leadership for the settlement of eastern questions – in the future Jews, Poles, Gypsies, Russians and Ukrainians will no longer be sentenced by regular courts of law where criminal cases are concerned, but instead dealt with by the Reichsführer SS.

The intention to kill members of persecuted groups by means of – literally – back-breaking work was rarely so openly stated as it was in this document detailing the agreement reached between the most senior representative of the German judiciary and the chief of the German police. On 13 October, Thierack notified Chief of the Party Chancellery Martin Bormann of this judicial licence to murder. Bormann, in turn, informed Hitler, who gave his explicit approval.[2]

It is conceivable that Thierack had adopted the wording of the agreement regarding 'annihilation through labour' from Reich Minister of Propaganda Goebbels, with whom he had met four days prior to his meeting with Himmler. After seeing Goebbels, Thierack noted: 'With regard to the annihilation of antisocial life, Dr Goebbels takes the view that Jews and Gypsies in general, Poles serving three or four years of penal servitude, Czechs and Germans sentenced to death, lifelong penal servitude or preventive detention, ought to be annihilated. The concept of annihilation through labour is, he says, the best.' The two men were evidently of one mind, and Goebbels was confident that they would be able to work well together. Following the meeting with Thierack, Goebbels himself noted in his diary regarding those destined for labour deployment in the east: 'Whoever dies of this work is no loss.'[3]

Himmler's 16 December deportation order prompted the Reich Criminal Police Office to convene a meeting to discuss its implications. This meeting was held on 15 January 1943 and attended by representatives of the host institution, the Racial Hygiene Research Centre within the Reich Public Health Authority, the SD and the Race and Settlement Main Office of the SS. In accordance with the agreements reached at this meeting, the Reich Criminal

Police Office – as Office V of the RSHA – issued regulations for the implementation of Himmler's deportation order two weeks later, on 29 January, under the title 'Admission of Gypsy cross-breeds, Roma Gypsies and Balkan Gypsies to a concentration camp'. The guidelines had Auschwitz in mind: 'Admission takes place as a family, regardless of the degree of mixed blood, to Auschwitz concentration camp (Gypsy camp)'. The choice most likely fell on Auschwitz because at the time the geographical dimensions of Birkenau were in the process of being considerably expanded. The RSHA regulations were sent to the Criminal Police regional headquarters, which were tasked with organising the transports to Auschwitz. Copies were also received by the commandant's office at Auschwitz, the head of the Party Chancellery, Himmler as Reich commissioner for the strengthening of German nationhood, the SS Economic Administration Main Office, the Main Office of the Order Police, Eichmann's Jewish desk, the higher SS and police leaders, the inspectors of the Security Police and the SD, and all State Police headquarters, among others.[4]

Certain categories of Roma were exempted from deportation to Auschwitz, including 'racially pure' Sinti and Lalleri (another Central European branch of the Roma living primarily in Czech lands), war invalids or decorated veterans, those doing jobs in the armaments industry regarded as vital for the war effort, those married to non-Roma and foreign nationals, as well as their respective spouses and children. However, in accordance with the results of the 15 January meeting, all the groups excluded from deportation – aside from 'racially pure' Roma and foreign nationals – were only spared this fate on the condition that they agree to be sterilised (provided they were twelve years of age or older), thus subjecting them to a form of delayed genocide. Indeed, approximately 2,000 Roma were later forcibly sterilised in the German Reich pursuant to these regulations. Moreover, many of the exemptions, including those granted to 'racially pure' Roma and foreign nationals, applied theoretically but not in practice; the regulations left local police authorities a wide margin of discretion – any Roma with a criminal record, for instance, were immediately struck from the list of exemptions. Just as German forces in the occupied territories rarely differentiated between itinerant and sedentary Roma, the local police organising the deportations took little notice of the stipulations regarding exemptions and frequently included members of the exempted groups in the transports to Birkenau.[5]

Deportation to the Government General

The Himmler–Thierack agreement and the former's subsequent deportation order were the latest steps in a process that had been under way for some time in different German-occupied territories. The persecution process against Sinti and Roma in the German Reich was characterised well into 1938 by numerous voluntary exclusion strategies taken on the initiative of local authorities. These strategies frequently anticipated nationwide regulations – such as the exclusion of Sinti and Roma from receiving welfare benefits or attending schools – and contributed considerably to the escalation of persecution of these minority groups. Forced displacement and the refusal to issue trade licences for travelling salespeople destroyed livelihoods and pushed those affected to the margins of society. National Socialist indoctrination was not required in order to accelerate the persecution of Sinti and Roma on the ground; instead, Nazi racial policies tied in with existing attitudes and sentiments, which in turn met with a readiness on the part of the majority of society to follow instructions from above.[6]

On the orders of Reichsführer SS and Chief of the German Police Heinrich Himmler, a Reich Central Agency for Combating the Gypsy Nuisance (*Reichszentrale zur Bekämpfung des Zigeunerunwesens*) was established within the Reich Criminal Police Office in Berlin on 1 October 1938. This completed a process that had been under way since 1936. The Reich Central Agency thus superseded the Gypsy Central Agency (*Zigeunerzentrale*), which the Bavarian State Ministry of the Interior had set up at the Munich police headquarters as early as 1899. The Munich authorities now transferred their files to the Reich Central Agency in Berlin. The new agency was tasked with the central coordination of measures for registering and persecuting Sinti and Roma. In a circular decree for 'Combating the Gypsy Plague' issued two months later, on 8 December, Himmler ordered all police authorities to report people 'who, to judge by their appearance, their habits and [their] customs, are regarded as Gypsies or Gypsy cross-breeds, as well as all people roaming around like Gypsies, to the Reich Criminal Police Office – Reich Central Agency for Combatting the Gypsy Nuisance – via the appropriate Criminal Police headquarters and Criminal Police regional headquarters'. With the aid of these arbitrary measures, Himmler's decree aimed at bringing about a 'definitive solution to the Gypsy question' on the basis of 'the nature of this race'.[7]

Shortly after the German invasion of Poland in September 1939, the first plans for the deportation of Sinti and Roma to the Government General began to emerge. On 21 September, Chief of the Security Police and the SD Reinhard Heydrich hosted a meeting in Berlin of the office heads of the future Reich Security Main Office, who were joined by the chiefs of the Einsatzgruppen operating at the time in Poland. Adolf Eichmann, then head of the Central Office for Jewish Emigration (*Zentralstelle für jüdische Auswanderung*) in Vienna, was also present. Heydrich condensed his instructions into four points:

1. Jews into the cities as quickly as possible.
2. Jews from the Reich to Poland.
3. The remaining 30,000 Gypsies to Poland as well.
4. Systematic sending forth of the Jews from the German territories with freight trains.

A common fate was thus envisaged for Jews and 'Gypsies' living in the German Reich in September 1939: deportation to German-occupied Poland. In the period between 1939 and 1941, the persecution of the Roma indeed ran more parallel to that of the Jews than it had done either before or would do after. Prior to the war, much of the persecution of Roma had resulted from the disproportionate impact of more general measures against those considered antisocial or work-shy, and only gradually had the 'Gypsy problem' been defined in clear racial terms. Between 1939 and 1941, however, it was intended to deport Jews and Roma together as part of the same vast programme of ethnic cleansing and demographic engineering. Both deportation programmes, with notable exceptions, went unrealised. The discriminatory measures of concentration and deprivation of freedom of movement, forced-labour exploitation, isolation and humiliation were often identical. Only from 1941 did the treatment and fate of Jews and Roma begin, on the whole, to diverge again.[8]

As so often, however, the persecution of Jews was also in this case pursued with greater zeal and swiftness than that of other victim groups. A mere month after the meeting of the future RSHA office heads on 21 September 1939, Eichmann seized the initiative and arranged for six transports carrying a total of more than 5,000 Jews from Ostrava (Mährisch-Ostrau), Vienna and Katowice, all cities located in territories annexed to the Reich since 1938, to be sent to the area around Nisko on the San river, in the far east of the Government General. Eichmann hoped that the transports would be ongoing and continuous – the Vienna authorities were anticipating a total deportation of 65,000 Jews. Before even the third transport could leave Vienna, however, the Nisko deportations were discontinued pending further notice. Gestapo chief Heinrich Müller informed Eichmann that deportations of Jews to occupied Poland required 'central coordination'. The stop order had clearly come from Himmler personally; he cited 'technical difficulties' as the reason for his decision. By virtue of his appointment as Reich commissioner for the strengthening of German nationhood on 7 October, Himmler had just obtained jurisdiction over the resettlement of ethnic Germans currently living outside the Reich. For the time being, this task evidently took priority over deporting Jews from East Upper Silesia, Austria or the Protectorate of Bohemia and Moravia.[9]

A deportation of German Jews did, however, take place on a much smaller scale within months of the discontinuation of the transports initiated by Eichmann. On 30 January 1940, Heydrich hosted a meeting of forty-five senior SS officers convened by Himmler with the purpose of reaching a common understanding regarding the 'implementation of the resettlement tasks decreed by the Führer'. There, Heydrich announced that 1,000 Jews from the city of Stettin, 'whose apartments are urgently required due to wartime necessities', would be deported to the Government General in mid-February. On 12 February, more than 1,100 Jews from Stettin – the third largest German city by area, after Berlin and Hamburg – and other parts of Pomerania, the Prussian province bordering the annexed Polish territories in the north, were indeed sent to Lublin. This was the first deportation of German Jews from the Old Reich.[10]

Though developments in anti-'Gypsy' policy did not proceed at quite the same tempo, the intention to deport all Sinti and Roma from the German Reich announced at the meeting of the future RSHA office heads on 21 September 1939 had clearly not been forgotten. On 17 October, a day before the first transport of Jews left Ostrava, the RSHA ordered that the 'Gypsies, who are later to be detained', be accommodated 'in special assembly camps until their final evacuation'. The Criminal Police were entrusted with making preparations for the establishment of such camps. This measure was designed to ensure quick and ready access to the Sinti and Roma when the time came to deport them. From this point on, Sinti and Roma living in the German Reich were no longer permitted to leave their place of residence or current abode; they otherwise risked being sent to a concentration camp. Chief of the Reich Criminal Police Office Arthur Nebe saw an opportunity to circumvent the construction of an assembly camp for Berlin's Sinti and Roma by including them in the deportations of Jews to the Nisko region. The envisaged camp would have accommodated not only the 850 people still living in wretched conditions on a caravan site enclosed with barbed wire in the Berlin suburb of Marzahn, people who had been forcibly relocated there in July 1936 away from the sight of visitors to that year's Summer Olympic Games, but also 1,000 living in rented accommodation in the centre of the capital. Eichmann was amenable to the idea and suggested to Nebe that a few train carriages containing Sinti and Roma simply be attached to the transports of Jews; the discontinuation of the Nisko deportations ultimately prevented this.[11]

There were nonetheless some dissenting voices. Reich Health Leader Leonardo Conti, for instance, believed as of late January 1940 that the short-term solution offered by deportations to the Government General would prevent 'a truly radical solution'. Conti had mass sterilisation in mind, thus rendering 'irrelevant' the continued presence of Roma on Reich territory. The head of the Racial Hygiene Research Centre, Dr Robert Ritter, shared Conti's assessment. At the aforementioned meeting of 30 January 1940, however, Heydrich reiterated the intention of deporting '30,000 Gypsies from Reich territory to the Government General'. On 29 February, Himmler told the Gauleiters and other Nazi Party functionaries: 'The Gypsies are a question in their own right. If possible, I want to get rid of them this year. There are [only] 30,000 in the whole Reich, but they nonetheless cause very substantial racial damage. Above all in the Ostmark [Austria], there are very many of them.' As of 4 March, Governor General Hans Frank was also expecting to receive 30,000 deported Roma. Almost another two months passed before Himmler, on 27 April, ordered the 'first transport of Gypsies' to be sent to the Government General in mid-May. It would represent only a partial fulfilment of the envisaged numbers, however, and encompass '2,500 people – comprising entire clans' from the Reich's western and north-western border areas.[12]

Starting in the early morning of 16 May 1940, less than a week after German forces had launched the invasion of France, the Criminal Police arrested several hundred Sinti and Roma in Hamburg, Cologne and Stuttgart, as well as dozens more in Bremen, Flensburg, Kiel, Düsseldorf, Aachen, Bonn, Essen, Hanover, Freiburg, Frankfurt, Mainz and numerous other western and northwestern German towns. Following these coordinated operations, the first deportation of 2,338 Sinti and Roma from Germany to occupied Poland took place on 20, 21 and 22 May, respectively, from three collection points: Hamburg (910 deportees), Cologne (938 deportees) and Asperg near Stuttgart (490 deportees). Upon arrival in the Government General – the Hamburg train (like the aforementioned Stettin transport of Jews) in Lublin, the Cologne train in Warsaw and the Asperg train in Radom – the deportation trains were, in the words of Governor General Frank, 'emptied into Gypsy camps'. Hardly any preparations had been made for the arrival of the Roma and they were shunted from one internment camp to another. So disastrous were conditions in the first internment camps, especially, that many of the deportees died of starvation, disease and SS cruelty. One of the deportees from Hamburg, Lani Rosenberg, later recalled how Roma were shot for nothing more than collecting water: 'I once saw how several eight- to twelve-year-old children had to lie on the ground, and the SS people then stamped around on the children with their spotless boots.' The number of German Sinti and Roma in the Government General increased to 2,800 by November 1940 due to the arrival there of relatives of those already deported in May. Around 80 per cent of the German Sinti and Roma deported to the Government General in May 1940 perished.[13]

As late as 31 July 1940, the higher SS and police leader in the Government General, Friedrich-Wilhelm Krüger, still expected to receive 30,000 'Gypsies' from the Old Reich. The same month, the Criminal Police authorities in Salzburg were told of an imminent deportation of Roma scheduled for late August. As in the case of the oft-postponed deportation of Jews, however, the deportation of Sinti and Roma was delayed indefinitely. On 4 September, the Reich Criminal Police Office noted in a letter to the Racial Policy Office of the NSDAP: 'Further resettlements are not anticipated for now, since the reception in the Government General at the present time is encountering difficulties. The final solution of the Gypsy problem is scheduled for after the war.' Of course, in September 1940, the period 'after the war' was not considered far off: a victorious conclusion of hostilities was expected at an early date. The RSHA order of 17 October 1939 forbidding Sinti and Roma from leaving their place of residence or current abode had deprived them of freedom of movement in preparation for deportation. They were stuck. Virtually all of the 'Gypsies', particularly in Austria and the Protectorate of Bohemia and Moravia, were now incarcerated in camps.[14]

Territorial Variations

Plans to deport Austrian Roma further east thus came to nothing in the summer of 1940, but in autumn 1941 a large deportation finally did take place. As we saw earlier, 5,000 Austrian Roma were deported to the Łódź Ghetto in early November 1941, where they were confined in a separate block of buildings within the perimeter of the Jewish ghetto. After hundreds had died from a typhus epidemic, the Germans sent the remaining 4,400 Roma to Chełmno extermination camp the following January, where they were murdered in gas vans. The experience of the deportation to Łódź and the existence of ghettos in occupied Poland made deportations of Roma conceivable once more; the ghettos provided an alternative to the construction of further assembly camps in the Reich. Though deportations of Roma on this scale were rare until early 1943, the expulsion of the 5,000 Austrian Roma was not a complete exception: after a wave of arrests across East Prussia, 2,000 Sinti were deported to Białystok prison in January and February 1942. Conditions in the prison were disastrous: starvation and a typhus epidemic led to numerous deaths; on some days, up to 20 Sinti perished. During the spring and summer, the survivors – 950 people – were transferred south to the city of Brest, where they would remain until their deportation to Auschwitz in April 1944. Hundreds of Roma, some of them from Germany, were sent to the Warsaw Ghetto between April and June 1942, where – in contrast to the Austrian Roma in Łódź – they lived alongside the Jews. Just as the Austrian Roma in Łódź and the East Prussian Sinti in Białystok who survived the typhus epidemics in those two places were then deported to Chełmno and Auschwitz-Birkenau, respectively, the final destination for the Roma in the Warsaw Ghetto was also an extermination camp, in this case Treblinka.[15]

Anti-Roma policy in other territories under German occupation was even more deadly. Around the time the 5,000 Austrian Roma were deported to the Łódź Ghetto, Einsatzgruppe D was embarking on a systematic annihilation of the Soviet Roma in southern Ukraine and on the Crimean Peninsula. By spring 1942, Roma were being murdered indiscriminately across all Soviet territories under German occupation, resulting in the death of around 30,000 in total. The approach towards the Roma taken by German occupation forces in Serbia was similarly radical. Between October and December 1941, a substantial proportion of the adult male Roma in Serbia were put to death by firing squads of the Security Police and, above all, the Wehrmacht. The Roma women and children were initially interned in Sajmište concentration camp. At the end of August 1942, the chief of the German Military Administration in Serbia, Harald Turner, proudly reported to General Alexander Löhr, the new Wehrmacht commander in Thessaloniki: 'Jew question, like the Gypsy question, completely eliminated: Serbia the only country in which Jew question and Gypsy question solved.'[16]

As with anti-Jewish policy, the action taken against local Roma populations by German occupation forces in the Soviet Union and Serbia transitioned to widespread, direct murder operations already during 1941 and was not (yet) reflected in measures adopted elsewhere in German-occupied Europe. However, the aforementioned proposals by Conti and Ritter for mass sterilisation demonstrate the existence in early 1940 of deliberations for more immediate and permanent measures for dealing with Roma in the Reich, too. On 10 October 1941, Heydrich, Eichmann, Karl Hermann Frank – higher SS and police leader in Prague – and others even debated sending Roma 'to Stahlecker in Riga'. Walter Stahlecker was chief of Einsatzgruppe A, while the subordinated Einsatzkommando 2 under Rudolf Batz was stationed at the time in Riga, so this could only mean one thing: shooting. This suggestion remained confined to paper, however, and another year would pass before a more uniform policy emerged for dealing with the remaining Roma communities across German-occupied Europe.[17]

'Gypsy Family Camp'

Back to the 23,000 Sinti and Roma in the 'Gypsy family camp' at Auschwitz-Birkenau in mid-1943: as a result of the overcrowded barracks, the poor sanitary conditions and lack of medical treatment, and the inadequate food supply, disease spread rapidly. The most common illnesses were scabies, measles, tuberculosis, typhus, smallpox and noma, an infection primarily affecting extremely impoverished and malnourished children and causing painful tissue degeneration in the face. After the war, the prisoner physician Lucie Adelsberger described the suffering of the children:

> The children's block in the Gypsy camp did not really differ much from the blocks of the adults, but the plight of these little things was even more heartrending. Like the adults, the children were all skin and bones, without muscles and without fat; their thin, parchment-like skin was chafed everywhere from being stretched over the hard bones of their skeleton, and became inflamed with festering wounds. Scabies covered the malnourished bodies from top to bottom, and drained them of their last bit of energy. Their mouths were eaten away by noma ulcers that gnawed deep into the skin, hollowed the jaws and riddled the cheeks like a cancer. [...] Weeks of diarrhoea dissolved their unresisting bodies until the constant drainage of substance left nothing. [...] Hunger and thirst, along with the cold and the pain, kept the children from getting some rest even at night. Their moans swelled like a hurricane and resounded through the entire block until exhaustion caused them to abate, only to start a new crescendo after a brief pause.

Entire families perished together in the 'Gypsy camp'. Elisabeth Guttenberger, who had been deported from Germany in spring 1943, later testified that she lost around thirty relatives, including both her parents and her four siblings. 'The children were the first to die,' she said. 'Day and night, they cried for bread; soon they had all starved.' The morgue in the infirmary was piled high with corpses of children, covered in rats. Many of the dead babies had been born inside the compound – pregnant women had also been deported to Birkenau; there were a total of 389 births in the 'family camp'.[18]

The annihilation of the Sinti and Roma in Auschwitz through disease and starvation was – like that of the Soviet soldiers in POW camps before them – intentional. As Rudolf Höß later expressed it: 'Now, the general conditions in Birkenau were anything but suitable for a family camp. Even if one intended to preserve these Gypsies only for the duration of the war, all necessary requirements were lacking.' The SS, who bore responsibility for the terrible condition in which the prisoners found themselves, responded to the outbreak of epidemics in the camp by murdering its inmates in the gas chambers. On 23 March 1943, 1,700 Roma from Białystok – men, women and children – were gassed in Birkenau. On the grounds of suspected typhus, they had been neither registered nor examined. Instead, they had been isolated in Blocks 20 and 22 of Auschwitz concentration camp prior to being gassed. In a further attempt to contain the typhus epidemic, more than 1,000 sick prisoners – 507 men and 528 women – from the 'Gypsy family camp' were gassed on 25 May; these victims were originally from Austria and had also been transported via Białystok.[19]

By the end of 1943, 70 per cent of the inhabitants of the 'Gypsy family camp' had perished as a result of disease, starvation, gassings and the brutality of the camp personnel. When former commandant Rudolf Höß returned to Auschwitz on 8 May 1944 to oversee the extermination of the Hungarian Jews, only around 6,000 people were still alive in the 'Gypsy camp'. A week later, the Auschwitz camp leadership decided to dissolve it and murder its remaining inmates to create space for the hundreds of thousands of new arrivals they were expecting from Hungary. The following day, on the evening of 16 May, the SS surrounded the compound and ordered the Sinti and Roma to leave the barracks. Only a fraction of the prisoners obeyed the order, however. Forewarned by the camp supervisor, ethnic German SS Sergeant Georg Bonigut, the majority instead offered resistance, took up arms – crowbars, spades, knives and stones – and barricaded themselves in their barracks. Some of them were former Wehrmacht soldiers; they called out that they had been in the military, knew what death looked like and would not die without a fight. As the SS had not counted on resistance, it broke off the operation.[20]

On the same day the SS surrounded the 'Gypsy family camp' in Birkenau, a total of 578 people identified as 'Gypsies or Gypsy cross-breeds', as well as all people 'roaming around like Gypsies' were arrested across the Netherlands and taken to the Westerbork transit camp for Jews on the orders of the commander of the Security Police and the SD in the Netherlands, Erich Naumann. The way in which the target groups were defined was reminiscent of Himmler's decree of 8 December 1938 for 'Combating the Gypsy Plague' in the German Reich. In Westerbork, a selection took place that led to the release of 279 people classified as 'Aryan antisocial elements'. On 19 May 1944, after their heads had been shaved and their valuables taken from them, 245 Roma who were chiefly members of Sinti families – 29 adult men and 38 adult women, 68 adolescent boys and girls aged between sixteen and twenty-one and 110 children under the age of sixteen – were put on freight trains and deported to Auschwitz. The commandant of Westerbork, Albert Konrad Gemmeker, had arranged for a film to be shot of daily life in the camp. The final version included sequences of the Roma and Sinti boarding the trains. One seven-second clip shows a nine-year-old Sinti girl, Settela Steinbach, peering through the crack of the sliding door of the train carriage. Her eyes dart left and right. It is the last visible reminder of the 245 Roma and Sinti deported from the Netherlands on 19 May 1944. The transport reached Auschwitz-Birkenau three days later, on 22 May, where the deportees were incarcerated in the 'Gypsy family camp'.[21]

To avoid a repetition of the defiance encountered on 16 May, the SS selected more than 1,500 Sinti and Roma deemed 'fit for work' – and thus capable of offering resistance – on 23 May, including the former Wehrmacht soldiers and their families, and transferred them from Birkenau to the Auschwitz main camp. On 1 August 1944, a final selection of the Sinti and Roma in the 'family camp' took place: 1,408 prisoners – 918 males, including 105 boys aged between nine and fourteen, and 490 women – responded to a call for the able-bodied to report for work; 2,897 inmates remained in their barracks. Late the following day, the SS surrounded the compound once more; although the Sinti and Roma again fought back, the SS forcibly removed them from the barracks. During the night, all the Sinti and Roma the SS could get its hands on were murdered in Crematoria II and V. The next morning, 3 August, members of the SS once more searched the cleared camp for survivors who had hidden the previous night; they found a woman and two children, whom they also killed. The 'Gypsy family camp', which had existed for seventeen months, was no more. During the night of 2–3 August 1944, the SS murdered a total of 4,200 men, women and children in the gas chambers of Birkenau, including 215 of the 245 Dutch Roma and Sinti deported in May. Settela Steinbach, her mother, two brothers, two sisters, aunt, two nephews and niece were among them.[22]

Of those prisoners who had been selected for work at the beginning of August 1944, the 918 males were sent to Buchenwald and the 490 females to

Ravensbrück women's concentration camp. They accounted for some of the total number of 3,191 Roma transported *back out* of Birkenau, though many of them were subsequently returned and gassed. A return transport from Buchenwald, for instance, arrived in Birkenau on 5 October 1944, containing 1,118 male prisoners, including 800 who had previously been sent from Auschwitz to Buchenwald. The majority of the new arrivals were gassed. In Ravensbrück, numerous women and girls died of illness and malnutrition or as a result of inhuman experiments in sterilisation with X-rays and injections into the uterus.[23]

More than 20,000 Roma in total perished in Auschwitz-Birkenau. At least 7,735 were gassed and 32 were shot following escape attempts. The remaining victims succumbed to the catastrophic living conditions in the so-called Gypsy family camp and the treatment meted out by the camp guards; the Roma died from disease and starvation, were beaten to death and shot. Across German-occupied Europe, a total of 200,000 Roma were deliberately murdered by the Nazi regime during the war years or died as a result of intentional starvation or denial of medical care. More than two-thirds of the Sinti and Roma living in the German Reich and the territories annexed to it perished in Nazi camps. Around 2,000 more were forcibly sterilised on the basis of Himmler's 16 December 1942 deportation order. It is thought that a further 500 Roma were sterilised in accordance with the Law for the Prevention of Offspring with Hereditary Diseases, which provided the legal foundation for the forced sterilisation of up to 400,000 men and women in Germany and Austria between 1934 and 1945.[24]

The National Socialist annihilation of the Roma constituted systematic mass murder that went beyond individual massacres. Without the active and effective participation of the civil service and the police, it would have been scarcely possible. By means of legislation and legal regulations, the Sinti and Roma in Germany had been subjected to discriminatory special laws long before the Nazi era. In Imperial Germany and during the Weimar years, the civil service and the police had made a point of expelling those stigmatised 'Gypsies' from towns and villages, thereby scuppering their attempts to adopt a permanently settled lifestyle. Once the political climate had fundamentally changed after 1933, it was not long before demands for more resolute measures could be heard. Indeed, it was not only the upper echelons of the Criminal Police but also mayors, welfare offices, local police chiefs, county commissioners, district authorities and regional governors who called for imprisonment in concentration camps or permanent expulsion as a way to 'solve' definitively the 'Gypsy problem'. The deportations of Roma to the Government General in 1940, to Łódź in 1941, to Białystok and Warsaw in 1942 and to Auschwitz-Birkenau from 1943 were widely welcomed among German civil servants and police officials as a radical variation on the customary anti-'Gypsy' policy. For all the emphasis placed on their supposedly antisocial behaviour and nomadic way of life, however, it ultimately mattered little in practice whether the individual Roma were itinerant or sedentary. They were killed because they were Roma.[25]

CHAPTER 11
DECENTRALISED 'EUTHANASIA' IN THE GERMAN REICH

Following the official stop to Operation T4 – the murder by gas of the mentally and physically disabled in the German Reich – on 24 August 1941, a second wave of mass killing commenced later the same year, gaining in intensity from summer 1942 onwards. This was the third major series of measures taken to kill the sick in Germany and the annexed territories following the Reich Committee scheme in the more than thirty so-called special children's wards and Operation T4 in the six killing centres. During this third phase, it was no longer gas but rather intentional neglect, over-doses of medication or – and above all – food deprivation that were employed to bring about the death of patients. More victims of 'euthanasia' perished after the stop order of August 1941 was issued than before. This local or decentralised 'euthanasia' campaign claimed the lives of almost 120,000 people between late 1941 and 1945.[1]

In fact, psychiatric patients in German mental hospitals suffered widespread starvation *throughout* the Second World War. The first major regional instance of large-scale fatalities as a result of starvation since the outbreak of the conflict occurred in winter 1939–40, when at least 1,500 mentally ill or disabled patients in the province of Saxony starved to death. This mass mortality was triggered by a drastic reduction in the food allotted to patients by order of the Saxon Ministry of the Interior. The victims had already been severely weakened by the system-atic cost-cutting measures of the previous years, so that when their food was once more reduced after the outbreak of war their bodies could offer no resis-tance. Saxony was not the only Prussian province where death by starvation among psychiatric patients occurred on a large scale prior to the start of Operation T4 in early 1940: this also happened in Hesse-Nassau, where the administrator of all state hospitals, Fritz Bernotat, had already promoted brutal austerity measures to reduce institutional costs well before 1939.[2]

The 'annihilation of worthless life', then, was not only Nazi Germany's first mass-killing programme; it also spanned the entire period of the Second World War. Even the official stop to Operation T4 in August 1941 did not lead to a discontinuation, however temporary, of the wider 'euthanasia' killings. In reality, the stop applied only to murder by gas in the six T4 killing centres. The Saxon Ministry of the Interior, for instance, entrusted Dr Ernst Leonhardt, acting director of Arnsdorf mental hospital near Dresden, which served as a transit institution for the Sonnenstein killing centre, 'with the continued implementation of the special operation' on 30 September, only five weeks after the official stop order. Child 'euthanasia' – which had never utilised gas chambers – not only continued without interruption but was indeed intensified; many of the 'special children's wards' were established only *after* the stop. Another strand of the 'euthanasia' killings that continued unchecked, irrespective of the August 1941 stop order, was the murder of concentration-camp inmates who were sick or no longer able to work.[3]

Operation 14f13

Even before the official stop to Operation T4 in August 1941, other Nazi organisations were keen to make use of the services provided by the T4 killing centres. German concentration camps were growing in number and size, but they did not yet possess the facilities to kill large numbers of prisoners at one time. Early in 1941, Reichsführer SS Heinrich Himmler – who had advised Viktor Brack to close the Grafeneck killing centre after being informed of the public knowledge and popular disquiet regarding that institution – conferred with Brack's boss, the head of the Chancellery of the Führer, Philipp Bouhler, concerning whether and how the personnel and facilities of T4 could be utilised for the concentration camps. Soon thereafter, in the spring of 1941, a new killing operation commenced, aimed at prisoners in the German concentration camps. The killing of concentration-camp inmates selected as 'sick' and 'no longer fit for work' in the gas chambers of the T4 killing centres was designated Operation 14f13 (*Aktion 14f13*). SS camp physicians pre-selected a pool of potential victims, and T4 physicians then visited the concentration camps – singly, in teams of two or three, or as panels of several physicians – to make the final selection of victims. In some concentration camps, the SS, who had plenty of leeway during their initial selections, encouraged those prisoners who had reported sick or unfit for work to volunteer for selection by holding out the prospect of a transfer to a 'recreation camp'. The first known selection took place in early April 1941, when physicians Friedrich Mennecke (also a captain in the SS), Theodor Steinmeyer and Otto Heboid visited Sachsenhausen concentration camp on the outskirts of Oranienburg, north of Berlin. In four days at Sachsenhausen, the three T4 physicians managed to 'process' between 350 and 400 prisoners.[4]

The T4 physicians made no attempt to perform a physical examination of the concentration-camp prisoners, and the speed with which they surveyed large numbers of inmates – at Buchenwald, two of them 'processed' 873 prisoners in two days – precluded any serious medical evaluation. In fact, prisoners' records and conduct determined their evaluation as much as their physical condition. This focus on behaviour applied especially to prisoners designated as racial aliens. Not surprisingly then, the T4 physicians judged Jewish 'patients' with particular severity. With Jews, they did not even bother to enact the pretence of a physical examination. In one of his innumerable letters home to his wife, Eva, whom he addressed as 'mummy', the aforementioned Mennecke described a selection he conducted in late November 1941 in Buchenwald concentration camp. It is illustrative of the superficial and cynical nature of the so-called examinations:

> To begin with, there were still about forty questionnaires to be completed for a first allotment of Aryans [...]. After that, the 'examination' of the patients took place, that is, the presentation of each individual and a comparison of the entries taken from the files. [...] As a second allotment, there then followed a total of 1,200 Jews, none of whom had first to be 'examined', but in whose case it is sufficient to learn from the files the reasons for their arrest (often very extensive!) and record them on the questionnaires. It is, therefore, entirely theoretical work, which will keep us busy up to and including Monday, and perhaps even longer.

After the inaugural trip to Sachsenhausen in April 1941, T4 physicians visited most of the main camps, including Auschwitz (May 1941), Buchenwald (June and November–December 1941), Mauthausen (June–July 1941), Dachau (September 1941), Ravensbrück (November 1941 and

January 1942), Groß-Rosen (January 1942), Flossenbürg (March 1942) and Neuengamme (April 1942). The physicians were sometimes accompanied during these trips by their wives or even their children. Mennecke's wife joined him on his trips to Buchenwald, Ravensbrück and Groß-Rosen, while Professor Paul Nitsche brought along his wife and daughter during his trip to southern Germany to carry out selections at Dachau.[5]

Operation 14f13 was a watershed in the history of the concentration camps: for the first time, camp inmates became victims of systematic mass murder. The actual killing of the selected prisoners, however, did not take place in the camps themselves. Prior to 24 August 1941, when Hitler ordered a stop to the murder of the disabled by gas, the victims of Operation 14f13 were gassed in facilities otherwise occupied with the killing of the disabled, specifically at Hartheim and Sonnenstein. For instance, a total of 1,031 prisoners from Sachsenhausen (269), Buchenwald (187, almost half of them Jews) and Auschwitz (575) concentration camps were deported to Sonnenstein in June and July 1941, where they were gassed. Not one of the 575 Auschwitz inmates was mentally ill. During this first phase of Operation 14f13 from April to August 1941, a total of around 2,500 concen-tration-camp prisoners were murdered in Hartheim and Sonnenstein. After the official stop to Operation T4 in late August 1941, only concentra-tion-camp prisoners were gassed in T4 killing centres. Four centres were still operational: Bernburg (successor to Brandenburg), Hadamar (successor to Grafeneck), Hartheim and Sonnenstein. Hadamar was never used for this purpose, however, and its gassing facilities were demolished at the end of July 1942 (though systematic killings of psychiatric patients by overdoses of medication, starvation rations or intentional neglect did resume there the following month). Although the gassing facilities at Sonnenstein were like-wise not dismantled until summer 1942, this killing centre was only used for gassing concentration-camp prisoners up to August 1941. Thus, after August 1941, Bernburg and Hartheim were the only killing centres used for Operation 14f13. During the following weeks and months, those responsible for 14f13 stepped up the murder of Jewish prisoners. This new approach was no doubt linked to the recent escalation of Nazi anti-Jewish policy in general: in summer 1941, the SS Einsatzgruppen had begun to murder hundreds of thousands of Jewish men, women and children in the occupied Soviet terri-tories. From now on, most Jews in the concentration camps would be assessed by the T4 physicians. The 1,200 Jewish men evaluated by Mennecke in Buchenwald in November 1941 comprised more than 85 per cent of all Jewish prisoners at that camp.[6]

Not long after the extension of Operation 14f13 in the second half of 1941, the programme was cut back. The camp commandants were informed of this curtailment on 26 March 1942 in a secret communication sent by Oswald Pohl's WVHA. From now on, only prisoners who were permanently unable to work would be sent to their deaths. All other prisoners, including those who might regain their fitness for work, were to be deployed for the German war effort. In any case, by this time, both the T4 personnel and the SS had embarked on a far bigger killing programme further east, in the Government General: Operation Reinhardt. The first transport of Jews had arrived at Bełżec extermination camp little more than a week earlier. By the time Operation 14f13 was curtailed in March 1942, some 6,500 concentration-camp prisoners had died in the T4 gas chambers inside a year. Though a scaled-back version of Operation 14f13 continued after the WVHA directive of 26 March, prisoner selections by T4 physicians in the concentration camps had come to an end by mid-1942. Thereafter, SS camp physicians themselves carried out prisoner selections autonomously, without questionnaires or T4 visits, though the actual killings still took place in the T4 centres.[7]

At Bernburg, the 14f13 killings continued to take place in the gas chambers until late 1942, by which time a total of around 5,000 men and women from concentration camps had been gassed there. The Bernburg victims were almost exclusively Jewish prisoners, many of them perfectly fit for work. Just as disabled Jews had been murdered in Grafeneck, Brandenburg and Bernburg in Operation T4, the gassing of Jewish prisoners in Bernburg during Operation 14f13 is a further example of the direct integration of the 'euthanasia' killing centres into the Holocaust. During 1942, primarily transports from Dachau concentration camp reached the Hartheim killing centre, the first on 15 January and the last on 8 December. A total of 2,593 concentration-camp prisoners from Dachau were murdered in Hartheim.[8]

On 27 April 1943, Richard Glücks wrote to fifteen concentration-camp commandants and conveyed an order by Himmler to limit 14f13 selections exclusively to prisoners with actual mental, not physical, disorders. This order effectively signalled the abandonment of the central programme for murdering prisoners deemed 'unfit for work' and officially ended SS–T4 collaboration in this particular area. The dismantling of the gassing installations at Bernburg in April 1943 coincided with the official winding-up of Operation 14f13. Though no transports from the concentration camps had been sent to Hartheim during 1943, gassings of prisoners resumed there – in contrast to Sonnenstein and Bernburg – in 1944. In the spring, a full year after the official termination of Operation 14f13, the commandant of Mauthausen concentration camp, Franz Ziereis, ordered the SS garrison physician, SS Captain Friedrich Entress, to restart the selections. During this third phase of killings, from April to November 1944, prisoners from Mauthausen and Gusen concentration camps were gassed at Hartheim. Finally, in December 1944, the gassing facilities at Hartheim were also demolished; Mauthausen prisoners were used for the job. By this time, a total of 10,000 prisoners from Mauthausen, Gusen, Dachau and Ravensbrück had been gassed in Hartheim alone. Hartheim Castle thus holds the dubious distinction of being the killing centre where not only the most victims perished during Operation T4 (1940–41) but also during Operation 14f13 (1941–42 and 1944). All in all, as many as 20,000 people were killed on the basis of SS–T4 collaboration in Operation 14f13, at least half of whom were Jews.[9]

Regional Starvation Initiatives

The first province to resume the transfer of psychiatric patients to other regions after the stop order of August 1941 was the Rhineland in summer 1942. The destinations included Hesse-Nassau, Saxony and Pomerania. In Hesse-Nassau and Pomerania, close associates of the local Gauleiters established killing centres for the second 'euthanasia' phase in the Reich. Saxony initially functioned as a reception area for patients from regions that were at risk of bombing, and developed from summer 1943 – like Pomerania and Hesse-Nassau before it – into a core region for the murder of the sick. The first inter-regional transfer of the second wave of 'euthanasia' killings fully reflected the measures adopted in disaster medicine to tackle the impact of the air war. After heavy air raids on Cologne at the end of May 1942, the Gauleiter there pushed for the evacuation of municipal retirement homes, in order to be able to use the buildings as auxiliary hospitals and sickbays.

During the weeks that followed, some psychiatric patients in the vicinity of Cologne were transferred to other institutions in the Rhine Province. In August 1942, another group of transfers took around 370 psychiatric patients from the Catholic nursing home of Hoven, in the town of Düren, to Hadamar. On the orders of Rudolf Hartung, head of the Cologne Gau office for public health, these patients had been forced to make space for residents of a Cologne retirement home that had been turned into an auxiliary hospital for sick soldiers and civilians after air raids had destroyed numerous Cologne healthcare facilities. Three months later, the majority of the patients transferred to Hadamar were dead, murdered by an overdose of sedatives.[10]

What started as an isolated case became, less than a year later, the default solution in emergency situations. Between May and July 1943, the cities of Essen, Düsseldorf and Cologne transferred not only numerous hospital patients but also 4,000 residents of psychiatric wards, above all those who had little or no contact with their relatives. For a quarter of them, the journey ended in the starvation institutions in the east, another quarter died in a Hessian killing centre, while others perished in Bavaria and Pomerania. The majority of these transfers in summer 1943 were carried out parallel to the evacuation of the infirm and casualties of bombing raids; as a result, unlike the T4 transports, they attracted little public attention. By the end of the war, around 6,000 psychiatric patients from the Rhine Province alone had lost their lives in this way. Similar series of transports are documented for the period from summer 1943 in the Ruhr region and in Hamburg, often carried out simultaneously with large-scale transfers of hospital patients requiring long-term care.[11]

Developments in southern Germany in 1942 and 1943 were different to those in the west of the Reich. First, the western provinces became targets of Allied bombing raids at a comparatively early stage, so that capacity bottlenecks in hospital care were a far more pressing problem there than in the south. Second, discussions in Bavaria took place directly between the Ministry of the Interior and the mental hospitals subordinated to it; local authorities were not involved to the same extent as in the Rhineland. Third, in Bavaria (and, likewise, Saxony) initiatives were taken to find 'solutions' on the ground to the capacity problems in hospital care by means of the institutionalisation of a regional 'euthanasia' system. Dr Walter Schultze, section head in the Bavarian Ministry of the Interior, hosted a meeting of asylum directors

on 17 November 1942 to discuss urgent food questions. During the conference, the director of the mental hospital in Kaufbeuren, Valentin Faltlhauser,
suggested dividing the sick into two categories according to their ability to
work. Those unfit for work would be fed a 'special diet', with which he had
already been experimenting in his own institution since August. The fare
proposed by Faltlhauser contained no fat, scarcely any meat and little in the
way of carbohydrates. The food saved in this way would be allocated to those
sick patients who worked. It was clear to all present at the conference that
Faltlhauser's proposal for solving the food problems aimed at a reduction in
the patient numbers. It was a continuation of the 'euthanasia' campaign by
other means, namely a 'gradual starvation of the sick', as one of the attendees
put it. In the wake of the conference, the Ministry of the Interior issued a
decree in which it called on psychiatric institutions to provide a better diet to
those patients 'who perform useful work or are undergoing therapeutic treatment, as well as those children still capable of learning [. . .], at the expense of
the other patients'. The selections carried out thereafter in Bavarian mental
institutions inevitably led to a rapid increase in mortality rates.[12]

Eglfing-Haar mental hospital near Munich soon joined Faltlhauser's Irsee
Monastery near Kaufbeuren in introducing the 'special diet'. From January
1943, patients at Eglfing-Haar subject to the special diet were grouped in two
buildings: numbers 22 and 25. These came to be known as the 'starvation
houses'. The ruthless enforcement of the special diet was overseen by director
Hermann Pfannmüller, who visited the kitchens at Eglfing-Haar three or four
times a week. He announced to one of the orderlies: 'We'll keep them without
fats or proteins and then they'll die of their own accord.' The introduction of
this starvation diet indeed resulted in the death of 444 patients at Eglfing-Haar.
During the course of 1943, the 'special diet' was also introduced in the Bavarian
mental hospitals in Ansbach, Erlangen, Klingenmünster and Mainkofen. From
February 1943, at least 2,503 psychiatric patients from Alsterdorf (Hamburg),
Aplerbeck, Eickelborn, Grafenberg, Hausen, Süchteln (all in the Rhineland or
Westphalia), Neuruppin (Brandenburg), Wiesloch, Emmendingen (Baden),
Frankenthal and Lörchingen (Lorraine) were transferred to Bavarian institutions. Further transfers from summer 1943 brought the total number of
patients in the ten Bavarian mental hospitals to 19,869 – 300 more than the
number accommodated in the *thirteen* Bavarian institutions in existence in
1939. The death rate at these hospitals was particularly high among the patients

transferred from elsewhere. They were either the subject of targeted killings or died as a result of the wretched living conditions.[13]

The central German regions had long been regarded as safe from air raids. Therefore, the cities in northern and western Germany affected by bombing attempted to evacuate their sick – both the physically infirm and psychiatric patients – further into the interior of the Reich. After heavy bombing raids on the Ruhr region, the province of Westphalia held out the prospect in June 1943 of transferring *all* its psychiatric patients. During the second half of that month, the Reich Association of Mental Hospitals began to draw up transfer plans for psychiatric patients in western Germany. By September 1943, the Düsseldorf Gau alone had evacuated around 2,800 sick people to central Germany. In some regions, however, free beds were very scarce. In Saxony, for instance, almost two-thirds of all psychiatric beds had, with the approval of the office of Gauleiter Martin Mutschmann, been appropriated for other purposes. As a result of the transfers from provinces in western Prussia, living conditions in the overcrowded Saxon mental hospitals deteriorated further. In this acute situation, and encouraged by Gauleiter Mutschmann, Paul Nitsche – former director of the Pirna-Sonnenstein mental asylum in Saxony and T4 physician in Operation 14f13, and current medical director of 'euthanasia' headquarters in Berlin – approached Karl Brandt, now Hitler's general commissioner for sanitation and health, at the end of June with 'a very specific proposal in the E. [= euthanasia] question'. In Nazi doublespeak, this meant once more murdering large numbers of the mentally sick.[14]

An Expanded Mandate

Nitsche had good reasons for approaching Brandt rather than, say, Reich Health Leader Leonardo Conti with his proposal. Brandt was not only widely known as the plenipotentiary of the original 'euthanasia' programme; as his escort physician and now general commissioner for sanitation and health, Brandt also had ready access to Hitler. On the basis of Nitsche's proposal, Brandt indeed succeeded in obtaining Hitler's approval for the authorisation of a group of around ten physicians once again to 'administer euthanasia in individual cases'. Having secured this mandate, Nitsche hosted a meeting of like-minded asylum directors and physicians on 17 August 1943 in Berlin. On 25 August, he wrote to Max de Crinis, who held a university chair in psychiatry in Cologne and at the Charité in Berlin and had accompanied Nitsche during his visit to Brandt: 'Concerning our initiative with Prof. Br. [= Brandt], [...] he has granted me the authorisation via Mr Blankenburg to proceed in accordance with the E.-proposal I presented to him verbally.' (Werner Blankenburg was Viktor Brack's deputy and head of Office IIb within Brack's Main Office II in the Chancellery of the Führer.) On the basis of this authorisation, which Nitsche subsequently referred to in internal correspondence as the 'E-mandate', the director of the Waldheim mental hospital in Saxony, Dr Gerhard Wischer, ordered the 'necessary medication' from Nitsche in Berlin on 13 September: 'By the way, the work discussed in Berlin [on 17 August] proceeds smoothly; I'm expecting an average of twenty to thirty treated patients per month. Neither with the staff nor on the part of the relatives have any difficulties arisen so far.'[15]

From late summer 1943 onwards, more than 9,000 patients died in the Saxon mental hospitals from an overdose of one of the barbiturates barbital or phenobarbital (a model developed by Nitsche himself in early 1940 and also used to murder children in the wards of the Reich Committee scheme) or a morphine–scopolamine combination. In their use of medication to kill patients, the Saxon health authorities fell back on regional models: as early as autumn 1939, Gauleiter Mutschmann had called on asylum directors in Saxony to sedate restless patients by administering an increased dose of sedatives and simultaneously reducing their food; patients' deaths were not only accepted but expressly desired. Alone in Großschweidnitz mental hospital, which had already served as a transit institution for the Sonnenstein killing centre during Operation T4, around 2,400 patients lost their lives between late summer 1943 and September 1944 after receiving an overdose of one of the aforementioned drugs. Around 80 per cent of the victims at Großschweidnitz during this period had been transferred there during the evacuation measures. In December 1943, a 'special children's ward' was also set up at Großschweidnitz. Indeed, the murders in Großschweidnitz spanned the entire period of the war. Under director Alfred Schulz, more than 5,700 patients were killed there between 1939 and the end of the war in May 1945. This figure does not include the approximately 2,500 patients sent from Großschweidnitz to the Sonnenstein killing centre.[16]

Despite appearances, however, Brandt's authorisation (and its approval by Hitler) did not signify the start of a new wave of transregional, centrally organised patient killings, that is, a resumption of the expanded 'euthanasia' programme that had been stopped in August 1941. First, the authorisation was limited to a small number of physicians, and an intensification of the killings is documented above all for the mental institutions in Saxony, not by chance the domain of the man whose proposal had prompted Brandt's authorisation in the first place, Paul Nitsche. This suggests that the geographical focus of Brandt's authorisation was central Germany. This mandate evidently served to reduce the overcrowding in the Saxon institutions caused by the transports from western Germany and, simultaneously, to create space for new transfers by means of killing the sick. The aforementioned Gerhard Wischer wrote to Nitsche accordingly on 4 November 1943: 'I [...] have plenty to do, as almost all new admissions from the area between Leipzig, Chemnitz and Meißen come to me. Of course, I could never accommodate these arrivals if I did not carry out corresponding measures for making space available – which proceed very smoothly. Having said that, I have a real shortage of necessary medication.' Second, neither Brandt nor anyone else in Berlin decided who or how many would be murdered; these decisions were left to the discretion of the individual institutions. The 'euthanasia' headquarters in Berlin were responsible, however, for providing the medication, as Wischer's letters to Nitsche from 13 September and 4 November, quoted above, demonstrate. Third, patient killings in Meseritz-Obrawalde (Pomerania) and Hadamar had already resumed in summer 1942, a full year *before* Brandt's authorisation. In Großschweidnitz (Saxony) they had never stopped. Indeed, Großschweidnitz, Hadamar and Meseritz-Obrawalde were the three central sites of killing during the second 'euthanasia' phase.[17]

Meseritz-Obrawalde – probably the most notorious killing hospital during the period of decentralised 'euthanasia' – had accommodated 900 patients in 1939, but during the war the institution was filled to capacity with at least 2,000 patients, for whom there were only three specialist physicians. Its conversion to a site of systematic patient killings began in winter 1941–42. This coincided with the appointment by Pomeranian Provincial Governor Franz Schwede-Coburg of Walter Grabowski as economic director in November 1941. Handicapped patients were transferred from more than thirty German cities, usually at night. Many patients from Hamburg arrived dead at Meseritz-Obrawalde, after travelling in unheated trains in the middle of winter. The first to be killed were those classified as unfit for work, patients who caused extra work for the nursing staff or were considered troublesome, anyone who attempted to escape or inform third parties of conditions at the asylum, and anyone voicing suspicions about the poisonings. The murders were committed by means of injection or oral administration of overdoses of painkillers or sedatives. The patients also died from a deliberately induced state of exhaustion and chronic undernourishment, while at the same time the systematic exploitation of the patients for labour was intensified. Between 1942 and 1945, a total of 18,000 patients were murdered at Meseritz-Obrawalde.[18]

Hadamar was the only institution utilised as a killing centre during both the first killing phase, when it used gas, and, after the stop order, in the period of decentralised 'euthanasia', when it used overdoses of medication, deliberate food deprivation or the intentional withholding of medical care. During this second phase of killings at Hadamar, from August 1942 to March 1945, a total of 4,411 patients were murdered. Most of them came from institutions in Bremen, Hamburg, the Rhineland, Hesse-Nassau, Brandenburg, Baden and Alsace. The circle of victims was extended beyond the mentally sick and disabled to include forced labourers suffering from tuberculosis, residents of large cities who had been bombed out and were experiencing severe mental trauma, Wehrmacht soldiers who could not cope with the psychological effects of combat and children in care who had a Jewish parent. The victims were no longer selected by the T4 headquarters in Berlin. Instead, every morning chief physician Dr Adolf Wahlmann decided with the assistance of his head nurse, Irmgard Huber, and head orderly, Heinrich Ruoff, who would be murdered that night. Sentenced to death after the war for his part in the killings at Hadamar, orderly Karl Willig stated before going to the gallows: 'I did my duty as a German official. God is my witness.'[19]

The independence of action displayed by medical personnel during the decentralised 'euthanasia' is perhaps best illustrated by events at Kaufbeuren-Irsee. There, patient killings continued even *after* Germany's unconditional surrender on 8 May 1945, which ended the Second World War in Europe. On 29 May, fully three weeks after the cessation of hostilities, the staff murdered a child for the last time when Sister Mina Wörle, the head nurse of the 'special children's ward', administered a lethal injection to four-year-old Richard

Jenne. At 1:10 p.m., Director Faltlhauser recorded the death of the child from 'typhus'. Though American troops had entered the town of Kaufbeuren in late April, they were deterred for several weeks from venturing inside the hospital by a large sign warning of an outbreak of the disease there. As a result, the routine killing was able to continue beyond the formal end of the war.[20]

Based on the present state of research, at least 196,000 mentally sick and disabled people – predominantly patients in psychiatric institutions – were murdered between 1939 and 1945 within the borders of the German Reich, including the annexed territories. If we add the approximately 80,000 killed in institutions in the occupied Polish, French and Soviet territories, as well as the 20,000 concentration-camp inmates murdered in the T4 facilities, the death toll rises to almost 300,000. The so-called euthanasia programme was deliberately launched by the National Socialist apparatus of power and implemented in a planned and systematic manner; as a general tendency, it resulted in the complete annihilation of a group of human beings clearly defined by the perpetrators. The objective of the murders was the racial–biological cleansing and strengthening of the German nation. The mentally and physically disabled had no way of escaping the categorisation imposed on them as 'life unworthy of life'.[21]

The range of killing methods used in the various 'euthanasia' programmes in the Reich and the occupied territories – gas, shooting and starvation, especially – seems emblematic of Nazi mass killings as a whole. Of these methods, it was above all starvation that was employed to murder psychiatric patients during the last three years of the war. Like poison gas and bullets, the Nazis used starvation on a huge scale to murder millions of human beings in the territories under their control. The victims belonged to different groups, they perished in different surroundings and contexts – captured Red Army soldiers in POW camps, residents of Soviet urban centres, ghettoised Jews in occupied Poland, psychiatric patients in German asylums – but they all suffered a protracted death brought about by deliberate starvation.

CHAPTER 12
SUPPRESSION OF THE WARSAW UPRISING

As discussed earlier, German preventive terror and reprisals resulted in the deaths of around a million people – generally unarmed civilians and mostly non-Jews. These people lived primarily in rural areas. In some cases, substantial numbers of urban dwellers under German occupation also fell victim to so-called pacification operations and anti-partisan warfare. Like the more than 1 million residents of Leningrad who were starved to death, these civilians were targeted by German occupation forces in deliberate policies of mass murder (rather than dying in aerial bombardments, however indiscriminate, or as a result of other acts of conventional warfare). The most devastating instance of mass killing of this type in an urban centre took place in August and September 1944 during the suppression of the Warsaw Uprising. In a city of 1 million people, as many as 185,000 civilians lost their lives in the slaughter unleashed by German forces.[1]

Following the discovery in April 1943 of the graves of 22,000 Polish officers murdered by the NKVD in Katyn Forest near Smolensk three years earlier, the Polish government-in-exile in London called for an independent investigation into the killings. Joseph Stalin responded by breaking off diplomatic relations with the Poles. On 4 January 1944, the Red Army crossed the old, pre-war Polish–Soviet border in its offensive against the Wehrmacht, occupying ever-greater swathes of what had been eastern Poland but was now western Belarus, and thus part of the Soviet Union. On 23 June, the Red Army launched Operation Bagration against Army Group Centre in Belarus, succeeding by early July in shattering the German front line. In response to the rapid advance of Soviet forces, the Polish Home Army (*Armia Krajowa*), whose allegiance was to the Polish government-in-exile in London, organised a series of offensives against German forces codenamed Operation Tempest. This included attempts in July to capture and occupy the formerly Polish cities of Vilnius and Lvov before the arrival of the Red Army. In both cases, the Home Army attack stalled long enough to allow the Soviets to arrive; although Home Army and Red Army units then cooperated in capturing both cities, Polish troops were thereafter promptly disarmed and often arrested by their Soviet counterparts.[2]

On 20 July, meanwhile, a handful of German military officers tried – and failed – to assassinate Adolf Hitler. This piece of news gave some hope to Polish Home Army commanders in Warsaw; it led some of them to believe that Germany had lost the will to fight, and that a bold blow might drive German forces from Warsaw before the Red Army could arrive. As it turned out, nothing could have been further from the truth. Two days later, on 22 July, the Red Army captured the first large city west of the Bug river, Chełm. The same day, the Committee for National Liberation was proclaimed 65km to the northwest, in Lublin, as the 'legitimate government' of Poland. The Lublin Committee had the backing of the Soviets and functioned in opposition to the London-based Polish government. It was furthermore clear by late July that it was the Red Army – whose offensive against the Wehrmacht had by now resulted in it occupying more than half of pre-war Poland – that would liberate the country. If the Home Army did nothing, Stalin's followers would most likely be installed in Warsaw, too.[3]

On 25 July, the Polish government in London granted the Home Army in Warsaw the authority to begin an uprising in the capital at a time of its choosing. Warsaw had in fact been excluded from the planning for Operation Tempest back in March; the Warsaw section of the Home Army had there-upon sent many of its arms to the east of the country, where they were subsequently lost to the Soviets in places such as Vilnius and Lvov. Given the nature of German anti-partisan tactics, an uprising in Warsaw looked to many like suicide. The argument in favour of the uprising was that the rebellion could not fail: whether or not the Poles defeated the Germans, the Red Army was moving fast and would arrive in Warsaw in a few days. On this logic, which prevailed, the only question seemed to be whether Poles would first make an effort to liberate their own capital. The Poles were caught between an approaching Red Army and occupying German forces. They could not defeat the Germans on their own, so they had to hope that the Soviet advance would prompt a German retreat and that there would be some interval between the Wehrmacht's withdrawal and the Red Army's arrival. The Poles in Warsaw hoped that the interval would not be too brief, so that they could establish themselves as the Polish government before the Soviets arrived. In fact, the interval was too long.[4]

A Three-Part Order

The uprising was launched as planned at 5 o'clock on the afternoon of Tuesday, 1 August 1944. The entire city erupted in waves of explosions, gunfire and movements of soldiers and civilians seeking cover. Fighting alongside the 40,000 Home Army troops were around 1,700 members of other resistance units, including the communist People's Army, and a motley collection of foreign nationals, some of whom were Hungarian and Italian deserters who chose to fight on the Polish side. The Home Army was equipped with a mere 1,000 rifles, 1,700 pistols, 300 machine pistols, 60 sub-machine guns, 7 machine guns, 35 anti-tank guns and 25,000 hand grenades. Even after capturing 6 howitzers, 7 mortars, 13 heavy and 57 light machine guns, 373 rifles, 103 pistols and 27 Panzerfaust anti-tank weapons during the first days of fighting, the Home Army still had nowhere near enough weapons to take on heavily defended German areas. It was little wonder, then, that the insurrectionists were unable to take key installations from the Germans, such as bridges, airports, railway stations and police and military outposts during the first crucial days of the uprising. By the end of the third day, the Home Army had admittedly captured more than 50km^2 of territory, including a large chunk of Żoliborz (one of the city's northern districts), much of the Old Town, the southern part of Śródmieście (the city's central district) and a huge sector of Wola (a district in the west of the city). In doing so, however, they had lost over 2,000 fighters, compared to just 500 German casualties.[5]

Though the Germans had made few preparations, they were not caught completely by surprise. It had been hard to disguise the mobilisation going on within the city. In fact, the SS and police leader in Warsaw, Paul Otto Geibel, placed his 5,000 SS and police personnel on full alert at 4 o'clock on the afternoon of the 1st, an hour before the uprising began. It was clear, however, that the Warsaw garrison alone would not be able to crush the insurgency. On the evening of the first day, the logbook of the German Ninth Army – stationed at the Vistula river, just east of Warsaw city centre – calmly noted 'the outbreak of the expected insurgency' and requested police forces to be brought in to crush the uprising. Thus, with the Wehrmacht stubbornly holding its positions, the uprising would be a matter for Heinrich Himmler's SS and German police. On 1 August, Hitler told Himmler that the city of Warsaw was to be completely destroyed. This was not the first time he had threatened the complete destruction of a metropolis. It had been the fate intended for Leningrad, Moscow and Kiev before military developments dictated otherwise. For the city of Warsaw, however, there would be no reprieve. Himmler placed overall command of operations in Warsaw in the hands of Erich von dem Bach-Zelewski. As higher SS and police leader for central Russia and chief of anti-partisan operations, Bach-Zelewski had been Himmler's most senior representative on the ground in the killing fields of Belarus, where he had overseen the murder of hundreds of thousands of civilians. On vacation when the Warsaw Uprising erupted, he was called back to meet Himmler in Cracow on 4 August.[6]

Atrocities were committed even before Bach-Zelewski assumed personal command in Warsaw. From the first day of the uprising, German forces already on the ground responded by rounding up large groups of Varsovians and taking them first to Gestapo headquarters on Szucha Avenue in the district of Śródmieście, and from there to the ruins of the former cadet school on nearby Bagatela Street. According to one witness:

> I saw piles of bodies. The victims were led up to these piles and then the killers approached with small firearms and shot them in the back of the head. Among those killed, I saw a man with a child in his arms. First the child was shot, then the child's father. Among the victims were children as young as 4. Young boys aged 14 were shot. I saw piles of dead old men, cripples, a man with false legs. [...] On 1st VIII, 980 people were shot. The pile was doused in petrol and naphtha and set alight. Starting from that day, similar executions were held daily. The shooting lasted all day. By my calculations, anywhere from 1,500 to 2,000 people were shot.

The victims of these mass shootings had been taken from their homes or off the streets in the immediate vicinity of Gestapo headquarters.[7]

After his meeting with Himmler in Cracow, Bach-Zelewski reached Warsaw on 5 August; it was day five of the uprising. Following the German withdrawal from Belarus, experienced anti-partisan units were available to reinforce the Warsaw garrison. These included the notorious SS Storm Brigade Dirlewanger, a penal unit named after its commander, Dr Oskar Dirlewanger, a sadistic, habitual criminal and – like Bach-Zelewski – another veteran of the slaughter in Belarus. Before being expanded to brigade size, it had been deployed for anti-partisan warfare in Belarus between February 1942 and summer 1944, first as the SS Special Battalion Dirlewanger and later as the SS Special Commando Dirlewanger. Its name may have changed, but its methods had not. In Belarus, it had been one of the most murderous of all German formations and killed at a conservative estimate 30,000 civilians. During Operation Cottbus in May and June 1943, it had forced locals to cross minefields on the access routes to partisan camps. Dirlewanger's forces started to arrive in Warsaw on 4 August: an advance guard of one battalion with 365 men. Two more battalions, a sub-machine-gun company, a mortar company and an anti-tank company followed. In all, the brigade had 16 officers, 865 men and a detachment of 677 Azerbaijani troops by the time it was ready to move on Warsaw.[8]

Bach-Zelewski's chief of operations in Warsaw was the higher SS and police leader in the Wartheland, Heinz Reinefarth. The newly arrived 'combat group' was placed under Reinefarth's command, and Himmler issued him with a three-part order:

1. Captured insurgents ought to be killed regardless of whether they are fighting in accordance with the Hague Convention or not.
2. The part of the population not fighting, women and children, should likewise be killed.
3. The whole town must be levelled to the ground, i.e. houses, streets, offices – everything that is in the town.

Though the order to level Warsaw had come from Hitler, it was Himmler who had added the directive to murder civilians. Even by Nazi standards, this was an extraordinary stipulation. In practice, German preventive terror and reprisals not uncommonly resulted in the indiscriminate killing of all residents of certain towns and villages, as we have seen. It was comparatively rare, however, for explicit orders to be issued in advance for the murder of all civilians in a given area – men, women and children – without distinction. This type of thing was normally reserved for Europe's Jewish population.

These orders to destroy Warsaw and kill all its inhabitants also received the support of the Wehrmacht. Heinz Guderian, appointed chief of the Army General Staff following the failed attempt on Hitler's life on 20 July 1944, passed them on down the chain of command, as did General Georg-Hans Reinhardt – who would be appointed commander of Army Group Centre on 16 August – and Lieutenant General Nikolaus von Vormann, the commander of the Ninth Army.[9]

The Wola Massacres

By 4 August, the advancing Red Army had managed to secure two bridgeheads on the west bank of the Vistula river: the road to Warsaw was clear. Contrary to Polish expectations, however, the Red Army now ceased its rapid advance from the east. Many residents of Warsaw woke up on the sunny morning of 5 August still hopeful that the Soviets were coming and that their ordeal would soon be over. In fact, the worst was yet to come. The principal reinforcements of the German garrison had by now arrived and SS Major General Reinefarth launched his assault on the working-class neighbourhood of Wola, in the west of the city. The operation began at 7 a.m. Reinefarth's combat group comprised SS, police and Wehrmacht units. Security Regiment 608 of the 203rd Security Division under Colonel Willi Schmidt moved towards the northern cemeteries. A group of three motorised police companies entered the city to the south of them, while two Dirlewanger battalions and an Azerbaijani battalion moved up Wolska Street, the neighbourhood's main thoroughfare.[10]

The Dirlewanger Brigade, which formed the nucleus of Reinefarth's combat group, had a military objective: to relieve German garrison headquarters in the Saxon Gardens, where city commander Major General Rainer Stahel was surrounded in the Brühl Palace. The brigade lifted the Home Army's barricades on Wolska Street by marching Poles in front of them and forcing them to do the work, using women and children as human shields in the meantime, and raping some of the women along the way. As they moved west, they destroyed each and every building, one by one, using gasoline and hand grenades. Dirlewanger's men likewise followed the other parts of Himmler's order to the letter: they spared no one, pitilessly murdering women, children, the elderly, the wounded and the sick. In the orphanage of the Orthodox church at 149 Wolska Street, they massacred

350 children, gunning them down, then smashing the children's skulls with their rifle butts. Similar scenes took place during the destruction of the hospital for female orphans run by the nuns of St Vincent de Paul, which was burned to the ground.[11]

No mercy was shown in Wola's other hospitals either. Men from the Dirlewanger Brigade arrived at the Wolski Hospital at noon on 5 August and drove everyone out, before shooting them – 2,000 people, including women and children – at the nearby railway viaduct on Górczewska Street. Wolski Hospital was burned down, killing those hiding inside and the sick and injured who had been unable to move. Another of Dirlewanger's targets that day was the St Lazarus Hospital, which contained approximately 300 sick, 300 wounded, the hospital staff and 600 civilians who had taken refuge in the hospital. Around 50 members of the medical and nursing staff were taken to St Stanisław Hospital. Apart from a small number of people who managed to hide or escape, everyone else was murdered: 600 people were burned in the cellars, while 335 people were shot in the courtyard. After Dirlewanger's men had removed the Germans who had been cared for by Poles, the whole building was burned down. The same fate befell the Charles and Mary Hospital the following afternoon. Only the St Stanisław Hospital at 37 Wolska Street was spared; here, Oskar Dirlewanger and his staff established their headquarters, painting a Red Cross emblem on the roof. Although it had not been the scene of a massacre, killing nonetheless continued here, too. A few days after the hospital had been occupied, the SS took two young Home Army prisoners, hanged them from a tree in the hospital courtyard and decorated their corpses with the red-and-white flag of Poland. On the very first evening, the men of the Dirlewanger Brigade brought some of the nurses back to camp; to the accompaniment of flute music, they stripped and gang-raped them, raised a gallows and then hanged the naked women along with a doctor. The seizure, rape and murder of young female members of the hospital staff would be repeated on subsequent nights. After raping Warsaw women, one SS captain was known for putting hand grenades in the vaginas of his victims and detonating them.[12]

Many people were shot in their homes, in cellars and attics, on staircases, in courtyards; many perished in the flames of the blazing houses. Across the street from Sowiński Park, the Germans set up three machine guns. They then emptied nearby residential buildings of all their tenants, including

Wacława Szlacheta, who was taken from her home on Wolska Street along with her husband, two sons and two daughters. After the males and females had been separated, they were lined up against the park railings. Then the Germans opened fire:

> I fell to the ground by the second post of the railings, counting from the gate. I was unhit. Bodies fell across my legs. My youngest daughter Alina was lying next to me, still alive. Lying on the pavement I could see and hear the German soldiers walking among those on the ground and kicking them to see if anyone was alive. Those who were, they finished off with one shot from their revolvers. I was on my stomach but my head was propped on a food basket and so I could more or less make out what was happening. In this way I was able to see a German soldier (I do not know what unit he was from) kick the woman next to me who was still alive and then shoot her. Then I saw him move to a pram in which the several months-old twins of my neighbour, Jakubczyk, were lying and shoot them. All the time I could hear the groans of the dying. [...] After lunch – I do not know the time exactly – a German finished off my daughter Alina.

Over a thousand civilians were murdered at Sowiński Park that day.[13]

Killing Warsaw civilians in their own homes proved to be a time-consuming process. No doubt owing to its thoroughness in implementing Himmler's orders to kill all residents of Warsaw, the Dirlewanger Brigade advanced only 400m on 5 August. Therefore, Reinefarth decided to have prisoners gathered in large groups and murdered en masse. To this end, the Germans established several central killing sites across Wola. In addition to Sowiński Park and the aforementioned railway viaduct on Górczewska Street, these included factories. In the days following the mass shootings at these locations, Polish workers were forced to burn the bodies. One of them, Franciszek Zasada, later described this gruesome task:

> In the farm machinery warehouse at 85 Wolska Street we found about 300 bodies in cassocks and about 80 in ordinary clothes. We burned them on the spot. On the same side as the warehouse, a little way down the street, at No. 83, we found the bodies of about 50 men who had been shot. Many of the bodies had bandages on them. At 60 Wolska Street, in

the yard of the macaroni factory, we found a pile of bodies about 2 metres high, 20 metres long and 15 metres wide. Most of them were men and only some women and children. It took us several hours to burn these bodies. At a rough guess there must have been over 2,000 of them.

Those women and children who had been separated from the men at the macaroni factory were led off and later shot elsewhere.[14]

On 8 August, the same work squad was sent to the Ursus factory at 55 Wolska Street to burn 5,000 more bodies – men, women and children who had been murdered there by German units three days earlier, on 5 August, in one of the largest mass shootings. It took the workers all day to burn the corpses. One of the few survivors of the massacre in the factory yard was Zofia Staworzynska. She testified the following year:

My daughter took my hand and we walked in the direction of the wall. When we were by the wall shots were fired at us. The first shot hit me in the neck. I fell and was hit three more times, once in the arm and twice near the heart. My daughter fell next to me, I heard another shot almost immediately, after which my daughter lay still. All the while more groups of Poles were being brought in, but I do not know how often. I do not know how long this went on since I was completely delirious. In the intervals between the shootings and just before evening the SS men and Ukrainians moved around finishing off the wounded (they finished off my daughter and the person lying next to me) and removing their jewellery. Trampling over me they broke my left arm (the one where I was wounded) and my right collar bone, and tore my ring off my fingers.

A resident from the same house, Wanda Lurie, was in the final month of pregnancy. She was ordered to the Ursus factory with her three children, aged four, six and twelve years: 'I went in last and kept back, always lagging behind in the hope that they would not kill a pregnant woman. However, I was taken in the last group. In the factory yard I saw a heap of bodies about a metre high.' She lost her children:

I went to the execution spot holding in my right hand the two small hands of my youngest children and in the left that of my eldest son. The children were crying and praying; the older, seeing the dead bodies, cried out that we were going to be killed and called for his father. The first shot hit my elder son, the second me and the third my younger children.

Wanda fell wounded, but lay alive under the mounting pile of dead, witnessing all the executions that took place. These stopped the next day, but the Germans came back with dogs. 'They walked and jumped on the corpses to see if any of the supposed dead were still alive. On the third day I felt the child move in my womb. I was determined that this child not die, and I looked around to find a way to escape.' Wanda managed to dig herself out from under the blood and bodies once the Germans had left, and hid in a cellar. On 20 August, with the fighting still raging above her, she gave birth to a healthy baby boy.[15]

The mass killing slowed somewhat on 6 August, possibly because bullets were in short supply and were needed elsewhere. Reinefarth complained that he did not have enough ammunition to kill all the civilians. In a recorded phone conversation with the commander of the Ninth Army, Lieutenant General Vormann, on 5 August, he said: 'What should I do with the civilians? I have less ammunition than prisoners.' Reinefarth's response when asked by Vormann about his losses illustrates that the German suppression of the Warsaw Uprising had nothing in common with regular combat: 'Our losses are six killed, twenty-four badly wounded, twelve slightly wounded; losses of the enemy including those shot are more than 10,000.' The German approach was reminiscent of their so-called large-scale operations conducted in occupied Belarus during the previous two years, only this time the mass slaughter was being carried out not in the countryside and small towns but in a major European city.[16]

In the course of only two days, the units of Reinefarth's combat group murdered in cold blood as many as 40,000 Polish civilians in Wola – men, women and children. Of these, the Dirlewanger Brigade alone slaughtered 12,500 civilians on 5 August. In terms of its death toll, the Wola massacres surpassed even the mass shooting of 33,771 Ukrainian Jews at Babi Yar on 29 and 30 September 1941 and were on the same scale as Operation Harvest Festival, during which 42,000 Jews had been murdered in the Lublin area on 3–5 November 1943 in the single largest mass shooting of Jews during the war. Some 100,000 civilians fled from Wola and the neighbouring district of

Ochota, where the Kaminski Brigade had been on the rampage, mostly to the Old Town and the city centre. The Kaminski Brigade was part of a second combat group under Brigadier Günther Rohr. The brigade itself was led by the eponymous Russian anti-communist collaborator Bronislav Kaminski, who – like Bach-Zelewski and Dirlewanger – was another veteran of the German terror in Belarus. Though fewer mass shootings were carried out in Ochota than in Wola, as Kaminski's troops were more interested in rape and plunder, many civilians were nonetheless murdered in groups or individually. One of the worst atrocities was committed at yet another hospital, the Radium Institute. There, over the course of a two-week period from 5 to 19 August, Kaminski's men murdered 170 patients and staff, often raping the women first, sometimes repeatedly, and finally burned the hospital building.[17]

The Destruction of an Entire City

With Wola retaken, Bach-Zelewski selected the Old Town as the next target of the German onslaught. The attack aimed to restore the communication and supply lines to the Ninth Army across the Kierbedź Bridge and, to the north of it, the Citadel Rail Bridge, both of which lay undestroyed just outside the Old Town. On 13 August, the newly formed 'von dem Bach Corps' – named for Bach-Zelewski – numbered almost 26,000 soldiers, twenty-six tanks, thirty-eight attack guns and several artillery units, one of them supplied with the biggest mortar of the Second World War (600mm, nicknamed 'Karl'); it also received air support. In addition, Reinefarth's combat group moved against the Old Town with some 8,000 men. In the south, they were supported by 5,000 soldiers under Major General Stahel, who had been relieved by Dirlewanger's troops on the afternoon of 6 August.[18]

The 39,000 German soldiers launched their offensive at 10 o'clock on the morning of 13 August. Within a few days, the Old Town lost about a third of its structures; casualties among civilians ran into the thousands, although Bach-Zelewski had officially called off the mass shootings of women and children in the wake of the slaughter in Wola and restricted the murder of civilians to men. This was not a humanitarian gesture, however, but rather a tactical calculation designed to achieve Hitler's objectives more effectively: the chaos caused by the mass slaughter was so immense that it was obstructing the Germans' own operations against rebel forces. As of 17 August, fewer than 5,000 Home Army soldiers defended an area just 1,200m wide by 600–1,100m long. Of the 75,000–100,000 civilians who were originally trapped in the Old Town centre, including many refugees from Wola and Ochota, at least 10,000 were still in the area now retaken by the Germans, but a good 40,000 remained in the rebel area. The rebels repelled several attacks each day, but gradually had to give up the ruins of the shot-up and bombed buildings. Reflecting on the vain hope of Varsovians that the Soviets might still save their city from complete ruin, Józef Szczepański, a poet serving in the Home Army, wrote: 'We await you, red plague / To deliver us from the black death.'[19]

During the course of 1 September, the rebels fired their last rounds of ammunition and used up their last reserves. In the afternoon, the fighting died down. That evening, the evacuation of the Old Town began, using the sewers. After an artillery barrage that lasted several hours, the Germans occupied the ruins of the Old Town the next day. Even now, the mass killing continued. The victims were mainly the sick and wounded in the hospitals and temporary first-aid stations. The Germans did not even spare the aged and crippled in various institutions. Particularly savage was the treatment of the wounded, who were murdered ruthlessly and often burned alive. Among the hospitals where Dirlewanger's men ran riot were those at 10 Freta Street (60 people gunned down, along with the staff), 7 Długa Street (400 people killed on the first and second floors alone), 24 Miodowa Street, 1/3 Kilińskiego Street, the Crooked Lantern at 25 Podwale Street and the smaller Black Swan at 46 Podwale Street (30 people killed). Some of the civilians and less sick were evacuated from the Old Town and many of them were shot along the way on Podwale and Wąski Dunaj streets, on Castle Square and in the neighbourhood of Mariensztat. The Germans shot and burned hundreds of wounded, including 430 people in a single hospital on Długa Street. Though the mass killing of civilians did not quite reach the scale of the massacres in Wola, a total of 30,000 civilians (as well as 5,000 members of the Home Army) were nonetheless murdered in the Old Town between 13 August and 2 September. Some 35,000 civilians were sent to concentration camps or transported to the Reich for forced labour.[20]

During the month of September, fighting – and killing – continued in other parts of Warsaw still held by the rebels. On 7 September, Bach-Zelewski and the command of the Ninth Army received orders from Führer Headquarters to treat members of the Home Army as regular troops in surrender negotiations. The mass slaughter of the preceding five weeks had only stiffened Polish resistance and the Germans were now seeking a way to bring the fighting to an end. It is significant that Bach-Zelewski drew up detailed plans for the general evacuation of Warsaw on 30 September, without waiting for an agreement with the Home Army to be signed: the end was in sight. The capitulation of the surviving Polish forces was signed on 2 October 1944 and the exodus began the following day. Five days later, Himmler dined with Bach-Zelewski at the former's East Prussian field head-quarters and issued him with concrete orders for the destruction of the entire city of Warsaw, building by building, block by block. By this time, huge swathes of the city were already in ruins but most of Warsaw was still standing and many of its inhabitants were still present. A total of around 185,000 Warsaw civilians had been killed by the Germans in the course of August and September. A further 15,000 Polish soldiers had fallen in battle. Now the Germans evacuated the survivors – 600,000 people – to a transit camp at Pruszków (Dulag 121), established for this purpose. From there, some 60,000 people would be sent to concentration camps and another 90,000 to forced-labour assignments in the Reich. More than 13,000 of those sent to concentration camps were deported to Auschwitz, almost 10 per cent of whom were children and adolescents.[21]

The destruction of the city was carried out systematically; some districts were burned and blown up house by house. Special demolition squads armed with flamethrowers, mines and bombs were sent in to level every-thing – homes and churches, museums and archives, theatres and cinemas, hospitals and factories, tramlines and gas pipes. During the destruction, there were instances of people being thrown into the flames alive. By the time the demolition crews had finished, almost 85 per cent of Warsaw had been destroyed; 30 per cent of the destruction happened *after* capitulation. The Old Town, dating from the 1300s, and the fifteenth-century New Town, with all their medieval, Baroque and Neoclassical glories, were turned into rubble and ashes. Out of 957 buildings classified as historical monuments, 782 were totally destroyed and 141 partly destroyed. Only 34 survived, because the Germans did not have time to set the charges once the Soviet advance resumed. Of 105 million cubic metres of buildings in the city,

73.6 million vanished. As of January 1945, the left bank of Warsaw (80 per cent of the pre-war city) had scarcely a single undamaged building; it had no water, no light, no telephones, no public transport. The railways were not functioning; there were no means of communication with the rest of the country. Visiting Warsaw shortly after its liberation, Supreme Allied Commander General Dwight D. Eisenhower said: 'I have seen many towns destroyed during the war, but nowhere have I been faced with such extent of destruction executed with such bestiality.'[22]

For their 'heroic deeds' in suppressing the Warsaw Uprising, three of the unit commanders were decorated by Hitler: Bach-Zelewski, Reinefarth and Dirlewanger. The latter was especially congratulated by Governor General Hans Frank, who expressed his appreciation for 'the exemplary action of his combat group during the fighting in Warsaw', at a reception held in Dirlewanger's honour at Wawel Castle, Frank's residence in Cracow, on 16 October 1944. The extent of the slaughter in Warsaw is summed up in a statement made by Reinefarth, reported in issue 294 of the German daily newspaper *Ostdeutscher Beobachter* (published in Poznań from 1939 to 1945) of 5 November, concerning the 'heroic action' of his combat group during the Warsaw Uprising: 'We have both defeated the enemy and dealt him losses amounting to about a quarter of a million people.'[23]

Two days after the reception held in his honour at Wawel Castle, Dirlewanger was sent with his brigade to assist in the suppression of another uprising. On 29 August 1944, while the fighting in Warsaw was at its height, a broad-based coalition of Slovak resistance forces comprising conservatives, social democrats and communists had launched an armed insurrection. Its aim was the overthrow of Jozef Tiso's Slovak Republic, a client state of Nazi Germany. Wehrmacht and Waffen SS swiftly intervened and succeeded in quashing the uprising by the end of October. The Nazi leadership seized the opportunity to murder Slovaks suspected of aiding the rebels and Jews who had thus far evaded deportation. At least 4,000 civilians – around a quarter of them women and children – fell victim to targeted punitive measures on Slovak soil between September 1944 and March 1945; half of them were Jews. These killings were carried out first and foremost by Einsatzgruppe H, which had been specially set up for the task. In a series of mass shootings, one of its subordinate units, Einsatzkommando 14, murdered 743 people (half of them Jews, the rest Roma, partisans and rebels), including

280 women and 99 children, in the municipality of Kremnička alone and at least 400 people of all ages in the village of Nemecká; the latter were shot over a lime kiln and their corpses then burned. Furthermore, between September and March, around 30,000 Slovak citizens – including at least 12,000 Jews – were deported to German camps. Almost 8,000 of the Jewish deportees were sent to Auschwitz, where the majority were immediately gassed.[24]

CONCLUSION

In deliberate policies of mass murder, Nazi Germany killed approximately 13 million people in the space of less than six years from summer 1939 to late spring 1945. These were not 'casualties of war' resulting from bombing raids, military hostilities and general privation, but victims of premeditated mass murder targeted as part of Germany's strategy for winning a global conflict. In the context of seven major killing campaigns, Nazi Germany intentionally killed 300,000 mentally and physically disabled people, up to 100,000 members of the Polish ruling classes and elites, approximately 5.8 million European Jews, 200,000 European Roma, at least 2 million residents of Soviet cities, up to 3.3 million Soviet POWs, around 1 million unarmed civilians in primarily rural areas during preventive terror operations and reprisals in the occupied territories (even after accounting for actual partisans among the dead) and another 185,000 civilian residents of Warsaw (see Appendix I). Starvation, shooting and gassing, in that order, were the preferred killing methods. Substantial numbers of disabled people, Jews, Roma and Soviet POWs fell victim to each of these three methods. This once more illustrates how many of the killing operations worked on parallel lines. In addition to the three principal killing methods, numerous other victims were stabbed or beaten to death, drowned, burned alive or given lethal injections.[1]

If we factor in the hundreds of thousands of people who, between 1933 and 1945, were executed following mock trials by Nazi courts, worked, beaten or tortured to death in concentration camps, or shot on German soil during the final months of the war as the net tightened around the perpetrators, then the total number of civilians and other non-combatants who fell victim to premeditated murder by Nazi perpetrators approaches 14 million. Over the course of March 1945, for instance, more than 18,000 prisoners lost their lives at Bergen-Belsen. At no point in the history of the concentration camps did so many prisoners die so fast of disease and deprivation as in Bergen-Belsen during this one month. It is revealing how Gestapo chief Heinrich Müller justified the killings carried out during the final phase of the war: 'We will not make the same mistake that was made in 1918. We will not leave our enemies in Germany alive.' Avoiding a repetition of the defeat in the First World War and the ensuing crisis of 1918 remained a touchstone for the Nazis to the very end. Some of the prisoners who died in the prisons and camps throughout the Nazi era, as well as some of those who fell victim to the crimes committed during its final months, notably in Bergen-Belsen, fall into the seven major victim groups addressed in this book: for instance, the Jews, Roma and Soviet POWs who were killed at Auschwitz and other camps or the Jews who perished on death marches. Other victims, however, cannot easily be categorised as part of a clearly definable victim group: for instance, most of the camp prisoners sent on death marches were non-Jews. They were undoubtedly victims of Nazi mass terror, and this terror, furthermore, had a very high mortality rate. This book, by contrast, addresses the major victim groups of mass killing, where the death toll for each group reached at least into the tens of thousands. For these reasons, the additional victims of Nazi terror are not examined in detail here, though they were no less victims of Nazi murder than those who are at the centre of this study.[2]

Around two-thirds of the 13 million victims addressed in this book were killed on Soviet territory within the borders of 22 June 1941, when German forces launched Operation Barbarossa. It was in this theatre of war that the military conflict was most brutally fought and in which more of Nazi Germany's mass crimes were committed than on any other front. The number of dead that Germany's war against the Soviet Union cost exceeded that of the other fronts several times over. It is particularly the death toll among civilians and other non-combatants that stands out here. Alongside the 2 million starved inhabitants of Soviet cities and the 3.3 million Soviet POWs mentioned above, German forces murdered at least 17,000 psychiatric patients, 2.6 million Jews, 30,000 Roma and up to 600,000 rural-dwelling civilians in so-called anti-partisan operations (see Appendix I). More than 6 million additional Soviet civilians died directly or indirectly from the war as a result of starvation in rural and small-town settings and behind the Soviet front, Wehrmacht scorched-earth operations during its retreat west, German bombing raids and military hostilities, killings by Soviet partisans behind

German lines or crimes committed by the Stalinist regime against its own people. The exacerbation of mortality among refugees and evacuees caused by the war was considerable, though some of the wider knock-on effects of the German invasion are difficult to reconstruct and assess.

As we know, the German perpetrators often kept detailed records and submitted lengthy reports cataloguing their killing operations. The almost daily incident reports compiled by the RSHA on the basis of dispatches sent back to Berlin by the Einsatzgruppen – a total of 195 documents issued between 23 June 1941 and 24 April 1942 – are a case in point. After successfully decoding German radio transmissions from the eastern front, British intelligence analysts from the Government Code and Cypher School even noted in August 1941: 'the [higher SS and police] leaders of the three sectors stand somewhat in competition with each other as to their "scores"'. Nonetheless, there is reason to believe that the tallies recorded by some German units, rather than being inflated, were in fact too *low*. According to the figures submitted, for instance, by Einsatzkommando 9 to its superiors in the staff of Einsatzgruppe B and then forwarded on to Berlin, the commando shot a total of 11,449 people (the vast majority of whom were Jews) during the first four months of its deployment in the occupied Soviet territories under the command of Alfred Filbert. Based on a thorough examination of all available primary source material, however, EK 9 in fact killed at a conservative estimate just over 18,000 people during these four months, though it might easily have been several thousands more. Thus, as the presiding judge at Filbert's trial suspected as early as 1962, the figures reported back to Berlin were indeed too low. There is evidence to suggest that this applies to other commandos as well. For example, the sum of reported six-day tallies for EK 5 (Einsatzgruppe C) exceeded the unit's reported overall number. As the data was passed from the detachments via the commandos and the group staffs to Berlin, mistakes were almost certainly introduced, contents were mixed up, information was omitted. In short, then, further research might well reveal that the numbers of civilians and other non-combatants murdered by Nazi Germany were even higher. The total of 13 million civilians and other non-combatants killed in deliberate Nazi policies of mass murder should, therefore, be regarded as a minimum figure.[3]

The mass murder of children is surely the most salient feature of National Socialist atrocities: from the first victims of the child 'euthanasia' campaign, via the 1.5 million murdered children of Jewish descent, to the so-called gang children (*Bandenkinder*) in the occupied Soviet territories. Especially young children succumbed to the starvation policy in various occupied territories; infant mortality assumed horrendous proportions. The ruthless murder of so many children in particular is a crime without historical precedent. Numerous children, furthermore, were deported, compelled to carry out heavy labour, sent to camps or subjected to barbaric medical experiments. Others were stolen from their parents and given up for forced adoption. The crimes committed against these defenceless victims are a vivid illustration of the moral degeneration of the perpetrators.[4]

And so to the perpetrators. This book has focused on German and Austrian perpetrators. The participation of local actors in the atrocities discussed – though extensive in some parts of German-occupied Europe, such as Lithuania and Ukraine – has featured here just occasionally and then only briefly. We have heard about the local Belarusian police who participated in massacres of Jews in the Minsk Ghetto, the Ukrainian at Sobibór who sliced a child in pieces with a spade or the Azerbaijanis among the Dirlewanger forces who slaughtered tens of thousands in the Warsaw neighbourhood of Wola. However, the Nazi mass-killing programmes were a German project, conceived of, set in motion by and driven forward through the agency of Germans. Furthermore, the vast majority of perpetrators were German (Reich or ethnic) or Austrian, and the vast majority of victims were killed by them, sometimes exclusively so: though substantial numbers of local collaborators can be found in parts of the Holocaust and some anti-partisan operations, many of the undertakings, such as the 'euthanasia' campaign, the extermination of Soviet POWs and the mass murder of Roma, were exclusively German crimes (even if the *persecution* of the victims that preceded the killing was not). The same applies to the elimination of the Polish elites: the Selbstschutz units that played such a prominent role in decimating the ranks of the Polish leadership were recruited from among ethnic Germans native to Poland – this was a crime committed in contested multi-ethnic borderlands, not a crime of collaboration.[5]

Nazi mass atrocities were not unique; genocides were committed before the Nazis and have been committed since. But Nazi genocide and mass killing can perhaps be seen as an extreme case of collective violence in view of the dimensions, intensity and nature of the crimes committed. In this sense, they remain unparalleled and continue to inform our understanding and categorisation of mass killing. Alone the sheer number of Nazi perpetrators active over an extended period of time, operating often in multiple contexts and against several victim groups, requires explanation. Hundreds of thousands of mass murderers were at large simultaneously. These perpetrators, mainly but not exclusively men, were not from one single generation; they transcended multiple peer groups. Some of the most merciless and radical killers had spent their formative years in the Imperial Germany of the 1890s and early 1900s: Hermann Pfannmüller, who killed disabled children at Eglfing-Haar mental hospital, was born in 1886; Gustav von Bechtolsheim, whose 707th Infantry Division murdered more than 10,000 Jews in Belarus in autumn 1941, was born in 1889; Paul Blobel, who shot Jewish children in the city of Belaya Tserkov after having done the same to their parents, was born in 1894. Other perpetrators, by contrast, had still been children themselves when the Nazis assumed power in Germany in 1933: Gerhard Sommer, a company commander in the Waffen SS who participated in the massacre of hundreds of inhabitants – including children – of the Italian village of Sant'Anna di Stazzema, was born in 1921; Fritz Swoboda, an Austrian NCO in the Waffen SS who shot residents of the Czech village of Lidice and later remarked more than once in US captivity that his greatest ambition was to kill every Frenchman between the ages of fourteen and sixty and every Italian between the ages of sixteen and fifty, was born in 1922.[6]

The Nazi perpetrators at the shooting pits, on the selection ramps and in the mental asylums spanned several generations. If not a peer group, then, what did these people have in common? They were certainly united by a shared national trauma that cut across age groups and social backgrounds. Defeat in the First World War, the obliteration of German great-power ambitions (loss of colonies and substantial swathes of Reich territory; military and economic subjugation) and the tumultuous fallout of 1918–19 caused an individual and collective trauma in German society. This affected not merely those who consciously experienced these events but also – by means of intergenerational transmission – their progeny, who suffered a secondary traumatisation. In this situation, ethnic–nationalist sentiments already present in the belated nation-state were radicalised further. Not only was there a widespread conviction that what had gone wrong in 1918 had to be put right, but also a fervent belief that radical measures of an unprecedented nature were imperative in order to achieve this and to avoid a repetition of 1918, the constant and inescapable point of reference for the Nazi perpetrators. The ends justified any and all means. When the next, inevitable European (and later global) war came in 1939, the full force of Nazi revisionist violence – informed by an obsessive crusade to racially and socially purify and strengthen the German nation and, by extension, the pan-European Nazi empire – was unleashed; genocide and mass killing became a form of warfare in their own right.[7]

There are features and patterns common to all modern genocides, but there were also specifically Nazi motivations for mass killing. There is not a monocausal explanation or single explanatory model for the actions of the perpetrators. The answer we seek can be found only in the interaction of several factors converging in specific historical circumstances. The conduct of the Holocaust perpetrators, for instance, cannot be explained in terms of their ideology alone, and yet cannot be understood without it, for anti-Semitism provided at all times a general absolution for their actions. However, more than half of the victims of deliberate Nazi policies of mass murder were not Jewish. Anti-Semitism as a motivating factor cannot explain why German (and Austrian) perpetrators massacred Belarusian villagers, starved German psychiatric patients or gassed Austrian Roma. However, anti-Semitism was only one, albeit central, component of Nazi ideology: radical ethnic nationalism and biological racism were also key elements, and they are indispensable for explaining Nazi atrocities against non-Jewish victims. These profound ideological convictions were not held by a few fanatics but by hundreds of thousands of people at the same time. These people came not only from elite Nazi organisations such as the SS but also in substantial numbers from the Wehrmacht, which – with a total of 18 million members between 1935 and 1945 – constituted a cross section of the German male population at the time. Very many perpetrators, therefore, came not from the fringes but from the heart of German society. The prevalence of radical ideological convictions during the years in question point to a shared and defining historical context. The perpetrators were less 'ordinary men' than ordinary Germans during an extraordinary time in German history. Arguing that there was a German predisposition for mass violence does not mean that the Germans were biologically predisposed to kill because they were Germans, but rather that these specific generations of Germans, by virtue of a certain set of circumstances and the events of the preceding decades, were particularly radicalised and more inclined to pursue extreme solutions to perceived problems.[8]

There is another reason why context is a key explanatory factor. The Nazi state placed at the disposal of its followers means of violence normally beyond the reach of most people; it then authorised the use of extreme violence against several groups that had been relentlessly dehumanised and declared fair game: psychiatric patients, Jews, Slavs, Roma and others. In the context of the war, these groups no longer enjoyed any legal protection whatsoever and could be killed with impunity. Many of the perpetrators were members of state organisations such as the Wehrmacht, the police and paramilitaries such as the SS, but the killings committed by hospital personnel during the period of decentralised 'euthanasia', for instance, demonstrate that membership in a state organisation was by no means necessary for participation in mass killing. Decisive, instead, was the fact that the Nazi regime created a framework that allowed its followers, under cover of war, to commit acts that would have been scarcely imaginable in other circumstances. Only in this way can we explain how it was possible for hundreds of thousands of murderers to settle back into normal civilian life after the war and reintegrate into German society as schoolteachers (Artur Wilke), bank managers (Alfred Filbert), physicians (Werner Catel), town mayors (Heinz Reinefarth) or salesmen (Kurt Eimann). During the Nazi period in general and the war in particular, conduct once considered wrong and unlawful now seemed right and justified; it was not only permitted but in fact desired and, therefore, 'legitimate' (or at least legitimated). When the war ended and the Nazi era with it, this behaviour was again deemed wrong and unlawful. The unity of and three-way interplay between the shared national trauma of 1918, ideological radicalisation and sanctioning from above are crucial to understanding the actions of the Nazi perpetrators.[9]

Emphasising that ordinary people, acting under certain circumstances, commit extraordinary evil does not preclude the possibility that certain types of individual may be more likely than others to engage in destructive conformity. There must be a reason why some people act in a certain way in a given situation, yet others do not; by the same token, circumstance alone does not explain why some people commit crimes with more enthusiasm than others or why some people do not limit themselves to following orders but actually display initiative. It is important, therefore, to supplement the question as to why people participate in mass murder by asking how extensive and enthusiastic this participation is. Numerous disturbing examples of enthusiasm and initiative have been cited in this book. However, individual disposition is of little help in explaining why (though not 'how enthusiastically') Nazi perpetrators committed atrocities, for the simple reason that these people on the whole *did not* react differently in a given situation. The vast majority of them reacted in the same way, that is, they killed innocent men, women and children. Few (prospective) perpetrators took advantage of the opportunities available to them to avoid participation in atrocities. A small number did ask for transfers away from the killing fields, request redeployment before or after the massacres started, or refuse to take part in shootings of defenceless Jews, and the fact that not a single case is documented in which one of these people suffered any severe consequences for their refusal to participate, such as death, imprisonment or transfer to a penal battalion, should give us pause for thought.[10]

Nonetheless, the number of those who did refuse to participate remained a tiny minority. Why was this? First, for the reasons discussed above, there was extensive agreement between the Nazi leadership and the frontline perpetrators when it came to ideological convictions and war aims; this applies not just to the SS and the police but also to the Wehrmacht. Illustrative of this are the results of the US opinion polls conducted over the course of 1944 among the Wehrmacht soldiers held captive at Fort Hunt, Virginia. There was approval for the person of Adolf Hitler among almost 64 per cent of those interrogated by the Americans. Among the soldiers born in or after 1923, that is, those who were ten years of age or younger at the time of the Nazi takeover of power, the rate of approval for Hitler was more than 74 per cent. Thus, three out of four members of the youngest age group continued to hold faith with Hitler, even at this late stage of the war. These findings complement the results of a survey of 1,400 Austrian former members of the Wehrmacht conducted after the war. Asked to name the four most important aims of the Wehrmacht, 78.4 per cent of those surveyed said 'more living space', 62.1 per cent the 'struggle against Bolshevism', 41.6 per cent the 'struggle against world Jewry' and 36.3 per cent 'racial purity'. These percentages – citing not just a selection but the *four main objectives* of the Wehrmacht in the eyes of those surveyed – demonstrate that its members by no means perceived the Wehrmacht as a purely military apparatus free from ideology. On the contrary, the Wehrmacht was for its members an instrument of the National Socialist regime that not only strove to accomplish its military but also its ideological and political objectives, such as the 'struggle against world Jewry' and 'racial purity'. Asked for their personal opinion, 26.4 per cent of the former soldiers surveyed stated that 'the Jews' had been the main culprits in the outbreak of the Second World War. Given that anti-Semitic attitudes were something of a taboo in the post-war period, in Austria as in Germany, it seems likely that this percentage would have been considerably higher during the war itself, when those surveyed were still members of the Wehrmacht. The letters sent home by German soldiers from the eastern front also reveal these shared beliefs and common convictions.[11]

Second, the largely internalised convictions of most soldiers established a fundamental and deep-rooted loyalty to the (Nazi) state and, in turn, to their comrades that went beyond conventional group conformity and peer pressure. This was heightened in wartime during deployment on the frontline and in the rear areas. Sebastian Haffner, one of the most perceptive contemporary commentators on National Socialism, wrote a youth memoir in 1939 that ended with an account of his own experiences in autumn 1933 in a camp for legal trainees in Jüterbog in the Prussian province of Brandenburg. Haffner explicitly denounced comradeship as an engine of moral decay, a 'poison':

> this comradeship can become one of the most terrible means of dehumanisation – and has become so in the hands of the Nazis. [...] The fact that it makes one happy for a while does not in the least change that. It corrupts and depraves a person like no alcohol or opium can. It makes humans incapable of leading an independent, responsible, civilised life. In fact, it is actually a means of de-civilisation. [...] To begin with the central feature: comradeship completely removes the feeling of personal responsibility [...]. The person who lives in comradeship is relieved of any concern for his existence, any hardship in the struggle for survival. [...] It is even worse that comradeship relieves a person of responsibility for himself, before God and one's conscience. He does what everyone does; he has no choice. He has no time to think [...]. His comrades are

290

his conscience and they give absolution for everything, provided he does what everyone else does. [...] Comradeship inevitably sets the intellectual tone at the lowest possible level, accessible to everyone. It cannot tolerate discussion [...]. In comradeship, no thoughts are allowed to flourish, just mass sentiments of the most primitive kind – and these are inescapable; to escape them would mean placing oneself beyond the boundaries of comradeship.

Very few were able or willing to remove themselves from the community of comrades. As Haffner commented on participation in play-fighting and telling dirty jokes at the camp in Jüterbog: 'You were a bad comrade if you did not take part.' This applied all the more so in extreme situations, for example in wartime, even if it meant killing defenceless civilians. Importantly, furthermore, it was not only comrades who gave 'absolution for everything', as Haffner put it; this was state-sponsored comradeship, and it was also the (Nazi) state that provided absolution.[12]

Of course, it is not enough to obliterate feelings of personal responsibility for people to commit atrocities. Yes, the Nazi perpetrators knew that the state gave them absolution for what they did. More than this, however, their shared trauma, resentment and ideological convictions convinced them that they were victims and, therefore, justified in what they were doing – righting, as they saw it, a past wrong. Widespread, radicalised ethnic-nationalist sentiments identified a target for this revisionist violence; indeed, multiple targets. As Haffner recognised, there is no community-building without boundaries, without the Other. The group needs the Other in order to become a community. The sociologist Albert K. Cohen observed that nothing unites the members of a group like a common enemy, though this ancient wisdom was already known in Aristotle's day. Of course, the Other could be a disliked superior or an outsider, someone who marched to a different drumbeat. But the Other could also be an outgroup – Jews, Roma, 'useless eaters', 'Slavic sub-humans'. This is the Janus face of comradeship.[13]

People can commit terrible atrocities when they believe they have been wronged. Like most perpetrators of genocide and mass killing, the Nazis were not only convinced that they were victims but also that what they were doing was right and necessary. They believed it was necessary in order to rectify what had gone wrong in 1918 and, in the new war, to avoid a repetition thereof. They believed it was necessary in order to remove any perceived threat to building a strong, healthy, racially pure German nation. In this line of thinking, whatever was necessary was justified, and whatever was justified was, surely, right. How could it be otherwise? The old moral order of universal rights – the morality of the civilised world – had been replaced by a new ethnic–nationalist morality that emerged from defeat in the First World War, its tumultuous aftermath and societal perceptions of these experiences: this became the new Nazi morality. One of the central figures in the annihilation was Heinrich Himmler. On 4 October 1943, he gave a wide-ranging speech to SS generals in Poznań:

> I also want to mention candidly to you a very difficult chapter. It ought to be addressed quite frankly between us, and nonetheless we will never speak about it in public. [...] I am now referring to the evacuation of the Jews, the extermination of the Jewish people. It's one of those things that are easily said: 'The Jewish people are being exterminated,' says every party comrade, 'of course, it's in our programme, elimination of the Jews, extermination, we're doing it.' And then they all turn up, the dutiful 80 million Germans, and each one has his decent Jew. Of course, they say, the others are all pigs, but this one is a splendid Jew. Of all those who speak in this way, none has seen it, none has endured it. Most of you here will know what it means when 100 corpses lie next to each other, when 500 lie there or when 1,000 lie there. To have endured this and at the same time to have remained decent — aside from exceptions due to human weakness — has made us tough. It is a glorious chapter in our history that has not and will never be written. Because we know how difficult it would be for us if we still had Jews as secret saboteurs, agitators and rabble-rousers in every city, what with the bombing raids, with the burden and with the hardships of the war. If the Jews were still part of the German racial corpus, we would now most likely be in the same state as we were in 1916–17.[14]

This chapter of German history *has* been written. It is a chapter of moral degeneration. This book has shown that more than just a few Nazi perpetrators were sadists, people who derived pleasure from killing. Nonetheless, these sadists still comprised a minority of the perpetrators. Every instance of mass killing reveals a percentage of sadists, just as every society contains a percentage of sadists. It is the non-sadistic majority of Nazi perpetrators, however, whose actions we must strive to explain – those hundreds of thousands of ordinary Germans who killed millions of human beings. Dismissing *them* as sadists or, worse, as monsters prevents us from understanding how human beings can, and do, plumb such depths.

APPENDIX I

VICTIMS OF NAZI MASS-KILLING CAMPAIGNS

Mass-killing Campaign	Total Number of Victims	Number of Victims in the German-occupied Soviet Territories
European Jews	5.8 million	2.6 million*
Soviet prisoners of war	3.3 million	3.3 million
Soviet urban dwellers	2 million	2 million
Civilians killed during anti-partisan operations – in the countryside (across Europe) – in Warsaw	1 million 185,000	600,000 —
Mentally and physically disabled (across Europe)	300,000	17,000
European Roma	200,000	30,000
Polish ruling classes and elites	100,000	—
	12.885 million	**8.547 million**

* On the territory of the Soviet Union within the borders of 22 June 1941.

APPENDIX II
COMPARATIVE RANKS FOR 1942

SS	German Army	British Army	US Army
Reichsführer-SS	Generalfeldmarschall	Field Marshal	General of the Army
SS-Oberst-Gruppenführer	Generaloberst	General	General
SS-Obergruppenführer	General	Lieutenant General	Lieutenant General
SS-Gruppenführer	Generalleutnant	Major General	Major General
SS-Brigadeführer	Generalmajor	Brigadier	Brigadier General
SS-Oberführer	*[no equivalent]*	*[no equivalent]*	*[no equivalent]*
SS-Standartenführer	Oberst	Colonel	Colonel
SS-Obersturmbannführer	Oberstleutnant	Lieutenant Colonel	Lieutenant Colonel
SS-Sturmbannführer	Major	Major	Major
SS-Hauptsturmführer	Hauptmann	Captain	Captain
SS-Obersturmführer	Oberleutnant	Lieutenant	First Lieutenant
SS-Untersturmführer	Leutnant	Second Lieutenant	Second Lieutenant
- - - - - - - - - -	- - - - - - - - - -	- - - - - - - - - -	- - - - - - - - - -
SS-Hauptscharführer	Oberfeldwebel	Warrant Officer Class I	Master Sergeant
SS-Oberscharführer	Feldwebel	Warrant Officer (Class II)	Technical Sergeant
SS-Scharführer	Unterfeldwebel	Staff Sergeant	Staff Sergeant
SS-Unterscharführer	Unteroffizier	Sergeant	Sergeant
SS-Rottenführer	Obergefreiter	Corporal	Corporal
SS-Sturmmann	Gefreiter	Lance Corporal	Private First Class
SS-Mann	Soldat	Private	Private

[1] This table is adapted from Kay et al., eds., *Nazi Policy*, p. 321; Shepherd, *Hitler's Soldiers*, pp. 548–9.

ENDNOTES

EPIGRAPHS

1. British Library Sound Archive (hereafter BLSA), Jewish Survivors of the Holocaust oral history collection, shelf mark C410/036, testimony of Josef Perl, September 1988, 4 of 4, 68:28–34.
2. Primo Levi, *I sommersi e i salvati* (Turin: Einaudi, 1986), p. 3.

NOTE ON PLACE NAMES AND CONVENTIONS

1. For 'Government General', see, for instance, the report from Alexander Kirk, chargé d'affaires at the US embassy in Berlin, to the US secretary of state in Washington, 6 March 1940, reproduced in: Paul R. Bartrop and Michael Dickerman, eds, *The Holocaust: An Encyclopedia and Document Collection, Volume 3: Holocaust Testimonies* (Santa Barbara, CA: ABC-CLIO, 2017), doc. 57, p. 1136; Polish Ministry of Information, *The Black Book of Poland* (New York: G.P. Putnam's Sons, 1942), p. 10.
2. For 'Nazi' and 'Nazis', see, for instance, 'Boycott of Jews', *The Times*, 3 April 1933, p. 14; Sebastian Haffner, *Geschichte eines Deutschen. Die Erinnerungen 1914–1933* (Munich: dtv, 2002), pp. 105, 128–32, 195–6 and 198–200. Though Haffner's memoirs were not published until 2000, they were written in 1939 and left untouched thereafter.

INTRODUCTION

1. For the quote, see Saul Friedländer, 'On the Possibility of the Holocaust: An Approach to a Historical Synthesis', in Yehuda Bauer and Nathan Rotenstreich, eds, *The Holocaust as Historical Experience: Essays and a Discussion* (New York: Holmes & Meier, 1981), pp. 1–21, here p. 2. See also the excellent discussion in Mark Levene, *Genocide in the Age of the Nation-State, Volume I: The Meaning of Genocide* (London/New York: I.B. Tauris, 2005), pp. 38–9.
2. For the figure of between 200,000 and 250,000, see Dieter Pohl, *Holocaust. Die Ursachen, das Geschehen, die Folgen* (Freiburg im Breisgau: Herder, 2000), p. 124; Wendy Lower, *Hitler's Furies: German Women in the Nazi Killing Fields* (Boston, MA: Houghton Mifflin Harcourt, 2013), p. 244, n. 154. For the figure of more than 500,000, see Konrad Kwiet, 'Rassenpolitik und Völkermord', in Wolfgang Benz, Hermann Graml and Hermann Weiß, eds, *Enzyklopädie des Nationalsozialismus* (Munich: dtv, 2001 [1997]), pp. 50–65, here p. 62.
3. On the Wehrmacht's perpetration of war crimes, see Dieter Pohl, *Die Herrschaft der Wehrmacht. Deutsche Militärbesatzung und einheimische Bevölkerung in der Sowjetunion 1941–1944* (Munich: Oldenbourg, 2008), pp. 348–9. For the figures of 18 and 10 million, see Christian Hartmann, *Wehrmacht im Ostkrieg. Front und militärisches Hinterland 1941/42* (Munich: Oldenbourg, 2009), pp. 12–13 and 16, fn. 29. For a spatial approach to Nazi (and Soviet) mass murder, see Timothy Snyder, *Bloodlands: Europe between Stalin*

296

and Hitler (New York: Basic Books, 2010). See also the discussion of local collaborators in the Conclusion in this book.

4. For the Yang Su definition, see Yang Su, 'Mass Killings in the Cultural Revolution: A Study of Three Provinces', in Joseph Esherick, Paul Pickowicz and Andrew George Walder, eds, *The Chinese Cultural Revolution as History* (Stanford, CA: Stanford University Press, 2006), pp. 96–123, here p. 98.

5. For the relevant passages in Lemkin's book, see Raphael Lemkin, *Axis Rule in Occupied Europe: Laws of Occupation, Analysis of Government, Proposals for Redress* (Washington, DC: Carnegie Endowment for International Peace, 1944), pp. 79–95. On Lemkin, see also Dominik J. Schaller and Jürgen Zimmerer, eds, *The Origins of Genocide: Raphael Lemkin as a Historian of Mass Violence* (Abingdon, Oxon: Routledge, 2009).

6. On the flaws of the UN definition, see Levene, *Genocide*, vol. 1, pp. 35–6. On developments since the late 1990s, see Dominik J. Schaller, 'From Lemkin to Clooney: The Development and State of Genocide Studies', *Genocide Studies and Prevention: An International Journal*, vol. 6, no. 3 (2011), pp. 245–56, esp. pp. 246–7. For genocide as an 'essentially contested concept', see Dan Stone, ed., *The Historiography of Genocide* (Houndmills: Palgrave Macmillan, 2008), p. 4. A useful and workable definition of genocide is offered by political scientist Adrian Gallagher: 'When a collective source of power (usually a State) intentionally uses its power base to implement a process of destruction in order to destroy a group (as defined by the perpetrator), in whole or in substantial part, dependent upon relative group size.' See Adrian Gallagher, *Genocide and its Threat to Contemporary International Order* (Houndmills: Palgrave Macmillan, 2013), p. 37.

7. For the alternative definition of 'mass killing' quoted, see Ervin Staub, *Overcoming Evil: Genocide, Violent Conflict, and Terrorism* (Oxford/New York: Oxford University Press, 2011), p. 100. On gender, see Elisa von Joeden-Forgey, 'Gender and Genocide', in Donald Bloxham and A. Dirk Moses, eds, *The Oxford Handbook of Genocide Studies* (Oxford: Oxford University Press, 2010), pp. 61–80, here p. 62. For one attempt to replace the genocide model, see Christian Gerlach, *Extremely Violent Societies: Mass Violence in the Twentieth-Century World* (Cambridge: Cambridge University Press, 2010). I am currently preparing a book on genocide in historical perspective. For a brilliant conceptual dissection, see Levene, *Genocide*, vol. 1, pp. 35–89.

8. On German plans exceeding actual violence and on differences between German and Soviet violence, see Christian Gerlach and Nicolas Werth, 'State Violence – Violent Societies', in Michael Geyer and Sheila Fitzpatrick, eds, *Beyond Totalitarianism: Stalinism and Nazism Compared* (Cambridge: Cambridge University Press, 2009), pp. 133–79, esp. pp. 175–9. On the General Plan East, see Karl Heinz Roth, '"Generalplan Ost" – "Gesamtplan Ost": Forschungsstand, Quellenprobleme, neue Ergebnisse', in Mechthild Rössler and Sabine Schleiermacher, eds, *Der 'Generalplan Ost': Hauptlinien der national-sozialistischen Planungs- und Vernichtungspolitik* (Berlin: Akademie, 1993), pp. 25–95; Alex J. Kay, *Exploitation, Resettlement, Mass Murder: Political and Economic Planning for German Occupation Policy in the Soviet Union, 1940–1941* (New York/Oxford: Berghahn Books, 2006), pp. 99–102.

9. See the discussion in Timothy Snyder, 'Hitler vs. Stalin: Who Killed More?', *New York Review of Books*, 10 March 2011, and Ian Johnson, 'Who Killed More? Hitler, Stalin, or Mao?', *New York Review of Books*, 5 February 2018; the comparative studies by Dietrich Beyrau, *Schlachtfeld der Diktatoren. Osteuropa im Schatten von Hitler und Stalin* (Göttingen: Vandenhoeck & Ruprecht, 2000), Stephen Wheatcroft, 'The Scale and Nature of German and Soviet Repression and Mass Killings, 1930–45', *Europe-Asia Studies*, vol. 48, no. 8 (December 1996), pp. 1319–53, Gerlach and Werth, 'State Violence', and Hans-Heinrich Nolte, 'Comparing Soviet and Nazi Mass Crimes', in Alex J. Kay and David Stahel, eds, *Mass Violence in Nazi-Occupied Europe* (Bloomington, IN: Indiana University Press, 2018), pp. 265–91; and the arguments of Jürgen Zarusky, 'Timothy Snyders "Bloodlands". Kritische Anmerkungen zur Konstruktion einer Geschichtslandschaft', *Vierteljahreshefte für Zeitgeschichte*, vol. 60, no. 1 (January 2012), pp. 1–31. On killings

during the Cultural Revolution, see also Yang Su, *Collective Killings in Rural China during the Cultural Revolution* (Cambridge/New York: Cambridge University Press, 2011). For 1 million victims of deliberate mass killing under Stalin, see Beyrau, *Schlachtfeld*, p. 119; Wheatcroft, 'The Scale and Nature', p. 1348. For the Soviet famine death tolls, see Zarusky, 'Timothy Snyders "Bloodlands"', p. 6.

10. See the literature cited in the previous note. For the Gulag death toll of 1.6 million, see Stephen A. Barnes, *Death and Redemption: The Gulag and the Shaping of Soviet Society* (Princeton, NJ/Oxford: Princeton University Press, 2011), p. 1; A.I. Kokurin and N.V. Petrov, eds, *Gulag (Glavnoe upravlenie lagerei), 1917–1960* (Moscow: Mezhdunarodnyi fond 'Demokratiia', 2000), doc. 103, p. 441. On the higher number of perpetrators in Nazi Germany than in Stalin's USSR, see Donald Bloxham, 'Organized Mass Murder: Structure, Participation, and Motivation in Comparative Perspective', *Holocaust and Genocide Studies*, vol. 22, no. 2 (autumn 2008), pp. 203–45, here p. 229. On Soviet perpetrators, see also Lynne Viola, 'The Question of the Perpetrator in Soviet History', *Slavic Review*, vol. 72, no. 1 (spring 2013), pp. 1–23. On the National Socialist 'war against children', see chapter 10.5 (pp. 1074–92) of Christian Gerlach, *Kalkulierte Morde. Die deutsche Wirtschafts- und Vernichtungspolitik in Weißrußland 1941 bis 1944* (Hamburg: Hamburger Edition, 1999). I use the term 'children' to refer to all those under the age of eighteen. Where I use the term 'adolescents', this is to be understood as referring to teenage children.

11. See Dieter Pohl, *Verfolgung und Massenmord in der NS-Zeit 1933–1945*, 3rd rev. edn (Darmstadt: Wissenschaftliche Buchgesellschaft, 2011 [2003]), pp. 3–4.

12. See Dieter Gosewinkel, 'Citizenship in Germany and France at the Turn of the Twentieth Century: Some New Observations on an Old Comparison', in Geoff Ely and Jan Palmowski, eds, *Citizenship and National Identity in Twentieth-Century Germany* (Stanford, CA: Stanford University Press, 2008), pp. 27–39.

13. See Sven Keller, 'Volksgemeinschaft and Violence: Some Reflections on Interdependencies', in Bernhard Gotto and Martina Steber, eds, *Visions of Community in Nazi Germany: Social Engineering and Private Lives* (Oxford: Oxford University Press, 2014), pp. 226–39. For the Haffner quote, see Haffner, *Geschichte eines Deutschen*, p. 23. On the turmoil of 1918 and the immediate post-war years, see Robert Gerwarth, *November 1918: The German Revolution* (Oxford: Oxford University Press, 2020); Robert Gerwarth, *The Vanquished: Why the First World War Failed to End, 1917–1923* (London: Allen Lane, 2016).

14. Christian Gerlach, *The Extermination of the European Jews* (Cambridge: Cambridge University Press, 2016), pp. 36–8. On German Southwest Africa, see also Jürgen Zimmerer, *Deutsche Herrschaft über Afrikaner. Staatlicher Machtanspruch und Wirklichkeit im kolonialen Namibia* (Münster: LIT, 2001). On German East Africa, see also Felicitas Becker and Jigal Beez, eds, *Der Maji-Maji-Krieg in Deutsch-Ostafrika 1905–1907* (Berlin: Ch. Links, 2005). On Belgium and France in 1914, see also John Horne and Alan Kramer, *German Atrocities 1914: A History of Denial* (New Haven, CT/London: Yale University Press, 2001). On continuities in German military culture dating back further still, to 1870, see Isabel V. Hull, *Absolute Destruction: Military Culture and the Practices of War in Imperial Germany* (Ithaca, NY: Cornell University Press, 2005), pp. 91–196. See, furthermore, the recent discussion in Bastian Matteo Scianna, 'A Predisposition to Brutality? German Practices against Civilians and *francs-tireurs* during the Franco-Prussian War 1870–1871 and their Relevance for the German "Military *Sonderweg*" Debate', *Small Wars & Insurgencies*, vol. 30, nos. 4–5 (2019), pp. 968–93.

15. On Jewish emancipation and education in Prussia and the German Reich, see Götz Aly, *Warum die Deutschen? Warum die Juden? Gleichheit, Neid und Rassenhass 1800–1933* (Frankfurt am Main: S. Fischer, 2011), pp. 37–48, esp. p. 42. On the role of the Enlightenment in Jewish emancipation, see also Philippe Burrin, *Nazi Anti-Semitism: From Prejudice to the Holocaust*, trans. from French by Janet Lloyd (New York/London: The New Press, 2005 [2000/2004]), pp. 19–22. For the Goebbels quote, see Tilman Tarach,

Der ewige Sündenbock. Heiliger Krieg, die 'Protokolle der Weisen von Zion' und die Verlogenheit der sogenannten Linken im Nahostkonflikt, 3rd rev. edn (Freiburg/Zurich: Edition Telok, 2010), p. 283.

16. Richard J. Evans, 'Wie einzigartig war die Ermordung der Juden durch die Nationalsozialisten?', in Günter Morsch and Bertrand Perz, eds, *Neue Studien zu national-sozialistischen Massentötungen durch Giftgas. Historische Bedeutung, technische Entwicklung, revisionistische Leugnung* (Berlin: Metropol, 2011), pp. 1–10, here p. 4. See also Jeffrey Herf, *The Jewish Enemy: Nazi Propaganda during World War II and the Holocaust* (Cambridge, MA: Harvard University Press, 2006); Hans-Erich Volkmann, ed., *Das Russlandbild im Dritten Reich* (Cologne: Böhlau, 1994). On the limitations of comparing colonialism with Nazi rule in Eastern Europe, see Robert Gerwarth and Stephan Malinowski, 'Der Holocaust als "kolonialer Genozid"? Europäische Kolonialgewalt und nationalsozialistischer Vernichtungskrieg', *Geschichte und Gesellschaft*, vol. 33 (2007), pp. 439–66, here pp. 455–9 (even if the examples cited of development, indirect rule and the training of local 'elites' are derived predominantly from British and French colonial practices rather than German ones).

17. The interplay between ideology and egotism is explored for one frontline Holocaust perpetrator in Alex J. Kay, *The Making of an SS Killer: The Life of Colonel Alfred Filbert, 1905–1990* (Cambridge: Cambridge University Press, 2016), esp. pp. 122–6. On the culture of resentment, see Burrin, *Nazi Anti-Semitism*, esp. pp. 89–91. For two case studies of German attitudes and policies in Eastern Europe, see Stephan Lehnstaedt, 'The Minsk Experience: German Occupiers and Everyday Life in the Capital of Belarus', in Alex J. Kay, Jeff Rutherford and David Stahel, eds, *Nazi Policy on the Eastern Front, 1941: Total War, Genocide, and Radicalization* (Rochester, NY: University of Rochester Press, 2012), pp. 240–66; Alexander Prusin, 'A Community of Violence: The SiPo/SD and its Role in the Nazi Terror System in Generalbezirk Kiew', *Holocaust and Genocide Studies*, vol. 21, no. 1 (spring 2007), pp. 1–30.

CHAPTER 1 KILLING THE SICK IN THE GERMAN REICH AND POLAND

1. See Heinz Faulstich, *Hungersterben in der Psychiatrie 1914–1949: Mit einer Topographie der NS-Psychiatrie* (Freiburg im Breisgau: Lambertus, 1998), pp. 25–83.

2. Philipp Rauh, 'Der Krieg gegen die "nutzlosen Esser". Psychiatriepatienten als Opfer der NS-"Euthanasie"', in Christoph Dieckmann and Babette Quinkert, eds, *Kriegführung und Hunger 1939–1945. Zum Verhältnis von militärischen, wirtschaftlichen und politischen Interessen* (Göttingen: Wallstein, 2015), pp. 33–58, here pp. 35–9. On Sweden, see Kristina Engwall, 'Starved to Death? Nutrition in Asylums during the World Wars', *Scandinavian Journal of Disability Research*, vol. 7, no. 1 (2005), pp. 2–22, here p. 13. For the Hitler quote, see Institut für Zeitgeschichte, ed., *Hitler. Reden, Schriften, Anordnungen: Februar 1925 bis Januar 1933, Band III: Zwischen den Reichstagswahlen, Juli 1928–September 1930, Teil 2: März 1929–Dezember 1929* (Munich: K.G. Saur, 1994), doc. 64, p. 348.

3. On the removal of barriers to state-sanctioned measures, see Ian Kershaw, '"Working towards the Führer." Reflections on the Nature of the Hitler Dictatorship', *Contemporary European History*, vol. 2, no. 2 (July 1993), pp. 103–18, here pp. 114–15. For the figure of 300,000 sterilisations, see Udo Benzenhöfer and Hanns Ackermann, *Die Zahl der Verfahren und der Sterilisationen nach dem Gesetz zur Verhütung erbkranken Nachwuchses* (Münster: Kontur, 2015), pp. 26–7. For the date of 1 January 1940 for Austria, see 'Verordnung über die Einführung des Gesetzes zur Verhütung erbkranken Nachwuchses und des Gesetzes zum Schutze der Erbgesundheit des deutschen Volkes in der Ostmark', *Reichsgesetzblatt*, 1939, Part 1, 14 November 1939, pp. 2230–2, here p. 2232 (§11). For the figure of 5,000 deaths, see Asmus Nitschke, *Die 'Erbpolizei' im Nationalsozialismus. Zur Alltagsgeschichte der Gesundheitsämter im Dritten Reich* (Opladen/Wiesbaden: Westdeutscher Verlag, 1999), pp. 111–12. On suicide, see Michael Burleigh, 'Psychiatry, German Society and the Nazi "Euthanasia" Programme', in Omer Bartov, ed., *The*

Holocaust: Origins, Implementation, Aftermath (London/New York: Routledge, 2000), pp. 43-62, here p. 50. For Hitler's comments to Wagner, see Manfred Vasold, 'Medizin', in Benz et al., eds, *Enzyklopädie*, pp. 235-50, here p. 245. See also Harvard Law School Library, Nuremberg Trials Project (hereafter HLSL), Trial Transcripts, Trial Transcript for NMT 1: Medical Case, Testimony of defendant Karl Brandt, HLSL Seq. No. 2419, 4 February 1947, p. 2402.

4. On Wagner and Nitsche, see Rauh, 'Krieg gegen die "nutzlosen Esser"', p. 44. For both Bernotat quotes, see Peter Sandner, *Verwaltung des Krankenmordes. Der Bezirksverband Nassau im Nationalsozialismus* (Gießen: Psychosozial-Verlag, 2003), pp. 320-1. For the 1938 quote, see Henry Friedlander, *The Origins of Nazi Genocide: From Euthanasia to the Final Solution* (Chapel Hill, NC/London: University of North Carolina Press, 1995), p. 62.

5. This important case has been reconstructed by Ulf Schmidt, 'Reassessing the Beginning of the "Euthanasia" Programme', *German History*, vol. 17, no. 4 (October 1999), pp. 543-50. For the surname of the child, see Ulf Schmidt, *Karl Brandt: The Nazi Doctor – Medicine and Power in the Third Reich* (London: Hambledon Continuum, 2007), pp. 117-18. On Catel killing the baby, see Udo Benzenhöfer, 'NS-"Kindereuthanasie": "Ohne jede moralische Skrupel"', *Deutsches Ärzteblatt*, vol. 97, no. 42 (October 2000), pp. A2766-72, here p. A2766. On the legal amendment of June 1935, see Friedlander, *Origins of Nazi Genocide*, p. 30.

6. Friedlander, *Origins of Nazi Genocide*, pp. 40-1 and 45-6; Benzenhöfer, 'NS-"Kindereuthanasie"', pp. A2768-70.

7. Voluntary testimony by Ludwig Lehner (Nbg. Doc. NO-863), 30 March 1947, quoted in Ernst Klee, *'Euthanasie' im NS-Staat. Die 'Vernichtung lebensunwerten Lebens'* (Frankfurt am Main: Fischer Taschenbuch, 1985), pp. 88-9. On the guided tours, see Michael Burleigh, *Death and Deliverance: 'Euthanasia' in Germany, c. 1900-1945* (Cambridge: Cambridge University Press, 1994), pp. 43-6.

8. On the 'special children's wards' and the instructions of September 1941, see Klee, *'Euthanasie'*, pp. 300-4. On parents, see Friedlander, *Origins of Nazi Genocide*, pp. 59-60.

9. Thomas Beddies, 'Die Einbeziehung von Minderjährigen in die nationalsozialistischen Medizinverbrechen – dargestellt am Beispiel der brandenburgischen Landesanstalt Görden', *Praxis der Kinderpsychologie und Kinderpsychiatrie*, vol. 58, no. 7 (2009), pp. 518-29, here pp. 520-1 and 524. On the cause of death and the two examples from Eglfing-Haar, see Julia Katzur, 'Die "Kinderfachabteilung" in der Heil- und Pflegeanstalt Eglfing-Haar und die nationalsozialistische "Kindereuthanasie" zwischen 1940-1945', unpublished doctoral thesis, Technische Universität München, 2017, pp. 107-8 and 129.

10. See Götz Aly, *Die Belasteten. 'Euthanasie' 1939-1945: Eine Gesellschaftsgeschichte* (Frankfurt am Main: S. Fischer, 2014), esp. pp. 153-61. For the Eglfing-Haar example, see Gerhard Schmidt, *Selektion in der Heilanstalt 1939-1945. Neuausgabe mit ergänzenden Texten*, ed. Frank Schneider (Berlin/Heidelberg: Springer, 2012), p. 137. On the added strain resulting from the war, see Katzur, '"Kinderfachabteilung"', pp. 161 and 168.

11. For the Eglfing-Haar figures and on those discharged, see Katzur, '"Kinderfachabteilung"', pp. 127-8. On Mosbach, see Klee, *'Euthanasie'*, p. 308 (emphasis in the original).

12. Petra Fuchs et al., 'Minderjährige als Opfer der Krankenmordaktion "T4"', in Thomas Beddies and Kristina Hübener, eds, *Kinder in der NS-Psychiatrie* (Berlin: be.bra, 2004), pp. 55-70; Benzenhöfer, 'NS-"Kindereuthanasie"', p. A2772. Gerrit Hohendorf puts the number of deaths during the child 'euthanasia' programme at 6,800; letter to the author, 5 December 2019.

13. Friedlander, *Origins of Nazi Genocide*, pp. 62-8; Ian Kershaw, *Hitler 1936-1945: Nemesis* (London: Allen Lane, 2000), pp. 252-5 and 259-61. For Hitler's letter of authorisation, see HLSL, Evidence Files, PS-630, signed A[dolf] Hitler, 1 September 1939.

14. Rauh, 'Krieg gegen die "nutzlosen Esser"', p. 46; Ulrike Winkler and Gerrit Hohendorf, 'The Murder of Psychiatric Patients by the SS and the Wehrmacht in Poland and the Soviet Union, Especially in Mogilev, 1939-1945', in Kay and Stahel, eds, *Mass Violence*, pp. 147-70, here pp. 148-9; Friedlander, *Origins of Nazi Genocide*, pp. 136-7. For the

Schwede-Coburg quote and on Eimann shooting first, see Klee, 'Euthanasie', pp. 95 and 97.

15. On the Fort VII killings and on Dziekanka, see Michael Alberti, *Die Verfolgung und Vernichtung der Juden im Reichsgau Wartheland 1939–1945* (Wiesbaden: Harrassowitz, 2006), pp. 326–7. On Himmler's visit, see Peter Longerich, *Heinrich Himmler*, trans. from German by Jeremy Noakes and Lesley Sharpe (Oxford: Oxford University Press, 2012 [2008]), p. 431. On the murders in mobile gas vans and the subsequent use of the cleared institutions, see Winkler and Hohendorf, 'Murder of Psychiatric Patients', p. 148. On the transit camp in Działdowo, see Sascha Topp et al., 'Die Provinz Ostpreußen und die nationalsozialistische "Euthanasie": SS–"Aktion Lange" und "Aktion T4"', *Medizinhistorisches Journal*, vol. 43, no. 1 (2008), pp. 20–55, here p. 39; Götz Aly, 'Endlösung'. *Völkerverschiebung und der Mord an den europäischen Juden* (Frankfurt am Main: S. Fischer, 1995), pp. 188–9.

16. National Holocaust Centre and Museum, Laxton (hereafter NHCM), video testimony of Barbara Stimler, November 1998, 23:17–24:03.

17. Volker Rieß, *Die Anfänge der Vernichtung 'lebensunwerten Lebens' in den Reichsgauen Danzig-Westpreußen und Wartheland 1939/40* (Frankfurt am Main: Peter Lang, 1995), p. 355; Zdzisław Jaroszewski, ed., *Zagłada chorych psychicznie w Polsce 1939–1945* (Warsaw: Wydawnictwo Naukowe PWN, 1993), pp. 16–17. For the quote, see Klee, 'Euthanasie', p. 114. On the Chełm ruse, see Friedlander, *Origins of Nazi Genocide*, pp. 274–81.

18. On ethnic Germans and the Reich commissioner, see Rauh, 'Krieg gegen die "nutzlosen Esser"', pp. 47–8. For the figure of 16,500, see Winkler and Hohendorf, 'Murder of Psychiatric Patients', p. 148.

19. Rauh, 'Krieg gegen die "nutzlosen Esser"', pp. 48–9.

20. Ibid., pp. 49–50; Dan Diner, 'Rationalisierung und Methode. Zu einem neuen Erklärungsversuch der "Endlösung"', *Vierteljahrshefte für Zeitgeschichte*, vol. 40, no. 3 (July 1992), pp. 359–82, here p. 369.

21. From a report by Pohlisch on the question of psychogenic reactions to air attacks among the Rhenish population, dated 6 July 1943, quoted in Rauh, 'Krieg gegen die "nutzlosen Esser"', p. 50.

22. Rauh, 'Krieg gegen die "nutzlosen Esser"', pp. 50–1.

23. Ibid., pp. 51–2.

24. Friedlander, *Origins of Nazi Genocide*, pp. 86–9. On the 70,000 expected victims, see Klee, 'Euthanasie', p. 102. For the Brack quote, see HLSL, Trial Transcripts, Trial Transcript for NMT 1: Medical Case, Testimony of defendant Karl Brandt, HLSL Seq. Nos. 7799–800, 16 May 1947, pp. 7652–3.

25. Rauh, 'Krieg gegen die "nutzlosen Esser"', pp. 33–4 (quote: p. 33). On the treatment of those maligned as 'useless eaters', see Kay and Stahel, eds, *Mass Violence*, part III (pp. 121–70).

26. For the letters from Else von Löwis, Walter Buch and Himmler to Buch, see HLSL, Evidence Files, NO-001 and NO-002. The letter from Himmler to Brack is quoted in Klee, 'Euthanasie', p. 291. On the closure and replacement of Brandenburg and Grafeneck, see also Friedlander, *Origins of Nazi Genocide*, pp. 106–108.

27. Friedlander, *Origins of Nazi Genocide*, p. 93.

28. Ibid., p. 108.

29. Annette Hinz-Wessels, 'Antisemitismus und Krankenmord. Zum Umgang mit jüdischen Anstaltspatienten im Nationalsozialismus', *Vierteljahrshefte für Zeitgeschichte*, vol. 61, no. 1 (January 2013), pp. 65–92; Friedlander, *Origins of Nazi Genocide*, pp. 263–83; Peter Longerich, *Der ungeschriebene Befehl. Hitler und der Weg zur 'Endlösung'* (Munich: Piper, 2001), p. 76.

30. Friedlander, *Origins of Nazi Genocide*, p. 111; Rauh, 'Krieg gegen die "nutzlosen Esser"', pp. 52–3; Pohl, *Verfolgung und Massenmord*, p. 32. For the Klemperer quote, see Victor Klemperer, *Tagebücher 1940–1941*, ed. Walter Nowojski (Berlin: Aufbau, 1995), p. 156 (entry for 22 August 1941). See also the entry for 21 May 1941 in Klemperer, *Tagebücher 1940–1941*, p. 90.

31. On Protestant denunciations and Galen's knowledge of the 'euthanasia' programme since July 1940, see Beth A. Griech-Polelle, *Bishop von Galen: German Catholicism and National Socialism* (New Haven, CT/London: Yale University Press, 2002), pp. 59–60 and 73–8. On the war-related factors, see Rauh, 'Krieg gegen die "nutzlosen Esser"', pp. 52–3. On the stalling of the military campaign against the Soviet Union, see David Stahel, *Operation Barbarossa and Germany's Defeat in the East* (Cambridge: Cambridge University Press, 2009), pp. 153–451.

32. National Archives and Records Administration, RG 338, T-1021, roll 18, frames 98 and 102. On the Hadamar celebrations and on other sources suggesting a possible total figure of 80,000 murdered patients, see Friedlander, *Origins of Nazi Genocide*, p. 110.

33. Friedlander, *Origins of Nazi Genocide*, pp. 111 and 150–2; Winfried Süß, *Der 'Volkskörper' im Krieg. Gesundheitspolitik, Gesundheitsverhältnisse und Krankenmord im nationalsozialistischen Deutschland 1939-1945* (Munich: Oldenbourg, 2003), pp. 313–14; Georg Lilienthal, 'NS-"Euthanasie"-Mordopfer und Wege des Gedenkens', in Sybille Quack, ed., *Dimensionen der Verfolgung. Opfer und Opfergruppen im Nationalsozialismus* (Munich: Deutsche Verlags-Anstalt, 2003), pp. 251–77, here pp. 256–7, 259 and 262. On the 'special children's wards', see Klee, *'Euthanasie'*, p. 379.

34. Friedlander, *Origins of Nazi Genocide*, p. 152. On Eglfing-Haar, see also Süß, *'Volkskörper'*, p. 324. On the so-called decentralised 'euthanasia', see also Chapter 11 in this book.

35. On parallels between 'euthanasia' and Holocaust, see Friedlander, *Origins of Nazi Genocide*, pp. 281–302; Longerich, *Der ungeschriebene Befehl*, pp. 75–6.

CHAPTER 2 DECAPITATION OF POLISH SOCIETY

1. On the Heydrich–Wagner agreement, see Philip T. Rutherford, *Prelude to the Final Solution: The Nazi Program for Deporting Ethnic Poles, 1939-1941* (Lawrence, KS: University Press of Kansas, 2007), p. 41; Michael Wildt, *Generation des Unbedingten. Das Führungskorps des Reichssicherheitshauptamtes*, rev. edn (Hamburg: Hamburger Edition, 2003 [2002]), pp. 426–8. For the Halder quote, see Christian Hartmann and Sergej Slutsch, 'Franz Halder und die Kriegsvorbereitungen im Frühjahr 1939. Eine Ansprache des Generalstabschefs des Heeres', *Vierteljahrshefte für Zeitgeschichte*, vol. 45, no. 3 (July 1997), pp. 467–95, here p. 493.

2. Rutherford, *Prelude to the Final Solution*, pp. 42–3; Dorothee Weitbrecht, 'Ermächtigung zur Vernichtung. Die Einsatzgruppen in Polen im Herbst 1939', in Klaus-Michael Mallmann and Bogdan Musial, eds, *Genesis des Genozids. Polen 1939-1941* (Darmstadt: Wissenschaftliche Buchgesellschaft, 2004), pp. 57–70, here p. 58.

3. For the Himmler quote, see Jochen Böhler, *Auftakt zum Vernichtungskrieg. Die Wehrmacht in Polen 1939* (Frankfurt am Main: Fischer Taschenbuch, 2006), pp. 204–5. For the Heydrich quote, see Bundesarchiv Berlin-Lichterfelde (hereafter BArch Berlin), R 58/825, fols 1–3, 'Vermerk: Amtschefbesprechung am 7. 9. 1939', Stabskanzlei, I 11 Rf./Fh., dated 8 September 1939, here fol. 2. On the 'self-defence' units, see Christian Jansen and Arno Weckbecker, *Der 'Volksdeutsche Selbstschutz' in Polen 1939/40* (Munich: Oldenbourg, 1992), pp. 34–5. On the 3 per cent, see Rutherford, *Prelude to the Final Solution*, p. 43. For the Hitler quote, see Snyder, *Bloodlands*, p. 126.

4. See Böhler, *Auftakt*, esp. pp. 241–2; Jochen Böhler, '"Tragische Verstrickung" oder Auftakt zum Vernichtungskrieg? Die Wehrmacht in Polen 1939', in Mallmann and Musial, eds, *Genesis des Genozids*, pp. 36–56. For a figure of 16,000 Poles murdered by the Wehrmacht up to the end of the Polish campaign in early October, see Alexander B. Rossino, *Hitler Strikes Poland: Blitzkrieg, Ideology, and Atrocity* (Lawrence, KS: University Press of Kansas, 2003), pp. 86–7. On 1914 as a reference point, see Horne and Kramer, *German Atrocities*, p. 406; Wildt, *Generation*, pp. 437–8.

5. Böhler, *Auftakt*, pp. 100–6 and 115–17; Böhler, '"Tragische Verstrickung"', p. 40.

6. Böhler, *Auftakt*, pp. 205–6 (Braemer quote: p. 206).

7. Ibid., pp. 205–8 (Braemer quote: p. 208); Weitbrecht, 'Ermächtigung zur Vernichtung', p. 61; Helmut Krausnick, 'Die Einsatzgruppen vom Anschluß Österreichs bis zum

Feldzug gegen die Sowjetunion. Entwicklung und Verhältnis zur Wehrmacht', in Helmut Krausnick and Hans-Heinrich Wilhelm, *Die Truppe des Weltanschauungskrieges. Die Einsatzgruppen der Sicherheitspolizei und des SD 1938–1942* (Stuttgart: Deutsche Verlags-Anstalt, 1981), pp. 11–278, here pp. 55–62 (Einsatzgruppe IV quote: p. 62).

8. Böhler, *Auftakt*, pp. 172–3 (quote: p. 172). After the war, Polish eyewitnesses estimated the number of victims at around 400 (ibid., p. 172, fn. 748).

9. Böhler, '"Tragische Verstrickung"', p. 49; Böhler, *Auftakt*, pp. 171–2 and 175.

10. Böhler, *Auftakt*, pp. 174 and 176.

11. Ibid., pp. 211–14; Alexander B. Rossino, 'Nazi Anti-Jewish Policy during the Polish Campaign: The Case of the Einsatzgruppe von Woyrsch', *German Studies Review*, vol. 24, no. 1 (February 2001), pp. 35–53, here pp. 39–42.

12. Weitbrecht, 'Ermächtigung zur Vernichtung', pp. 64–5 (quote: p. 65); Böhler, *Auftakt*, pp. 240 and 246. On the shootings in Świecie, see also Jansen and Weckbecker, *Der 'Volksdeutsche Selbstschutz'*, pp. 117–19.

13. For the Heydrich quote, see Christopher R. Browning, with contributions by Jürgen Matthäus, *The Origins of the Final Solution: The Evolution of Nazi Jewish Policy, September 1939–March 1942* (London: William Heinemann, 2004), pp. 31–2. On the annexation order, see Rutherford, *Prelude to the Final Solution*, p. 58. On the meeting of 17 October, see Krausnick, 'Einsatzgruppen', pp. 85–6.

14. Krausnick, 'Einsatzgruppen', pp. 87–93 (Einsatzkommando 16 quote: pp. 88–9). For the quote from *The Black Book*, see Polish Ministry of Information, *Black Book*, pp. 28–9. On Greiser and Himmler, see Catherine Epstein, *Model Nazi: Arthur Greiser and the Occupation of Western Poland* (Oxford: Oxford University Press, 2010), pp. 153–6.

15. Polish Ministry of Information, *Black Book*, p. 30. Between 1939 and 1945, Gdynia was renamed Gotenhafen.

16. Institute of National Remembrance, *The Destruction of the Polish Elite: Operation AB – Katyn* (Warsaw: Instytut Pamięci Narodowej, 2009), p. 54; Magdalena Gawin, '"Flurbereinigung". Der Zusammenhang zwischen der Vernichtung der polnischen Intelligenz und der nationalsozialistischen Rassenhygiene', in Piotr Madajczyk and Paweł Popieliński, eds, *Social Engineering. Zwischen totalitärer Utopie und 'Piecemeal-Pragmatismus'* (Warsaw: Instytut Studiów Politycznych PAN, 2014), pp. 118–40, here pp. 123 and 140.

17. Krausnick, 'Einsatzgruppen', pp. 90–4 (Rasch quote: p. 94); Jens Banach, *Heydrichs Elite. Das Führerkorps der Sicherheitspolizei und des SD 1936–1945*, 3rd rev. edn (Paderborn: Ferdinand Schöningh, 2002 [1998]), pp. 226–8.

18. Browning, *Origins of the Final Solution*, pp. 31–3. For the total number of victims of Selbstschutz units and the proportion killed in West Prussia, see Jansen and Weckbecker, *Der 'Volksdeutsche Selbstschutz'*, pp. 155–6 and 211–29. For the figure of 40,000, see Maria Wardzyńska, *Był rok 1939. Operacja niemieckiej policji bezpieczeństwa w Polsce – Intelligenzaktion*, (Warsaw: Instytut Pamięci Narodowej, 2009), p. 182.

19. For the figures of 60,000 and 5,000, see Pohl, *Verfolgung und Massenmord*, p. 49. See also the figures cited in Bogdan Musial, *Deutsche Zivilverwaltung und Judenverfolgung im Generalgouvernement. Eine Fallstudie zum Distrikt Lublin 1939–1944* (Wiesbaden: Harrassowitz, 1999), p. 106; Gerlach, *Extermination*, p. 292. For the 7,000 Jews, see Rossino, *Hitler Strikes Poland*, p. 234. On deportations, see Rutherford, *Prelude to the Final Solution*, pp. 88–97. On expulsions across the San river, see Böhler, '"Tragische Verstrickung"', p. 46. On Hitler and Rosenberg, see Browning, *Origins of the Final Solution*, p. 27.

20. Snyder, *Bloodlands*, pp. 146–7; Krausnick, 'Einsatzgruppen', pp. 100–1. For the Frank quote, see Yasemin Shooman, 'Die Rotunde von Zamość', in Wolfgang Benz and Barbara Distel, eds, *Der Ort des Terrors. Geschichte der nationalsozialistischen Konzentrationslager, Band 9* (Munich: C.H. Beck, 2009), pp. 497–510, here p. 498.

21. Robert Seidel, *Deutsche Besatzungspolitik in Polen: Der Distrikt Radom 1939–1945* (Paderborn: Ferdinand Schöningh, 2006), pp. 186–8.

22. Institute of National Remembrance, *Destruction of the Polish Elite*, pp. 57–61. On operations against Dobrzański's unit and the killings in the Leśny Stadium and the Brzask Forest, see also Seidel, *Deutsche Besatzungspolitik*, pp. 189–91. For a figure of around 300 murdered in Firlej, see Polish Ministry of Information, *Black Book*, p. 52.
23. Institute of National Remembrance, *Destruction of the Polish Elite*, pp. 62–6; Snyder, *Bloodlands*, p. 147. On large transports arriving at the Pawiak prison, see Pilecki Institute, Testimony Database – Chronicles of Terror, testimony of former prisoner Janina Kozak, 21 May 1946, and testimony of former nurse Stanisława Sroka, 21 May 1946. For the figure of 1,700 people murdered in the Kampinos Forest, see Wardzyńska, *Był rok 1939*, p. 243.
24. Institute of National Remembrance, *Destruction of the Polish Elite*, pp. 67–8.
25. For the figure of 3,500 Poles, see Wardzyńska, *Był rok 1939*, p. 270. For the 3,000 common criminals, see Snyder, *Bloodlands*, p. 147. Both figures are also given by Longerich, *Heinrich Himmler*, p. 438. For a total death toll of 6,500 during Operation AB and on the concentration camps, see Institute of National Remembrance, *Destruction of the Polish Elite*, pp. 69–70 and 81. See also Shooman, 'Rotunde', p. 498. Dieter Pohl cites a total figure of '4,000 Poles': Pohl, *Verfolgung und Massenmord*, p. 49. On Auschwitz, see Chapter 9 in this book. For the total figure of 100,000 killed between late summer 1939 and late summer 1940, see Wardzyńska, *Był rok 1939*, p. 74. Christian Gerlach cites a figure of 60,000–80,000 Polish civilians murdered by early 1940: Gerlach, *Extermination*, p. 292. For the Hitler quote, see Krausnick, 'Einsatzgruppen', p. 33. For the Greiser quote, see Polish Ministry of Information, *Black Book*, p. 73.

CHAPTER 3 HOLOCAUST BY BULLETS

1. On the massacres of black African troops in French service, see Raffael Scheck, *Hitler's African Victims: The German Army Massacres of Black French Soldiers in 1940* (New York: Cambridge University Press, 2006).
2. Pohl, *Herrschaft*, p. 78; Ben Shepherd, *Terror in the Balkans: German Armies and Partisan Warfare* (Cambridge, MA: Harvard University Press, 2012), pp. 87–8; Walter Manoschek, *'Serbien ist judenfrei'. Militärische Besatzungspolitik und Judenvernichtung in Serbien 1941/42* (Munich: Oldenbourg, 1993), pp. 31–2.
3. Manoschek, *'Serbien ist judenfrei'*, p. 35.
4. Pohl, *Herrschaft*, p. 79; Manoschek, *'Serbien ist judenfrei'*, pp. 39–40 (quote: p. 39). On the Fuchs order, see Walter Manoschek, 'Die Vernichtung der Juden in Serbien', in Ulrich Herbert, ed., *Nationalsozialistische Vernichtungspolitik 1939–1945. Neue Forschungen und Kontroversen* (Frankfurt am Main: Fischer Taschenbuch, 1998), pp. 209–34, here p. 211.
5. Manoschek, *'Serbien ist judenfrei'*, pp. 41–2; Jürgen Förster, *Die Wehrmacht im NS-Staat. Eine strukturgeschichtliche Analyse* (Munich: Oldenbourg, 2009), pp. 87–8.
6. Shepherd, *Terror in the Balkans*, pp. 89–92. On the Ustasha, see Alexander Korb, *Im Schatten des Weltkriegs. Massengewalt der Ustaša gegen Serben, Juden und Roma in Kroatien, 1941–1945* (Hamburg: Hamburger Edition, 2013).
7. Shepherd, *Terror in the Balkans*, pp. 95 and 99–100 (quote: p. 99).
8. Manoschek, *'Serbien ist judenfrei'*, pp. 43–4.
9. Quoted in Manoschek, 'Vernichtung der Juden', p. 215. Geissler is a pseudonym.
10. On the shootings in July and August and for the Hitler quote, see Manoschek, 'Vernichtung der Juden', p. 216. On Wehrmacht complicity and on the alliance between Chetniks and communist partisans, see Shepherd, *Terror in the Balkans*, pp. 101, 110 and 120.
11. Browning, *Origins of the Final Solution*, pp. 337–8. For the quote, see Shepherd, *Terror in the Balkans*, p. 121.
12. Manoschek, *'Serbien ist judenfrei'*, pp. 84–5 (including both quotes).
13. On German reprisals and the policy of murdering hostages, see Shepherd, *Terror in the Balkans*, pp. 103–4 and 121–2; Manoschek, 'Vernichtung der Juden', p. 216. On the equation of Jews with communists, see Shepherd, *Terror in the Balkans*, p. 101; Browning,

Origins of the Final Solution, p. 339. On the new role of the Wehrmacht, see Manoschek, 'Vernichtung der Juden', p. 222.

14. Browning, *Origins of the Final Solution*, pp. 340-1 (quotes: p. 341). On the propaganda company and on the Mountain Corps Signals Detachment, see Manoschek, 'Serbien ist judenfrei', pp. 88-9 and 92.

15. Manoschek, 'Vernichtung der Juden', p. 225.

16. Browning, *Origins of the Final Solution*, pp. 343-4 (quote: p. 343).

17. Ibid., p. 344. On the collaborators, see Manoschek, 'Vernichtung der Juden', p. 226; Klaus Schmider, *Partisanenkrieg in Jugoslawien 1941-1944* (Hamburg: Mittler, 2002), p. 73. For the quotes, see Manoschek, 'Serbien ist judenfrei', p. 165.

18. Manoschek, 'Serbien ist judenfrei', pp. 96-7 and 165-6 (first quote: p. 166; second quote: p. 97). On the 433rd Infantry Regiment and the 2,200 victims, see Shepherd, *Terror in the Balkans*, p. 123. For the figure of 250 Roma, see Michael Zimmermann, *Rassenutopie und Genozid. Die nationalsozialistische 'Lösung der Zigeunerfrage'* (Hamburg: Christians, 1996), p. 253. For the date of events in Valjevo, see Milovan Pisarri, *The Suffering of the Roma in Serbia during the Holocaust*, trans. from Serbian by Nataša Dinić (Belgrade: Forum for Applied History, 2014), p. 68.

19. On Böhme and the official figures, see Manoschek, 'Serbien ist judenfrei', p. 166. For the actual death toll of up to 30,000 civilians, see ibid.; Pohl, *Verfolgung und Massenmord*, p. 122. For the figures of 5,000 Jews and 2,500 Roma, see Pisarri, *Suffering of the Roma*, p. 156. Dieter Pohl suggests that the number of Jewish dead by the end of 1941 was closer to 6,000: Pohl, *Verfolgung und Massenmord*, p. 79.

20. Browning, *Origins of the Final Solution*, p. 345. On difficulties in fulfilling the old quota as a key reason for the reduction, see Schmider, *Partisanenkrieg*, p. 83.

21. Browning, *Origins of the Final Solution*, pp. 341 and 346 (Turner quote: p. 341). On the gassing of the women, children and elderly Jews in Sajmište concentration camp the following year, see Chapter 8 in this book.

22. For the quotes, see Adolf Hitler, *Mein Kampf. Zwei Bände in einem Band* (Munich: Zentralverlag der NSDAP, 1943 [1925–26]), pp. 751-2. On Hitler's decision to invade the Soviet Union, see Kay, *Exploitation*, pp. 26-46.

23. Kay, *Making of an SS Killer*, pp. 41-3; Alex J. Kay, 'Transition to Genocide, July 1941: Einsatzkommando 9 and the Annihilation of Soviet Jewry', *Holocaust and Genocide Studies*, vol. 27, no. 3 (winter 2013), pp. 411-42, here pp. 412-14. On the Einsatzgruppen's official title, see Klaus-Michael Mallmann, 'Menschenjagd und Massenmord. Das neue Instrument der Einsatzgruppen und -kommandos 1938-1945', in Gerhard Paul and Klaus-Michael Mallmann, eds, *Die Gestapo im Zweiten Weltkrieg. 'Heimatfront' und besetztes Europa* (Darmstadt: Wissenschaftliche Buchgesellschaft, 2000), pp. 291-316, here p. 304.

24. Kay, *Making of an SS Killer*, p. 42.

25. Ibid.; Kay, 'Transition to Genocide', pp. 413-14. Quote from 'Guidelines for the Conduct of the Troops in Russia' in Bundesarchiv-Militärarchiv, Freiburg im Breisgau (hereafter BArch-MA), RH 22/12, fols 114–15, 'Richtlinien für das Verhalten der Truppe in Rußland', undated [19 May 1941], here fol. 114 (emphasis in the original).

26. Kay, *Making of an SS Killer*, pp. 41-2; Kay, 'Transition to Genocide', p. 416.

27. Kay, 'Transition to Genocide', pp. 416-17 (all quotes: p. 417). On the civilian internment camps, see Gerlach, *Kalkulierte Morde*, pp. 504-5.

28. Longerich, *Der ungeschriebene Befehl*, pp. 100 and 202-4. On SK 1a, see Christoph Dieckmann, *Deutsche Besatzungspolitik in Litauen 1941-1944, Band 1* (Göttingen: Wallstein, 2011), p. 384, fn. 381. An Advance Commando Moscow, which was to fulfil special tasks in the Soviet capital, was also part of EG B.

29. On the killings by EK Tilsit, see Longerich, *Der ungeschriebene Befehl*, p. 202; Browning, *Origins of the Final Solution*, pp. 253-5. For the Jäger quote, see 'Ereignismeldung UdSSR' (hereafter EM) 19 (11 July 1941), reproduced in: Klaus-Michael Mallmann, Andrej Angrick, Jürgen Matthäus and Martin Cüppers, eds, *Die 'Ereignismeldungen UdSSR' 1941. Dokumente der Einsatzgruppen in der Sowjetunion I* (Darmstadt: Wissenschaftliche Buchgesellschaft,

2011), p. 103. On EKs 5 and 6, see *Trials of War Criminals before the Nuernberg Military Tribunals under Control Council Law No. 10*, vol. 4 (Washington, DC: U.S. Government Printing Office, 1950), Affidavit of Erwin Schulz, 26 May 1947, pp. 135–8, here pp. 136–8. On EK 9, see Kay, *Making of an SS Killer*, pp. 55 and 72; Kay, 'Transition to Genocide', p. 415. On Einsatzgruppe z.b.V., see EM 43 (5 August 1941), p. 231. On SK 10b, see Andrej Angrick, *Besatzungspolitik und Massenmord. Die Einsatzgruppe D in der südlichen Sowjetunion 1941–1943* (Hamburg: Hamburger Edition, 2003), pp. 150–3; Andrej Angrick, 'Die Einsatzgruppe D', in Peter Klein, ed., *Die Einsatzgruppen in der besetzten Sowjetunion 1941/42. Die Tätigkeits- und Lageberichte des Chefs der Sicherheitspolizei und des SD* (Berlin: Edition Hentrich, 1997), pp. 88–110, here p. 92.

30. Pohl, *Herrschaft*, pp. 243–82; Johannes Hürter, 'Hitler's Generals in the East and the Holocaust', in Kay and Stahel, eds, *Mass Violence*, pp. 17–40, here pp. 27–8.
31. On Signals Detachment 537 of the 286th Security Division, Infantry Regiment 691 (also subordinated to the 286th Security Division), units of the 339th Infantry Division, the 707th Infantry Division, the 62nd Infantry Division and the 454th Security Division, and on the second battalion of Infantry Regiment 350 of the 221st Security Division, see Jörn Hasenclever, *Wehrmacht und Besatzungspolitik. Die Befehlshaber der rückwärtigen Heeresgebiete 1941–1943* (Paderborn: Ferdinand Schöningh, 2010), pp. 496–7, 501–2, 506–7, 519 and 553–4. On the 12th Company of Infantry Regiment 354 of the 286th Security Division and the 707th Infantry Division, see Gerlach, *Kalkulierte Morde*, pp. 586–7 and 617–20. On the 25th Infantry Division and the 707th Infantry Division, see Ben H. Shepherd, *Hitler's Soldiers: The German Army in the Third Reich* (New Haven, CT/London: Yale University Press, 2016), pp. 173–6. On the 72nd Infantry Division, the 707th Infantry Division and Wehrmacht participation in general, see Pohl, *Herrschaft*, pp. 265, 340 and 342. On the Seventeenth Army, see Manfred Oldenburg, *Ideologie und militärisches Kalkül. Die Besatzungspolitik der Wehrmacht in der Sowjetunion 1942* (Cologne: Böhlau, 2004), p. 48. On the Sixth Army, see Browning, *Origins of the Final Solution*, p. 259. On the Eleventh Army in Simferopol, see Shepherd, *Hitler's Soldiers*, pp. 181–2; Mallmann et al., eds, '*Ereignismeldungen UdSSR*', p. 897, fn. 9.
32. On Police Battalion 309 and the 221st Security Division, see Jürgen Matthäus, 'Controlled Escalation: Himmler's Men in the Summer of 1941 and the Holocaust in the Occupied Soviet Territories', *Holocaust and Genocide Studies*, vol. 21, no. 2 (autumn 2007), pp. 218–42, here pp. 223–4; Gerlach, *Kalkulierte Morde*, pp. 542–3. On Police Battalion 307, see Pohl, *Herrschaft*, p. 256; Browning, *Origins of the Final Solution*, p. 259. On the 162nd Infantry Division, see Gerlach, *Kalkulierte Morde*, p. 547. On Police Battalions 316 and 322, see Longerich, *Der ungeschriebene Befehl*, p. 102.
33. For the total of 63,000 killed by the end of July, see Christian Gerlach, 'Die Ausweitung der deutschen Massenmorde in den besetzten sowjetischen Gebieten im Herbst 1941. Überlegungen zur Vernichtungspolitik gegen Juden und sowjetische Kriegsgefangene', in Christian Gerlach, *Krieg, Ernährung, Völkermord. Deutsche Vernichtungspolitik im Zweiten Weltkrieg*, rev. edn (Zurich/Munich: Pendo, 2001 [1998]), pp. 11–78, here pp. 54–5. On 90 per cent of the victims being Jews, see Gerlach, *Krieg, Ernahrung, Volkermord*, p. 54; Longerich, *Der ungeschriebene Befehl*, p. 99; Browning, *Origins of the Final Solution*, p. 260. On reprisals as a pretext, see Dieter Pohl, 'Die Wehrmacht und der Mord an den Juden in den besetzten sowjetischen Gebieten', in Wolf Kaiser, ed., *Täter im Vernichtungskrieg. Der Überfall auf die Sowjetunion und der Völkermord an den Juden* (Berlin: Propyläen, 2002), pp. 39–53, here p. 43.
34. Longerich, *Der ungeschriebene Befehl*, pp. 99–101. On the near-complete absence of pogroms in Belarus, see Gerlach, *Kalkulierte Morde*, pp. 536–7. On Nebe, see EM 31 (23 July 1941), p. 166; EM 43 (5 August 1941), p. 233; EM 67 (29 August 1941), p. 369.
35. Kay, 'Transition to Genocide', pp. 417–18. On Army Group Centre, see Stahel, *Operation Barbarossa*, pp. 153–451, esp. pp. 211–12 and 246–8; David Stahel, 'Radicalizing Warfare: The German Command and the Failure of Operation Barbarossa', in Kay et al., eds, *Nazi Policy*, pp. 19–44, esp. pp. 25–9.

36. Kay, 'Transition to Genocide', pp. 417–18; Dieckmann, *Deutsche Besatzungspolitik*, vol. 1, pp. 267–79. On the nine undermanned and insufficient security divisions, see Hasenclever, *Wehrmacht und Besatzungspolitik*, pp. 143–9; Ben Shepherd, *War in the Wild East: The German Army and Soviet Partisans* (Cambridge, MA: Harvard University Press, 2004), pp. 46–52. For the Halder quote, see Franz Halder, *Kriegstagebuch, Band 3: Der Rußlandfeldzug bis zum Marsch auf Stalingrad* (Stuttgart: W. Kohlhammer, 1964), p. 38 (entry for 3 July 1941). For the Keitel letter, see BArch-MA, RW 4/v. 578, fols 105–6, OKW/WFSt/Abt. L Nr. 441158/41 g. Kdos. Chefs., 5 July 1941, here fol. 105 (emphasis in the original).
37. Kay, 'Transition to Genocide', pp. 418–19; Dieckmann, *Deutsche Besatzungspolitik*, vol. 1, pp. 401–7, and vol. 2, pp. 923–6. For the Goebbels quotes, see Elke Fröhlich, ed., *Die Tagebücher von Joseph Goebbels. Teil II: Diktate 1941–1945, Band 1: Juli–September 1941* (Munich: K.G. Saur, 1996), pp. 53 (entry for 12 July 1941) and 118 (entry for 24 July 1941). For Directive No. 34, see 'Weisung Nr. 34 für die Kriegführung', 30 July 1941, reproduced in: Walther Hubatsch, ed., *Hitlers Weisungen für die Kriegführung, 1939–1945*, 2nd exp. edn (Koblenz: Bernard & Graefe, 1983 [1962]), pp. 168–171. For the Einsatzgruppen quote, see Krausnick, 'Einsatzgruppen', p. 267.
38. Kay, 'Transition to Genocide', p. 419. On the First World War and military legitimation, see Pohl, 'Wehrmacht', p. 49. On perceived military necessity, see also Jeff Rutherford, *Combat and Genocide on the Eastern Front: The German Infantry's War, 1941–1944* (Cambridge: Cambridge University Press, 2014), esp. pp. 7–10. For Bormann quoting Hitler, see Nbg. Doc.221–L, 'Aktenvermerk', 16 July 1941, reproduced in: Internationaler Militärgerichtshof, ed., *Der Prozess gegen die Hauptkriegsverbrecher vor dem Internationalen Militärgerichtshof, Nürnberg, 14. November 1945–1. Oktober 1946*, 42 vols (Nuremberg: Sekretariat des Gerichtshofs, 1947–49) (hereafter IMG), vol. 38, p. 92. For the supplement to the OKW directive, see Nbg. Doc. 052-C, 'Ergänzung zur Weisung Nr. 33', 23 July 1941, reproduced in: IMG, vol. 34, p. 259.
39. Kay, 'Transition to Genocide', p. 419. For the OKH directive, see BArch-MA, RH 26-403/4a, 'Betr. Behandlung feindlicher Zivilpersonen und russischer Kriegsgefangener im rückwärtigen Heeresgebiet', Az. 453 Gr. R Wes, Nr 1332/41 geh., General z.b.V. beim Befehlshaber des Heeres, 25 July 1941. For the Nebe quote, see BArch Berlin, R 58/215, fols 48–65, 'Ereignismeldung UdSSR Nr. 34', 26 July 1941, here fol. 59.
40. Kay, 'Transition to Genocide', pp. 419–20. For the quotes from the 17 July decree, see 'Erlaß des Führers über die polizeiliche Sicherung der neu besetzten Ostgebiete vom 17. Juli 1941', reproduced in: Martin Moll, ed., *'Führer-Erlasse' 1939–1945* (Stuttgart: Franz Steiner, 1997), p. 188.
41. Kay, 'Transition to Genocide', p. 420.
42. Kay, *Making of an SS Killer*, pp. 57–8 (including all quotes); Kay, 'Transition to Genocide', pp. 412, 420–1 and 427–8.
43. Kay, *Making of an SS Killer*, pp. 58–9 (Greiffenberger quote: p. 58); Kay, 'Transition to Genocide', pp. 422–3.
44. Kay, *Making of an SS Killer*, p. 59 (including all quotes); Kay, 'Transition to Genocide', p. 424.
45. Kay, *Making of an SS Killer*, pp. 59–60 (including both quotes); Kay, 'Transition to Genocide', p. 424.
46. Kay, 'Transition to Genocide', pp. 425–6.
47. Ibid., p. 426. On the SS Cavalry Brigade, see Henning Pieper, *Fegelein's Horsemen and Genocidal Warfare: The SS Cavalry Brigade in the Soviet Union* (Basingstoke: Palgrave Macmillan, 2015), esp. pp. 79–121. On the 1st SS Infantry Brigade, see Longerich, *Der ungeschriebene Befehl*, p. 106.
48. Browning, *Origins of the Final Solution*, p. 291. See also Saul Friedländer, *The Years of Extermination: Nazi Germany and the Jews, 1939–1945* (New York: HarperCollins, 2007), pp. 215–19. On the military chaplains, see Lauren Faulkner Rossi, *Wehrmacht Priests:*

Catholicism and the Nazi War of Annihilation (Cambridge, MA: Harvard University Press, 2015), p. 148.

49. All examples cited in Gerlach, *Kalkulierte Morde*, p. 1075, apart from the example with the skullcap, in Harald Welzer, *Täter. Wie aus ganz normalen Menschen Massenmörder werden* (Frankfurt am Main: S. Fischer, 2005), p. 185. In general, see Gerlach, *Kalkulierte Morde*, pp. 1074–92; Welzer, *Täter*, pp. 173–88.

50. For the quote and the analysis, see Gerlach, *Kalkulierte Morde*, pp. 588–9.

51. Nonna Bannister, with Denise George and Carolyn Tomlin, *The Secret Holocaust Diaries. The Untold Story of Nonna Bannister* (Carol Stream, IL: Tyndale, 2009), pp. 7–12. Although it contains the story of the Jewish baby, the book's title is misleading, as Nonna Lisowskaja Bannister was not Jewish and, as such, not a victim of the Holocaust, that is, the annihilation of Europe's Jews – or those deemed Jewish – by the Nazi regime and its accomplices.

52. Guenter Lewy, *Perpetrators: The World of the Holocaust Killers* (New York: Oxford University Press, 2017), pp. 34–5 (quote: p. 35). On the prevalence of such occurrences, see Welzer, *Täter*, p. 187.

53. Karel C. Berkhoff, 'Dina Pronicheva's Story of Surviving the Babi Yar Massacre: German, Jewish, Soviet, Russian, and Ukrainian Records', in Ray Brandon and Wendy Lower, eds, *The Shoah in Ukraine: History, Testimony, Memorialization* (Bloomington, IN: Indiana University Press in association with the United States Holocaust Memorial Museum, 2008), pp. 291–317, here pp. 291–2.

54. For the Klemperer quotes, see Victor Klemperer, *Tagebücher 1942*, ed. Walter Nowojski (Berlin: Aufbau, 1995), pp. 9 and 68 (entries for 13 January and 19 April 1942; emphasis in the original). For the Cohn quote, see Willy Cohn, *Als Jude in Breslau 1941*, ed. Joseph Walk (Gerlingen: Bleicher, 1984), p. 106 (entry for 11 October 1941). On German civilians' knowledge of killing operations against Jews, see also Peter Fritzsche, 'Babi Yar, but Not Auschwitz: What Did Germans Know about the Final Solution?', in Susanna Schrafstetter and Alan E. Steinweis, eds, *The Germans and the Holocaust: Popular Responses to the Persecution and Murder of the Jews* (New York/Oxford: Berghahn Books, 2016), pp. 85–104.

55. BLSA, Jewish Survivors of the Holocaust oral history collection, shelf mark C410/036, testimony of Josef Perl, September 1988, 2 of 4, 5:21–14:16. On the indiscriminate killing by early October 1941, see Longerich, *Der ungeschriebene Befehl*, pp. 104–8.

56. On Vitebsk and Surazh, see Kay, *Making of an SS Killer*, pp. 61–2. On Babi Yar, see Berkhoff, 'Dina Pronicheva's Story', pp. 303–4. On voyeurism, see Welzer, *Täter*, pp. 203–5; Gerhard Paul, 'Lemberg '41: Bilder der Gewalt – Bilder als Gewalt – Gewalt an Bildern', in Martin Cüppers, Jürgen Matthäus and Andrej Angrick, eds, *Naziverbrechen. Täter, Taten, Bewältigungsversuche* (Darmstadt: Wissenschaftliche Buchgesellschaft, 2013), pp. 191–212, here pp. 205–8.

57. On the extermination camps, see especially Chapters 8 and 9 in this book. On the distinction between sexual and sexualised violence, see Waitman Wade Beorn, 'Bodily Conquest: Sexual Violence in the Nazi East', in Kay and Stahel, eds, *Mass Violence*, pp. 195–215, here pp. 196–7. On Yanavichy, see Kay, *Making of an SS Killer*, p. 65. On Brest and on the lists of unmarried Jewish women, see Regina Mühlhäuser, *Eroberungen. Sexuelle Gewalttaten und intime Beziehungen deutscher Soldaten in der Sowjetunion, 1941–1945* (Hamburg: Hamburger Edition, 2010), pp. 134–5 and 139. On Bauska, see Bernhard Press, *The Murder of the Jews in Latvia, 1941–1945*, trans. from German by Laimdota Mazzarins (Evanston, IL: Northwestern University Press, 2000 [1992]), pp. 47–8.

58. Ray Brandon, 'The First Wave', unpublished manuscript, 2009, pp. 1–7. I am grateful to Ray for providing me with a copy of his text, and for his further elaboration of its contents on 4 February 2020. On the 707th Infantry Division, see Gerlach, *Kalkulierte Morde*, pp. 617–20; Peter Lieb, 'Täter aus Überzeugung? Oberst Carl von Andrian und die Judenmorde der 707. Infanteriedivision 1941/42', *Vierteljahrshefte für Zeitgeschichte*,

vol. 50, no. 4 (October 2002), pp. 523–57. On the frozen ground, see Yitzhak Arad, *The Holocaust in the Soviet Union* (Lincoln, NE: University of Nebraska Press, 2009), pp. 157 and 251; Lewy, *Perpetrators*, p. 35. On the impact of adverse 'weather conditions' on the shootings, see also EM 145 (12 December 1941), p. 876.

59. On technical modifications in the gas vans, see Chapter 4 in this book. On Hitler's decision to murder all European Jews, and on Chełmno and Bełżec, see Chapter 8 in this book.

60. Friedländer, *Years of Extermination*, pp. 359–60. On the number of ghettos in the occupied Soviet Union, see Il'ja Al'tman, *Opfer des Hasses. Der Holocaust in der UdSSR 1941–1945*, trans. from Russian by Ellen Greifer (Gleichen: Muster-Schmidt, 2008 [2002]), pp. 113 and 131.

61. On the stagnation of the German advance and on Einsatzgruppe D, see Andrej Angrick, Klaus-Michael Mallmann, Jürgen Matthäus and Martin Cüppers, eds, *Deutsche Besatzungsherrschaft in der UdSSR 1941–1945. Dokumente der Einsatzgruppen in der Sowjetunion II* (Darmstadt: Wissenschaftliche Buchgesellschaft, 2013), pp. 19–20. On the later establishment of stationary posts within Einsatzgruppe C, see Gert Robel, 'Sowjetunion', in Wolfgang Benz, ed., *Dimension des Völkermords. Die Zahl der jüdischen Opfer des Nationalsozialismus* (Munich: Oldenbourg, 1991), pp. 499–560, here pp. 517–18. On the sub-commandos of Einsatzgruppe C, see Dieter Pohl, 'Die Einsatzgruppe C 1941/42', in Klein, ed., *Einsatzgruppen*, pp. 71–87, here p. 81. On the reinforcements, see Lewy, *Perpetrators*, p. 35.

62. Arad, *Holocaust in the Soviet Union*, pp. 149–50, 251–3, 258–60, 325–6 and 328. On the deportations to Treblinka and Sobibór, see also Yitzhak Arad, *The Operation Reinhard Death Camps: Belzec, Sobibor, Treblinka*, rev. and exp. edn (Bloomington, IN: Indiana University Press, 2018 [1987]), pp. 168–76.

63. Arad, *Holocaust in the Soviet Union*, pp. 254–6 (quote from the ghetto: p. 256); Gerlach, *Kalkulierte Morde*, pp. 700–1, 704–5 and 707 (Kube quote: p. 705). For the death toll of 10,000, see Gerlach, *Kalkulierte Morde*, p. 704; Pohl, *Verfolgung und Massenmord*, p. 96.

64. On Rovno and Lutsk, see Arad, *Holocaust in the Soviet Union*, pp. 264–5. On Hitler's headquarters and the Jews of Vinnitsa, see Friedländer, *Years of Extermination*, p. 361.

65. Friedländer, *Years of Extermination*, pp. 361–2. On Müller's letter to Jäger, see also Longerich, *Holocaust*, p. 318. On the Baltic countries in 1942, see Arad, *Holocaust in the Soviet Union*, pp. 260–2.

66. Friedländer, *Years of Extermination*, p. 363. On Chełmno, see Chapter 8 in this book. For the quotes from Rauff's report, see Claude Lanzmann, *Shoah*, trans. from French by Nina Börnsen and Anna Kamp (Reinbek bei Hamburg: Rowohlt Taschenbuch, 2011), pp. 144–7. On the gas van sent from Serbia to Minsk via Berlin, see Manoschek, 'Vernichtung der Juden', pp. 230–1; Gerlach, *Kalkulierte Morde*, pp. 765–6.

67. Arad, *Holocaust in the Soviet Union*, p. 267; Gerlach, *Kalkulierte Morde*, pp. 717–18; Mühlhäuser, *Eroberungen*, p. 139. For the total death toll of 19,000, see Pohl, *Verfolgung*, p. 96.

68. On ghetto dissolutions throughout 1942, see Longerich, *Der ungeschriebene Befehl*, p. 108. On Belarus and Ukraine, see Arad, *Holocaust in the Soviet Union*, pp. 258 and 273. On Białystok, see Sara Bender, *The Jews of Białystok during World War II and the Holocaust*, trans. from Hebrew by Yaffa Murciano (Waltham, MA: Brandeis University Press, 2008 [1997]), p. 172. For the death toll of 2.6 million Jews on Soviet territory, see Arad, *Holocaust in the Soviet Union*, p. 525; Dieter Pohl, 'Just How Many? On the Death Toll of Jewish Victims of Nazi Crimes', in Alfred Kokh and Pavel Polian, eds, *Denial of the Denial, or The Battle of Auschwitz: The Demography and Geopolitics of the Holocaust. The View from the Twenty-First Century* (Brighton, MA: Academic Studies Press, 2012), pp. 129–48, here p. 147, n. 43. For higher death tolls of 2.825 and 2.9 million, see Al'tman, *Opfer des Hasses*, pp. 366–7, and Robel, 'Sowjetunion', p. 560, respectively. The main discrepancy can be found in the figures for the number of Jewish dead in Belarus: Gerlach's total of up to 550,000 is far more consistent with Arad (up to 582,000) than with Al'tman (810,000); see Gerlach, *Kalkulierte Morde*, p. 1158; Arad, *Holocaust in the Soviet Union*, p. 525; Al'tman, *Opfer des Hasses*, p. 367.

69. For the term 'Holocaust by bullets', see Patrick Desbois, *The Holocaust by Bullets: A Priest's Journey to Uncover the Truth Behind the Murder of 1.5 Million Jews*, trans. from French by Catherine Spencer (New York: Palgrave Macmillan, 2008).

CHAPTER 4 MURDER OF PSYCHIATRIC PATIENTS AND ROMA IN THE SOVIET UNION

1. Winkler and Hohendorf, 'Murder of Psychiatric Patients', pp. 149–51; Pohl, *Verfolgung und Massenmord*, p. 33.
2. Pohl, *Verfolgung und Massenmord*, p. 33. On Mogilev, see Andrei Zamoiski, 'Einheimische Mediziner und die nationalsozialistischen Krankenmorde in der Stadt Mahilëŭ', in Alexander Friedman and Rainer Hudeman, eds, *Diskriminiert – vernichtet – vergessen. Behinderte in der Sowjetunion, unter nationalsozialistischer Besatzung und im Ostblock 1917–1991* (Stuttgart: Franz Steiner, 2016), pp. 415–22.
3. Winkler and Hohendorf, 'Murder of Psychiatric Patients', p. 151.
4. Pohl, *Herrschaft*, p. 274. On Choroszcz, see Winkler and Hohendorf, 'Murder of Psychiatric Patients', p. 150; Gerlach, *Kalkulierte Morde*, pp. 1067–8.
5. Peter Witte et al., eds, *Der Dienstkalender Heinrich Himmlers 1941/42* (Hamburg: Christians, 1999), p. 195 (entry for 15 August 1941); Mathias Beer, 'Die Entwicklung der Gaswagen beim Mord an den Juden', *Vierteljahrshefte für Zeitgeschichte*, vol. 35, no. 3 (July 1987), pp. 403–17, here p. 407; Gerlach, *Kalkulierte Morde*, p. 1068; Longerich, *Heinrich Himmler*, pp. 533–4. For Bach-Zelewski's account of Himmler's visit, see Yad Vashem Archives (hereafter YVA), O.18/90, Statement by Erich von dem Bach-Zelewski, undated, fols 52–55 ('humane' quote: fol. 55).
6. Beer, 'Entwicklung der Gaswagen', pp. 407–9; Winkler and Hohendorf, 'Murder of Psychiatric Patients', pp. 156–7. On the transport of carbon monoxide canisters, see also Alberti, *Verfolgung*, p. 409. For the number of victims, see Witte et al., eds, *Dienstkalender*, p. 195, fn. 15; Gerlach, *Kalkulierte Morde*, p. 1068.
7. Friedländer, *Years of Extermination*, p. 234; Beer, 'Entwicklung der Gaswagen', pp. 409 and 413–15.
8. On Halder and Wagner, see Christian Gerlach, 'Militärische "Versorgungszwänge", Besatzungspolitik und Massenverbrechen: Die Rolle des Generalquartiermeisters des Heeres und seiner Dienststellen im Krieg gegen die Sowjetunion', in Norbert Frei, Sybille Steinbacher and Bernd C. Wagner, eds, *Ausbeutung, Vernichtung, Öffentlichkeit: Neue Studien zur nationalsozialistischen Lagerpolitik* (Munich: K.G. Saur, 2000), pp. 175–208, here p. 194. On Himmler and Lange, see Witte et al., eds, *Dienstkalender*, p. 225, fn. 4. On lethal injections, see Boris N. Kovalev, 'Vernichtung von psychisch kranken und behinderten Menschen unter der deutschen Okkupation im Nordwesten Russlands', in Friedman and Hudeman, eds, *Diskriminiert*, pp. 373–84, here p. 377–83. On Novgorod, see also Alberti, *Verfolgung*, p. 409. On Poltava, see Beer, 'Entwicklung der Gaswagen', p. 412; Friedländer, *Years of Extermination*, p. 234; Krausnick, 'Einsatzgruppen', p. 193.
9. On Mogutovo, see EM 94 (25 September 1941), pp. 554–5. On Kherson and Dnepropetrovsk, see Pohl, *Herrschaft*, p. 275. For the figure of 760 patients, see Ulrike Winkler and Gerrit Hohendorf, '"Nun ist Mogiljow frei von Verrückten". Die Ermordung der PsychiatriepatientInnen in Mogilew 1941/42', in Babette Quinkert, Philipp Rauh and Ulrike Winkler, eds, *Krieg und Psychiatrie 1914–1950* (Göttingen: Wallstein, 2010), pp. 75–103, here p. 82. On Mariupol and on 'beggars' and 'vagrants', see Pohl, *Verfolgung und Massenmord*, pp. 33–4.
10. EM 135 (19 November 1941), p. 817.
11. On Makarevskaya Pustin, see Krausnick, 'Einsatzgruppen', pp. 268–70 (quotes: p. 269); Johannes Hürter, 'Die Wehrmacht vor Leningrad: Krieg und Besatzungspolitik der 18. Armee im Herbst und Winter 1941/42', *Vierteljahrshefte fur Zeitgeschichte*, vol. 49, no. 3 (July 2001), pp. 377–440, here pp. 435–6. On Huber, see Angrick et al., eds, *Deutsche*

Besatzungsherrschaft, p. 249, n. 3. On Kashchenko, see Winkler and Hohendorf, 'Murder of Psychiatric Patients', p. 151. On EK 3, see Friedländer, *Years of Extermination*, p. 362.

12. Gerlach, *Kalkulierte Morde*, pp. 1071–2 (including all quotes); Viktoria Latysheva, Alexander Friedman and Alexander Pesetsky, 'Die Wehrmacht, die deutsche Zivilverwaltung und die Ermordung geistig behinderter Kinder in Červen' (Gebiet Minsk) im Mai 1942', in Friedman and Hudeman, eds, *Diskriminiert*, pp. 453–7.

13. On Yeysk, see Angrick, *Besatzungspolitik und Massenmord*, pp. 648–51 (quote: p. 650). For the total of 17,000, see Winkler and Hohendorf, 'Murder of Psychiatric Patients', p. 152; Winkler and Hohendorf, '"Nun ist Mogiljow frei"', pp. 81–3.

14. Pohl, *Herrschaft*, p. 272; Martin Holler, *Der nationalsozialistische Völkermord an den Roma in der besetzten Sowjetunion (1941–1944)* (Heidelberg: Dokumentations- und Kulturzentrum Deutscher Sinti und Roma, 2009), p. 66; Christopher R. Browning, 'The Nazi Empire', in Bloxham and Moses, eds, *Oxford Handbook*, pp. 407–25, here pp. 414–15.

15. On the Wehrmacht and on Berezovka, see Pohl, *Herrschaft*, p. 273. On EK 3, see Zimmermann, *Rassenutopie*, p. 260. On Einsatzgruppe B, EK 9 and Heydrich's orders, see Kay, *Making of an SS Killer*, p. 65.

16. On Mogilev and Marina Gorka, see Gerlach, *Kalkulierte Morde*, p. 1064. On Army Group Centre and on Bryansk, see Holler, *Völkermord an den Roma*, pp. 61 and 66.

17. Holler, *Völkermord an den Roma*, pp. 53–9 (quote: p. 57).

18. Pohl, *Herrschaft*, pp. 272–3. For the 5 November quote, see Zimmermann, *Rassenutopie*, p. 265. For the 24 November quote, see United States Holocaust Memorial Museum (hereafter USHMM), RG-53.002M, reel 2, Kommandant in Weißruthenien, Befehl Nr. 24, 24 November 1941. I am grateful to Martin Holler for bringing this source to my attention. For the 10 October quote and on the chief of the Army Field Police, see Gerlach, *Kalkulierte Morde*, pp. 1064–5.

19. On the group staff, see EM 94 (28 September 1941), p. 557. On SK 4a, see EM 119 (20 October 1941), p. 706.

20. Martin Holler, 'The Nazi Persecution of Roma in Northwestern Russia: The Operational Area of the Army Group North, 1941–1944', in Anton Weiss-Wendt, ed., *The Nazi Genocide of the Roma: Reassessment and Commemoration* (New York/Oxford: Berghahn Books, 2013), pp. 153–80, esp. pp. 156–7; Holler, *Völkermord an den Roma*, pp. 31–3 ('itinerant' and 'free from suspicion' quotes: p. 31). On Liepāja, see Zimmermann, *Rassenutopie*, p. 269 (including quote); Wolfgang Curilla, *Die deutsche Ordnungspolizei und der Holocaust im Baltikum und in Weißrussland 1941–1944* (Paderborn: Ferdinand Schöningh, 2006), pp. 194 and 248.

21. Zimmermann, *Rassenutopie*, pp. 269–71.

22. Holler, 'Nazi Persecution of Roma', pp. 157 and 172; Holler, *Völkermord an den Roma*, pp. 32–3, 44 and 48. On the seventy-one Roma killed by Einsatzgruppe A, see also Arolsen Archives, ITS Digital Archive, 2273000, fols 384–409, 'Ereignismeldung UdSSR Nr. 195', 24 April 1942, here fol. 402; Zimmermann, *Rassenutopie*, p. 260.

23. On Novorzhev, see Krausnick, 'Einsatzgruppen', pp. 276–7 (including quotes). On Pushkinskie Gory, Porkhov and the area of the 281st Security Division, see Holler, 'Nazi Persecution of Roma', pp. 163–4; Holler, *Völkermord an den Roma*, pp. 40–2.

24. On Nikolayev, see Angrick, *Besatzungspolitik und Massenmord*, p. 252; Holler, *Völkermord an den Roma*, pp. 80–1. On the Crimea, see Holler, *Völkermord an den Roma*, p. 78. On Kerch, see Mikhail Tyaglyy, 'Were the "Chingene" Victims of the Holocaust? Nazi Policy toward the Crimean Roma, 1941–1944', *Holocaust and Genocide Studies*, vol. 23, no. 1 (spring 2009), pp. 26–53, here p. 35 (including quote). On those killed during the period from mid-January to the end of March 1942, see Zimmermann, *Rassenutopie*, p. 263. For the quote from 8 April 1942, see Martin Holler, 'Extending the Genocidal Program: Did Otto Ohlendorf Initiate the Systematic Extermination of Soviet "Gypsies"?', in Kay et al., eds, *Nazi Policy*, pp. 267–88, here p. 271.

25. Zimmermann, *Rassenutopie*, pp. 264–5 (Schubert quote: p. 265). On the Eleventh Army, Hauck and the identity of the shooters, see Mallmann et al., eds, *'Ereignismeldungen UdSSR'*, p. 897, fn. 9. For the date of 9 December, the figure of 600 and the Lashkevich

quote, see Tyaglyy, 'Were the "Chingene"', pp. 36 and 38–9. For the figure of 600, see also Zimmermann, *Rassenutopie*, p. 264.

26. Holler, *Völkermord an den Roma*, pp. 79–80 (including first, second, fourth and fifth quotes). For the 'nomadic people' quote, see Holler, 'Extending the Genocidal Program', p. 280. For the 'no lesser threat' and 'than the parents themselves' quotes, see Zimmermann, *Rassenutopie*, p. 261.

27. Holler, 'Extending the Genocidal Program', pp. 267–88.

28. For the total number of 30,000 and the figure of 6,000 for Belarus, see Donald Kenrick and Grattan Puxon, *Gypsies under the Swastika* (Hatfield: University of Hertfordshire Press, 2009), pp. 91 and 96. Christian Gerlach gives a figure of at least 3,000 for Belarus but emphasises that this number is based on samples and that the actual total was probably substantially higher: Gerlach, *Kalkulierte Morde*, p. 1066. On the Extraordinary State Commission and the treatment of Roma from spring 1942, see Holler, *Völkermord an den Roma*, pp. 51, 59 and 112.

CHAPTER 5 STARVATION POLICY AGAINST THE SOVIET URBAN POPULATION

1. On the following, see Alex J. Kay, '"The Purpose of the Russian Campaign Is the Decimation of the Slavic Population by Thirty Million": The Radicalization of German Food Policy in Early 1941', in Kay et al., eds, *Nazi Policy*, pp. 101–29; Kay, *Exploitation*. For the Hitler quote, see Carl J. Burckhardt, *Meine Danziger Mission, 1937–1939* (Munich: Georg D.W. Callwey, 1960), p. 348.

2. Kay, '"Purpose of the Russian Campaign"', pp. 101–2. For the quotes from Directive No. 21, see Hubatsch, ed., *Hitlers Weisungen*, pp. 86–7. On pre-invasion planning for German occupation policy in the Soviet Union, see Kay, *Exploitation*, pp. 26–178.

3. Kay, '"Purpose of the Russian Campaign"', p. 102. On Belgium and Norway, see Kay, *Exploitation*, p. 123.

4. Kay, '"Purpose of the Russian Campaign"', p. 102.

5. Ibid., pp. 102–3.

6. Ibid., pp. 103 and 105. For the Thomas quote, see BArch-MA, RW 19/164, fol. 126, 'Vortrag Hauptmann Emmerich beim Amtschef', 30 January 1941. For the Reich Food Estate quote, see BArch-MA, RW 19/164, fol. 150, 'Vortrag Obstlt. Matzky, Major Knapp, Hptm. Emmerich beim Amtschef', 12 February 1941. On the German–Soviet trade agreements of 11 February 1940 and 10 January 1941, see Alex J. Kay, 'German Economic Plans for the Occupied Soviet Union and their Implementation, 1941–1944', in Timothy Snyder and Ray Brandon, eds, *Stalin and Europe: Imitation and Domination, 1928–1953* (Oxford/New York: Oxford University Press, 2014), pp. 163–89, here pp. 163–4.

7. Kay, '"Purpose of the Russian Campaign"', p. 105. For the Thomas quote, see Georg Thomas, *Geschichte der deutschen Wehr- und Rüstungswirtschaft (1918–1943/45)*, ed. Wolfgang Birkenfeld (Boppard am Rhein: Harald Boldt, 1966), p. 517 (emphasis in the original). For the Göring quote, see BArch-MA, RW 19/164, fol. 180, 'Vortrag Amtschef beim Reichsmarschall', 26 February 1941, and BArch-MA, RW 19/185, fol. 171, 'Aktennotiz über Vortrag beim Reichsmarschall am 26.2.1941', 27 February 1941.

8. Kay, '"Purpose of the Russian Campaign"', pp. 105–6. The war-game paper is quoted in Gerlach, 'Militärische "Versorgungszwänge"', p. 184. For the quote from the Special Instructions, see Norbert Müller, ed., *Okkupation, Raub, Vernichtung: Dokumente zur Besatzungspolitik der faschistischen Wehrmacht auf sowjetischem Territorium, 1941 bis 1944* (Berlin: Militärverlag der DDR, 1980), doc. 4, p. 35.

9. Kay, '"Purpose of the Russian Campaign"', p. 106. For the Göring quote, see BArch-MA, RW 19/164, fol. 228, 'Vortrag bei Reichsmarschall Göring am 19.3.41', 20 March 1941.

10. Kay, '"Purpose of the Russian Campaign"', pp. 106–7.

11. Ibid., p. 107. For the quotes from the decree signed by Körner, see Bundesarchiv Koblenz (hereafter BArch Koblenz), N 1094/II 20, Mappe III, 'Geheime Reichssache!', 12 April

1941. For the reference to a 'secret decree', see the letter from Backe to Darré in BArch Koblenz, N 1094/II 20, Mappe III, 'Geheime Reichssache!', 25 June 1941.

12. Alex J. Kay, 'Germany's Staatssekretäre, Mass Starvation and the Meeting of 2 May 1941', *Journal of Contemporary History*, vol. 41, no. 4 (October 2006), pp. 685–700. For the quote from the memorandum, see Nbg. Doc. 2718-PS, 'Aktennotiz über Ergebnis der heutigen Besprechung mit den Staatssekretären über Barbarossa', 2 May 1941, reproduced in: IMG, vol. 31, p. 84.

13. Kay, '"Purpose of the Russian Campaign"', p. 108.

14. For the Glaise quote, see Peter Broucek, ed., *Ein General im Zwielicht: Die Erinnerungen Edmund Glaises von Horstenau, Band 3: Deutscher Bevollmächtigter General in Kroatien und Zeuge des Untergangs des 'Tausendjährigen Reiches'* (Vienna: Böhlau, 1988), pp. 107–8. For the Goebbels quotes, see Elke Fröhlich, ed., *Die Tagebücher von Joseph Goebbels. Teil I: Aufzeichnungen 1923–1941, Band 9: Dezember 1940–Juli 1941* (Munich: K.G. Saur, 1998), pp. 283–4 (entry for 1 May 1941) and 293–4 (entry for 6 May 1941). For the Schubert quote, see BArch-MA, RW 19/739, fol. 272, 'Betr. Studie Südost', 13 May 1941. On Rosenberg's meetings with Backe and Körner, and for further information on the above, see Kay, '"Purpose of the Russian Campaign"', pp. 108–9.

15. BArch-MA, RW 19/473, fols 177–9, 'Dr. Claussen über die Ernährungslage', signed Eicke, 14 May 1941 (quotes: fols 177–8).

16. Kay, '"Purpose of the Russian Campaign"', pp. 109–10.

17. For the Backe quotes, see BArch-MA, RW 19/739, fols 124–5. For the Keitel quote, see Müller, ed., *Okkupation*, doc. 7, p. 45 (emphasis in the original).

18. Nbg. Doc. 126-EC, 'Wirtschaftspolitische Richtlinien für Wirtschaftsorganisation Ost, Gruppe Landwirtschaft', 23 May 1941, reproduced in: IMG, vol. 36, pp. 135–57 (quotes: pp. 138, 140–1 and 145). See also Kay, '"Purpose of the Russian Campaign"', pp. 110–11.

19. Kay, '"Purpose of the Russian Campaign"', pp. 111–12. For the Backe quote, see Nbg. Doc. 089-USSR, '12 Gebote', 1 June 1941, reproduced in: IMG, vol. 39, p. 371.

20. Kay, '"Purpose of the Russian Campaign"', p. 112. For the Himmler quote, see Bach-Zelewski's post-war testimony at Nuremberg on 7 January 1946, reproduced in: IMG, vol. 4, pp. 535–6. It is not clear on what basis Lizzie Collingham claims that 'the regime's agrarian vision for the east generated plans to murder up to 100 million people': Lizzie Collingham, *The Taste of War: World War Two and the Battle for Food* (London: Allen Lane, 2011), p. 5.

21. Kay, '"Purpose of the Russian Campaign"', p. 112; Kay, *Exploitation*, p. 104; Christoph Dieckmann, 'Das Scheitern des Hungerplans und die Praxis der selektiven Hungerpolitik im deutschen Krieg gegen die Sowjetunion', in Dieckmann and Quinkert, eds, *Kriegführung und Hunger*, pp. 88–122, here pp. 94–5. See also Jürgen Zimmerer, 'Climate Change, Environmental Violence and Genocide', *The International Journal of Human Rights*, vol. 18, no. 3 (2014), pp. 265–80, here pp. 273–5. For the Goebbels quote, see Fröhlich, ed., *Tagebücher von Joseph Goebbels*, part 1, vol. 9, p. 330 (entry for 23 May 1941).

22. For the Jeckeln quote, see Bundesarchiv-Zwischenarchiv, Dahlwitz-Hoppegarten, ZM 1683, vol. 1, fol. 105, post-war testimony in Riga on 2 January 1946. For the Six quote, see Rudolf-Christoph Freiherr von Gersdorff, *Soldat im Untergang* (Frankfurt am Main: Ullstein, 1977), p. 93.

23. Kay, '"Purpose of the Russian Campaign"', pp. 113 and 126, n. 76. For the Keitel quote, see BArch Berlin, R 26 IV/33a, 'Richtlinien für die Führung der Wirtschaft (Fall Barbarossa)', 16 June 1941, signed Wilhelm Keitel, in 'Richtlinien für die Führung der Wirtschaft in den neubesetzten Ostgebieten (Grüne Mappe)'.

24. Kay, '"Purpose of the Russian Campaign"', pp. 113–14. For the Green Folder quote, see BArch Berlin, R 26 IV/33a, 'Richtlinien für die Führung der Wirtschaft in den neubesetzten Ostgebieten (Grüne Mappe)', p. 18.

25. For the Rosenberg quote, see Nbg. Doc. 1058-PS, 'Rede des Reichsleiters A. Rosenberg vor den engsten Beteiligten am Ostproblem am 20. Juni 1941', reproduced in: IMG, vol. 26, p. 622.

26. Kay, *Exploitation*, pp. 50–3, 144 and 200.
27. For the Bach-Zelewski quote, see his post-war testimony at Nuremberg on 7 January 1946, reproduced in: IMG, vol. 4, p. 539. For the Richter quote, see BArch Berlin, R 6/60a, fol. 1, 'Auszug aus einem Feldpostbrief von Leutnant Dr. Friedrich Richter, Referent für Ostfragen vom Vierjahresplan, vom 26.5.1943'.
28. Dieckmann, 'Scheitern des Hungerplans', pp. 98 and 111; Jörg Ganzenmüller, 'Hungerpolitik als Problemlösungsstrategie. Der Entscheidungsprozess zur Blockade Leningrads und zur Vernichtung seiner Zivilbevölkerung', in Babette Quinkert and Jörg Morré, eds, *Deutsche Besatzung in der Sowjetunion 1941–1944. Vernichtungskrieg, Reaktionen, Erinnerung* (Paderborn: Ferdinand Schöningh, 2014), pp. 34–53, here pp. 34–7.
29. Kay, '"Purpose of the Russian Campaign"', p. 115 (including Sauckel quote). For the Göring quotes and Ciano's report on the conversation, see Ministero degli Affari Esteri, ed., *I Documenti Diplomatici Italiani. Nona Serie: 1939–1943*, vol. 7 (Rome: Istituto Poligrafico e Zecca dello Stato, 1987), doc. 786, p. 802.
30. Dieckmann, 'Scheitern des Hungerplans', pp. 105–7. On Soviet Jews living in towns and cities, see Kay, *Exploitation*, p. 136. On Vitebsk, see Kay, *Making of an SS Killer*, pp. 67–8. On Leningrad, see Jörg Ganzenmüller, *Das belagerte Leningrad, 1941 bis 1944. Die Stadt in den Strategien von Angreifern und Verteidigern* (Paderborn: Ferdinand Schöningh, 2005), here pp. 238–9. On Kiev, see Karel C. Berkhoff, *Harvest of Despair: Life and Death in Ukraine under Nazi Rule* (Cambridge, MA: Harvard University Press, 2004), pp. 164–86. On Kharkov, see Norbert Kunz, 'Das Beispiel Charkow: Eine Stadtbevölkerung als Opfer der deutschen Hungerstrategie 1941/42', in Christian Hartmann, Johannes Hürter and Ulrike Jureit, eds, *Verbrechen der Wehrmacht: Bilanz einer Debatte* (Munich: C.H. Beck, 2005), pp. 136–44.
31. Ganzenmüller, 'Hungerpolitik', pp. 37–8.
32. Ibid., p. 42. For the Halder quote, see Halder, *Kriegstagebuch*, vol. 3, p. 53 (entry for 8 July 1941).
33. Ganzenmüller, 'Hungerpolitik', pp. 38–9.
34. For the first Wagner quote, see Gerlach, 'Militärische "Versorgungszwänge"', pp. 196–8. For the second Wagner quote and on Army Group North, see Ganzenmüller, 'Hungerpolitik', p. 46. For the Manstein quote, see Christian Streit, *Keine Kameraden. Die Wehrmacht und die sowjetischen Kriegsgefangenen 1941–1945*, 4th rev. edn (Bonn: Dietz, 1997 [1978]), pp. 163–4.
35. Ganzenmüller, *Das belagerte Leningrad*, pp. 40–1 (including both quotes); Ganzenmüller, 'Hungerpolitik', pp. 41–2.
36. Ganzenmüller, *Das belagerte Leningrad*, pp. 237–8.
37. Ibid., pp. 238, 255 and 268–9.
38. For the diary entries, see Walter Kempowski, *Das Echolot – Barbarossa '41. Ein kollektives Tagebuch* (Munich: Penguin Verlag, 2019), pp. 378 (9 December), 392–4 (10 December) and 469 (15 December 1941), and Anna Reid, *Leningrad: Tragedy of a City under Siege, 1941–44* (London: Bloomsbury, 2011), p. 273 (6 January 1942). On the evacuation slots, the departure of Yura's mother and sister and their respective fates, see Reid, *Leningrad*, p. 273. On the food situation, the lifting of the siege and the death toll, see Ganzenmüller, *Das belagerte Leningrad*, pp. 239 and 241.
39. Jeff Rutherford, 'The Radicalization of German Occupation Policies: The Wirtschaftsstab Ost and the 121st Infantry Division in Pavlovsk, 1941', in Kay et al., eds, *Nazi Policy*, pp. 130–54, here p. 137; Rutherford, *Combat and Genocide*, pp. 175–6.
40. Rutherford, 'Radicalization', pp. 142 and 153, n. 84.
41. Ibid., pp. 142–3.
42. On the number of deaths from starvation in Kiev and Kharkov, see Karel C. Berkhoff, '"Wir sollen verhungern, damit Platz für die Deutschen geschaffen wird." Hungersnöte in den ukrainischen Städten im Zweiten Weltkrieg', in Quinkert and Morré, eds, *Deutsche Besatzung*, pp. 54–75, here pp. 66–7. On swathes of territory stripped bare, see Johannes Hürter, *Hitlers*

Heerführer: Die deutschen Oberbefehlshaber im Krieg gegen die Sowjetunion, 1941/42 (Munich: Oldenbourg, 2006), p. 493.

43. Kay, '"Purpose of the Russian Campaign"', pp. 128–9, n. 95; Streit, *Keine Kameraden*, p. 369, n. 199. For the 778 days, see Karl Schlögel, *Entscheidung in Kiew. Ukrainische Lektionen* (Munich: Carl Hanser, 2015), p. 112.
44. Berkhoff, '"Wir sollen verhungern"', pp. 56–7; Berkhoff, *Harvest of Despair*, p. 169. For the figure of 900,000, see Schlögel, *Entscheidung in Kiew*, p. 112.
45. Berkhoff, '"Wir sollen verhungern"', p. 60 (including all quotes).
46. Ibid., p. 57; Kunz, 'Beispiel Charkow', pp. 140–1.
47. Berkhoff, '"Wir sollen verhungern"', pp. 57–8; Kunz, 'Beispiel Charkow', pp. 136–40 and 143–4.
48. Berkhoff, '"Wir sollen verhungern"', pp. 58–9. On infant mortality, see A.V. Skorobohatov, *Kharkiv u chasy nimets'koï okupatsiï (1941–1943)* (Kharkiv: Prapor, 2004), p. 306.
49. Berkhoff, '"Wir sollen verhungern"', pp. 60 and 64; Berkhoff, *Harvest of Despair*, p. 181.
50. Berkhoff, '"Wir sollen verhungern"', pp. 55, 65 and 74, n. 89.
51. On those regions particularly affected by famine and on western Russia, see Dieckmann, 'Scheitern des Hungerplans', p. 113. On Rzhev, see Pohl, *Herrschaft*, p. 197; Gerlach, *Kalkulierte Morde*, p. 289; Nicholas Terry, 'The German Army Group Centre and the Soviet Civilian Population, 1942–1944: Forced Labour, Hunger and Population Displacement on the Eastern Front', unpublished PhD thesis, King's College London, 2005, pp. 196–202. I am grateful to Nick for providing me with a copy of his thesis.
52. For the Steblin-Kamenskii quotes, see Oleg Beyda, '"Rediscovering Homeland": Russian Interpreters in the Wehrmacht, 1941–1943', in Amanda Laugesen and Richard Gehrmann, eds, *Communication, Interpreting and Language in Wartime: Historical and Contemporary Perspectives* (Cham: Palgrave Macmillan, 2020), pp. 131–52, here pp. 140–1. On this and other examples, see Alex J. Kay and David Stahel, 'Crimes of the Wehrmacht: A Re-evaluation', *Journal of Perpetrator Research*, vol. 3, no. 1 (2020), pp. 95–127, here pp. 101–8, esp. p. 104. For the Strauß quote, see Hürter, *Hitlers Heerführer*, p. 455.
53. Quoted in Paul Kohl, *Der Krieg der deutschen Wehrmacht und der Polizei 1941–1944. Sowjetische Überlebende berichten* (Frankfurt am Main: Fischer Taschenbuch, 1995), pp. 191–5.
54. On starvation under German military administration, see Pohl, *Herrschaft*, pp. 188–94 and 198–9. On famines elsewhere in Nazi-occupied Europe, see Berkhoff, '"Wir sollen verhungern"', p. 54. On the Netherlands, see Ingrid de Zwarte, *The Hunger Winter: Fighting Famine in the Occupied Netherlands, 1944–1945* (Cambridge: Cambridge University Press, 2020). On Athens and Greece in general, see Violetta Hionidou, *Famine and Death in Occupied Greece, 1941–1944* (Cambridge: Cambridge University Press, 2006).
55. Ganzenmüller, *Das belagerte Leningrad*, p. 51; Kay, '"Purpose of the Russian Campaign"', pp. 115–16.

CHAPTER 6 EXTERMINATION OF CAPTIVE RED ARMY SOLDIERS

1. Kay, *Exploitation*, pp. 159–61 (Jodl and Warlimont quotes: p. 160; emphasis in the original). For the number of prisoners expected, see Streit, *Keine Kameraden*, p. 76.
2. Christoph Dieckmann, *Deutsche Besatzungspolitik in Litauen 1941–1944, Band 2* (Göttingen: Wallstein, 2011), p. 1329.
3. For the figure of 360,000 and on France, see Streit, *Keine Kameraden*, pp. 83 and 358, n. 18. For the figure of 800,000 and on death rates, see Gerlach, *Kalkulierte Morde*, pp. 791–6. On Georg Thomas, Army Group North and the Sixteenth Army, see Dieckmann, *Deutsche Besatzungspolitik*, vol. 2, pp. 1377–8.
4. Nbg. Doc. 022-PS, 'Bericht. Betrifft: Gefangenenlager in Minsk', signed Dorsch, 10 July 1941, reproduced in: IMG, vol. 25, pp. 81–2. For the date of the visit and on the 286th Security Division, the open field and the extreme heat, see Gerlach, *Kalkulierte Morde*, pp. 789–90.

5. Gerlach, 'Ausweitung', p. 33. On cases of cannibalism in Belarusian camps, see Gerlach, *Kalkulierte Morde*, p. 807. On Shepetovka and Krivoy Rog, see Karel C. Berkhoff, 'The "Russian" Prisoners of War in Nazi-Ruled Ukraine as Victims of Genocidal Massacre', *Holocaust and Genocide Studies*, vol. 15, no. 1 (spring 2001), pp. 1–32, here pp. 13–14. On the death penalty, see Dieckmann, *Deutsche Besatzungspolitik*, vol. 2, p. 1349.
6. Gerlach, 'Ausweitung', pp. 34–5. On the orders, see Gerlach, *Kalkulierte Morde*, p. 849; the quotes are taken from testimony given during legal proceedings in the 1960s. On Globocnik, see Curilla, *Ordnungspolizei*, p. 626.
7. Gerlach, *Kalkulierte Morde*, pp. 797–9 (Riecke/Wagner and Wagner quotes: p. 799); Dieckmann, 'Scheitern des Hungerplans', pp. 114–15. For the Göring quote, see Streit, *Keine Kameraden*, pp. 143–4 (emphasis in the original).
8. Gerlach, 'Ausweitung', pp. 40–1 (Wagner quote, cited by Wilhelm Hasse, chief of staff of the Eighteenth Army: p. 40). Georg von Sodenstern, chief of staff of Army Group Centre, produced a similar account of Wagner's comments at the Orsha meeting; see Rüdiger Overmans, Andreas Hilger and Pavel Polian, eds, *Rotarmisten in deutscher Hand. Dokumente zu Gefangenschaft, Repatriierung und Rehabilitierung sowjetischer Soldaten des Zweiten Weltkrieges* (Paderborn: Ferdinand Schöningh, 2012), p. 529, fn. 72. For the figure of 83,000 in November, see Streit, *Keine Kameraden*, p. 134. For the Göring quote, recounted by Ciano, see Galeazzo Ciano, *Diario 1939–1943. Volume secondo, 1941–1943* (Milan: Rizzoli, 1946), p. 98, entry for 24–26 November 1941. For the share of 55 per cent, see Pohl, *Herrschaft*, p. 219.
9. Quoted in Dieckmann, *Deutsche Besatzungspolitik*, vol. 2, p. 1346.
10. On the basic decision and on Göring, see Kay, *Exploitation*, p. 141. On 1942 and the selection of those deemed 'fit for work', see Dieckmann, *Deutsche Besatzungspolitik*, vol. 2, pp. 1339–40. On Dulag 220 and in general, see Gerlach, 'Ausweitung', pp. 49–52.
11. Gerlach, 'Ausweitung', pp. 41–2. For the figure of 500,000, see Rolf Keller, 'Arbeitseinsatz und Hungerpolitik. Sowjetische Kriegsgefangene im Deutschen Reich 1941/42', in Dieckmann and Quinkert, eds, *Kriegführung und Hunger*, pp. 123–54, here p. 126.
12. Streit, *Keine Kameraden*, pp. 128, 356, n. 2, and 357, n. 5. For the total of 3.35 million, see ibid., p. 136; Gerlach, 'Ausweitung', p. 50. For the figure of at least 265,000 in the Reich and on conditions there, see Keller, 'Arbeitseinsatz und Hungerpolitik', p. 149. On civilian forced labourers in Germany, see Gerlach, *Extermination*, p. 230; Pohl, *Herrschaft*, p. 318. For the Einsatzgruppe comparison, see Gerlach, 'Ausweitung', pp. 52–3.
13. For the Rosenberg quote, see Nbg. Doc. 081-PS, 'Betr.: Kriegsgefangene', 28 February 1942, reproduced in: IMG, vol. 25, pp. 156–61. Rosenberg's letter is analysed in Streit, *Keine Kameraden*, p. 377, n. 338. For Rosenberg's comments on the Hague Convention, see BArch Berlin, R 90/256a, 'Die Zivilverwaltung in den besetzten Ostgebieten (Braune Mappe), Teil I: Reichskommissariat Ostland', 3 September 1941, p. 25. The quotation is from Article 4 of the Annex to the Convention respecting the Laws and Customs of War on Land (Hague IV) from 1907; see James Brown Scott, ed., *The Hague Conventions and Declarations of 1899 and 1907* (New York: Oxford University Press, 1915), p. 108.
14. Streit, *Keine Kameraden*, pp. 134–5; Gerlach, 'Ausweitung', pp. 46–7. On 'diseases of famine', see John R. Butterly and Jack Shepherd, *Hunger: The Biology and Politics of Starvation* (Lebanon, NH: University Press of New England, 2010), pp. 218–23.
15. KONTAKTE-КОНТАКТЫ – Verein für Kontakte zu Ländern der ehemaligen Sowjetunion, Freitagsbriefe, 'Grigorij Pawlowitsch Donskoj – Neuer Freitagsbrief Nr. 88', dated 21 November 2005, published on 21 June 2019. I am grateful to Christian Streit for bringing this piece of testimony to my attention.
16. Pohl, *Herrschaft*, pp. 207–9. See also Gerlach, *Kalkulierte Morde*, p. 803. On Army Group Centre and on the distance of 400km, and for the Tettau quote, see Streit, *Keine Kameraden*, pp. 164 and 169. Christoph Dieckmann cites an example of an order to shoot the sick and wounded issued by the captain of an infantry battalion: Dieckmann, *Deutsche Besatzungspolitik*, vol. 2, p. 1336. On the number of Soviet prisoners taken in the battle of Kiev, see also David Stahel, *Kiev 1941: Hitler's Battle for Supremacy in the East*

(Cambridge: Cambridge University Press, 2012), pp. 301–2. For use of the term 'death marches', see Berkhoff, '"Russian" Prisoners', pp. 5–10.

17. Both quotes in Berkhoff, '"Russian" Prisoners', p. 7.

18. Ibid., pp. 7–8 and 10 (first quote: p. 8; second quote: p. 10).

19. Ibid., pp. 8–9.

20. Gerlach, 'Ausweitung', p. 48; Gerlach, *Kalkulierte Morde*, p. 810 (including Reinecke quote). On transportation in open freight trains, see Gerlach, *Kalkulierte Morde*, p. 803. On the Reich and the Government General, see Pohl, *Herrschaft*, p. 211. On Stalag XI C (311), see Streit, *Keine Kameraden*, pp. 172 and 376, n. 298.

21. Gerlach, 'Ausweitung', pp. 48–9; Gerlach, *Kalkulierte Morde*, pp. 810–11. See also Terry, 'German Army Group Centre', p. 164.

22. Pohl, *Herrschaft*, p. 229. On the decline in death rates in summer 1942, see Streit, *Keine Kameraden*, p. 246. On Stalag 352, see Gerlach, *Kalkulierte Morde*, p. 832.

23. Felix Römer, *Der Kommissarbefehl: Wehrmacht und NS-Verbrechen an der Ostfront 1941/42* (Paderborn: Ferdinand Schöningh, 2008), pp. 561–2; Felix Römer, 'The Wehrmacht in the War of Ideologies: The Army and Hitler's Criminal Orders on the Eastern Front', in Kay et al., eds, *Nazi Policy*, pp. 73–100, here pp. 88 and 93.

24. Kay, *Making of an SS Killer*, p. 75.

25. Römer, *Kommissarbefehl*, pp. 359–60. For the quotes from the Commissar Order, see BArch-MA, RW 4/v. 578, fols 41–4, 'Richtlinien für die Behandlung politischer Kommissare', 6 June 1941, here fol. 44.

26. On the 17 July guidelines, see Kay, 'Transition to Genocide', p. 414. For the 17 July quote, see BArch Berlin, R 58/272, fols 46–58, 'Einsatzbefehl Nr. 8, Betr. Richtlinien für die in die Stalags und Dulags abzustellenden Kommandos des Chefs der Sicherheitspolizei und des SD', 17 July 1941, second enclosure: 'Anlage 2. Richtlinien für die in die Stalags abzustellenden Kommandos des Chefs der Sicherheitspolizei und des SD', here fol. 56. For the October quote, see Klein, ed., *Einsatzgruppen*, doc. 22, p. 359. For the number of Jewish Red Army soldiers in German captivity and the percentage of survivors, and for the Bondarets quote, see Arad, *Holocaust in the Soviet Union*, pp. 377–8 and 381. For a similar figure of between 70,000 and 90,000 dead Jewish soldiers, see Pohl, 'Wehrmacht', p. 41.

27. Pohl, *Herrschaft*, pp. 235–6. For the quote from the Guidelines for the Conduct of the Troops in Russia, see BArch-MA, RH 22/12, fols 114–15, 'Richtlinien für das Verhalten der Truppe in Rußland', undated [19 May 1941], here fol. 114 (emphasis in the original). On the circulation of these guidelines, see Römer, *Kommissarbefehl*, p. 86, fn. 199. For the quote from the Commissar Order, see BArch-MA, RW 4/v. 578, fols 41–4, 'Richtlinien für die Behandlung politischer Kommissare', 6 June 1941, here fol. 42. Karel Berkhoff argues that the German identification of Soviet POWs as 'Russians' (and thus irreversibly 'Bolshevised') resulted in a 'genocidal massacre' lasting from mid-1941 to at least the end of 1942: Berkhoff, '"Russian" Prisoners', pp. 1–32, esp. pp. 1–3 and 21–2.

28. Felix Römer, 'Gewaltsame Geschlechterordnung. Wehrmacht und "Flintenweiber" an der Ostfront 1941/42', in Klaus Latzel, Franka Maubach and Silke Satjukow, eds, *Soldatinnen. Gewalt und Geschlecht im Krieg vom Mittelalter bis heute* (Paderborn: Ferdinand Schöningh, 2011), pp. 331–51, here pp. 335–7 (Kluge quote: p. 335; Hammer quote: p. 336).

29. Ibid., pp. 337–46 and 348–51 (NCO quote: p. 337).

30. Pohl, *Herrschaft*, pp. 236–7. On Stalag 358, see Berkhoff, '"Russian" Prisoners', p. 15. On Stalag 324, the camps in Latvia, the hospital in Gomel and the fact that in Belarus more killings targeted the sick than political opponents, see Gerlach, *Kalkulierte Morde*, pp. 850 and 855.

31. Reinhard Otto and Rolf Keller, 'Soviet Prisoners of War in Nazi Concentration Camps: Current Knowledge and Research Desiderata', in Kay and Stahel, eds, *Mass Violence*, pp. 123–46, esp. pp. 125–6, 128 and 135–6; Nikolaus Wachsmann, *KL: A History of the Nazi Concentration Camps* (London: Little, Brown, 2015), pp. 277–87. See also Reinhard Otto and Rolf Keller, *Sowjetische Kriegsgefangene im System der Konzentrationslager* (Vienna: new

academic press, 2019); Rolf Keller, *Sowjetische Kriegsgefangene im Deutschen Reich 1941/42. Behandlung und Arbeitseinsatz zwischen Vernichtungspolitik und kriegswirtschaftlichen Zwängen* (Göttingen: Wallstein, 2011), pp. 419–23. On the OKW order and on the camps receiving POWs in October 1941, see Reinhard Otto, *Wehrmacht, Gestapo und sowjetische Kriegsgefangene im deutschen Reichsgebiet 1941/42* (Munich: Oldenbourg, 1998), pp. 188–9.

32. Gerlach, *Kalkulierte Morde*, pp. 852–3.
33. On the area of operations and for the figure of at least 120,000 in territories under civil administration, see Pohl, *Herrschaft*, p. 237. For the figure of 33,000 in Germany until July 1942, see Otto and Keller, *Sowjetische Kriegsgefangene*, p. 145. On prisoner shootings in Belarus, see Gerlach, *Kalkulierte Morde*, p. 855. For the total figure of 140,000, see Alfred Streim, *Die Behandlung sowjetischer Kriegsgefangener im 'Fall Barbarossa'. Eine Dokumentation* (Heidelberg/Karlsruhe: C.F. Müller Juristischer, 1981), p. 244; Christian Streit, 'Keine Kameraden. Die Wehrmacht und die sowjetischen Kriegsgefangenen', in Verein 'KONTAKTE-КОНТАКТЫ' e.V., ed., *'Ich werde es nie vergessen'. Briefe sowjetischer Kriegsgefangener 2004–2006* (Berlin: Ch. Links, 2007), pp. 11–21, here p. 17.
34. For the figures of 3.3 million and 5.7 million, see Streit, *Keine Kameraden*, pp. 244–6; Gerlach, *Kalkulierte Morde*, pp. 857–8; Hans-Adolf Jacobsen, 'Kommissarbefehl und Massenexekutionen sowjetischer Kriegsgefangener', in Martin Broszat, Hans-Adolf Jacobsen and Helmut Krausnick, *Anatomie des SS-Staates, Band 2: Konzentrationslager, Kommissarbefehl, Judenverfolgung* (Olten/Freiburg im Breisgau: Walter-Verlag, 1965), pp. 161–279, here p. 197. As the authors themselves emphasise, the article by Reinhard Otto, Rolf Keller and Jens Nagel, 'Sowjetische Kriegsgefangene in deutschem Gewahrsam 1941–1945: Zahlen und Dimensionen', *Vierteljahrsheft e fur Zeitgeschichte*, vol. 56, no. 4 (October 2008), pp. 557–602, here p. 559, fn. 5, does not address the number of deaths among Soviet POWs but rather the number of individual prisoner *registrations*. For the regional figures, see Dieckmann, *Deutsche Besatzungspolitik*, vol. 2, p. 1340. On the areas under military administration and the total of 1 million deaths there, see also Pohl, *Herrschaft*, 240. On prisoners shot immediately after being captured, see Streit, *Keine Kameraden*, p. 405, n. 45. It is important to point out here that Streit's figure of 3.3 million dead did not include prisoners shot immediately after being captured.
35. For the figure of 200,000 deaths in Army Group Centre's zone of operations, see Terry, 'German Army Group Centre', p. 260. For the other figures, see Chapter 5 in this book. Hans-Heinrich Nolte estimates that as many as 7 million Soviet citizens starved on both sides of the front: Hans-Heinrich Nolte, 'Kriegskinder: Zu den Differenzen zwischen Russland und Deutschland', *Zeitgeschichte*, vol. 36, no. 5 (September–October 2009), pp. 311–23, here p. 319.

CHAPTER 7 PREVENTIVE TERROR AND REPRISALS AGAINST CIVILIANS

1. For the figure of 26.6 million, see Mark Harrison, 'Counting the Soviet Union's War Dead: Still 26–27 Million', *Europe-Asia Studies*, vol. 71, no. 6 (2019), pp. 1036–47; Nolte, 'Kriegskinder', p. 319; Peter Jahn, '27 Millionen', *Die Zeit*, 14 June 2007, p. 90; Hartmann, *Wehrmacht im Ostkrieg*, p. 790; John Barber and Mark Harrison, *The Soviet Home Front 1941–1945: A Social and Economic History of the USSR in World War II* (London: Longman, 1991), pp. 40–1. For the total figure of 14.6 million Red Army dead, see Lev Lopukhovsky and Boris Kavalerchik, *The Price of Victory: The Red Army's Casualties in the Great Patriotic War*, trans. from Russian by Harold Orenstein (Barnsley: Pen & Sword, 2017). On the 3.3 million Soviet POWs who died, see Chapter 6 in this book.
2. Pohl, *Verfolgung und Massenmord*, pp. 124–5; Kay, 'Transition to Genocide', pp. 418–19. On German pre-invasion expectations, see Kay, *Exploitation*, pp. 158–63.
3. Pohl, *Verfolgung und Massenmord*, p. 125. For the text of the so-called Jurisdiction Decree Barbarossa, see BArch-MA, RW 4/v. 577, fols 72–5, 'Erlass über die Ausübung der Kriegsgerichtsbarkeit im Gebiet "Barbarossa" und über besondere Massnahmen der Truppe', 13 May 1941, here fol. 73.

4. Römer, 'Wehrmacht', pp. 75–6. On the importance of troop leaders for the German conduct of war, see Felix Römer, *Comrades: The Wehrmacht from Within*, trans. from German by Alex J. Kay (Oxford: Oxford University Press, 2019), pp. 216–52.

5. Römer, 'Wehrmacht', p. 76.

6. Gerlach, *Kalkulierte Morde*, pp. 503–7.

7. Ibid., pp. 507–9; Krausnick, 'Einsatzgruppen', p. 236. For the Nebe quote, see EM 21 (13 July 1941), pp. 113–14. On the shooting of Asian or Asian-looking prisoners, see Chapter 6 in this book.

8. Kay, 'Transition to Genocide', p. 419. For the OKH directive, see BArch-MA, RH 26-403/4a, 'Betr. Behandlung feindlicher Zivilpersonen und russischer Kriegsgefangener im rückwärtigen Heeresgebiet', Az. 453 Gr. R Wes, Nr 1332/41 geh., General z.b.V. beim Befehlshaber des Heeres, 25 July 1941.

9. Gerlach, *Kalkulierte Morde*, pp. 870–2 and 955. Nicholas Terry notes that more than one-third of these villages were located in Vitebsk province: Terry, 'German Army Group Centre', pp. 226–7.

10. Dieckmann, *Deutsche Besatzungspolitik*, vol. 1, p. 299.

11. Gerlach, *Kalkulierte Morde*, pp. 872, 875 and 883. For the total of 63,257 partisans killed in the rear area of Army Group Centre as of 1 March 1942 and the 638 German dead, see also Timothy P. Mulligan, 'Reckoning the Cost of People's War: The German Experience in the Central USSR', *Russian History*, vol. 9, no. 1 (1982), pp. 27–48, here p. 32. On the stalling of the military campaign against the Soviet Union in summer 1941, see Stahel, *Operation Barbarossa*, pp. 153–451. See also the discussion in Chapter 3 in this book.

12. Gerlach, *Kalkulierte Morde*, pp. 873 and 876 (Schenckendorff quote: p. 876; emphasis in the original). On the SS Cavalry Brigade, see Martin Cüppers, *Wegbereiter der Shoah. Die Waffen-SS, der Kommandostab Reichsführer-SS und die Judenvernichtung 1939–1945* (Darmstadt: Wissenschaftliche Buchgesellschaft, 2005), p. 202. On Einsatzgruppe B, see 'Tätigkeits- und Lagebericht Nr. 7 der Einsatzgruppen der Sicherheitspolizei und des SD in der UdSSR (Berichtszeit v. 1.11.–30.11.1941)', reproduced in: Klein, ed., *Einsatzgruppen*, p. 251. On Sonderkommando 7a, see EM 108 (9 October 1941), p. 659.

13. The programme of the anti-partisan warfare seminar, the list of participants and the text of Schenckendorff's opening remarks can all be found in BArch-MA, WF-03/13302. On the conference in general, see Waitman W. Beorn, 'A Calculus of Complicity: The Wehrmacht, the Anti-Partisan War, and the Final Solution in White Russia, 1941–42', *Central European History*, vol. 44, no. 2 (June 2011), pp. 308–37, here pp. 316–24. On the repetition of the seminar, see Krausnick, 'Einsatzgruppen', p. 248, fn. 548. On the involvement of the Wehrmacht in massacres of Jews, see Hartmann, *Wehrmacht im Ostkrieg*, pp. 657–8. In general, see also Walter Manoschek, '"Wo der Partisan ist, ist der Jude, und wo der Jude ist, ist der Partisan". Die Wehrmacht und die Shoah', in Gerhard Paul, ed., *Die Täter der Shoah. Fanatische Nationalsozialisten oder ganz normale Deutsche?* (Göttingen: Wallstein, 2002), pp. 167–85. On Wehrmacht shootings of Jews, see also Chapter 3 in this book.

14. Gerlach, *Kalkulierte Morde*, pp. 875–84. See also the discussion in Hartmann, *Wehrmacht im Ostkrieg*, pp. 578–82; Klaus Jochen Arnold, *Die Wehrmacht und die Besatzungspolitik in den besetzten Gebieten der Sowjetunion: Kriegführung und Radikalisierung im 'Unternehmen Barbarossa'* (Berlin: Duncker & Humblot, 2005), pp. 474–7. On Korück 580, and also on the treatment of Red Army fugitives and civilian refugees by the 221st Security Division, see Shepherd, *War in the Wild East*, pp. 103–7 (quote: p. 104). For the 37,934 prisoners taken up to the end of September, see Tsentralnyi arkhiv Ministerstva oborony Rossiiskoi Federatsii, Podolsk, 500-12454-227, 'Gefangene und Beute (22.6.–27.9.41)', Abt. Ic/A.O., 30 September 1941, fol. 124. I am grateful to Nicholas Terry for bringing this source to my attention.

15. Gerlach, *Kalkulierte Morde*, p. 884; Pohl, *Verfolgung und Massenmord*, p. 126.

16. Hasenclever, *Wehrmacht und Besatzungspolitik*, pp. 383–4. For the von Bechtolsheim quotes, see Lieb, 'Täter aus Überzeugung?', here p. 550. On the actual number of dead, see

Gerlach, *Kalkulierte Morde*, pp. 887 and 889; Pohl, *Herrschaft*, p. 285. For the figure of forty-seven firearms captured, see Gerlach, *Kalkulierte Morde*, p. 889.

17. Gerlach, *Kalkulierte Morde*, p. 887.

18. On Himmler's appointment, see ibid., pp. 921–3; Longerich, *Heinrich Himmler*, pp. 625–7. On the acceleration of the extermination of Jews in July 1942, see Chapters 3, 8 and 9 in this book. On the large-scale operations, see Pohl, *Verfolgung und Massenmord*, p. 127; Gerlach, *Kalkulierte Morde*, pp. 899–904.

19. See the post-war testimony of Jacob Grigoriev at Nuremberg on 26 February 1946, reproduced in: IMG, vol. 8, pp. 257–61. I am grateful to Ben Shepherd for bringing this piece of testimony to my attention.

20. Gerlach, *Kalkulierte Morde*, pp. 902, 950 and 969–71 (Bach-Zelewski quote: p. 950; 78th Storm Division quote: p. 970 [emphasis in the original]; Gottberg quote: p. 971). On Bach-Zelewski's appointment as chief of anti-gang formations, see Philip W. Blood, *Hitler's Bandit Hunters: The SS and the Nazi Occupation of Europe* (Washington, DC: Potomac Books, 2006), p. 121.

21. Timm C. Richter, 'Belarusian Partisans and German Reprisals', in Snyder and Brandon, eds, *Stalin and Europe*, pp. 207–32, here p. 221 (including Treuenfeld quote); Snyder, *Bloodlands*, p. 242; Gerlach, *Kalkulierte Morde*, pp. 907–13 (Wilke quote: p. 909; Frentzel quote: p. 911). For the weapons hauls, see Gerlach, *Kalkulierte Morde*, pp. 900–1. For the partisan figures, see Gerlach, *Kalkulierte Morde*, p. 861; Bogdan Musial, *Sowjetische Partisanen 1941–1944. Mythos und Wirklichkeit* (Paderborn: Ferdinand Schöningh, 2009), p. 319.

22. Shepherd, *War in the Wild East*, pp. 189–94.

23. Gerlach, *Kalkulierte Morde*, pp. 891–2 and 900–2 (quote: p. 891).

24. Richter, 'Belarusian Partisans', p. 222; Gerlach, *Kalkulierte Morde*, pp. 899–904; Pohl, *Herrschaft*, pp. 293–4. For the Auschwitz comparison, see Gerlach, *Extermination*, p. 299.

25. Richter, 'Belarusian Partisans', p. 223; Pohl, *Verfolgung und Massenmord*, pp. 127–8. On Hermann Göring and for all the figures (dead, forced labourers, cattle and farm machines), see Gerlach, *Kalkulierte Morde*, pp. 902 and 907.

26. Pohl, *Verfolgung und Massenmord*, p. 127. On Kortelisy, see Berkhoff, *Harvest of Despair*, pp. 280–1.

27. For 345,000 dead in Belarus, see Gerlach, *Kalkulierte Morde*, pp. 957–8; Richter, 'Belarusian Partisans', p. 224. For the figure of 10 per cent and for German losses, see Gerlach, *Kalkulierte Morde*, pp. 866 and 958. For 640,000 dead across the Soviet Union, see Gerlach, *Extermination*, p. 288, fn. 4. For a total of half-a-million dead, see Pohl, *Verfolgung und Massenmord*, p. 128. On anti-partisan operations as a war against Soviet peasants, see Gerlach, *Kalkulierte Morde*, pp. 898, 907, 909 and 943; Pohl, *Verfolgung und Massenmord*, p. 128.

28. See Chapter 3 in this book.

29. Shepherd, *Terror in the Balkans*, pp. 125–6 (all quotes: p. 126).

30. Manoschek, *'Serbien ist judenfrei'*, pp. 61–4 ('insubordination' quote: p. 64); Shepherd, *Terror in the Balkans*, p. 127 (including 'incurred losses' quote).

31. Shepherd, *Terror in the Balkans*, pp. 126–8 (including 342nd quotes [emphasis in the original]: pp. 126–7). On Metković and the shooting of eighty-four prisoners two days later, see Ben Shepherd, 'Bloodier than Boehme: The 342nd Infantry Division in Serbia', in Ben Shepherd and Juliette Pattinson, eds, *War in a Twilight World: Partisan and Anti-Partisan Warfare in Eastern Europe, 1939–45* (Houndmills: Palgrave Macmillan, 2010), pp. 189–209, here p. 196 (including 'hostile activities' quote).

32. Shepherd, *Terror in the Balkans*, pp. 128 and 131; Schmider, *Partisanenkrieg*, p. 71 (including quote).

33. Manoschek, *'Serbien ist judenfrei'*, pp. 11–12 and 166; Pohl, *Verfolgung und Massenmord*, pp. 79 and 122–3; Pisarri, *Suffering of the Roma*, p. 156. On Rendulic and for the figures of 30,000 and 19,000, see Schmider, *Partisanenkrieg*, p. 331. For a total figure of 45,000 Serbian civilians killed during so-called reprisal measures, see Karl-Heinz Schlarp,

Wirtschaft und Besatzung in Serbien, 1941–1944. Ein Beitrag zur nationalsozialistischen Wirtschaftspolitik in Südosteuropa (Wiesbaden: Franz Steiner, 1986), p. 161. For the total of 200,000 across Yugoslavia, see Gerlach, *Extermination*, p. 288, fn. 4.

34. Pohl, *Verfolgung und Massenmord*, pp. 123–4; Mark Mazower, *Inside Hitler's Greece: The Experience of Occupation, 1941–44* (New Haven, CT/London: Yale University Press, 1993), pp. 173–4 (Kondomari), 179–80 (Kalavryta, Klisura), 191–2 (Komeno) and 212 (Distomo).

35. Mazower, *Inside Hitler's Greece*, pp. 192–5 (quotes: p. 195).

36. Pohl, *Verfolgung und Massenmord*, p. 124; Mazower, *Inside Hitler's Greece*, pp. 191 and 228. On the numbers of towns and villages destroyed, see Antonio J. Muñoz, *The German Secret Field Police in Greece, 1941–1944* (Jefferson, NC: McFarland, 2018), p. 90. For the figure of 100,000 dead, see Gerlach, *Extermination*, p. 288, fn. 4.

37. Mazower, *Inside Hitler's Greece*, pp. 40–1; Mark Mazower, *Hitler's Empire: Nazi Rule in Occupied Europe* (London: Allen Lane, 2008), p. 280 (including Göring quote). See also Hionidou, *Famine and Death*, esp. p. 158. On the transport of grain, see Polymeris Voglis, 'Surviving Hunger: Life in the Cities and the Countryside during the Occupation', in Robert Gildea, Olivier Wieviorka and Anette Warring, eds, *Surviving Hitler and Mussolini: Daily Life in Occupied Europe* (Oxford/New York: Berg, 2006), pp. 16–41, here p. 23.

38. On partisan strongholds, see Gerlach, *Extermination*, pp. 291–3. On Italy, see Carlo Gentile, *Wehrmacht und Waffen-SS im Partisanenkrieg: Italien 1943–1945* (Paderborn: Ferdinand Schöningh, 2012), pp. 14–15; Pohl, *Verfolgung und Massenmord*, pp. 131–2. On Poland, see Pohl, *Verfolgung und Massenmord*, p. 121; Gerlach, *Extermination*, p. 288, fn. 4. On Slovakia, see Rolf-Dieter Müller, *An der Seite der Wehrmacht. Hitlers ausländische Helfer beim 'Kreuzzug gegen den Bolschewismus' 1941–1944* (Berlin: Ch. Links, 2007), p. 105. On the Slovak National Uprising, see also Chapter 12 in this book.

39. Peter Lieb, *Konventioneller Krieg oder NS-Weltanschauungskrieg? Kriegführung und Partisanenbekämpfung in Frankreich 1943/44* (Munich: Oldenbourg, 2007), pp. 15, 25, 297, 368 and 412–15. For the 200 hostages killed by the end of 1941, see Thomas Fontaine, 'Chronologie: Répression et persécution en France occupée 1940–1944', *Violence de masse et Résistance – Réseau de recherche*, 7 December 2009; Pohl, *Verfolgung und Massenmord*, p. 130.

40. Gerlach, *Extermination*, p. 288, and the literature cited there in fn. 4. On the elimination of the Polish elites and the suppression of the Warsaw Uprising, respectively, see Chapters 2 and 12 in this book.

41. Gerlach, 'Ausweitung', p. 11. For the figure of 1 in every 500 people on the planet, see Peter Fritzsche, *Life and Death in the Third Reich* (Cambridge, MA: Harvard University Press, 2008), p. 186.

CHAPTER 8 HOLOCAUST BY GAS: OPERATION REINHARDT

1. Gerlach, *Extermination*, pp. 99 and 124; Stephan Lehnstaedt, *Der Kern des Holocaust. Bełżec, Sobibór, Treblinka und die Aktion Reinhardt* (Munich: C.H. Beck, 2017), pp. 8 and 83–7. For the figure of at least 1.37 million, see Sara Berger, *Experten der Vernichtung. Das T4-Reinhardt-Netzwerk in den Lagern Belzec, Sobibor und Treblinka* (Hamburg: Hamburger Edition, 2013), p. 254. See also Peter Witte and Stephen Tyas, 'A New Document on the Deportation and Murder of Jews during "Einsatz Reinhardt" 1942', *Holocaust and Genocide Studies*, vol. 15, no. 3 (winter 2001), pp. 468–86. On Auschwitz, see Chapter 9 in this book.

2. On Frank and on Himmler, see Witte et al., eds, *Dienstkalender*, pp. 233–4 (entry for 13 October 1941). On Globocnik, Bełżec and Wirth, see Lehnstaedt, *Kern des Holocaust*, pp. 34–5 and 41. On territorial proposals for resettling Jews, see Kay, *Exploitation*, pp. 108–14. On the visits to Bełżec by Brack and Bouhler, see Friedländer, *Years of Extermination*, p. 284. On Bełżec generally, see also Robert Kuwałek, *Das Vernichtungslager Bełżec* (Berlin: Metropol, 2013).

3. On Karl Litzmann, see Alberti, *Verfolgung*, p. 50, fn. 75. On conditions in the Łódź Ghetto and its selection by Hitler, see Gerlach, *Extermination*, pp. 73–4 and 76. On Frank's opposition, see also Aly, *'Endlösung'*, pp. 201–2. On Himmler and Greiser and the leasehold in Chełmno, see Peter Klein, 'Kulmhof/Chełmno', in Wolfgang Benz and Barbara Distel, eds, *Der Ort des Terrors. Geschichte der nationalsozialistischen Konzentrationslager, Band 8* (Munich: C.H. Beck, 2008), pp. 301–28, here p. 305. On Greiser obtaining the agreement of Hitler and Himmler, see Patrick Montague, *Chełmno and the Holocaust: The History of Hitler's First Death Camp* (Chapel Hill, NC/London: University of North Carolina Press, 2012), pp. 34–5; Epstein, *Model Nazi*, p. 185.
4. Klein, 'Kulmhof/Chełmno', pp. 306–8. On the delivery of the gas vans and the identity of the first victims, see Friedländer, *Years of Extermination*, pp. 284 and 316.
5. On the deportations of 15 October to 4 November, see Christian Gerlach, 'Die Wannsee-Konferenz, das Schicksal der deutschen Juden und Hitlers politische Grundsatzentscheidung, alle Juden Europas zu ermorden', in Gerlach, *Krieg, Ernährung, Völkermord*, pp. 79–152, here p. 89. This is the expanded version of an article published under the same title in *WerkstattGeschichte*, vol. 18 (1997), pp. 7–44. On the deportation of the Austrian Roma, see Steiermärkisches Landesarchiv, Landesregierung 384 Zi 1–1940, 'Betrifft: Abschiebung von Zigeunern', S – V A 2 b Nr. 81/41 g II, signed Werner, 1 October 1941. On the typhus epidemic, see Klein, 'Kulmhof/Chełmno', p. 308; Friedländer, *Years of Extermination*, pp. 316–17. On deportations to Chełmno between January and May 1942, see Klein, 'Kulmhof/Chełmno', pp. 308–9. The figure of 97,000 is quoted in Lanzmann, *Shoah*, p. 144. On large-scale and smaller transports, see Montague, *Chełmno*, p. 127. For the figures of 145,000 and 7,196 Jewish dead, see Montague, *Chełmno*, pp. 185 and 190; Klein, 'Kulmhof/Chełmno', pp. 310 and 317.
6. For the Heydrich quote, see Witte et al., eds, *Dienstkalender*, p. 238, fn. 52. On the general prohibition of Jewish emigration, see Browning, *Origins of the Final Solution*, p. 369; Peter Longerich, *Holocaust: The Nazi Persecution and Murder of the Jews* (Oxford: Oxford University Press, 2010), p. 285. On territorial proposals for resettling Jews, see Kay, *Exploitation*, pp. 108–14. On deportations of Jews from the German Reich, see Gerlach, 'Wannsee-Konferenz', pp. 87–95; Gerlach, *Extermination*, pp. 73–8. For the 41,000 Jews and the forty-two transports, see Dieckmann, *Deutsche Besatzungspolitik*, vol. 2, p. 961.
7. On deportations of Jews from the German Reich and on Hitler's decision to murder all European Jews, see Gerlach, 'Wannsee-Konferenz', pp. 87–125 (Himmler quote: p. 88); Gerlach, *Extermination*, pp. 73–84. See also Ian Kershaw, *Fateful Choices: Ten Decisions That Changed the World, 1940–1941* (London: Allen Lane, 2007), pp. 431–70. On the Kaunas and Riga shootings, see also Dieckmann, *Deutsche Besatzungspolitik*, vol. 2, pp. 961–7. For the Hitler quote, see Fröhlich, ed., *Die Tagebücher von Joseph Goebbels: Teil II*, p. 498 (entry for 13 December 1941).
8. On technical principles, see Friedländer, *Years of Extermination*, p. 234. On the trial gassings, see Robert Kuwałek, 'Bełżec', in Benz and Distel, eds, *Ort des Terrors, Band 8*, pp. 331–71, here p. 338; Berger, *Experten*, p. 47. On the three gas chambers and the death throes of the victims, see Berger, *Experten*, pp. 49–50 and 53. On Lubycza Królewska, see Kuwałek, 'Bełżec', p. 339.
9. On the transport from Żółkiew, see Dieter Pohl, *Nationalsozialistische Judenverfolgung in Ostgalizien 1941–1944. Organisation und Durchführung eines staatlichen Massenverbrechens* (Munich: Oldenbourg, 1997), pp. 189–90. On the transports from Lvov and Lublin, see Kuwałek, 'Bełżec', pp. 340 and 343. On the herding of Jews into the trains and on shooting operations, see Lehnstaedt, *Kern des Holocaust*, pp. 64–7. For the Thomas Blatt quote, see Thomas Toivi Blatt, *From the Ashes of Sobibor: A Story of Survival* (Evanston, IL: Northwestern University Press, 1997), p. 43.
10. On the start of construction at Sobibór and killing operations there, see Gerlach, *Extermination*, p. 92. On the SS visit in autumn 1941, see Jules Schelvis, *Sobibor: A History of a Nazi Death Camp*, trans. from Dutch by Karin Dixon (London: Bloomsbury, 2014),

pp. 26–7; Browning, *Origins of the Final Solution*, p. 365. On the three gas chambers, see Berger, *Experten*, p. 63. On the respective size of Bełżec and Sobibór, see Lehnstaedt, *Kern des Holocaust*, pp. 54–5. Sobibór was later expanded to a size of 60 hectares; see Lehnstaedt, *Kern des Holocaust*, p. 59; Barbara Distel, 'Sobibór', in Benz and Distel, eds, *Ort des Terrors, Band 8*, pp. 375–404, here p. 376. On the appointment of Stangl, the trial gassing, the first phase of killing operations, repair work and the expansion of the gas chambers, see Distel, 'Sobibór', pp. 380–2 and 390.

11. On the construction of Treblinka, see Gerlach, *Extermination*, p. 92; Berger, *Experten*, p. 72. On Krüger's appointment, the decision to expand operations, the death tolls in Bełżec and Sobibór as of late June, and the July order, see Lehnstaedt, *Kern des Holocaust*, pp. 36 and 69–70. On the decision to expand operations, see also Longerich, *Holocaust*, pp. 332–5. The same figures for the death tolls in Bełżec and Sobibór can also be found in Berger, *Experten*, pp. 52, 55 and 64. On the new gas chambers in Bełżec, see Arad, *Operation Reinhard*, pp. 110–11. For the Himmler quote, see Nbg. Doc. NO-5574, 'Geheim', Tgb.-Nr. 36/40/42 gv, signed H[einrich] Himmler, 19 July 1942, reproduced in: Jüdisches Historisches Institut Warschau, ed., *Faschismus – Getto – Massenmord. Dokumentation über Ausrottung und Widerstand der Juden in Polen während des Zweiten Weltkrieges* (Berlin: Rütten & Loening, 1960), doc. 229, p. 303. On Operation Reinhardt being named after Heydrich and on the spelling 'Reinhardt', see also Witte and Tyas, 'A New Document', pp. 474–5; Longerich, *Heinrich Himmler*, pp. 571 and 909, n. 74.

12. On the size of Treblinka, see Lehnstaedt, *Kern des Holocaust*, p. 56. On Eberl and Stangl, see Wolfgang Benz, 'Treblinka', in Benz and Distel, eds, *Ort des Terrors, Band 8*, pp. 407–43, here pp. 418–19; Lehnstaedt, *Kern des Holocaust*, pp. 82–3. On Globocnik and Wirth, see Berger, *Experten*, pp. 122–3. For the Wiernik quote, see Jankiel Wiernik, 'One Year in Treblinka', in Alexander Donat, ed., *The Death Camp Treblinka: A Documentary* (New York: Holocaust Library, 1979), pp. 147–88, here p. 151. Wiernik's account was first published in Polish in 1944, shortly after his escape from Treblinka. On Jews dying of thirst, see Gerlach, *Extermination*, p. 93.

13. For the 70,000 deaths before July 1942, see Pohl, 'Just How Many?', p. 135. On the 'great deportation' from the Warsaw Ghetto, see Yisrael Gutman, *The Jews of Warsaw, 1939–1943: Ghetto, Underground, Revolt*, trans. from Hebrew by Ina Friedman (Bloomington, IN: Indiana University Press, 1982), pp. 197–227, esp. pp. 197, 204 and 213; Havi Ben-Sasson, '"At the Present Time, Jewish Warsaw Is Like a Cemetery": Life in the Warsaw Ghetto during the Great Deportation', in Moshe Zimmermann, ed., *On Germans and Jews under the Nazi Regime: Essays by Three Generations of Historians. A Festschrift in Honor of Otto Dov Kulka* (Jerusalem: Magnes Press, 2006), pp. 353–83, here p. 353. For the diary entry, see Abraham I. Katsh, *Scroll of Agony: The Warsaw Diary of Chaim A. Kaplan*, trans. from Hebrew by Abraham I. Katsh (Bloomington, IN: Indiana University Press, 1999 [1965]), p. 396. On the ghettos in the Radom District, see Seidel, *Deutsche Besatzungspolitik*, pp. 310–30.

14. Pohl, *Verfolgung und Massenmord*, pp. 94–5; Lehnstaedt, *Kern des Holocaust*, p. 70. For the figure of 7,000 and on the Częstochowa trains, see Alfred C. Mierzejewski, *The Most Valuable Asset of the Reich: A History of the German National Railway, Volume 2: 1933–1945* (Chapel Hill, NC/London: University of North Carolina Press, 2000), p. 121. On the installation of gas chambers in Majdanek, see Barbara Schwindt, *Das Konzentrations- und Vernichtungslager Majdanek: Funktionswandel im Kontext der 'Endlösung'* (Würzburg: Königshausen & Neumann, 2005), pp. 156–7.

15. Pohl, *Verfolgung und Massenmord*, p. 95; Gerlach, *Extermination*, p. 197. For the Berek Freiberg quote, see Lehnstaedt, *Kern des Holocaust*, pp. 77–8. On the labour squads, see Berger, *Experten*, pp. 223–38. On the absence of crematoria in the Operation Reinhardt camps, see Gerlach, *Extermination*, pp. 120–1.

16. Lehnstaedt, *Kern des Holocaust*, pp. 80–1 (quote: p. 81). On Jews not doing any of the killing, see Berger, *Experten*, p. 224.

17. For the individual deportation figures for Sobibór, see Distel, 'Sobibór', p. 382; Berger, *Experten*, p. 253. For the Treblinka figures, see Berger, *Experten*, p. 253; Lehnstaedt, *Kern*

des Holocaust, p. 86. For the total of 1.3 million from the Government General, see Lehnstaedt, *Kern des Holocaust*, pp. 85–6.

18. On Majdanek as a selection site, see Gerlach, *Extermination*, p. 197, fn. 80. On the July 1943 deportation, see Distel, 'Sobibór', pp. 382–3 (including Freiberg quote).

19. Pohl, *Verfolgung und Massenmord*, p. 93; Lewi Stone, 'Quantifying the Holocaust: Hyperintense Kill Rates during the Genocide', *Science Advances*, vol. 5, no. 1 (January 2019), pp. 1–10. On the deportation of Hungary's Jews to Auschwitz, see Chapter 9 in this book.

20. Lehnstaedt, *Kern des Holocaust*, pp. 85 and 136. On Operation 1005, see Andrej Angrick, *'Aktion 1005'. Spurenbeseitigung von NS-Massenverbrechen 1942–1945: Eine 'geheime Reichssache' im Spannungsfeld von Kriegswende und Propaganda* (Göttingen: Wallstein, 2018). On Himmler's visit to Treblinka, see Arad, *Operation Reinhard*, pp. 206–8; Wiernik, 'One Year', p. 169. According to Sara Berger, 'approximately 500,000 people' were murdered in Bełżec: Berger, *Experten*, p. 255.

21. On the termination of the mass murder and the Treblinka uprising, see Lehnstaedt, *Kern des Holocaust*, pp. 111–12 and 134; Berger, *Experten*, pp. 269–74. On the Warsaw Ghetto uprising, see Barbara Engelking and Jacek Leociak, *The Warsaw Ghetto: A Guide to the Perished City*, trans. from Polish by Emma Harris (New Haven, CT: Yale University Press, 2009 [2001]), pp. 775–800. On the Białystok Ghetto uprising, see Bender, *Jews of Białystok*, pp. 243–76. On Jews from the Minsk Ghetto joining partisan units, see Barbara Epstein, *The Minsk Ghetto, 1941–1943: Jewish Resistance and Soviet Internationalism* (Berkeley/Los Angeles/London: University of California Press, 2008), esp. pp. 188–227. On Jewish resistance during the Holocaust, see Patrick Henry, ed., *Jewish Resistance against the Nazis* (Washington, DC: Catholic University of America Press, 2014).

22. On the Sobibór uprising, see Lehnstaedt, *Kern des Holocaust*, pp. 114–16; Berger, *Experten*, pp. 274–7. On the units involved in the hunt for Jews, see Berger, *Experten*, p. 276. On survivors of the camps, see Lehnstaedt, *Kern des Holocaust*, pp. 108 and 120. According to Sara Berger, 'just over fifty' of those who fled Treblinka survived the war, two women among them: Berger, *Experten*, p. 272.

23. On the dissolution of Treblinka, the transfers to Sobibór and Globocnik's declaration, see Berger, *Experten*, pp. 270 and 273–4. On the Białystok Jews and Treblinka's final victims, see Lehnstaedt, *Kern des Holocaust*, p. 137. On the dissolution of Sobibór, see Lehnstaedt, *Kern des Holocaust*, p. 137; Berger, *Experten*, p. 277. On the total death tolls in Treblinka and Sobibór, see Lehnstaedt, *Kern des Holocaust*, p. 85. According to Wolfgang Benz, the number of victims of Treblinka was 'at least 900,000': Benz, 'Treblinka', p. 409. Sara Berger gives for Treblinka a figure of 'approximately 900,000 people murdered' and for Sobibór a figure of 'approximately 200,000': Berger, *Experten*, p. 255. For Auschwitz and 1944, see Gerlach, *Extermination*, p. 124. For the figure of 178 million Reichsmarks, see Nbg. Doc. 4024-PS, 'Vorläufiger Abschlussbericht der Kasse Aktion "Reinhardt" Lublin per 15. Dezember 1943', signed [Odilo] Globocnik, reproduced in: IMG, vol. 34, pp. 81–9, here p. 89. On ideological motives taking precedence over economic considerations, see Lehnstaedt, *Kern des Holocaust*, pp. 141 and 145–51 (Fischer quote: p. 150).

24. Lehnstaedt, *Kern des Holocaust*, pp. 135, 138 and 141–3. On the 18,400 prisoners and the loudspeakers, see also Friedländer, *Years of Extermination*, p. 559. On the nine hours, see Tomasz Kranz, 'Lublin-Majdanek – Stammlager', in Wolfgang Benz and Barbara Distel, eds, *Der Ort des Terrors. Geschichte der nationalsozialistischen Konzentrationslager, Band 7* (Munich: C.H. Beck, 2008), pp. 33–84, here p. 52. On the single largest massacre, see Wachsmann, *KL*, p. 331.

25. Gerlach, *Extermination*, pp. 119–21. On Majdanek, see Lehnstaedt, *Kern des Holocaust*, p. 193, n. 12. For the Suchomel quote, see Lanzmann, *Shoah*, p. 88. For the duration of Suchomel's deployment in Treblinka, see Berger, *Experten*, p. 413. On the staff at Treblinka, see Benz, 'Treblinka', p. 407. On the second sweep of mass-shooting operations in the occupied territories of the Soviet Union, see Chapter 3 in this book.

26. Browning, *Origins of the Final Solution*, pp. 421–2. On the completion of Sajmište concentration camp, see Manoschek, 'Serbien ist judenfrei', p. 69.

27. Browning, *Origins of the Final Solution*, p. 422. For the names of the drivers, see Manoschek, 'Vernichtung der Juden', p. 230.
28. Manoschek, *'Serbien ist judenfrei'*, pp. 179–81; Browning, *Origins of the Final Solution*, p. 423.
29. For the Schäfer quotes, see Browning, *Origins of the Final Solution*, p. 423. For the 17,000 victims, see Manoschek, 'Vernichtung der Juden', pp. 209–10. On the deployment of the gas van in Minsk, see Manoschek, 'Vernichtung der Juden', pp. 230–1; Gerlach, *Kalkulierte Morde*, pp. 765–6.

CHAPTER 9 THE GATES OF HELL: AUSCHWITZ

1. On the number of deportees, the death toll and the proportion of Jews among the dead, see Franciszek Piper, 'The Number of Victims', in Yisrael Gutman and Michael Berenbaum, eds, *Anatomy of the Auschwitz Death Camp* (Bloomington, IN: Indiana University Press, 1994), pp. 61–76, here pp. 68–71; Wachsmann, *KL*, p. 628; Pohl, 'Just How Many?', p. 142. On Auschwitz's pre-eminence in Holocaust memory, its multiple missions and the number of Jews in the concentration camps in early 1942, see Wachsmann, *KL*, pp. 292 and 295. On Auschwitz as the first camp for non-German-speaking prisoners, Polish inmates in 1940 and 1941, and the proportion of Jews in 1942 and 1943, see Wolfgang Benz et al., 'Auschwitz', in Wolfgang Benz and Barbara Distel, eds, *Der Ort des Terrors. Geschichte der nationalsozialistischen Konzentrationslager, Band 5* (Munich: C.H. Beck, 2007), pp. 79–173, here p. 99.
2. Benz et al., 'Auschwitz', pp. 80–1 and 83. On Bach-Zelewski, see Charles Sydnor, 'Auschwitz I Main Camp', in Geoffrey P. Megargee, ed., *The United States Holocaust Memorial Museum Encyclopedia of Camps and Ghettos, 1933–1945, Vol. I: Early Camps, Youth Camps, and Concentration Camps and Subcamps under the SS-Business Administration Main Office (WVHA), Part A* (Bloomington, IN: Indiana University Press, 2009), pp. 204–8, here p. 204. On Auschwitz being part of the German Reich, see Sybille Steinbacher, *Auschwitz. Geschichte und Nachgeschichte* (Munich: C.H. Beck, 2004), p. 18.
3. Benz et al., 'Auschwitz', pp. 81 and 83. On the prisoners from Tarnów, see also Wachsmann, *KL*, pp. 202–3.
4. Wolfgang Benz and Barbara Distel, 'Einleitung', in Benz and Distel, eds, *Ort des Terrors, Band 5*, pp. 9–14, here pp. 10–11. On the satellite camp in Gliwice-Sośnica, see Benz et al., 'Auschwitz', p. 83.
5. Benz et al., 'Auschwitz', pp. 100–1 (including quote).
6. Ibid., p. 101.
7. Report from Auschwitz, 1945, excerpts reproduced in: Zentrum für Politische Schönheit, ed., *An die Nachwelt: Letzte Nachrichten und Zeitzeugnisse von NS-Opfern gegen das Vergessen* (Berlin: Zentrum für Politische Schönheit, 2019), pp. 27–32, here pp. 28–9. For the full report, see Witold Pilecki, *Witold's Report from Auschwitz*, ed. Józef Brynkus, Michał Siwiec-Cielebon and Wiesław Jan Wysocki, trans. from Polish by Karolina Linda Potocka and Witold Wybrański (Ząbki: Apostolicum, 2017), here pp. 6, 38, 42 and 103. On Pilecki, see also Jack Fairweather, *The Volunteer: The True Story of the Resistance Hero Who Infiltrated Auschwitz* (London: WH Allen, 2019).
8. Sydnor, 'Auschwitz I', p. 205. On the grading of concentration camps, see HLSL, Evidence Files, NO-743, 'Betrifft: Einstufung der Konzentrationslager', IV C 2 Allg.Nr.4865/40 g., signed [Reinhard] Heydrich, 2 January 1941. For the SS personnel figures, see Benz et al., 'Auschwitz', pp. 98–9.
9. On the first crematorium, see Benz et al., 'Auschwitz', p. 121. On the tests using Zyklon B, see ibid., p. 121; Wachsmann, *KL*, pp. 267–8; Friedländer, *Years of Extermination*, p. 236; Otto, *Wehrmacht*, pp. 90–1. On Soviet POWs, see also Chapter 6 in this book.
10. Benz et al., 'Auschwitz', pp. 121–2; Wachsmann, *KL*, pp. 268–9. For the three nights, see Otto, *Wehrmacht*, p. 91.
11. On the gas chamber in the morgue, see Benz et al., 'Auschwitz', p. 122. On orders to construct Majdanek and Birkenau, see Kranz, 'Lublin-Majdanek', pp. 34–5; Wachsmann, *KL*,

pp. 278–9. For September (rather than 1 March) as the date of the order to construct Birkenau, see Jan Erik Schulte, 'Vom Arbeits- zum Vernichtungslager. Die Entstehungsgeschichte von Auschwitz-Birkenau 1941/42', *Vierteljahrshefte für Zeitgeschichte*, vol. 50, no. 1 (January 2002), pp. 41–69, here pp. 50–2; Steinbacher, *Auschwitz*, pp. 71–2. For the Kammler quote, see Schulte, 'Vom Arbeits- zum Vernichtungslager', p. 50.

12. On construction work at Birkenau, see Wachsmann, *KL*, p. 279. On the 10,000 Soviet POWs deployed to construct Birkenau, see Franciszek Piper, 'Auschwitz II – Birkenau Main Camp', in Megargee, ed., *Encyclopedia of Camps and Ghettos, Vol. I, Part A*, pp. 209–14, here p. 210. On Birkenau's surface area, see Benz et al., 'Auschwitz', p. 108. On Soviet POWs in concentration camps, see also Chapter 6 in this book.

13. On this and the following, see Wachsmann, *KL*, pp. 279, 292 and 295–7. Verena Walter incorrectly claims: 'From late 1941, at the latest early 1942, Auschwitz functioned [...] as a site of mass extermination of the European Jews.' See Benz et al., 'Auschwitz', p. 140. On the Wannsee Conference, see also Longerich, *Holocaust*, p. 307. For the quotes from the conference minutes, see Politisches Archiv des Auswärtigen Amtes, Berlin, Inland II g, Nr. 177, R 100857, fols 166–80, 'Besprechungsprotokoll', undated, here fol. 172. On Himmler's meeting with Pohl and for the Hitler quote, see Witte et al., eds, *Dienstkalender*, p. 326 (entry for 25 January 1942).

14. On the general prohibition of Jewish emigration, see Browning, *Origins of the Final Solution*, p. 369; Longerich, *Holocaust*, p. 285. On Himmler's phone call with Heydrich, see Witte et al., eds, *Dienstkalender*, p. 327 (entry for 25 January 1942). For Himmler's message to Glücks, see HLSL, Evidence Files, NO-500, 'Fernschreiben', signed H[einrich] Himmler, 25 January 1942. On the gassing of Jews, see Gerlach, *Extermination*, pp. 78, fn. 52, and 97.

15. Wachsmann, *KL*, pp. 296–7 and 302. On Himmler's visit to Ravensbrück and his briefing of Pohl, see also Witte et al., eds, *Dienstkalender*, pp. 368–9 (entries for 3 and 4 March 1942). On the transfer of the Inspectorate of the Concentration Camps to Pohl and the establishment of the WVHA, see Schulte, 'Vom Arbeits- zum Vernichtungslager', p. 46. On the 999 female prisoners, see Danuta Czech, 'Kalendarium der wichtigsten Ereignisse aus der Geschichte des KL Auschwitz', in Danuta Czech et al., eds, *Auschwitz 1940-1945. Studien zur Geschichte des Konzentrations- und Vernichtungslagers Auschwitz, Band V: Epilog*, trans. from Polish by Jochen August (Oświęcim: Verlag des Staatlichen Museums Auschwitz-Birkenau, 1999), pp. 109–240, here p. 138; Witte et al., eds, *Dienstkalender*, p. 368, fn. 4.

16. Czech, 'Kalendarium', pp. 139–41 and 147. On Danneker and the French transports, see Schulte, 'Vom Arbeits- zum Vernichtungslager', pp. 62–3 (quotes: p. 62). On Jews as the largest group from mid-1942, see Franciszek Piper, *Auschwitz 1940-1945. Studien zur Geschichte des Konzentrations- und Vernichtungslagers Auschwitz, Band III: Vernichtung*, trans. from Polish by Jochen August (Oświęcim: Verlag des Staatlichen Museums Auschwitz-Birkenau, 1999), p. 11. On deaths among new arrivals and on the Žilina transport, see Wachsmann, *KL*, pp. 298–9. On the 999 Jewish women from Slovakia, see also Heather Dune Macadam, *The Nine Hundred: The Extraordinary Young Women of the First Official Jewish Transport to Auschwitz* (London: Hodder & Stoughton, 2020).

17. Wachsmann, *KL*, pp. 300–2; Schulte, 'Vom Arbeits- zum Vernichtungslager', pp. 64–5. On Katowice and Mildner, see Sybille Steinbacher, *'Musterstadt' Auschwitz. Germanisierungspolitik und Judenmord in Ostoberschlesien* (Munich: K.G. Saur, 2000), p. 280.

18. On the first selection, see Schulte, 'Vom Arbeits- zum Vernichtungslager', p. 67; Czech, 'Kalendarium', p. 148. On the typical sequence of events, see Piper, 'Auschwitz II', p. 211. For the Primo Levi quote, see Levi, *I sommersi e i salvati*, p. 39. On selections of Special Squad members, see Wachsmann, *KL*, p. 350. On the Special Squad in general, see Gideon Greif, *We Wept without Tears: Testimonies of the Jewish Sonderkommando from Auschwitz* (New Haven, CT/London: Yale University Press, 2005); Pavel Polian, *Briefe aus der Hölle. Die Aufzeichnungen des jüdischen Sonderkommandos Auschwitz*, trans. from Russian by Roman Richter (Darmstadt: wbg Theiss, 2019).

19. For the figure of 2,200, see Wachsmann, *KL*, p. 350. For the Venezia quotes, see NHCM, video testimony of Shlomo Venezia, 12 April 1999. On this episode, see also Shlomo Venezia, *Meine Arbeit im Sonderkommando Auschwitz. Das erste umfassende Zeugnis eines Überlebenden*, trans. from Italian by Dagmar Mallett (Munich: Blessing, 2008), pp. 159–60.

20. For the figures of 232,000 and 216,000, see Benz et al., 'Auschwitz', p. 150. For the figure of 2,500 and on the hardships and punishments, see Wachsmann, *KL*, pp. 310 and 356–7. For the Anna Palarczyk quote and on the drownings and lethal injections, see Hermann Langbein, *People in Auschwitz*, trans. from German by Harry Zohn (Chapel Hill, NC/London: University of North Carolina Press, 2004), pp. 233–5. On children and adolescents in Auschwitz, see also Helena Kubica, 'Children and Adolescents in Auschwitz', in Tadeusz Iwaszko et al., eds, *Auschwitz, 1940–1945: Central Issues in the History of the Camp, Vol. 2: The Prisoners – Their Life and Work*, trans. from Polish by William Brand (Oświęcim: Auschwitz-Birkenau State Museum, 2000), pp. 201–90; Verena Buser, *Überleben von Kindern und Jugendlichen in den Konzentrationslagern Sachsenhausen, Auschwitz und Bergen-Belsen* (Berlin: Metropol, 2011).

21. Wachsmann, *KL*, pp. 304 and 306–7.

22. On Himmler's two-day visit, see Czech, 'Kalendarium', pp. 150–1; Jean-Claude Pressac with Robert-Jan van Pelt, 'The Machinery of Mass Murder at Auschwitz', in Gutman and Berenbaum, eds, *Anatomy*, pp. 183–245, here p. 215; Witte et al., eds, *Dienstkalender*, pp. 491–3 (entries for 17 and 18 July 1942). On the converted farmhouse and the new cremation facilities and gas chambers, see Wachsmann, *KL*, pp. 304 and 314. On the designations of the new crematoria, see Pressac, 'Machinery', p. 218. On Chełmno and on Himmler's order to Globocnik, see Chapter 8 in this book.

23. Wachsmann, *KL*, p. 315 (including second Hejblum quote). For the first Hejblum quote, see also Angrick, 'Aktion 1005', p. 208. On Blobel, see also Franciszek Piper, 'Gas Chambers and Crematoria', in Gutman and Berenbaum, eds, *Anatomy*, pp. 157–82, here p. 163. On Blobel's activities in Chełmno, see Nicholas Terry, 'Covering Up Chelmno: Nazi Attempts to Obfuscate and Obliterate a Nazi Extermination Camp', *Dapim: Studies on the Holocaust*, vol. 32, no. 3 (2018), pp. 188–205, here pp. 199–201.

24. On the four new crematoria becoming operational and on Crematoria IV and V later being out of service, see Pressac, 'Machinery', pp. 232–7; Greif, *We Wept without Tears*, p. 9. For Bischoff's letter, see Robert Jan van Pelt, *The Case for Auschwitz: Evidence from the Irving Trial* (Bloomington, IN: Indiana University Press, 2002), pp. 342–3. For the quote from the escapees' report, see Alfred Wetzler, *Escape from Hell: The True Story of the Auschwitz Protocol*, ed. Péter Várnai, trans. from Slovak by Ewald Osers (New York/Oxford: Berghahn Books, 2007 [1964]), Appendix II, p. 250 (emphasis in the original). On the correct number of furnaces, see Pelt, *Case for Auschwitz*, pp. 342, 345 and 350; Pressac, 'Machinery', pp. 232–5. On the transfer of all registered Jews to Birkenau, see Sydnor, 'Auschwitz I', p. 205.

25. On the extension of the railway tracks and the construction of a new ramp, see USHMM, Claude Lanzmann Shoah Collection, RG-60.5016, FILM ID 3230, video testimony of Rudolf Vrba, November 1978, 03:03:01–11; Rudolf Vrba, 'The Preparations for the Holocaust in Hungary: An Eyewitness Account', in Randolph L. Braham and Scott Miller, eds, *The Nazis' Last Victims: The Holocaust in Hungary* (Detroit: Wayne State University Press, 1998), pp. 55–101, here p. 68; NHCM, video recording of talk given by Trude Levi, 2003. On Hungarian salami, see Vrba, 'Preparations', pp. 69–70.

26. On the 2 May arrivals, see Czech, 'Kalendarium', p. 201. On large-scale deportations from 14 May to 9 July, the subsequent transports and the three-day journey, and for the figures of 425,000 deportees until 9 July and 430,000 deportees in total, see Christian Gerlach and Götz Aly, *Das letzte Kapitel. Realpolitik, Ideologie und der Mord an den ungarischen Juden 1944/1945* (Stuttgart/Munich: Deutsche Verlags-Anstalt, 2002), pp. 274–6 and 286. See also YVA, O.18/240, 'Zusammenstellung der in der Zeit vom 16.V. bis 20.9.1944 im Konzentrationslager Auschwitz II Birkenau eingetroffenen Transporte/Maenner',

5 August 1945. On the three-week period from 16 May to 8 June, see Benz et al., 'Auschwitz', p. 149.

27. For the figures of 320,000 immediately gassed and 110,000 selected for work, and on the four transports rerouted to Strasshof, see Gerlach and Aly, *Das letzte Kapitel*, pp. 276, 295–6 and 375. See also YVA, O.18/240, 'Zusammenstellung der in der Zeit vom 16.V. bis 20.9.1944 im Konzentrationslager Auschwitz II Birkenau eingetroffenen Transporte/ Maenner', 5 August 1945. On Höß, open-air pits and bypassing the gas chambers, see Wachsmann, *KL*, pp. 458 and 460–1. On Veesenmayer, see Benz et al., 'Auschwitz', p. 149; Czech, 'Kalendarium', p. 208.

28. On the female Hungarian Jews sent to Plaszów, see Angelina Awtuszewska-Ettrich, 'Płaszów – Stammlager', in Benz and Distel, eds, *Ort des Terrors, Band 8*, pp. 235–87, here pp. 275 and 277–8. For the Josef Perl quote, see BLSA, Jewish Survivors of the Holocaust oral history collection, shelf mark C410/036, testimony of Josef Perl, September 1988, 2 of 4, 18:22–19:18. Göth's dogs were in fact Great Danes.

29. On the escape and the writing, translation and distribution of the report, see Vrba, 'Preparations', pp. 72–83. See also Wachsmann, *KL*, p. 494; Miroslav Karny, 'The Vrba and Wetzler Report', in Gutman and Berenbaum, eds, *Anatomy*, pp. 553–68. For the Wetzler quote, see Wetzler, *Escape from Hell*, p. 196. On Horthy, see Gerlach and Aly, *Das letzte Kapitel*, pp. 331–3.

30. On deportations in 1944, see Wachsmann, *KL*, pp. 458; Benz et al., 'Auschwitz', pp. 141–3. For the figure of 74 per cent, see Piper, 'Auschwitz II', p. 211. On the Special Squad uprising, see Wachsmann, *KL*, pp. 537–40. On Crematorium IV, see also Pressac, 'Machinery', p. 234. On the killed and wounded SS guards, see also Czech, 'Kalendarium', p. 225.

31. Benz et al., 'Auschwitz', pp. 155–6.

32. Wachsmann, *KL*, pp. 572–7, 579–81 and 586. On the preservation of labour and the absence of an order to murder all prisoners, see Daniel Blatman, 'The Death Marches and the Final Phase of Nazi Genocide', in Jane Caplan and Nikolaus Wachsmann, eds, *Concentration Camps in Nazi Germany: The New Histories* (Abingdon, Oxon: Routledge, 2010), pp. 167–85, here pp. 175 and 182.

33. Wachsmann, *KL*, pp. 546, 559 and 582.

34. Ibid., p. 585. On the heterogeneity of the evacuated prisoners and the Holocaust as a questionable framework, see also Blatman, 'Death Marches', p. 170. According to Dieter Pohl, Jewish prisoners were probably more likely than non-Jews to be shot if they were unable to continue: Dieter Pohl, 'The Holocaust and the Concentration Camps', in Caplan and Wachsmann, eds, *Concentration Camps*, pp. 149–66, here p. 159.

35. Wachsmann, *KL*, pp. 558–60, 577–8, 584–5 and 763, n. 89. On the chaotic circumstances, the decentralised process and the increase in indiscriminate killings from January 1945, see Blatman, 'Death Marches', pp. 181–2; Pohl, 'Holocaust', p. 160. For the figure of 250,000 deaths, see Daniel Blatman, *The Death Marches: The Final Phase of Nazi Genocide*, trans. from Hebrew by Chaya Galai (Cambridge, MA: Harvard University Press, 2011), pp. 2 and 12. Christian Gerlach and Götz Aly suggest that estimates of death rates of between a third and a half of all concentration camp prisoners during the death marches are most likely 'far too high': Gerlach and Aly, *Das letzte Kapitel*, p. 413.

36. Andreas Kossert, 'Endlösung on the "Amber Shore": The Massacre in January 1945 on the Baltic Seashore – A Repressed Chapter of East Prussian History', *Leo Baeck Institute Yearbook*, vol. 49 (2004), pp. 3–21, here pp. 4 and 11–17 (quote: p. 16). On the factory building, see Blatman, *Death Marches*, p. 120. Blatman makes no mention of the apparent plan to murder the Jews by burying them alive inside a disused shaft of the amber mine.

37. Wachsmann, *KL*, p. 589. On Mieste, the freight trains, the damaged tracks, the hundreds killed before arrival in Gardelegen, the home guard and the paratroopers, see Blatman, *Death Marches*, pp. 298–310, 323–5 and 333.

38. Piper, 'Number of Victims', pp. 68–71. Some of Piper's figures are amended slightly here in order to account for the arrival of around 8,000 fewer Hungarian Jews than he states.

For the figure of 430,000 Hungarian Jews, see Gerlach and Aly, *Das letzte Kapitel*, pp. 274 and 276. For 1.1 million deaths, see also Wachsmann, *KL*, p. 628. For 900,000 Jewish dead, see Pohl, 'Just How Many?', p. 142.

CHAPTER 10 GENOCIDE OF THE EUROPEAN ROMA

1. On Poles as the second largest and Roma as the third largest group, and on sanitary conditions in the 'Gypsy camp', see Wachsmann, *KL*, pp. 461–2. On the arrival of the first transport of Sinti, see Czech, 'Kalendarium', p. 173. On construction of the new sector, see Martin Luchterhandt, *Der Weg nach Birkenau. Entstehung und Verlauf der nationalsozialistischen Verfolgung der 'Zigeuner'* (Lübeck: Schmidt-Römhild, 2000), pp. 273–4. On March and July 1943, see Zimmermann, *Rassenutopie*, p. 327.
2. For the Himmler–Thierack agreement, see HLSL, Evidence Files, PS-654, 'Besprechung mit Reichsfuehrer SS Himmler am 18.9.1942 in seinem Feldquartier', 18 September 1942. On Himmler's deportation order, and on Bormann and Hitler, see Zimmermann, *Rassenutopie*, pp. 300–1.
3. For the Thierack quote, see Marc Buggeln and Michael Wildt, 'Arbeit im Nationalsozialismus (Einleitung)', in Marc Buggeln and Michael Wildt, eds, *Arbeit im Nationalsozialismus* (Munich: DeGruyter/Oldenbourg, 2014), pp. ix–xxxvii, here p. xxvi. For the Goebbels quote, see Fröhlich, ed., *Die Tagebücher von Joseph Goebbels. Teil II*, p. 504 (entry for 15 September 1942).
4. On the 15 January meeting, see Karola Fings, 'A "Wannsee Conference" on the Extermination of the Gypsies? New Research Findings Regarding 15 January 1943 and the Auschwitz Decree', *Dapim: Studies on the Holocaust*, vol. 27, no. 3 (2013), pp. 174–94, here pp. 174–5. On the 29 January regulations and on Auschwitz, see Zimmermann, *Rassenutopie*, pp. 303–4 (all quotes: p. 303).
5. On the exemptions and the implementation of the 29 January regulations, see Zimmermann, *Rassenutopie*, pp. 303–4 and 308–9; Kenrick and Puxon, *Gypsies under the Swastika*, pp. 36–9; Fings, 'A "Wannsee Conference"', pp. 181–2. For the figure of 2,000 sterilisations, see Fings, 'A "Wannsee Conference"', p. 190.
6. Karola Fings, 'Der Völkermord an den Sinti und Roma im Deutschen Reich. Lokale Initiative und nationalsozialistische Rassenpolitik', *Einsicht. Bulletin des Fritz Bauer Instituts*, vol. 11 (2019), pp. 6–15, here pp. 7 and 14.
7. On the establishment of the Reich Central Agency, see Monika Nakath, 'NS-Terror gegen Sinti und Roma in der Provinz Brandenburg. Dokumente aus dem Brandenburgischen Landeshauptarchiv (BLHA)', *Brandenburgische Archive*, vol. 35 (2018), pp. 46–50, here p. 47. On the Munich-based Gypsy Central Agency, see Till Bastian, *Sinti und Roma im Dritten Reich. Geschichte einer Verfolgung* (Munich: C.H. Beck, 2001), pp. 21–2. Circular decree quoted in Wolfgang Wippermann, '"The Definitive Solution to the Gypsy Question": The Pan-European Genocide of the European Roma', in Kay and Stahel, eds, *Mass Violence*, pp. 81–93, here p. 81.
8. BArch Berlin, R 58/825, fols 26–30, 'Vermerk: Amtschef und Einsatzgruppenleiterbesprechung', Stabskanzlei, I 11 Rf./Fh., 27 September 1939, here fol. 29. On parallels in the persecution of Jews and Roma, see Browning, *Origins of the Final Solution*, p. 184.
9. On the October 1939 deportations, see Browning, *Origins of the Final Solution*, pp. 37–43 (Müller quote: p. 41; Himmler quote: p. 42); Wolf Gruner, 'Von der Kollektivausweisung zur Deportation der Juden aus Deutschland (1938–1945). Neue Perspektiven und Dokumente', in Birthe Kundrus and Beate Meyer, eds, *Die Deportation der Juden aus Deutschland. Pläne – Praxis – Reaktionen 1938–1945* (Göttingen: Wallstein, 2004), pp. 21–62, here pp. 34–5.
10. On the meeting hosted by Heydrich, see BArch Berlin, R 58/1032, 'Betrifft: Besprechung am 30. Januar 1940', IV D 4 – III ES, 30 January 1940, fols 35–43 (quotes: fols 35 and 41). On the February 1940 deportation, see Browning, *Origins of the Final Solution*, p. 64.

11. Zimmermann, *Rassenutopie*, pp. 96–7 and 168–9 (quotes: p. 169). On Nebe and the Berlin Roma, see also Browning, *Origins of the Final Solution*, p. 40.
12. On Conti and Ritter and on the order of 27 April, see Zimmermann, *Rassenutopie*, pp. 171–2. On the 30 January meeting, see BArch Berlin, R 58/1032, fols 35–43, 'Betrifft: Besprechung am 30. Januar 1940', IV D 4 – III ES, 30 January 1940, here fol. 40. For the Himmler quote of 29 February, see Heinrich Himmler, *Geheimreden 1933 bis 1945 und andere Ansprachen*, ed. Bradley F. Smith and Agnes F. Peterson (Frankfurt am Main: Propyläen, 1974), p. 139. On Frank, see Luchterhandt, *Weg nach Birkenau*, p. 157, fn. 12.
13. On the arrests and for the number of deportees from Hamburg and Asperg, see Zimmermann, *Rassenutopie*, pp. 173–4. On the deportations, see Fings, 'Völkermord', pp. 12–13. For the number of deportees from Cologne, on conditions in the internment camps and for the Lani Rosenberg quote, see Luchterhandt, *Weg nach Birkenau*, pp. 159–60 and 164–7.
14. Browning, *Origins of the Final Solution*, p. 183. On the 4 September letter, see Guenter Lewy, *The Nazi Persecution of the Gypsies* (Oxford/New York: Oxford University Press, 2000), p. 76.
15. On the Austrian Roma deported to the Łódź Ghetto and on Chełmno, see Chapter 8 in this book. On deportations of Roma becoming conceivable once more, see Luchterhandt, *Weg nach Birkenau*, p. 196. On the East Prussian Sinti, see Martin Holler, 'Deadly Odyssey: East Prussian Sinti in Białystok, Brest-Litovsk, and Auschwitz-Birkenau', in Kay and Stahel, eds, *Mass Violence*, pp. 94–120, here pp. 97–8, 100, 102 and 106–7. On Roma in the Warsaw Ghetto and their deportation to Treblinka, see Arad, *Operation Reinhard*, pp. 192–3; Karolina Wróbel, 'The Roma inside the Warsaw Ghetto's Walls', *Czas Kultury/English*, vol. 6 (2009), pp. 92–103.
16. On the mass murder of Soviet and Serbian Roma, see Chapters 4 and 3, respectively, in this book. For the Turner quote, see Manoschek, 'Serbien ist judenfrei', p. 195.
17. On sending Roma to Stahlecker in Riga, see Luchterhandt, *Weg nach Birkenau*, p. 195. On EK 2 in Riga, see Andrej Angrick and Peter Klein, *The 'Final Solution' in Riga: Exploitation and Annihilation, 1941–1944*, trans. from German by Ray Brandon (New York/Oxford: Berghahn Books, 2009), esp. pp. 197–200.
18. On conditions and diseases, see Benz et al., 'Auschwitz', p. 116. For the Adelsberger quote, see Hermann Langbein, *Menschen in Auschwitz* (Frankfurt am Main: Ullstein, 1980), pp. 271–2. On Elisabeth Guttenberger, see Wachsmann, *KL*, pp. 462–3 (quote: p. 462). For the figure of 389 births, see Luchterhandt, *Weg nach Birkenau*, p. 297.
19. Benz et al., 'Auschwitz', p. 117; Czech, 'Kalendarium', pp. 177 and 179–80; Zimmermann, *Rassenutopie*, p. 337. For the Höß quote, see Zimmermann, *Rassenutopie*, p. 339.
20. Zimmermann, *Rassenutopie*, p. 340. On Bonigut, see Lewy, *Nazi Persecution*, p. 163. On the former Wehrmacht soldiers, see Luchterhandt, *Weg nach Birkenau*, p. 300.
21. On the arrests, the selection at Westerbork and the deportation to Auschwitz, see Zimmermann, *Rassenutopie*, pp. 312–15. On the ages and gender of the 245 Roma and their arrival at Auschwitz, and on the film and Settela Steinbach, see Aad Wagenaar, *Settela*, new edn, trans. from Dutch by Janna Eliot (Marshwood: Lamorna Publications, 2016), pp. 1, 19–20 and 109–10.
22. Benz et al., 'Auschwitz', pp. 117–18; Czech, 'Kalendarium', pp. 211–12; Zimmermann, *Rassenutopie*, pp. 315 and 343. On the 23 May selection, see also Luchterhandt, *Weg nach Birkenau*, p. 301. On the woman and two children, see Holler, 'Deadly Odyssey', p. 109. For the figure of 4,200, see Fings, 'Völkermord', p. 13. On Settela Steinbach and her family, see Wagenaar, *Settela*, p. 112.
23. On the August 1944 selection and the return transport, see Czech, 'Kalendarium', pp. 212–13 and 223. For the figure of 3,191 transported out of Birkenau, see Luchterhandt, *Weg nach Birkenau*, pp. 305–6. On conditions in Ravensbrück, see Holler, 'Deadly Odyssey', p. 109.
24. Zimmermann, *Rassenutopie*, pp. 343–4. Zimmermann's figure of 5,600 for the number of Sinti and Roma who were gassed is too low: 1,700 were gassed in March 1943; 1,035 in

May 1943; 4,200 on 2–3 August 1944; and 800 on 5 October 1944. See also Yehuda Bauer, 'Gypsies', in Gutman and Berenbaum, eds, *Anatomy*, pp. 441–55, here, p. 449; Fings, 'Völkermord', p. 413. On escape attempts and shootings, see Zimmermann, *Rassenutopie*, pp. 335–6. For the total figure of 200,000, see Fings, 'Völkermord', p. 13; Anton Weiss-Wendt, 'Introduction', in Weiss-Wendt, ed., *Nazi Genocide of the Roma*, pp. 1–26, here p. 1. For the proportion of two-thirds, see Browning, 'Nazi Empire', p. 416. For the figure of 2,000 forcibly sterilised, see Fings, 'Völkermord', p. 13; Zimmermann, *Rassenutopie*, pp. 362 and 376. On the Law for the Prevention of Offspring with Hereditary Diseases, see Chapter 1 in this book.
25. Zimmermann, *Rassenutopie*, p. 376.

CHAPTER 11 DECENTRALISED 'EUTHANASIA' IN THE GERMAN REICH

1. Rauh, 'Krieg gegen die "nutzlosen Esser"', p. 53; Beddies, 'Einbeziehung', p. 523. For the figure of almost 120,000, see Faulstich, *Hungersterben*, p. 582.
2. Rauh, 'Krieg gegen die "nutzlosen Esser"', pp. 53–4. On Hesse-Nassau, see also Sandner, *Verwaltung*, p. 582.
3. Friedlander, *Origins of Nazi Genocide*, pp. 111 and 151–2; Süß, 'Volkskörper', p. 314. On Arnsdorf and on the 'special children's wards', see Klee, '*Euthanasie*', pp. 267, 379 and 417 (quote: p. 417).
4. Friedlander, *Origins of Nazi Genocide*, pp. 142–6. On the recreation camps, see Astrid Ley, 'Die "Aktion 14f13" in den Konzentrationslagern', in Morsch and Perz, eds, *Neue Studien*, pp. 231–43, here p. 232.
5. Friedlander, *Origins of Nazi Genocide*, pp. 146–7. For the Mennecke quote, see Peter Chroust, ed., *Friedrich Mennecke. Innenansichten eines medizinischen Täters im Nationalsozialismus: Eine Edition seiner Briefe 1935–1947, Band 1* (Hamburg: Hamburger Institut für Sozialforschung, 1987), pp. 243–4. On the camps visited and the attendance of wives and children, see Wachsmann, *KL*, pp. 246 and 248–9.
6. On Operation 14f13 as a watershed in the history of the camps, see Nikolaus Wachsmann, 'The Dynamics of Destruction: The Development of the Concentration Camps, 1933–1945', in Caplan and Wachsmann, eds, *Concentration Camps*, pp. 17–43, here pp. 28–9. On the pre- and post-August 1941 periods, see Friedlander, *Origins of Nazi Genocide*, pp. 148–9 and 152. On Sonnenstein, see Boris Böhm and Thomas Schilter, 'Pirna-Sonnenstein. Von der Reformpsychiatrie zur Tötung psychisch Kranker und Behinderter', in Stiftung Sächsische Gedenkstätten, ed., *Nationalsozialistische Euthanasieverbrechen. Beiträge zur Aufarbeitung ihrer Geschichte in Sachsen* (Dresden: Michel Sandstein Verlag, 2004), pp. 30–66, here pp. 53–6. For the figure of 2,500, see Walter Grode, *Die 'Sonderbehandlung 14f13' in den Konzentrationslagern des Dritten Reiches. Ein Beitrag zur Dynamik faschistischer Vernichtungspolitik* (Frankfurt am Main: Peter Lang, 1987), p. 88. On Jewish prisoners, see Wachsmann, *KL*, p. 254. On the mass murder of Soviet Jews, see Chapter 3 in this book.
7. On the curtailment of Operation 14f13 and for the figure of 6,500, see Wachsmann, *KL*, pp. 255–6. On Operation Reinhardt, see Chapter 8 in this book. On the end of T4 visits to the camps, see Ley, '"Aktion 14f13"', pp. 234 and 240.
8. On Bernburg, see Ute Hoffmann and Dietmar Schulze, '... *wird heute in eine andere Anstalt verlegt'. Nationalsozialistische Zwangssterilisation und 'Euthanasie' in der Landes-Heil- und Pflegeanstalt Bernburg – eine Dokumentation* (Dessau: Regierungspräsidium Dessau, 1997), pp. 74 and 76. On the end of gassings in Bernburg by late 1942, see Ley, '"Aktion 14f13"', p. 234. On Hartheim, see Florian Schwanninger, 'Hartheim 1940–1944', in Morsch and Perz, eds, *Neue Studien*, pp. 118–30, here p. 126.
9. For the Glücks letter, see Nbg. Doc. 1933-PS, 'Aktion 14 f 13 in den Konzentrationslagern', 27 April 1943, reproduced in: IMG, vol. 29, pp. 173–4. On Hartheim, see Schwanninger, 'Hartheim', pp. 127–8. For the death toll of 20,000, see Hinz-Wessels, 'Antisemitismus und Krankenmord', p. 91; Friedlander, *Origins of Nazi Genocide*, p. 150. For the estimate of at least 10,000 Jewish victims of Operation 14f13, see Lewy, *Perpetrators*, p. 13.

10. Winfried Süß, 'Dezentralisierter Krankenmord. Zum Verhältnis von Zentralgewalt und Regionalgewalten in der 'Euthanasie' seit 1942', in Horst Möller, Jürgen John and Thomas Schaarschmidt, eds, *NS-Gaue – regionale Mittelinstanzen im zentralistischen 'Führerstaat'* (Munich: Oldenbourg, 2007), pp. 123–35, here p. 125.
11. Süß, 'Dezentralisierter Krankenmord', p. 125; Süß, *'Volkskörper'*, pp. 336–7.
12. On the differences in regional developments and the November conference, see Süß, *'Volkskörper'*, pp. 321–2 and 337–8 (quote: p. 322). On the decree of the Bavarian Ministry of the Interior from 30 November, see Rauh, 'Krieg gegen die "nutzlosen Esser"', pp. 54–5 (quote: p. 54).
13. On the starvation houses at Eglfing-Haar and Kaufbeuren-Irsee, see Süß, *'Volkskörper'*, p. 324; Burleigh, *Death and Deliverance*, pp. 241–2 (including Pfannmüller quote). On the number of deaths at Eglfing-Haar, see Katzur, '"Kinderfachabteilung"', p. 15. On the introduction of the 'special diet' elsewhere, see Süß, *'Volkskörper'*, p. 324. On the February 1943 transfers, the patient numbers and the death rates, see Hans-Ludwig Siemen, 'Die bayerischen Heil- und Pflegeanstalten während des Nationalsozialismus', in Michael von Cranach and Hans-Ludwig Siemen, eds, *Psychiatrie im Nationalsozialismus. Die Bayerischen Heil- und Pflegeanstalten zwischen 1933 und 1945* (Munich: Oldenbourg, 2012), pp. 417–74, here pp. 452–3.
14. Süß, 'Dezentralisierter Krankenmord', pp. 129–30 (quote: p. 130). On the Reich Association of Mental Hospitals and the timing of Nitsche's proposal, see Süß, *'Volkskörper'*, p. 356.
15. On Brandt's access to Hitler, see Schmidt, *Karl Brandt*, p. 229. On Hitler's approval, see Süß, 'Dezentralisierter Krankenmord', pp. 130–1 (quote: p. 131). On the 17 August meeting and for the Wischer quotes, see Klee, *'Euthanasie'*, pp. 426–7. On Nitsche's letter to de Crinis and the 'E-mandate', see Süß, *'Volkskörper'*, pp. 356–7. On Blankenburg, see Friedlander, *Origins of Nazi Genocide*, pp. 40 and 42.
16. On deaths from late summer 1943 and on Gauleiter Mutschmann, see Süß, 'Dezentralisierter Krankenmord', p. 131. On Nitsche's phenobarbital model, Großschweidnitz as a transit institution and the total number of dead there, see Klee, *'Euthanasie'*, pp. 267, 433 and 451. On the 'special children's ward' at Großschweidnitz, see Benzenhöfer, 'NS-"Kindereuthanasie"', p. A2770.
17. Süß, 'Dezentralisierter Krankenmord', pp. 132–3; Süß, *'Volkskörper'*, pp. 357–9. Wischer quoted in Anika Burkhardt, *Das NS-Euthanasie-Unrecht vor den Schranken der Justiz: Eine strafrechtliche Analyse* (Tübingen: Mohr Siebeck, 2015), p. 160, fn. 457.
18. On the 2,000 patients, the three physicians, winter 1941–42 and the causes of death, see Beddies, 'Einbeziehung', p. 525. On the appointment of Grabowski and patients from Hamburg, see Friedlander, *Origins of Nazi Genocide*, pp. 160 and 166. On the arrival of patients, the first to be killed and the total number of deaths, see Klee, *'Euthanasie'*, pp. 405–6, 408 and 410.
19. Georg Lilienthal, 'Der Gasmord in Hadamar', in Morsch and Perz, eds, *Neue Studien*, pp. 140–50, here pp. 148–9. Willig quoted in Burleigh, *Death and Deliverance*, p. 273.
20. Friedlander, *Origins of Nazi Genocide*, pp. 162–3; Melvyn Conroy, *Nazi Eugenics: Precursors, Policy, Aftermath* (Stuttgart: ibidem, 2017), pp. 169–70.
21. Hans-Walter Schmuhl, '"Euthanasie" und Krankenmord', in Robert Jütte et al., *Medizin und Nationalsozialismus. Bilanz und Perspektiven der Forschung* (Göttingen: Wallstein, 2011), pp. 214–55, here p. 214. See also Faulstich, *Hungersterben*, p. 582. Like Hans-Walther Schmuhl, the German Association for Psychiatry, Psychotherapy and Psychosomatics concludes for these reasons that the Nazi 'euthanasia' must be regarded as genocide; see 'Früherer Dekan war "Mittäter" beim NS-Massenmord', *Westfälische Nachrichten*, 28 December 2011.

CHAPTER 12 SUPPRESSION OF THE WARSAW UPRISING

1. For the 1 million in Warsaw, see Alexandra Richie, *Warsaw 1944: Hitler, Himmler, and the Warsaw Uprising* (New York: Farrar, Straus and Giroux, 2013), p. 194. For the death toll,

see Włodzimierz Borodziej, *The Warsaw Uprising of 1944*, trans. from German by Barbara Harshav (Madison, WI: University of Wisconsin Press, 2006), p. 130.

2. On Katyn and on the Polish–Soviet border, see Włodzimierz Borodziej, 'Der Warschauer Aufstand', in Bernhard Chiari, ed., *Die polnische Heimatarmee. Geschichte und Mythos der Armia Krajowa seit dem Zweiten Weltkrieg* (Munich: Oldenbourg, 2003), pp. 217–53, here pp. 217–18. On Vilnius and Lvov, see Grzegorz Mazur, 'Die Aktion "Burza"', in Chiari, ed., *Heimatarmee*, pp. 255–74, here pp. 258–60 and 263–5.

3. Snyder, *Bloodlands*, pp. 299–300. On the capture of Chełm, see Borodziej, 'Warschauer Aufstand', p. 220. On the Lublin Committee, see Richie, *Warsaw 1944*, p. 165.

4. Snyder, *Bloodlands*, p. 300; Borodziej, *Warsaw Uprising*, pp. 61–4.

5. Richie, *Warsaw 1944*, pp. 194–8 and 214.

6. On Geibel and the Warsaw garrison, on Hitler's instructions to Himmler and on Bach-Zelewski's appointment, see ibid., pp. 224, 245 and 250. On the Ninth Army, see Norman Davies, *Rising '44: The Battle for Warsaw* (London: Macmillan, 2003), p. 248. On the intended destruction of Leningrad, Moscow and Kiev, see Chapter 5 in this book.

7. Statement by the witness Wohlschläger, October 1944, reproduced in: Edward Serwański and Irena Trawińska, eds, *Documenta Occupationis Tuetonicae, Vol. II: German Crimes in Warsaw 1944*, trans. from Polish by Graham Crawford, Thomas Anessi and Krzysztof Kotkowski (Poznań: Instytut Zachodni, 2019 [1946]), pp. 168–9.

8. On Bach-Zelewski's arrival and the composition of the Dirlewanger Brigade, see Richie, *Warsaw 1944*, pp. 250 and 253. On the Dirlewanger Brigade as a penal unit, see Hellmuth Auerbach, 'Die Einheit Dirlewanger', *Vierteljahrshefte für Zeitgeschichte*, vol. 10, no. 3 (July 1962), pp. 250–63, esp. pp. 253–60. On the Dirlewanger unit in Belarus, see Gerlach, *Kalkulierte Morde*, pp. 217, 899–902, 928 and 958; Christian Ingrao, *Les chasseurs noirs: La brigade Dirlewanger* (n.pl. [Paris]: Perrin, 2006), p. 50. On Operation Cottbus, see Chapter 7 in this book.

9. Richie, *Warsaw 1944*, pp. 245 and 257 (quote). On Guderian, Reinhardt and Vormann, see ibid., p. 19; Patrycja Grzebyk, 'Hidden in the Glare of the Nuremberg Trial: Impunity for the Wola Massacre as the Greatest Debacle of Post-War Trials', *MPI Luxembourg Working Paper Series*, no. 7 (2019), pp. 1–16, here p. 7.

10. On the bridgeheads, see Christopher Duffy, *Red Storm on the Reich: The Soviet March on Germany, 1945* (New York: Athenium, 1991), p. 11. On the cessation of the Red Army's advance, see Snyder, *Bloodlands*, p. 302. On the sunny morning, the 7 a.m. start and the units comprising the combat group, see Richie, *Warsaw 1944*, pp. 257 and 260.

11. On the Dirlewanger Brigade, see Snyder, *Bloodlands*, p. 304. On the human shields, see also Pilecki Institute, Testimony Database – Chronicles of Terror, undated letter from Włodzimierz Włodarski, chief economic supervisor at St Stanisław Hospital, pp. 2–3. On Stahel, see Borodziej, *Warsaw Uprising*, p. 78. On the orphans, see Richie, *Warsaw 1944*, p. 284.

12. On Wolski Hospital and the Charles and Mary Hospital, see Johanna K.M. Hanson, *The Civilian Population and the Warsaw Uprising of 1944* (Cambridge: Cambridge University Press, 1982), p. 88. On St Lazarus Hospital, see Janusz Gumkowski and Kazimierz Leszczynski, *Poland under Nazi Occupation*, trans. from Polish by Edward Rothert (Warsaw: Polonia, 1961), pp. 201 and 203; Richie, *Warsaw 1944*, pp. 292–3. On Dirlewanger's headquarters, see Hanson, *Civilian Population*, p. 88; Richie, *Warsaw 1944*, p. 296. On the Home Army prisoners, see Richie, *Warsaw 1944*, p. 298. On the nurses, see Snyder, *Bloodlands*, p. 304. On the Home Army prisoners and the rape of nurses from St Stanisław Hospital, see also Pilecki Institute, Testimony Database – Chronicles of Terror, undated letter from Włodzimierz Włodarski, chief economic supervisor at St Stanisław Hospital, pp. 3–4. On the hand grenades, see Ingrao, *Les chasseurs noirs*, p. 182.

13. Gumkowski and Leszczynski, *Poland under Nazi Occupation*, pp. 187–9 and 201 (quote: pp. 188–9). For the figure of 1,000, see Richie, *Warsaw 1944*, p. 272.

14. On the killing sites and the 400m advance, see Richie, *Warsaw 1944*, pp. 268 and 299–300. On the Polish workers, see Gumkowski and Leszczynski, *Poland under Nazi Occupation*,

pp. 206–7 (quote: p. 207). On the women and children, see Hanson, *Civilian Population*, pp. 87–8. Hanson estimates the number shot at the macaroni factory at between 2,000 and 4,000.

15. On the burning and the 5,000 bodies and for the testimony of Zofia Staworzynska, see Gumkowski and Leszczynski, *Poland under Nazi Occupation*, pp. 193 (quote) and 207–8. A figure of 'more than 5,000 people' is also given by Hanson, *Civilian Population*, p. 88; Richie, *Warsaw 1944*, p. 270. On Wanda Lurie, the dogs and the birth of her baby, see Richie, *Warsaw 1944*, pp. 270–2 (third quote: pp. 271–2). For the first and second quotes from Wanda, see Hanson, *Civilian Population*, p. 89. The complete testimony is also reproduced in Serwański and Trawińska, eds, *Documenta*, vol. II, pp. 37–41.

16. On the phone conversation, see Borodziej, *Warsaw Uprising*, p. 81 (first quote); Richie, *Warsaw 1944*, p. 276 (second quote). On the 'large-scale operations', see Chapter 7 in this book.

17. For the figure of 40,000 civilians, see Snyder, *Bloodlands*, p. 304; Borodziej, *Warsaw Uprising*, p. 81; Hanson, *Civilian Population*, p. 90. Norman Davies gives a figure of 35,000 murdered on 5 August alone: Davies, *Rising '44*, p. 279. For the figure of 12,500 killed by the Dirlewanger Brigade on 5 August, see Ingrao, *Les chasseurs noirs*, p. 53. On Babi Yar and 'Harvest Festival', see Chapters 3 and 8, respectively, in this book. For the 100,000 refugees, see Borodziej, *Warsaw Uprising*, p. 130. On the Kaminski Brigade in Ochota, see Hanson, *Civilian Population*, pp. 90–1. On the Radium Institute, see Richie, *Warsaw 1944*, pp. 323–6.

18. Borodziej, *Warsaw Uprising*, pp. 97–9.

19. Ibid., pp. 81 and 99–100. On Bach-Zelewski calling off mass shootings of women and children, see also Davies, *Rising '44*, pp. 252–3; Hanson, *Civilian Population*, p. 86. For the Szczepański quote, see Snyder, *Bloodlands*, p. 308.

20. On the rebels, the evacuation and the artillery barrage, and for the figures, see Borodziej, *Warsaw Uprising*, p. 106. For 30,000 civilians killed in the Old Town, see also Snyder, *Bloodlands*, p. 305. On the sick and wounded in the hospitals and on the evacuees, see Gumkowski and Leszczynski, *Poland under Nazi Occupation*, p. 212. For the figures of dead at individual hospitals, see Richie, *Warsaw 1944*, pp. 462 and 464.

21. On the orders from Führer Headquarters, the surrender and the exodus, and for the figures of 185,000 civilian and 15,000 military dead, see Borodziej, *Warsaw Uprising*, pp. 112, 127 and 130. On plans for the general evacuation, see Davies, *Rising '44*, p. 408. On Himmler dining with Bach-Zelewski, see Matthias Uhl et al., eds, *Die Organisation des Terrors. Der Dienstkalender Heinrich Himmlers 1943–1945* (Munich: Piper, 2020), p. 906 (entry for 7 October 1944). On Himmler's orders and the evacuation of the survivors, see Snyder, *Bloodlands*, pp. 307–8. According to Gerlach, 'probably 170,000–180,000 people (mostly civilians) were killed': Gerlach, *Extermination*, p. 299. For the figure of 600,000 evacuees, see Gerlach, *Extermination*, p. 299. On those sent to Auschwitz, see Benz et al., 'Auschwitz', p. 150.

22. On the demolition, see Gumkowski and Leszczynski, *Poland under Nazi Occupation*, p. 183; Richie, *Warsaw 1944*, p. 16. For the figure of 85 per cent, see Halik Kochanski, *The Eagle Unbowed: Poland and the Poles in the Second World War* (Cambridge, MA: Harvard University Press, 2012), p. 532. On the Old Town and the New Town, the historical monuments and the cubic metreage of buildings, see Robert Bevan, *The Destruction of Memory: Architecture at War* (London: Reaktion Books, 2006), pp. 97–8. On the historical monuments and Warsaw in January 1945, and for the Eisenhower quote, see Stanislaw Jankowski, 'Warsaw: Destruction, Secret Town Planning, 1939–44, and Postwar Reconstruction', in Jeffry M. Diefendorf, ed., *Rebuilding Europe's Bombed Cities* (Houndmills: Palgrave Macmillan, 1990), pp. 77–93, here pp. 79–80.

23. Gumkowski and Leszczynski, *Poland under Nazi Occupation*, p. 214.

24. On the uprising, see Vilém Prečan, 'The Slovak National Uprising: The Most Dramatic Moment in the Nation's History', in Mikuláš Teich, Dušan Kováč and Martin D. Brown, eds, *Slovakia in History* (Cambridge: Cambridge University Press, 2011), pp. 206–28, esp.

pp. 206–12. On the 4,000 civilians, the mass shootings and the deportation of 12,000 Jews, see Lenka Šindelářová, *Finale der Vernichtung. Die Einsatzgruppe H in der Slowakei 1944/1945* (Darmstadt: Wissenschaftliche Buchgesellschaft, 2013), pp. 82, 104–6 and 115–17. The figure of 400 killed in Nemecká should be regarded as a minimum figure. Due to the burning of the bodies, it is difficult to determine how many actually died. A total of 900 victims is frequently cited in the secondary literature; see Šindelářová, *Finale der Vernichtung*, p. 117, fn. 302. On half of the victims of the Kremnička massacres being Jewish and on the deportation of almost 8,000 Jews to Auschwitz, see Gila Fatran, 'Die Deportation der Juden aus der Slowakei 1944–1945', *Bohemia: Zeitschrift für Geschichte und Kultur der böhmischen Länder*, vol. 37, no. 1 (1996), pp. 98–119, here pp. 115 and 117. For the total figure of 30,000 deportees, see Pohl, *Verfolgung und Massenmord*, p. 130.

CONCLUSION

1. For the figure of 5.8 million Jews, see Pohl, 'Just How Many?', p. 143; Christoph Dieckmann, 'Bilanz der Massenvernichtungs-Maschinerie der Nazis', paper presented at the Bundeszentrale für politische Bildung, Bonn, 21 January 2019.
2. On Nazi courts, see Nikolaus Wachsmann, *Hitler's Prisons: Legal Terror in Nazi Germany* (New Haven, CT/London: Yale University Press, 2004). On prisoner deaths in SS concentration camps, see the table in Wachsmann, *KL*, p. 628. On Nazi crimes during the final months of the war, see Sven Keller, *Volksgemeinschaft am Ende. Gesellschaft und Gewalt 1944/45* (Munich: Oldenbourg, 2013); Andrej Angrick, 'Abendrot des Dritten Reichs – oder vom somnambulen Kannibalismus eines Regimes im Untergang', in Cüppers et al., eds, *Naziverbrechen*, pp. 117–31. On Bergen-Belsen, see Wachsmann, *KL*, pp. 565–8. For the Müller quote, see Helmuth James von Moltke, *Briefe an Freya 1939–1945*, ed. Beate Ruhm von Oppen, 2nd rev. and exp. edn (Munich: C.H. Beck, 1991), p. 626. On death marches during the final months of the war, see Blatman, *Death Marches*, here p. 10.
3. For the 'Incident Reports USSR' (*Ereignismeldungen UdSSR*), see BArch Berlin, R 58/214–21; Arolsen Archives, ITS Digital Archive, 2273000. For the GCCS quote, see The National Archives, Kew, HW 16/6, Summary of German Police Decodes, Nos. 275–323 (Most Secret), 21 August 1941, p. 4. For the figure of 11,449, see BArch Berlin, R 58/218, fols 307–15, 'Ereignismeldung UdSSR Nr. 125', 26 October 1941, here fol. 310. For the figure of 18,000 and a discussion of the accuracy of the Einsatzgruppen figures, see Kay, *Making of an SS Killer*, pp. 70–5. On the figures submitted by the commandos tending to be too low, see also Robel, 'Sowjetunion', pp. 542–3; Gerlach, *Kalkulierte Morde*, p. 27, fn. 64. On EK 5 and the passing on of information, see Brandon, 'First Wave', p. 2.
4. Pohl, *Verfolgung und Massenmord*, p. 154.
5. On Eastern European involvement and cooperation in Nazi crimes, see Christoph Dieckmann, Babette Quinkert and Tatjana Tönsmeyer, eds, *Kooperation und Verbrechen. Formen der 'Kollaboration' im östlichen Europa 1939–1945* (Göttingen: Wallstein, 2003). On non-German violence, see Gerlach, *Extermination*, pp. 368–403. On contested borderlands, see Brendan Karch, *Nation and Loyalty in a German-Polish Borderland: Upper Silesia, 1848–1960* (Cambridge/New York: Cambridge University Press, 2018); Gaëlle Fisher and Caroline Mezger, eds, *The Holocaust in the Borderlands: Interethnic Relations and the Dynamics of Violence in Occupied Eastern Europe* (Göttingen: Wallstein, 2019).
6. For a strong emphasis on generation as an explanatory approach, see Wildt, *Generation*, esp. pp. 23–9. On the limitations of this approach, see Gerhard Paul, 'Von Psychopathen, Technokraten des Terrors und "ganz gewöhnlichen Deutschen". Die Täter der Shoah im Spiegel der Forschung', in Paul, ed., *Täter der Shoah*, pp. 13–90, here pp. 62–4; Bernd Weisbrod, 'Generation und Generationalität in der Neueren Geschichte', *Aus Politik und Zeitgeschichte*, vol. 8 (2005), pp. 3–9, here pp. 6–7; Kay, *Making of an SS Killer*, p. 123. On Sommer, see Gentile, *Wehrmacht und Waffen-SS*, pp. 279–81. On Swoboda, see Römer, *Comrades*, pp. 308–15.

7. Three examples of the growing literature on intergenerational, historical trauma are Linda O'Neill et al., 'Hidden Burdens: A Review of Intergenerational, Historical and Complex Trauma, Implications for Indigenous Families', *Journal of Child & Adolescent Trauma*, vol. 11, no. 2 (June 2018), pp. 173–86; Amit Shrira, Ravit Menashe and Moshe Bensimon, 'Filial Anxiety and Sense of Obligation among Offspring of Holocaust Survivors', *Aging & Mental Health*, vol. 23, no. 6 (2019), pp. 752–61; Peter Sichrovsky, *Born Guilty: Children of Nazi Families*, trans. from German by Jean Steinberg (New York: Basic Books, 1988). See also the discussion in the Introduction to this book and the literature cited there.

8. On the interaction of different factors, see Lewy, *Perpetrators*, pp. 118–36, esp. p. 124. On anti-Semitism, see Klaus-Michael Mallmann, '"Mensch, ich feiere heut' den tausendsten Genickschuß". Die Sicherheitspolizei und die Shoah in Westgalizien', in Paul, ed., *Täter der Shoah*, pp. 109–36, here p. 124. On ordinary men, see Christopher R. Browning, *Ordinary Men: Reserve Police Battalion 101 and the Final Solution in Poland*, exp. edn (London: Penguin, 1998 [1992]); Raul Hilberg, *The Destruction of the European Jews*, 3rd edn, vol. III (New Haven, CT/London: Yale University Press, 2003), p. 1060. On ordinary Germans, see Abram de Swaan, *The Killing Compartments: The Mentality of Mass Murder* (New Haven, CT: Yale University Press, 2015), p. 255. In general, see the discussion in Kay, *Making of an SS Killer*, pp. 122–6.

9. On means of violence, see Lewy, *Perpetrators*, p. 122. On sanctioning from above, see Mallmann, '"Mensch, ich feiere heut"', p. 124; Kay, *Making of an SS Killer*, p. 123. On state organisations, see Stefan Kühl, *Ganz normale Organisationen. Zur Soziologie des Holocaust* (Berlin: Suhrkamp, 2014), esp. pp. 22–5.

10. On certain types of individual, see Janine Natalya Clark, 'Genocide, War Crimes and the Conflict in Bosnia: Understanding the Perpetrators', *Journal of Genocide Research*, vol. 11, no. 4 (2009), pp. 421–45, here pp. 426–7. On different degrees of enthusiasm, see Donald Bloxham, 'Motivation und Umfeld. Vergleichende Anmerkungen zu den Ursachen genozidaler Täterschaft', in Cüppers et al., eds, *Naziverbrechen*, pp. 62–74, here p. 73. On opportunities not taken, see Lewy, *Perpetrators*, pp. 20 and 136; Clark, 'Genocide, War Crimes', pp. 433–4. On perhaps the most well-known example of perpetrators declining the offer to opt out of a shooting, the Józefów massacre of July 1942, see Browning, *Ordinary Men*, pp. 71–7. For examples of successful redeployment requests in Einsatzgruppe B and on the absence of punishment for refusal to participate in killings, see Kay, *Making of an SS Killer*, pp. 41 and 101.

11. Kay and Stahel, 'Crimes of the Wehrmacht', pp. 24–8. On ideological convictions among Wehrmacht soldiers and for the results of the Fort Hunt opinion polls, see Römer, *Comrades*, pp. 38–78. On the survey of former Austrian soldiers, see Manoschek, '"Wo der Partisan ist"', pp. 177–8. On soldiers' letters, see Michaela Kipp, 'The Holocaust in the Letters of German Soldiers on the Eastern Front (1939–44)', *Journal of Genocide Research*, vol. 9, no. 4 (2007), pp. 601–15.

12. Haffner, *Geschichte eines Deutschen*, pp. 278–81 and 283. On the importance of group conformity and peer pressure in the killing process, see Browning, *Ordinary Men*, pp. 174–5, 184–6 and 189; Welzer, *Täter*, pp. 82–91. On comradeship, see Thomas Kühne, *Belonging and Genocide: Hitler's Community, 1918–1945* (New Haven, CT/London: Yale University Press, 2010), esp. pp. 55–136; Römer, *Comrades*, pp. 118–53. See also the discussion in Frank Bajohr, 'Neuere Täterforschung', in Oliver von Wrochem, ed., *Nationalsozialistische Täterschaften. Nachwirkungen in Gesellschaft und Familie* (Berlin: Metropol, 2016), pp. 19–31, here pp. 28–9.

13. On what Philippe Burrin terms a 'culture of resentment', see Burrin, *Nazi Anti-Semitism*, pp. 89–91. On the boundaries of community-building and the Other, see Thomas Kühne, *The Rise and Fall of Comradeship: Hitler's Soldiers, Male Bonding and Mass Violence in the Twentieth Century* (Cambridge: Cambridge University Press, 2017), p. 116.

14. On subjective victimhood, see Snyder, *Bloodlands*, pp. 399–400; Kay, *Making of an SS Killer*, pp. 124–6. For another example of genocidal perpetrators 'blaming the victims', see

Helen M. Hintjens, 'Explaining the 1994 Genocide in Rwanda', *The Journal of Modern African Studies*, vol. 37, no. 2 (1999), pp. 241–86, here pp. 262–7. On the old moral order and the morality of the civilised world, see Kühne, *Belonging and Genocide*, pp. 91–2. On Nazi morality, see also Wolfgang Bialas, 'Nationalsozialistische Ethik und Moral. Konzepte, Probleme, offene Fragen', in Wolfgang Bialas and Lothar Fritze, eds, *Ideologie und Moral im Nationalsozialismus* (Göttingen: Vandenhoeck & Ruprecht, 2014), pp. 23–63; Raphael Gross, *Anständig geblieben. Nationalsozialistische Moral* (Frankfurt am Main: S. Fischer, 2010); Claudia Koonz, *The Nazi Conscience* (Cambridge, MA: Harvard University Press, 2003). For the Himmler quote, see Nbg. Doc. 1919-PS, 'Rede des Reichsführer-SS bei der SS-Gruppenführertagung in Posen am 4. Oktober 1943', reproduced in: IMG, vol. 29, pp. 110–73, here pp. 145–6.

BIBLIOGRAPHY

ARCHIVES

Bundesarchiv (Federal Archives), Berlin-Lichterfelde
Bundesarchiv (Federal Archives), Koblenz
Bundesarchiv-Militärarchiv (Federal Military Archives), Freiburg im Breisgau
Bundesarchiv-Zwischenarchiv (Federal Archives – Intermediate Archives), Dahlwitz-Hoppegarten
National Archives, The, Kew
National Archives and Records Administration, College Park, MA
Politisches Archiv des Auswärtigen Amtes (Political Archives of the Foreign Office), Berlin
Steiermärkisches Landesarchiv (Styrian Provincial Archives), Graz
Tsentralnyi arkhiv Ministerstva oborony Rossiiskoi Federatsii (Central Archives of the Ministry of Defence of the Russian Federation), Podolsk
United States Holocaust Memorial Museum, Washington, DC
Yad Vashem Archives, Jerusalem

ELECTRONIC SOURCES

Arolsen Archives, ITS Digital Archive, https://collections.arolsen-archives.org/archive/
British Library Sound Archive, Jewish Survivors of the Holocaust oral history collection, https://sounds.bl.uk/Oral-history/Jewish-Holocaust-survivors
Harvard Law School Library, Nuremberg Trials Project, https://nuremberg.law.harvard.edu/
KONTAKTE-КОНТАКТЫ – Verein für Kontakte zu Ländern der ehemaligen Sowjetunion, Freitagsbriefe, https://kontakte-kontakty.de/freitagsbriefe/
National Holocaust Centre and Museum, Laxton, Testimony, https://www.holocaust.org.uk/oral-testimony
Pilecki Institute, Testimony Database – Chronicles of Terror, https://www.chroniclesofterror.pl/dlibra
United States Holocaust Memorial Museum, Claude Lanzmann Shoah Collection, https://collections.ushmm.org/search/catalog/irn1000017

PRINTED PRIMARY SOURCES AND MEMOIRS

Angrick, Andrej, Klaus-Michael Mallmann, Jürgen Matthäus and Martin Cüppers, eds, *Deutsche Besatzungsherrschaft in der UdSSR 1941–1945. Dokumente der Einsatzgruppen in der Sowjetunion II* (Darmstadt: Wissenschaftliche Buchgesellschaft, 2013).
Bannister, Nonna, with Denise George and Carolyn Tomlin, *The Secret Holocaust Diaries. The Untold Story of Nonna Bannister* (Carol Stream, IL: Tyndale, 2009).
Bartrop, Paul R., and Michael Dickerman, eds, *The Holocaust: An Encyclopedia and Document Collection, Volume 3: Holocaust Testimonies* (Santa Barbara, CA: ABC-CLIO, 2017).

Blatt, Thomas Toivi, *From the Ashes of Sobibor: A Story of Survival* (Evanston, IL: Northwestern University Press, 1997).

'Boycott of Jews', *The Times*, 3 April 1933, p. 14.

Broucek, Peter, ed., *Ein General im Zwielicht: Die Erinnerungen Edmund Glaises von Horstenau, Band 3: Deutscher Bevollmächtigter General in Kroatien und Zeuge des Untergangs des 'Tausendjährigen Reiches'* (Vienna: Böhlau, 1988).

Burckhardt, Carl J., *Meine Danziger Mission, 1937–1939* (Munich: Georg D.W. Callwey, 1960).

Chroust, Peter, ed., *Friedrich Mennecke. Innenansichten eines medizinischen Täters im Nationalsozialismus: Eine Edition seiner Briefe 1935–1947, Band 1* (Hamburg: Hamburger Institut für Sozialforschung, 1987).

Ciano, Galeazzo, *Diario 1939–1943. Volume secondo, 1941–1943* (Milan: Rizzoli, 1946).

Cohn, Willy, *Als Jude in Breslau 1941*, ed. Joseph Walk (Gerlingen: Bleicher, 1984).

Fröhlich, Elke, ed., *Die Tagebücher von Joseph Goebbels. Teil I: Aufzeichnungen 1923–1941, Band 9: Dezember 1940–Juli 1941* (Munich: K.G. Saur, 1998).

Fröhlich, Elke, ed., *Die Tagebücher von Joseph Goebbels. Teil II: Diktate 1941–1945, Band 1: Juli–September 1941, Band 2: Oktober–Dezember 1941, Band 5: Juli–September 1942* (Munich: K. G. Saur, 1995–96).

Gersdorff, Rudolf-Christoph Freiherr von, *Soldat im Untergang* (Frankfurt am Main: Ullstein, 1977).

Haffner, Sebastian, *Geschichte eines Deutschen. Die Erinnerungen 1914–1933* (Munich: dtv, 2002).

Halder, Franz, *Kriegstagebuch, Band 3: Der Rußlandfeldzug bis zum Marsch auf Stalingrad* (Stuttgart: W. Kohlhammer, 1964).

Himmler, Heinrich, *Geheimreden 1933 bis 1945 und andere Ansprachen*, ed. Bradley F. Smith and Agnes F. Peterson (Frankfurt am Main: Propyläen, 1974).

Hitler, Adolf, *Mein Kampf. Zwei Bände in einem Band* (Munich: Zentralverlag der NSDAP, 1943 [1925–26]).

Hubatsch, Walther, ed., *Hitlers Weisungen für die Kriegführung, 1939–1945*, 2nd exp. edn (Koblenz: Bernard & Graefe, 1983 [1962]).

Institut für Zeitgeschichte, ed., *Hitler. Reden, Schriften, Anordnungen: Februar 1925 bis Januar 1933, Band III: Zwischen den Reichstagswahlen, Juli 1928–September 1930, Teil 2: März 1929–Dezember 1929* (Munich: K. G. Saur, 1994).

Internationaler Militärgerichtshof, ed., *Der Prozess gegen die Hauptkriegsverbrecher vor dem Internationalen Militärgerichtshof, Nürnberg, 14. November 1945–1. Oktober 1946*, vols 4, 8, 25–26, 29, 31, 34, 36, 38–39 (Nuremberg: Sekretariat des Gerichtshofs, 1947–49).

Jüdisches Historisches Institut Warschau, ed., *Faschismus – Getto – Massenmord. Dokumentation über Ausrottung und Widerstand der Juden in Polen während des Zweiten Weltkrieges* (Berlin: Rütten & Loening, 1960).

Katsh, Abraham I., *Scroll of Agony: The Warsaw Diary of Chaim A. Kaplan*, trans. from Hebrew by Abraham I. Katsh (Bloomington, IN: Indiana University Press, 1999 [1965]).

Kempowski, Walter, *Das Echolot – Barbarossa '41. Ein kollektives Tagebuch* (Munich: Penguin Verlag, 2019).

Klein, Peter, ed., *Die Einsatzgruppen in der besetzten Sowjetunion 1941/42. Die Tätigkeits- und Lageberichte des Chefs der Sicherheitspolizei und des SD* (Berlin: Edition Hentrich, 1997).

Klemperer, Victor, *Tagebücher 1940–1941*, ed. Walter Nowojski (Berlin: Aufbau, 1995).

Klemperer, Victor, *Tagebücher 1942*, ed. Walter Nowojski (Berlin: Aufbau, 1995).

Kohl, Paul, *Der Krieg der deutschen Wehrmacht und der Polizei 1941–1944. Sowjetische Überlebende berichten* (Frankfurt am Main: Fischer Taschenbuch, 1995).

Kokurin, A.I., and N.V. Petrov, eds, *Gulag (Glavnoe upravlenie lagerei), 1917–1960* (Moscow: Mezhdunarodnyi fond 'Demokratiia', 2000).

Lanzmann, Claude, *Shoah*, trans. from French by Nina Börnsen and Anna Kamp (Reinbek bei Hamburg: Rowohlt Taschenbuch, 2011).

Lemkin, Raphael, *Axis Rule in Occupied Europe: Laws of Occupation, Analysis of Government, Proposals for Redress* (Washington, DC: Carnegie Endowment for International Peace, 1944).

Levi, Primo, *I sommersi e i salvati* (Turin: Einaudi, 1986).

Mallmann, Klaus-Michael, Andrej Angrick, Jürgen Matthäus and Martin Cüppers, eds, *Die 'Ereignismeldungen UdSSR' 1941. Dokumente der Einsatzgruppen in der Sowjetunion I* (Darmstadt: Wissenschaftliche Buchgesellschaft, 2011).

Ministero degli Affari Esteri, ed., *I documenti diplomatici Italiani. Nona serie: 1939–1943*, vol. 7 (Rome: Istituto Poligrafico e Zecca dello Stato, 1987).

Moll, Martin, ed., *'Führer-Erlasse' 1939–1945* (Stuttgart: Franz Steiner, 1997).

Moltke, Helmuth James von, *Briefe an Freya 1939–1945*, ed. Beate Ruhm von Oppen, 2nd rev. and exp. edn (Munich: C.H. Beck, 1991).

Müller, Norbert, ed., *Okkupation, Raub, Vernichtung: Dokumente zur Besatzungspolitik der faschistischen Wehrmacht auf sowjetischem Territorium, 1941 bis 1944* (Berlin: Militärverlag der DDR, 1980).

Overmans, Rüdiger, Andreas Hilger and Pavel Polian, eds, *Rotarmisten in deutscher Hand. Dokumente zu Gefangenschaft, Repatriierung und Rehabilitierung sowjetischer Soldaten des Zweiten Weltkrieges* (Paderborn: Ferdinand Schöningh, 2012).

Pilecki, Witold, *Witold's Report from Auschwitz*, ed. Józef Brynkus, Michał Siwiec-Cielebon and Wiesław Jan Wysocki, trans. from Polish by Karolina Linda Potocka and Witold Wybrański (Ząbki: Apostolicum, 2017).

Polian, Pavel, *Briefe aus der Hölle. Die Aufzeichnungen des jüdischen Sonderkommandos Auschwitz*, trans. from Russian by Roman Richter (Darmstadt: wbg Theiss, 2019).

Polish Ministry of Information, *The Black Book of Poland* (New York: G.P. Putnam's Sons, 1942).

Reichsgesetzblatt, 1939, Part 1.

Scott, James Brown, ed., *The Hague Conventions and Declarations of 1899 and 1907* (New York: Oxford University Press, 1915).

Serwański, Edward, and Irena Trawińska, eds, *Documenta Occupationis Tuetonicae, Vol. II: German Crimes in Warsaw 1944*, trans. from Polish by Graham Crawford, Thomas Anessi and Krzysztof Kotkowski (Poznań: Instytut Zachodni, 2019 [1946]).

Thomas, Georg, *Geschichte der deutschen Wehr- und Rüstungswirtschaft (1918–1943/45)*, ed. Wolfgang Birkenfeld (Boppard am Rhein: Harald Boldt, 1966).

Trials of War Criminals before the Nuernberg Military Tribunals under Control Council Law No. 10, vol. 4 (Washington, DC: U.S. Government Printing Office, 1950).

Uhl, Matthias, Thomas Pruschwitz, Martin Holler, Jean-Luc Leleu and Dieter Pohl, eds, *Die Organisation des Terrors. Der Dienstkalender Heinrich Himmlers 1943–1945* (Munich: Piper, 2020).

Venezia, Shlomo, *Meine Arbeit im Sonderkommando Auschwitz. Das erste umfassende Zeugnis eines Überlebenden*, trans. from Italian by Dagmar Mallett (Munich: Blessing, 2008).

Vrba, Rudolf, 'The Preparations for the Holocaust in Hungary: An Eyewitness Account', in Randolph L. Braham and Scott Miller, eds, *The Nazis' Last Victims: The Holocaust in Hungary* (Detroit, MI: Wayne State University Press, 1998), pp. 55–101.

Wetzler, Alfred, *Escape from Hell: The True Story of the Auschwitz Protocol*, ed. Péter Várnai, trans. from Slovak by Ewald Osers (New York/Oxford: Berghahn Books, 2007 [1964]).

Wiernik, Jankiel, 'One Year in Treblinka', in Alexander Donat, ed., *The Death Camp Treblinka: A Documentary* (New York: Holocaust Library, 1979), pp. 147–88.

Witte, Peter, Michael Wildt, Martina Voigt, Dieter Pohl, Peter Klein, Christian Gerlach, Christoph Dieckmann and Andrej Angrick, eds, *Der Dienstkalender Heinrich Himmlers 1941/42* (Hamburg: Christians, 1999).

Zentrum für Politische Schönheit, ed., *An die Nachwelt: Letzte Nachrichten und Zeitzeugnisse von NS-Opfern gegen das Vergessen* (Berlin: Zentrum für Politische Schönheit, 2019).

SECONDARY LITERATURE

Alberti, Michael, *Die Verfolgung und Vernichtung der Juden im Reichsgau Wartheland 1939–1945* (Wiesbaden: Harrassowitz, 2006).

Al'tman, Il'ja, *Opfer des Hasses. Der Holocaust in der UdSSR 1941–1945*, trans. from Russian by Ellen Greifer (Gleichen: Muster-Schmidt, 2008 [2002]).

Aly, Götz, *Die Belasteten. 'Euthanasie' 1939–1945: Eine Gesellschaftsgeschichte* (Frankfurt am Main: S. Fischer, 2014).

Aly, Götz, *'Endlösung'. Völkerverschiebung und der Mord an den europäischen Juden* (Frankfurt am Main: S. Fischer, 1995).

Aly, Götz, *Warum die Deutschen? Warum die Juden? Gleichheit, Neid und Rassenhass 1800–1933* (Frankfurt am Main: S. Fischer, 2011).

Angrick, Andrej, 'Abendrot des Dritten Reichs – oder vom somnambulen Kannibalismus eines Regimes im Untergang', in Martin Cüppers, Jürgen Matthäus and Andrej Angrick, eds, *Naziverbrechen. Täter, Taten, Bewältigungsversuche* (Darmstadt: Wissenschaftliche Buchgesellschaft, 2013), pp. 117–31.

Angrick, Andrej, *'Aktion 1005'. Spurenbeseitigung von NS-Massenverbrechen 1942–1945: Eine 'geheime Reichssache' im Spannungsfeld von Kriegswende und Propaganda* (Göttingen: Wallstein, 2018).

Angrick, Andrej, *Besatzungspolitik und Massenmord. Die Einsatzgruppe D in der südlichen Sowjetunion 1941–1943* (Hamburg: Hamburger Edition, 2003).

Angrick, Andrej, 'Die Einsatzgruppe D', in Peter Klein, ed., *Die Einsatzgruppen in der besetzten Sowjetunion 1941/42. Die Tätigkeits- und Lageberichte des Chefs der Sicherheitspolizei und des SD* (Berlin: Edition Hentrich, 1997), pp. 88–110.

Angrick, Andrej, and Peter Klein, *The 'Final Solution' in Riga: Exploitation and Annihilation, 1941–1944*, trans. from German by Ray Brandon (New York/Oxford: Berghahn Books, 2009).

Arad, Yitzhak, *The Holocaust in the Soviet Union* (Lincoln, NE: University of Nebraska Press, 2009).

Arad, Yitzhak, *The Operation Reinhard Death Camps: Belzec, Sobibor, Treblinka*, rev. and exp. edn (Bloomington, IN: Indiana University Press, 2018 [1987]).

Arnold, Klaus Jochen, *Die Wehrmacht und die Besatzungspolitik in den besetzten Gebieten der Sowjetunion: Kriegführung und Radikalisierung im 'Unternehmen Barbarossa'* (Berlin: Duncker & Humblot, 2005).

Auerbach, Hellmuth, 'Die Einheit Dirlewanger', *Vierteljahrshefte für Zeitgeschichte*, vol. 10, no. 3 (July 1962), pp. 250–63.

Awtuszewska-Ettrich, Angelina, 'Płaszów – Stammlager', in Wolfgang Benz and Barbara Distel, eds, *Der Ort des Terrors. Geschichte der nationalsozialistischen Konzentrationslager, Band 8* (Munich: C.H. Beck, 2008), pp. 235–87.

Bajohr, Frank, 'Neuere Täterforschung', in Oliver von Wrochem, ed., *Nationalsozialistische Täterschaften. Nachwirkungen in Gesellschaft und Familie* (Berlin: Metropol, 2016), pp. 19–31.

Banach, Jens, *Heydrichs Elite. Das Führerkorps der Sicherheitspolizei und des SD 1936–1945*, 3rd rev. edn (Paderborn: Ferdinand Schöningh, 2002 [1998]).

Barber, John, and Mark Harrison, *The Soviet Home Front 1941–1945: A Social and Economic History of the USSR in World War II* (London: Longman, 1991).

Barnes, Stephen A., *Death and Redemption: The Gulag and the Shaping of Soviet Society* (Princeton, NJ/Oxford: Princeton University Press, 2011).

Bastian, Till, *Sinti und Roma im Dritten Reich. Geschichte einer Verfolgung* (Munich: C.H. Beck, 2001).

Bauer, Yehuda, 'Gypsies', in Yisrael Gutman and Michael Berenbaum, eds, *Anatomy of the Auschwitz Death Camp* (Bloomington, IN: Indiana University Press, 1994), pp. 441–55.

Becker, Felicitas, and Jigal Beez, eds, *Der Maji-Maji-Krieg in Deutsch-Ostafrika 1905–1907* (Berlin: Ch. Links, 2005).

Beddies, Thomas, 'Die Einbeziehung von Minderjährigen in die nationalsozialistischen Medizinverbrechen – dargestellt am Beispiel der brandenburgischen Landesanstalt Görden', *Praxis der Kinderpsychologie und Kinderpsychiatrie*, vol. 58, no. 7 (2009), pp. 518–29.

Beer, Mathias, 'Die Entwicklung der Gaswagen beim Mord an den Juden', *Vierteljahrshefte für Zeitgeschichte*, vol. 35, no. 3 (July 1987), pp. 403–17.

Bender, Sara, *The Jews of Białystok during World War II and the Holocaust*, trans. from Hebrew by Yaffa Murciano (Waltham, MA: Brandeis University Press, 2008 [1997]).

Ben-Sasson, Havi, '"At the Present Time, Jewish Warsaw Is Like a Cemetery": Life in the Warsaw Ghetto during the Great Deportation', in Moshe Zimmermann, ed., *On Germans and Jews under the Nazi Regime: Essays by Three Generations of Historians. A Festschrift in Honor of Otto Dov Kulka* (Jerusalem: Magnes Press, 2006), pp. 353–83.

Benz, Wolfgang, 'Treblinka', in Wolfgang Benz and Barbara Distel, eds, *Der Ort des Terrors. Geschichte der nationalsozialistischen Konzentrationslager, Band 8* (Munich: C.H. Beck, 2008), pp. 407–43.

Benz, Wolfgang and Barbara Distel, eds, *Der Ort des Terrors. Geschichte der nationalsozialistischen Konzentrationslager, Band 8* (Munich: C.H. Beck, 2008).

Benz, Wolfgang and Barbara Distel, 'Einleitung', in Wolfgang Benz and Barbara Distel, eds, *Der Ort des Terrors. Geschichte der nationalsozialistischen Konzentrationslager, Band 5* (Munich: C.H. Beck, 2007), pp. 9–14.

Benz, Wolfgang, Miriam Bistrovic, Claudia Curio, Barbara Distel, Franziska Jahn, Angelika Königseder, Brigitte Mihok and Verena Walter, 'Auschwitz', in Wolfgang Benz and Barbara Distel, eds, *Der Ort des Terrors. Geschichte der nationalsozialistischen Konzentrationslager, Band 5* (Munich: C.H. Beck, 2007), pp. 79–173.

Benzenhöfer, Udo, 'NS-"Kindereuthanasie": "Ohne jede moralische Skrupel"', *Deutsches Ärzteblatt*, vol. 97, no. 42 (October 2000), pp. A2766–72.

Benzenhöfer, Udo, and Hanns Ackermann, *Die Zahl der Verfahren und der Sterilisationen nach dem Gesetz zur Verhütung erbkranken Nachwuchses* (Münster: Kontur, 2015).

Beorn, Waitman W., 'A Calculus of Complicity: The Wehrmacht, the Anti-Partisan War, and the Final Solution in White Russia, 1941–42', *Central European History*, vol. 44, no. 2 (June 2011), pp. 308–37.

Beorn, Waitman Wade, 'Bodily Conquest: Sexual Violence in the Nazi East', in Alex J. Kay and David Stahel, eds, *Mass Violence in Nazi-Occupied Europe* (Bloomington, IN: Indiana University Press, 2018), pp. 195–215.

Berger, Sara, *Experten der Vernichtung. Das T4-Reinhardt-Netzwerk in den Lagern Belzec, Sobibor und Treblinka* (Hamburg: Hamburger Edition, 2013).

Berkhoff, Karel C., 'Dina Pronicheva's Story of Surviving the Babi Yar Massacre: German, Jewish, Soviet, Russian, and Ukrainian Records', in Ray Brandon and Wendy Lower, eds, *The Shoah in Ukraine: History, Testimony, Memorialization* (Bloomington, IN: Indiana University Press in association with the United States Holocaust Memorial Museum, 2008), pp. 291–317.

Berkhoff, Karel C., *Harvest of Despair: Life and Death in Ukraine under Nazi Rule* (Cambridge, MA: Harvard University Press, 2004).

Berkhoff, Karel C., 'The "Russian" Prisoners of War in Nazi-Ruled Ukraine as Victims of Genocidal Massacre', *Holocaust and Genocide Studies*, vol. 15, no. 1 (spring 2001), pp. 1–32.

Berkhoff, Karel C., '"Wir sollen verhungern, damit Platz für die Deutschen geschaffen wird." Hungersnöte in den ukrainischen Städten im Zweiten Weltkrieg', in Babette Quinkert and Jörg Morré, eds, *Deutsche Besatzung in der Sowjetunion 1941–1944. Vernichtungskrieg, Reaktionen, Erinnerung* (Paderborn: Ferdinand Schöningh, 2014), pp. 54–75.

Bevan, Robert, *The Destruction of Memory: Architecture at War* (London: Reaktion Books, 2006).

Beyda, Oleg, '"Rediscovering Homeland": Russian Interpreters in the Wehrmacht, 1941–1943', in Amanda Laugesen and Richard Gehrmann, eds, *Communication, Interpreting and Language in Wartime: Historical and Contemporary Perspectives* (Cham: Palgrave Macmillan, 2020), pp. 131–52.

Beyrau, Dietrich, *Schlachtfeld der Diktatoren. Osteuropa im Schatten von Hitler und Stalin* (Göttingen: Vandenhoeck & Ruprecht, 2000).

Bialas, Wolfgang, 'Nationalsozialistische Ethik und Moral. Konzepte, Probleme, offene Fragen', in Wolfgang Bialas and Lothar Fritze, eds, *Ideologie und Moral im Nationalsozialismus* (Göttingen: Vandenhoeck & Ruprecht, 2014), pp. 23–63.

Blatman, Daniel, 'The Death Marches and the Final Phase of Nazi Genocide', in Jane Caplan and Nikolaus Wachsmann, eds, *Concentration Camps in Nazi Germany: The New Histories* (Abingdon, Oxon: Routledge, 2010), pp. 167–85.

Blatman, Daniel, *The Death Marches: The Final Phase of Nazi Genocide*, trans. from Hebrew by Chaya Galai (Cambridge, MA: Harvard University Press, 2011).

Blood, Philip W., *Hitler's Bandit Hunters: The SS and the Nazi Occupation of Europe* (Washington, DC: Potomac Books, 2006).

Bloxham, Donald, 'Motivation und Umfeld. Vergleichende Anmerkungen zu den Ursachen genozidaler Täterschaft', in Martin Cüppers, Jürgen Matthäus and Andrej Angrick, eds, *Naziverbrechen. Täter, Taten, Bewältigungsversuche* (Darmstadt: Wissenschaftliche Buchgesellschaft, 2013), pp. 62–74.

Bloxham, Donald, 'Organized Mass Murder: Structure, Participation, and Motivation in Comparative Perspective', *Holocaust and Genocide Studies*, vol. 22, no. 2 (autumn 2008), pp. 203–45.

Böhler, Jochen, *Auftakt zum Vernichtungskrieg. Die Wehrmacht in Polen 1939* (Frankfurt am Main: Fischer Taschenbuch, 2006).

Böhler, Jochen, '"Tragische Verstrickung" oder Auftakt zum Vernichtungskrieg? Die Wehrmacht in Polen 1939', in Klaus-Michael Mallmann and Bogdan Musial, eds, *Genesis des Genozids. Polen 1939–1941* (Darmstadt: Wissenschaftliche Buchgesellschaft, 2004), pp. 36–56.

Böhm, Boris, and Thomas Schilter, 'Pirna-Sonnenstein. Von der Reformpsychiatrie zur Tötung psychisch Kranker und Behinderter', in Stiftung Sächsische Gedenkstätten, ed., *Nationalsozialistische Euthanasieverbrechen. Beiträge zur Aufarbeitung ihrer Geschichte in Sachsen* (Dresden: Michel Sandstein Verlag, 2004), pp. 30–66.

Borodziej, Włodzimierz, 'Der Warschauer Aufstand', in Bernhard Chiari, ed., *Die polnische Heimatarmee. Geschichte und Mythos der Armia Krajowa seit dem Zweiten Weltkrieg* (Munich: Oldenbourg, 2003), pp. 217–53.

Borodziej, Włodzimierz, *The Warsaw Uprising of 1944*, trans. from German by Barbara Harshav (Madison, WI: University of Wisconsin Press, 2006).

Brandon, Ray, 'The First Wave', unpublished manuscript, 2009.

Browning, Christopher R., *Ordinary Men: Reserve Police Battalion 101 and the Final Solution in Poland*, exp. edn (London: Penguin, 1998 [1992]).

Browning, Christopher R., 'The Nazi Empire', in Donald Bloxham and A. Dirk Moses, eds, *The Oxford Handbook of Genocide Studies* (Oxford: Oxford University Press, 2010), pp. 407–25.

Browning, Christopher R., with contributions by Jürgen Matthäus, *The Origins of the Final Solution: The Evolution of Nazi Jewish Policy, September 1939–March 1942* (London: William Heinemann, 2004).

Buggeln, Marc, and Michael Wildt, 'Arbeit im Nationalsozialismus (Einleitung)', in Marc Buggeln and Michael Wildt, eds, *Arbeit im Nationalsozialismus* (Munich: DeGruyter/ Oldenbourg, 2014), pp. ix–xxxvii.

Burkhardt, Anika, *Das NS-Euthanasie-Unrecht vor den Schranken der Justiz: Eine strafrechtliche Analyse* (Tübingen: Mohr Siebeck, 2015).

Burleigh, Michael, *Death and Deliverance: 'Euthanasia' in Germany, c. 1900–1945* (Cambridge: Cambridge University Press, 1994).

Burleigh, Michael, 'Psychiatry, German Society and the Nazi "Euthanasia" Programme', in Omer Bartov, ed., *The Holocaust: Origins, Implementation, Aftermath* (London/New York: Routledge, 2000), pp. 43–62.

Burrin, Philippe, *Nazi Anti-Semitism: From Prejudice to the Holocaust*, trans. from French by Janet Lloyd (New York/London: The New Press, 2005 [2000/2004]).

Buser, Verena, *Überleben von Kindern und Jugendlichen in den Konzentrationslagern Sachsenhausen, Auschwitz und Bergen-Belsen* (Berlin: Metropol, 2011).

Butterly, John R., and Jack Shepherd, *Hunger: The Biology and Politics of Starvation* (Lebanon, NH: University Press of New England, 2010).

Caplan, Jane, and Nikolaus Wachsmann, eds, *Concentration Camps in Nazi Germany: The New Histories* (Abingdon, Oxon: Routledge, 2010).

Clark, Janine Natalya, 'Genocide, War Crimes and the Conflict in Bosnia: Understanding the Perpetrators', *Journal of Genocide Research*, vol. 11, no. 4 (2009), pp. 421–45.

343

Collingham, Lizzie, *The Taste of War: World War Two and the Battle for Food* (London: Allen Lane, 2011).

Conroy, Melvyn, *Nazi Eugenics: Precursors, Policy, Aftermath* (Stuttgart: ibidem, 2017).

Cüppers, Martin, *Wegbereiter der Shoah. Die Waffen-SS, der Kommandostab Reichsführer-SS und die Judenvernichtung 1939–1945* (Darmstadt: Wissenschaftliche Buchgesellschaft, 2005).

Cüppers, Martin, Jürgen Matthäus and Andrej Angrick, eds, *Naziverbrechen. Täter, Taten, Bewältigungsversuche* (Darmstadt: Wissenschaftliche Buchgesellschaft, 2013).

Curilla, Wolfgang, *Die deutsche Ordnungspolizei und der Holocaust im Baltikum und in Weißrussland 1941–1944* (Paderborn: Ferdinand Schöningh, 2006).

Czech, Danuta, 'Kalendarium der wichtigsten Ereignisse aus der Geschichte des KL Auschwitz', in Danuta Czech, Aleksander Lasik, Stanisław Kłodziński and Andrzej Strzelecki, eds, *Auschwitz 1940–1945. Studien zur Geschichte des Konzentrations- und Vernichtungslagers Auschwitz, Band V: Epilog*, trans. from Polish by Jochen August (Oświęcim: Verlag des Staatlichen Museums Auschwitz-Birkenau, 1999), pp. 109–240.

Davies, Norman, *Rising '44: The Battle for Warsaw* (London: Macmillan, 2003).

Desbois, Patrick, *The Holocaust by Bullets: A Priest's Journey to Uncover the Truth behind the Murder of 1.5 Million Jews*, trans. from French by Catherine Spencer (New York: Palgrave Macmillan, 2008).

Dieckmann, Christoph, 'Bilanz der Massenvernichtungs-Maschinerie der Nazis', paper presented at the Bundeszentrale für politische Bildung, Bonn, 21 January 2019.

Dieckmann, Christoph, 'Das Scheitern des Hungerplans und die Praxis der selektiven Hungerpolitik im deutschen Krieg gegen die Sowjetunion', in Christoph Dieckmann and Babette Quinkert, eds, *Kriegführung und Hunger 1939–1945. Zum Verhältnis von militärischen, wirtschaftlichen und politischen Interessen* (Göttingen: Wallstein, 2015), pp. 88–122.

Dieckmann, Christoph, *Deutsche Besatzungspolitik in Litauen 1941–1944*, 2 vols (Göttingen: Wallstein, 2011).

Dieckmann, Christoph, Babette Quinkert and Tatjana Tönsmeyer, eds, *Kooperation und Verbrechen. Formen der 'Kollaboration' im östlichen Europa 1939–1945* (Göttingen: Wallstein, 2003).

Dieckmann, Christoph, and Babette Quinkert, eds, *Kriegführung und Hunger 1939–1945. Zum Verhältnis von militärischen, wirtschaftlichen und politischen Interessen* (Göttingen: Wallstein, 2015).

Diner, Dan, 'Rationalisierung und Methode. Zu einem neuen Erklärungsversuch der "Endlösung"', *Vierteljahrshefte für Zeitgeschichte*, vol. 40, no. 3 (July 1992), pp. 359–82.

Distel, Barbara, 'Sobibór', in Wolfgang Benz and Barbara Distel, eds, *Der Ort des Terrors. Geschichte der nationalsozialistischen Konzentrationslager, Band 8* (Munich: C.H. Beck, 2008), pp. 375–404.

Duffy, Christopher, *Red Storm on the Reich: The Soviet March on Germany, 1945* (New York: Athenium, 1991).

Engelking, Barbara, and Jacek Leociak, *The Warsaw Ghetto: A Guide to the Perished City*, trans. from Polish by Emma Harris (New Haven, CT: Yale University Press, 2009 [2001]).

Engwall, Kristina, 'Starved to Death? Nutrition in Asylums during the World Wars', *Scandinavian Journal of Disability Research*, vol. 7, no. 1 (2005), pp. 2–22.

Epstein, Barbara, *The Minsk Ghetto, 1941–1943: Jewish Resistance and Soviet Internationalism* (Berkeley/Los Angeles/London: University of California Press, 2008).

Epstein, Catherine, *Model Nazi: Arthur Greiser and the Occupation of Western Poland* (Oxford: Oxford University Press, 2010).

Evans, Richard J., 'Wie einzigartig war die Ermordung der Juden durch die Nationalsozialisten?', in Günter Morsch and Bertrand Perz, eds, *Neue Studien zu nationalsozialistischen Massentötungen durch Giftgas. Historische Bedeutung, technische Entwicklung, revisionistische Leugnung* (Berlin: Metropol, 2011), pp. 1–10.

Fairweather, Jack, *The Volunteer: The True Story of the Resistance Hero Who Infiltrated Auschwitz* (London: WH Allen, 2019).

Fatran, Gila, 'Die Deportation der Juden aus der Slowakei 1944–1945', *Bohemia: Zeitschrift für Geschichte und Kultur der böhmischen Länder*, vol. 37, no. 1 (1996), pp. 98–119.

Faulkner Rossi, Lauren, *Wehrmacht Priests: Catholicism and the Nazi War of Annihilation* (Cambridge, MA: Harvard University Press, 2015).

Faulstich, Heinz, *Hungersterben in der Psychiatrie 1914–1949: Mit einer Topographie der NS-Psychiatrie* (Freiburg im Breisgau: Lambertus, 1998).

Fings, Karola, 'A "Wannsee Conference" on the Extermination of the Gypsies? New Research Findings Regarding 15 January 1943 and the Auschwitz Decree', *Dapim: Studies on the Holocaust*, vol. 27, no. 3 (2013), pp. 174–94.

Fings, Karola, 'Der Völkermord an den Sinti und Roma im Deutschen Reich. Lokale Initiative und nationalsozialistische Rassenpolitik', *Einsicht. Bulletin des Fritz Bauer Instituts*, vol. 11 (2019), pp. 6–15.

Fisher, Gaëlle, and Caroline Mezger, eds, *The Holocaust in the Borderlands: Interethnic Relations and the Dynamics of Violence in Occupied Eastern Europe* (Göttingen: Wallstein, 2019).

Fontaine, Thomas, 'Chronologie: Répression et persécution en France occupée 1940–1944', *Violence de masse et Résistance – Réseau de recherche*, 7 December 2009.

Förster, Jürgen, *Die Wehrmacht im NS-Staat. Eine strukturgeschichtliche Analyse* (Munich: Oldenbourg, 2009).

Friedlander, Henry, *The Origins of Nazi Genocide: From Euthanasia to the Final Solution* (Chapel Hill, NC/London: University of North Carolina Press, 1995).

Friedländer, Saul, 'On the Possibility of the Holocaust: An Approach to a Historical Synthesis', in Yehuda Bauer and Nathan Rotenstreich, eds, *The Holocaust as Historical Experience: Essays and a Discussion* (New York: Holmes & Meier, 1981), pp. 1–21.

Friedländer, Saul, *The Years of Extermination: Nazi Germany and the Jews, 1939–1945* (New York: HarperCollins, 2007).

Friedman, Alexander, and Rainer Hudeman, eds, *Diskriminiert – vernichtet – vergessen. Behinderte in der Sowjetunion, unter nationalsozialistischer Besatzung und im Ostblock 1917–1991* (Stuttgart: Franz Steiner, 2016).

Fritzsche, Peter, 'Babi Yar, but Not Auschwitz: What Did Germans Know about the Final Solution?', in Susanna Schrafstetter and Alan E. Steinweis, eds, *The Germans and the Holocaust: Popular Responses to the Persecution and Murder of the Jews* (New York/Oxford: Berghahn Books, 2016), pp. 85–104.

Fritzsche, Peter, *Life and Death in the Third Reich* (Cambridge, MA: Harvard University Press, 2008).

'Früherer Dekan war "Mittäter" beim NS-Massenmord', *Westfälische Nachrichten*, 28 December 2011.

Fuchs, Petra, Maike Rotzoll, Paul Richter, Annette Hinz-Wessels and Gerrit Hohendorf, 'Minderjährige als Opfer der Krankenmordaktion "T4"', in Thomas Beddies and Kristina Hübener, eds, *Kinder in der NS-Psychiatrie* (Berlin: be.bra, 2004), pp. 55–70.

Gallagher, Adrian, *Genocide and its Threat to Contemporary International Order* (Houndmills: Palgrave Macmillan, 2013).

Ganzenmüller, Jörg, *Das belagerte Leningrad, 1941 bis 1944. Die Stadt in den Strategien von Angreifern und Verteidigern* (Paderborn: Ferdinand Schöningh, 2005).

Ganzenmüller, Jörg, 'Hungerpolitik als Problemlösungsstrategie. Der Entscheidungsprozess zur Blockade Leningrads und zur Vernichtung seiner Zivilbevölkerung', in Babette Quinkert and Jörg Morré, eds, *Deutsche Besatzung in der Sowjetunion 1941–1944. Vernichtungskrieg, Reaktionen, Erinnerung* (Paderborn: Ferdinand Schöningh, 2014), pp. 34–53.

Gawin, Magdalena, '"Flurbereinigung". Der Zusammenhang zwischen der Vernichtung der polnischen Intelligenz und der nationalsozialistischen Rassenhygiene', in Piotr Madajczyk and Paweł Popieliński, eds, *Social Engineering. Zwischen totalitärer Utopie und 'Piecemeal-Pragmatismus'* (Warsaw: Instytut Studiów Politycznych PAN, 2014), pp. 118–40.

Gentile, Carlo, *Wehrmacht und Waffen-SS im Partisanenkrieg: Italien 1943–1945* (Paderborn: Ferdinand Schöningh, 2012).

Gerlach, Christian, 'Die Ausweitung der deutschen Massenmorde in den besetzten sowjetischen Gebieten im Herbst 1941. Überlegungen zur Vernichtungspolitik gegen Juden und sowjetische Kriegsgefangene', in Christian Gerlach, *Krieg, Ernährung, Völkermord. Deutsche Vernichtungspolitik im Zweiten Weltkrieg*, rev. edn (Zurich/Munich: Pendo, 2001 [1998]), pp. 11–78.

Gerlach, Christian, 'Die Wannsee-Konferenz, das Schicksal der deutschen Juden und Hitlers politische Grundsatzentscheidung, alle Juden Europas zu ermorden', *WerkstattGeschichte*, vol. 18 (1997), pp. 7–44.

Gerlach, Christian, 'Die Wannsee-Konferenz, das Schicksal der deutschen Juden und Hitlers politische Grundsatzentscheidung, alle Juden Europas zu ermorden', in Christian Gerlach, *Krieg, Ernährung, Völkermord. Deutsche Vernichtungspolitik im Zweiten Weltkrieg*, rev. edn (Zurich/Munich: Pendo, 2001 [1998]), pp. 79–152.

Gerlach, Christian, *Extremely Violent Societies: Mass Violence in the Twentieth-Century World* (Cambridge: Cambridge University Press, 2010).

Gerlach, Christian, *Kalkulierte Morde. Die deutsche Wirtschafts- und Vernichtungspolitik in Weißrußland 1941 bis 1944* (Hamburg: Hamburger Edition, 1999).

Gerlach, Christian, 'Militärische "Versorgungszwänge", Besatzungspolitik und Massenverbrechen: Die Rolle des Generalquartiermeisters des Heeres und seiner Dienststellen im Krieg gegen die Sowjetunion', in Norbert Frei, Sybille Steinbacher and Bernd C. Wagner, eds, *Ausbeutung, Vernichtung, Öffentlichkeit: Neue Studien zur nationalsozialistischen Lagerpolitik* (Munich: K.G. Saur, 2000), pp. 175–208.

Gerlach, Christian, *The Extermination of the European Jews* (Cambridge: Cambridge University Press, 2016).

Gerlach, Christian, and Götz Aly, *Das letzte Kapitel. Realpolitik, Ideologie und der Mord an den ungarischen Juden 1944/1945* (Stuttgart/Munich: Deutsche Verlags-Anstalt, 2002).

Gerlach, Christian, and Nicolas Werth, 'State Violence – Violent Societies', in Michael Geyer and Sheila Fitzpatrick, eds, *Beyond Totalitarianism: Stalinism and Nazism Compared* (Cambridge: Cambridge University Press, 2009), pp. 133–79.

Gerwarth, Robert, *November 1918: The German Revolution* (Oxford: Oxford University Press, 2020).

Gerwarth, Robert, *The Vanquished: Why the First World War Failed to End, 1917–1923* (London: Allen Lane, 2016).

Gerwarth, Robert, and Stephan Malinowski, 'Der Holocaust als "kolonialer Genozid"? Europäische Kolonialgewalt und nationalsozialistischer Vernichtungskrieg', *Geschichte und Gesellschaft*, vol. 33 (2007), pp. 439–66.

Gosewinkel, Dieter, 'Citizenship in Germany and France at the Turn of the Twentieth Century: Some New Observations on an Old Comparison', in Geoff Ely and Jan Palmowski, eds, *Citizenship and National Identity in Twentieth-Century Germany* (Stanford, CA: Stanford University Press, 2008), pp. 27–39.

Greif, Gideon, *We Wept without Tears: Testimonies of the Jewish Sonderkommando from Auschwitz* (New Haven, CT/London: Yale University Press, 2005).

Griech-Polelle, Beth A., *Bishop von Galen: German Catholicism and National Socialism* (New Haven, CT/London: Yale University Press, 2002).

Grode, Walter, *Die 'Sonderbehandlung 14f13' in den Konzentrationslagern des Dritten Reiches. Ein Beitrag zur Dynamik faschistischer Vernichtungspolitik* (Frankfurt am Main: Peter Lang, 1987).

Gross, Raphael, *Anständig geblieben. Nationalsozialistische Moral* (Frankfurt am Main: S. Fischer, 2010).

Gruner, Wolf, 'Von der Kollektivausweisung zur Deportation der Juden aus Deutschland (1938–1945). Neue Perspektiven und Dokumente', in Birthe Kundrus and Beate Meyer, eds, *Die Deportation der Juden aus Deutschland. Pläne – Praxis – Reaktionen 1938–1945* (Göttingen: Wallstein, 2004), pp. 21–62.

Grzebyk, Patrycja, 'Hidden in the Glare of the Nuremberg Trial: Impunity for the Wola Massacre as the Greatest Debacle of Post-War Trials', *MPI Luxembourg Working Paper Series*, no. 7 (2019), pp. 1–16.

Gumkowski, Janusz, and Kazimierz Leszczynski, *Poland under Nazi Occupation*, trans. from Polish by Edward Rothert (Warsaw: Polonia, 1961).

Gutman, Yisrael, *The Jews of Warsaw, 1939–1943: Ghetto, Underground, Revolt*, trans. from Hebrew by Ina Friedman (Bloomington, IN: Indiana University Press, 1982).

Gutman, Yisrael, and Michael Berenbaum, eds, *Anatomy of the Auschwitz Death Camp* (Bloomington, IN: Indiana University Press, 1994).

Hanson, Johanna K.M., *The Civilian Population and the Warsaw Uprising of 1944* (Cambridge: Cambridge University Press, 1982).

Harrison, Mark, 'Counting the Soviet Union's War Dead: Still 26–27 Million', *Europe-Asia Studies*, vol. 71, no. 6 (2019), pp. 1036–47.

Hartmann, Christian, *Wehrmacht im Ostkrieg. Front und militärisches Hinterland 1941/42* (Munich: Oldenbourg, 2009).

Hartmann, Christian, and Sergej Slutsch, 'Franz Halder und die Kriegsvorbereitungen im Frühjahr 1939. Eine Ansprache des Generalstabschefs des Heeres', *Vierteljahrshefte für Zeitgeschichte*, vol. 45, no. 3 (July 1997), pp. 467–95.

Hasenclever, Jörn, *Wehrmacht und Besatzungspolitik. Die Befehlshaber der rückwärtigen Heeresgebiete 1941–1943* (Paderborn: Ferdinand Schöningh, 2010).

Henry, Patrick, ed., *Jewish Resistance against the Nazis* (Washington, DC: Catholic University of America Press, 2014).

Herf, Jeffrey, *The Jewish Enemy: Nazi Propaganda during World War II and the Holocaust* (Cambridge, MA: Harvard University Press, 2006).

Hilberg, Raul, *The Destruction of the European Jews*, 3rd edn, vol. III (New Haven, CT/ London: Yale University Press, 2003).

Hintjens, Helen M., 'Explaining the 1994 Genocide in Rwanda', *The Journal of Modern African Studies*, vol. 37, no. 2 (1999), pp. 241–86.

Hinz-Wessels, Annette, 'Antisemitismus und Krankenmord. Zum Umgang mit jüdischen Anstaltspatienten im Nationalsozialismus', *Vierteljahrshefte für Zeitgeschichte*, vol. 61, no. 1 (January 2013), pp. 65–92.

Hionidou, Violetta, *Famine and Death in Occupied Greece, 1941–1944* (Cambridge: Cambridge University Press, 2006).

Hoffmann, Ute, and Dietmar Schulze '… wird heute in eine andere Anstalt verlegt'. *Nationalsozialistische Zwangssterilisation und 'Euthanasie' in der Landes-Heil- und Pflegeanstalt Bernburg – eine Dokumentation* (Dessau: Regierungspräsidium Dessau, 1997).

Holler, Martin, 'Deadly Odyssey: East Prussian Sinti in Białystok, Brest-Litovsk, and Auschwitz-Birkenau', in Alex J. Kay and David Stahel, eds, *Mass Violence in Nazi-Occupied Europe* (Bloomington, IN: Indiana University Press, 2018), pp. 94–120.

Holler, Martin, *Der nationalsozialistische Völkermord an den Roma in der besetzten Sowjetunion (1941–1944)* (Heidelberg: Dokumentations- und Kulturzentrum Deutscher Sinti und Roma, 2009).

Holler, Martin, 'Extending the Genocidal Program: Did Otto Ohlendorf Initiate the Systematic Extermination of Soviet "Gypsies"?', in Alex J. Kay, Jeff Rutherford and David Stahel, eds, *Nazi Policy on the Eastern Front, 1941: Total War, Genocide, and Radicalization* (Rochester, NY: University of Rochester Press, 2012), pp. 267–88.

Holler, Martin, 'The Nazi Persecution of Roma in Northwestern Russia: The Operational Area of the Army Group North, 1941–1944', in Anton Weiss-Wendt, ed., *The Nazi Genocide of the Roma: Reassessment and Commemoration* (New York/Oxford: Berghahn Books, 2013), pp. 153–80.

Horne, John, and Alan Kramer, *German Atrocities 1914: A History of Denial* (New Haven, CT/ London: Yale University Press, 2001).

Hull, Isabel V., *Absolute Destruction: Military Culture and the Practices of War in Imperial Germany* (Ithaca, NY: Cornell University Press, 2005).

Hürter, Johannes, 'Die Wehrmacht vor Leningrad: Krieg und Besatzungspolitik der 18. Armee im Herbst und Winter 1941/42', *Vierteljahrshefte fur Zeitgeschichte*, vol. 49, no. 3 (July 2001), pp. 377–440.

Hürter, Johannes, 'Hitler's Generals in the East and the Holocaust', in Alex J. Kay and David Stahel, eds, *Mass Violence in Nazi-Occupied Europe* (Bloomington, IN: Indiana University Press, 2018), pp. 17–40.

Hürter, Johannes, *Hitlers Heerführer: Die deutschen Oberbefehlshaber im Krieg gegen die Sowjetunion, 1941/42* (Munich: Oldenbourg, 2006).

Ingrao, Christian, *Les chasseurs noirs: La brigade Dirlewanger* (n.pl. [Paris]: Perrin, 2006).

Institute of National Remembrance, *The Destruction of the Polish Elite: Operation AB – Katyn* (Warsaw: Instytut Pamięci Narodowej, 2009).

Jacobsen, Hans-Adolf, 'Kommissarbefehl und Massenexekutionen sowjetischer Kriegsgefangener', in Martin Broszat, Hans-Adolf Jacobsen and Helmut Krausnick, *Anatomie des SS-Staates, Band 2: Konzentrationslager, Kommissarbefehl, Judenverfolgung* (Olten/Freiburg im Breisgau: Walter-Verlag, 1965), pp. 161–279.

Jahn, Peter, '27 Millionen', *Die Zeit*, 14 June 2007, p. 90.

Jankowski, Stanislaw, 'Warsaw: Destruction, Secret Town Planning, 1939–44, and Postwar Reconstruction', in Jeffry M. Diefendorf, ed., *Rebuilding Europe's Bombed Cities* (Houndmills: Palgrave Macmillan, 1990), pp. 77–93.

Jansen, Christian, and Arno Weckbecker, *Der 'Volksdeutsche Selbstschutz' in Polen 1939/40* (Munich: Oldenbourg, 1992).

Jaroszewski, Zdzisław, ed., *Zagłada chorych psychicznie w Polsce 1939–1945* (Warsaw: Wydawnictwo Naukowe PWN, 1993).

Joeden-Forgey, Elisa von, 'Gender and Genocide', in Donald Bloxham and A. Dirk Moses, eds, *The Oxford Handbook of Genocide Studies* (Oxford: Oxford University Press, 2010), pp. 61–80.

Johnson, Ian, 'Who Killed More? Hitler, Stalin, or Mao?', *New York Review of Books*, 5 February 2018.

Karch, Brendan, *Nation and Loyalty in a German-Polish Borderland: Upper Silesia, 1848–1960* (Cambridge/New York: Cambridge University Press, 2018).

Karny, Miroslav, 'The Vrba and Wetzler Report', in Yisrael Gutman and Michael Berenbaum, eds, *Anatomy of the Auschwitz Death Camp* (Bloomington, IN: Indiana University Press, 1994), pp. 553–68.

Katzur, Julia, 'Die "Kinderfachabteilung" in der Heil- und Pflegeanstalt Eglfing-Haar und die nationalsozialistische "Kindereuthanasie" zwischen 1940–1945', unpublished doctoral thesis, Technische Universität München, 2017.

Kay, Alex J., *Exploitation, Resettlement, Mass Murder: Political and Economic Planning for German Occupation Policy in the Soviet Union, 1940–1941* (New York/Oxford: Berghahn Books, 2006).

Kay, Alex J., 'German Economic Plans for the Occupied Soviet Union and their Implementation, 1941–1944', in Timothy Snyder and Ray Brandon, eds, *Stalin and Europe: Imitation and Domination, 1928–1953* (Oxford/New York: Oxford University Press, 2014), pp. 163–89.

Kay, Alex J., 'Germany's Staatssekretäre, Mass Starvation and the Meeting of 2 May 1941', *Journal of Contemporary History*, vol. 41, no. 4 (October 2006), pp. 685–700.

Kay, Alex J., *The Making of an SS Killer: The Life of Colonel Alfred Filbert, 1905–1990* (Cambridge: Cambridge University Press, 2016).

Kay, Alex J., '"The Purpose of the Russian Campaign Is the Decimation of the Slavic Population by Thirty Million": The Radicalization of German Food Policy in Early 1941', in Alex J. Kay, Jeff Rutherford and David Stahel, eds, *Nazi Policy on the Eastern Front, 1941: Total War, Genocide, and Radicalization* (Rochester, NY: University of Rochester Press, 2012), pp. 101–29.

Kay, Alex J., 'Transition to Genocide, July 1941: Einsatzkommando 9 and the Annihilation of Soviet Jewry', *Holocaust and Genocide Studies*, vol. 27, no. 3 (winter 2013), pp. 411–42.

Kay, Alex J., and David Stahel, 'Crimes of the Wehrmacht: A Re-evaluation', *Journal of Perpetrator Research*, vol. 3, no. 1 (2020), pp. 95–127.

Kay, Alex J., Jeff Rutherford and David Stahel, eds, *Nazi Policy on the Eastern Front, 1941: Total War, Genocide, and Radicalization* (Rochester, NY: University of Rochester Press, 2012).

Kay, Alex J., and David Stahel, eds, *Mass Violence in Nazi-Occupied Europe* (Bloomington, IN: Indiana University Press, 2018).

Keller, Rolf, 'Arbeitseinsatz und Hungerpolitik. Sowjetische Kriegsgefangene im Deutschen Reich 1941/42', in Christoph Dieckmann and Babette Quinkert, eds, *Kriegführung und Hunger 1939–1945. Zum Verhältnis von militärischen, wirtschaftlichen und politischen Interessen* (Göttingen: Wallstein, 2015), pp. 123–54.

Keller, Rolf, *Sowjetische Kriegsgefangene im Deutschen Reich 1941/42. Behandlung und Arbeitseinsatz zwischen Vernichtungspolitik und kriegswirtschaftlichen Zwängen* (Göttingen: Wallstein, 2011).

Keller, Sven, *Volksgemeinschaft am Ende. Gesellschaft und Gewalt 1944/45* (Munich: Oldenbourg, 2013).

Keller, Sven, 'Volksgemeinschaft and Violence: Some Reflections on Interdependencies', in Bernhard Gotto and Martina Steber, eds, *Visions of Community in Nazi Germany: Social Engineering and Private Lives* (Oxford: Oxford University Press, 2014), pp. 226–39.

Kenrick, Donald, and Grattan Puxon, *Gypsies under the Swastika* (Hatfield: University of Hertfordshire Press, 2009).

Kershaw, Ian, *Fateful Choices: Ten Decisions That Changed the World, 1940–1941* (London: Allen Lane, 2007).

Kershaw, Ian, *Hitler 1936–1945: Nemesis* (London: Allen Lane, 2000).

Kershaw, Ian, '"Working Towards the Führer." Reflections on the Nature of the Hitler Dictatorship', *Contemporary European History*, vol. 2, no. 2 (July 1993), pp. 103–18.

Kipp, Michaela, 'The Holocaust in the Letters of German Soldiers on the Eastern Front (1939–44)', *Journal of Genocide Research*, vol. 9, no. 4 (2007), pp. 601–15.

Klee, Ernst, *'Euthanasie' im NS-Staat. Die 'Vernichtung lebensunwerten Lebens'* (Frankfurt am Main: Fischer Taschenbuch, 1985).

Klein, Peter, 'Kulmhof/Chełmno', in Wolfgang Benz and Barbara Distel, eds, *Der Ort des Terrors. Geschichte der nationalsozialistischen Konzentrationslager, Band 8* (Munich: C.H. Beck, 2008), pp. 301–28.

Kochanski, Halik, *The Eagle Unbowed: Poland and the Poles in the Second World War* (Cambridge, MA: Harvard University Press, 2012).

Koonz, Claudia, *The Nazi Conscience* (Cambridge, MA: Harvard University Press, 2003).

Korb, Alexander, *Im Schatten des Weltkriegs. Massengewalt der Ustaša gegen Serben, Juden und Roma in Kroatien, 1941–1945* (Hamburg: Hamburger Edition, 2013).

Kossert, Andreas, '*Endlösung* on the "Amber Shore": The Massacre in January 1945 on the Baltic Seashore – A Repressed Chapter of East Prussian History', *Leo Baeck Institute Yearbook*, vol. 49 (2004), pp. 3–21.

Kovalev, Boris N., 'Vernichtung von psychisch kranken und behinderten Menschen unter der deutschen Okkupation im Nordwesten Russlands', in Alexander Friedman and Rainer Hudeman, eds, *Diskriminiert – vernichtet – vergessen. Behinderte in der Sowjetunion, unter nationalsozialistischer Besatzung und im Ostblock 1917–1991* (Stuttgart: Franz Steiner, 2016), pp. 373–84.

Kranz, Tomasz, 'Lublin-Majdanek – Stammlager', in Wolfgang Benz and Barbara Distel, eds, *Der Ort des Terrors. Geschichte der nationalsozialistischen Konzentrationslager, Band 7* (Munich: C.H. Beck, 2008), pp. 33–84.

Krausnick, Helmut, 'Die Einsatzgruppen vom Anschluß Österreichs bis zum Feldzug gegen die Sowjetunion. Entwicklung und Verhältnis zur Wehrmacht', in Helmut Krausnick and Hans-Heinrich Wilhelm, *Die Truppe des Weltanschauungskrieges. Die Einsatzgruppen der Sicherheitspolizei und des SD 1938–1942* (Stuttgart: Deutsche Verlags-Anstalt, 1981), pp. 11–278.

Kubica, Helena, 'Children and Adolescents in Auschwitz', in Tadeusz Iwaszko, Helena Kubica, Franciszek Piper, Irena Strzelecka and Andrzej Strzelecki, eds, *Auschwitz, 1940–1945: Central Issues in the History of the Camp, Vol. 2: The Prisoners – Their Life and Work*, trans.

from Polish by William Brand (Oświęcim: Auschwitz-Birkenau State Museum, 2000), pp. 201–90.

Kühl, Stefan, *Ganz normale Organisationen. Zur Soziologie des Holocaust* (Berlin: Suhrkamp, 2014).

Kühne, Thomas, *Belonging and Genocide: Hitler's Community, 1918–1945* (New Haven, CT/ London: Yale University Press, 2010).

Kühne, Thomas, *The Rise and Fall of Comradeship: Hitler's Soldiers, Male Bonding and Mass Violence in the Twentieth Century* (Cambridge: Cambridge University Press, 2017).

Kunz, Norbert, 'Das Beispiel Charkow: Eine Stadtbevölkerung als Opfer der deutschen Hungerstrategie 1941/42', in Christian Hartmann, Johannes Hürter and Ulrike Jureit, eds, *Verbrechen der Wehrmacht: Bilanz einer Debatte* (Munich: C.H. Beck, 2005), pp. 136–44.

Kuwałek, Robert, 'Bełżec', in Wolfgang Benz and Barbara Distel, eds, *Der Ort des Terrors. Geschichte der nationalsozialistischen Konzentrationslager, Band 8* (Munich: C.H. Beck, 2008), pp. 331–71.

Kuwałek, Robert, *Das Vernichtungslager Bełżec* (Berlin: Metropol, 2013).

Kwiet, Konrad, 'Rassenpolitik und Völkermord', in Wolfgang Benz, Hermann Graml and Hermann Weiß, eds, *Enzyklopädie des Nationalsozialismus* (Munich: dtv, 2001 [1997]), pp. 50–65.

Langbein, Hermann, *Menschen in Auschwitz* (Frankfurt am Main: Ullstein, 1980).

Langbein, Hermann, *People in Auschwitz*, trans. from German by Harry Zohn (Chapel Hill, NC/London: University of North Carolina Press, 2004).

Latysheva, Viktoria, Alexander Friedman and Alexander Pesetsky, 'Die Wehrmacht, die deutsche Zivilverwaltung und die Ermordung geistig behinderter Kinder in Červen' (Gebiet Minsk) im Mai 1942', in Alexander Friedman and Rainer Hudeman, eds, *Diskriminiert – vernichtet – vergessen. Behinderte in der Sowjetunion, unter nationalsozialistischer Besatzung und im Ostblock 1917–1991* (Stuttgart: Franz Steiner, 2016), pp. 453–7.

Lehnstaedt, Stephan, *Der Kern des Holocaust. Bełżec, Sobibór, Treblinka und die Aktion Reinhardt* (Munich: C.H. Beck, 2017).

Lehnstaedt, Stephan, 'The Minsk Experience: German Occupiers and Everyday Life in the Capital of Belarus', in Alex J. Kay, Jeff Rutherford and David Stahel, eds, *Nazi Policy on the Eastern Front, 1941: Total War, Genocide, and Radicalization* (Rochester, NY: University of Rochester Press, 2012), pp. 240–66.

Levene, Mark, *Genocide in the Age of the Nation-State, Volume I: The Meaning of Genocide* (London/New York: I.B. Tauris, 2005).

Lewy, Guenter, *Perpetrators: The World of the Holocaust Killers* (New York: Oxford University Press, 2017).

Lewy, Guenter, *The Nazi Persecution of the Gypsies* (Oxford/New York: Oxford University Press, 2000).

Ley, Astrid, 'Die "Aktion 14f13" in den Konzentrationslagern', in Günter Morsch and Bertrand Perz, eds, *Neue Studien zu nationalsozialistischen Massentötungen durch Giftgas. Historische Bedeutung, technische Entwicklung, revisionistische Leugnung* (Berlin: Metropol, 2011), pp. 231–43.

Lieb, Peter, *Konventioneller Krieg oder NS-Weltanschauungskrieg? Kriegführung und Partisanenbekämpfung in Frankreich 1943/44* (Munich: Oldenbourg, 2007).

Lieb, Peter, 'Täter aus Überzeugung? Oberst Carl von Andrian und die Judenmorde der 707. Infanteriedivision 1941/42', *Vierteljahrshefte für Zeitgeschichte*, vol. 50, no. 4 (October 2002), pp. 523–57.

Lilienthal, Georg, 'Der Gasmord in Hadamar', in Günter Morsch and Bertrand Perz, eds, *Neue Studien zu nationalsozialistischen Massentötungen durch Giftgas. Historische Bedeutung, technische Entwicklung, revisionistische Leugnung* (Berlin: Metropol, 2011), pp. 140–50.

Lilienthal, Georg, 'NS-"Euthanasie"-Mordopfer und Wege des Gedenkens', in Sybille Quack, ed., *Dimensionen der Verfolgung. Opfer und Opfergruppen im Nationalsozialismus* (Munich: Deutsche Verlags-Anstalt, 2003), pp. 251–77.

Longerich, Peter, *Der ungeschriebene Befehl. Hitler und der Weg zur 'Endlösung'* (Munich: Piper, 2001).

Longerich, Peter, *Heinrich Himmler*, trans. from German by Jeremy Noakes and Lesley Sharpe (Oxford: Oxford University Press, 2012 [2008]).

Longerich, Peter, *Holocaust: The Nazi Persecution and Murder of the Jews* (Oxford: Oxford University Press, 2010).

Lopukhovsky, Lev, and Boris Kavalerchik, *The Price of Victory: The Red Army's Casualties in the Great Patriotic War*, trans. from Russian by Harold Orenstein (Barnsley: Pen & Sword, 2017).

Lower, Wendy, *Hitler's Furies: German Women in the Nazi Killing Fields* (Boston, MA: Houghton Mifflin Harcourt, 2013).

Luchterhandt, Martin, *Der Weg nach Birkenau. Entstehung und Verlauf der nationalsozialist-ischen Verfolgung der 'Zigeuner'* (Lübeck: Schmidt-Römhild, 2000).

Macadam, Heather Dune, *The Nine Hundred: The Extraordinary Young Women of the First Official Jewish Transport to Auschwitz* (London: Hodder & Stoughton, 2020).

Mallmann, Klaus-Michael, '"Mensch, ich feiere heut' den tausendsten Genickschuß". Die Sicherheitspolizei und die Shoah in Westgalizien', in Gerhard Paul, ed., *Die Täter der Shoah. Fanatische Nationalsozialisten oder ganz normale Deutsche?* (Göttingen: Wallstein, 2002), pp. 109–36.

Mallmann, Klaus-Michael, 'Menschenjagd und Massenmord. Das neue Instrument der Einsatzgruppen und -kommandos 1938–1945', in Gerhard Paul and Klaus-Michael Mallmann, eds, *Die Gestapo im Zweiten Weltkrieg. 'Heimatfront' und besetztes Europa* (Darmstadt: Wissenschaftliche Buchgesellschaft, 2000), pp. 291–316.

Manoschek, Walter, 'Die Vernichtung der Juden in Serbien', in Ulrich Herbert, ed., *Nationalsozialistische Vernichtungspolitik 1939–1945. Neue Forschungen und Kontroversen* (Frankfurt am Main: Fischer Taschenbuch, 1998), pp. 209–34.

Manoschek, Walter, *'Serbien ist judenfrei'. Militärische Besatzungspolitik und Judenvernichtung in Serbien 1941/42* (Munich: Oldenbourg, 1993).

Manoschek, Walter, '"Wo der Partisan ist, ist der Jude, und wo der Jude ist, ist der Partisan". Die Wehrmacht und die Shoah', in Gerhard Paul, ed., *Die Täter der Shoah. Fanatische Nationalsozialisten oder ganz normale Deutsche?* (Göttingen: Wallstein, 2002), pp. 167–85.

Matthäus, Jürgen, 'Controlled Escalation: Himmler's Men in the Summer of 1941 and the Holocaust in the Occupied Soviet Territories', *Holocaust and Genocide Studies*, vol. 21, no. 2 (autumn 2007), pp. 218–242.

Mazower, Mark, *Hitler's Empire: Nazi Rule in Occupied Europe* (London: Allen Lane, 2008).

Mazower, Mark, *Inside Hitler's Greece: The Experience of Occupation, 1941–44* (New Haven, CT/London: Yale University Press, 1993).

Mazur, Grzegorz, 'Die Aktion "Burza"', in Bernhard Chiari, ed., *Die polnische Heimatarmee. Geschichte und Mythos der Armia Krajowa seit dem Zweiten Weltkrieg* (Munich: Oldenbourg, 2003), pp. 255–74.

Mierzejewski, Alfred C., *The Most Valuable Asset of the Reich: A History of the German National Railway, Volume 2: 1933–1945* (Chapel Hill, NC/London: University of North Carolina Press, 2000).

Montague, Patrick, *Chełmno and the Holocaust: The History of Hitler's First Death Camp* (Chapel Hill, NC/London: University of North Carolina Press, 2012).

Morsch, Günter, and Bertrand Perz, eds, *Neue Studien zu nationalsozialistischen Massentötungen durch Giftgas. Historische Bedeutung, technische Entwicklung, revisionist-ische Leugnung* (Berlin: Metropol, 2011).

Mühlhäuser, Regina, *Eroberungen. Sexuelle Gewalttaten und intime Beziehungen deutscher Soldaten in der Sowjetunion, 1941–1945* (Hamburg: Hamburger Edition, 2010).

Müller, Rolf-Dieter, *An der Seite der Wehrmacht. Hitlers ausländische Helfer beim 'Kreuzzug gegen den Bolschewismus' 1941–1944* (Berlin: Ch. Links, 2007).

Mulligan, Timothy P., 'Reckoning the Cost of People's War: The German Experience in the Central USSR', *Russian History*, vol. 9, no. 1 (1982), pp. 27–48.

Muñoz, Antonio J., *The German Secret Field Police in Greece, 1941–1944* (Jefferson, NC: McFarland, 2018).

Musial, Bogdan, *Deutsche Zivilverwaltung und Judenverfolgung im Generalgouvernement. Eine Fallstudie zum Distrikt Lublin 1939–1944* (Wiesbaden: Harrassowitz, 1999).

Musial, Bogdan, *Sowjetische Partisanen 1941–1944. Mythos und Wirklichkeit* (Paderborn: Ferdinand Schöningh, 2009).

Nakath, Monika, 'NS-Terror gegen Sinti und Roma in der Provinz Brandenburg. Dokumente aus dem Brandenburgischen Landeshauptarchiv (BLHA)', *Brandenburgische Archive*, vol. 35 (2018), pp. 46–50.

Nitschke, Asmus, *Die 'Erbpolizei' im Nationalsozialismus. Zur Alltagsgeschichte der Gesundheitsämter im Dritten Reich* (Opladen/Wiesbaden: Westdeutscher Verlag, 1999).

Nolte, Hans-Heinrich, 'Comparing Soviet and Nazi Mass Crimes', in Alex J. Kay and David Stahel, eds, *Mass Violence in Nazi-Occupied Europe* (Bloomington, IN: Indiana University Press, 2018), pp. 265–91.

Nolte, Hans-Heinrich, 'Kriegskinder: Zu den Differenzen zwischen Russland und Deutschland', *Zeitgeschichte*, vol. 36, no. 5 (September–October 2009), pp. 311–23.

Oldenburg, Manfred, *Ideologie und militärisches Kalkül. Die Besatzungspolitik der Wehrmacht in der Sowjetunion 1942* (Cologne: Böhlau, 2004).

O'Neill, Linda, Tina Fraser, Andrew Kitchenham and Verna McDonald, 'Hidden Burdens: A Review of Intergenerational, Historical and Complex Trauma, Implications for Indigenous Families', *Journal of Child & Adolescent Trauma*, vol. 11, no. 2 (June 2018), pp. 173–86.

Otto, Reinhard, *Wehrmacht, Gestapo und sowjetische Kriegsgefangene im deutschen Reichsgebiet 1941/42* (Munich: Oldenbourg, 1998).

Otto, Reinhard, and Rolf Keller, 'Soviet Prisoners of War in Nazi Concentration Camps: Current Knowledge and Research Desiderata', in Alex J. Kay and David Stahel, eds, *Mass Violence in Nazi-Occupied Europe* (Bloomington, IN: Indiana University Press, 2018), pp. 123–46.

Otto, Reinhard, and Rolf Keller, *Sowjetische Kriegsgefangene im System der Konzentrationslager* (Vienna: new academic press, 2019).

Otto, Reinhard, Rolf Keller and Jens Nagel, 'Sowjetische Kriegsgefangene in deutschem Gewahrsam 1941–1945. Zahlen und Dimensionen', *Vierteljahrshefte für Zeitgeschichte*, vol. 56, no. 4 (October 2008), pp. 557–602.

Paul, Gerhard, 'Lemberg '41: Bilder der Gewalt – Bilder als Gewalt – Gewalt an Bildern', in Martin Cüppers, Jürgen Matthäus and Andrej Angrick, eds, *Naziverbrechen. Täter, Taten, Bewältigungsversuche* (Darmstadt: Wissenschaftliche Buchgesellschaft, 2013), pp. 191–212.

Paul, Gerhard, 'Von Psychopathen, Technokraten des Terrors und "ganz gewöhnlichen Deutschen". Die Täter der Shoah im Spiegel der Forschung', in Gerhard Paul, ed., *Die Täter der Shoah. Fanatische Nationalsozialisten oder ganz normale Deutsche?* (Göttingen: Wallstein, 2002), pp. 13–90.

Paul, Gerhard, ed., *Die Täter der Shoah. Fanatische Nationalsozialisten oder ganz normale Deutsche?* (Göttingen: Wallstein, 2002).

Pelt, Robert Jan van, *The Case for Auschwitz: Evidence from the Irving Trial* (Bloomington, IN: Indiana University Press, 2002).

Pieper, Henning, *Fegelein's Horsemen and Genocidal Warfare: The SS Cavalry Brigade in the Soviet Union* (Basingstoke: Palgrave Macmillan, 2015).

Piper, Franciszek, *Auschwitz 1940–1945. Studien zur Geschichte des Konzentrations- und Vernichtungslagers Auschwitz, Band III: Vernichtung*, trans. from Polish by Jochen August (Oświęcim: Verlag des Staatlichen Museums Auschwitz-Birkenau, 1999).

Piper, Franciszek, 'Auschwitz II – Birkenau Main Camp', in Geoffrey P. Megargee, ed., *The United States Holocaust Memorial Museum Encyclopedia of Camps and Ghettos, 1933–1945, Vol. I: Early Camps, Youth Camps, and Concentration Camps and Subcamps under the SS-Business Administration Main Office (WVHA), Part A* (Bloomington, IN: Indiana University Press, 2009), pp. 209–14.

Piper, Franciszek, 'Gas Chambers and Crematoria', in Yisrael Gutman and Michael Berenbaum, eds, *Anatomy of the Auschwitz Death Camp* (Bloomington, IN: Indiana University Press, 1994), pp. 157–82.

Piper, Franciszek, 'The Number of Victims', in Yisrael Gutman and Michael Berenbaum, eds, *Anatomy of the Auschwitz Death Camp* (Bloomington, IN: Indiana University Press, 1994), pp. 61–76.

Pisarri, Milovan, *The Suffering of the Roma in Serbia during the Holocaust*, trans. from Serbian by Nataša Dinić (Belgrade: Forum for Applied History, 2014).

Pohl, Dieter, 'Die Einsatzgruppe C 1941/42', in Peter Klein, ed., *Die Einsatzgruppen in der besetzten Sowjetunion 1941/42. Die Tätigkeits- und Lageberichte des Chefs der Sicherheitspolizei und des SD* (Berlin: Edition Hentrich, 1997), pp. 71–87.

Pohl, Dieter, *Die Herrschaft der Wehrmacht. Deutsche Militärbesatzung und einheimische Bevölkerung in der Sowjetunion 1941–1944* (Munich: Oldenbourg, 2008).

Pohl, Dieter, 'Die Wehrmacht und der Mord an den Juden in den besetzten sowjetischen Gebieten', in Wolf Kaiser, ed., *Täter im Vernichtungskrieg. Der Überfall auf die Sowjetunion und der Völkermord an den Juden* (Berlin: Propyläen, 2002), pp. 39–53.

Pohl, Dieter, *Holocaust. Die Ursachen, das Geschehen, die Folgen* (Freiburg im Breisgau: Herder, 2000).

Pohl, Dieter, 'Just How Many? On the Death Toll of Jewish Victims of Nazi Crimes', in Alfred Kokh and Pavel Polian, eds, *Denial of the Denial, or The Battle of Auschwitz: The Demography and Geopolitics of the Holocaust. The View from the Twenty-First Century* (Brighton, MA: Academic Studies Press, 2012), pp. 129–48.

Pohl, Dieter, *Nationalsozialistische Judenverfolgung in Ostgalizien 1941–1944. Organisation und Durchführung eines staatlichen Massenverbrechens* (Munich: Oldenbourg, 1997).

Pohl, Dieter, 'The Holocaust and the Concentration Camps', in Jane Caplan and Nikolaus Wachsmann, eds, *Concentration Camps in Nazi Germany: The New Histories* (Abingdon, Oxon: Routledge, 2010), pp. 149–66.

Pohl, Dieter, *Verfolgung und Massenmord in der NS-Zeit 1933–1945*, 3rd rev. edn (Darmstadt: Wissenschaftliche Buchgesellschaft, 2011 [2003]).

Prečan, Vilém, 'The Slovak National Uprising: The Most Dramatic Moment in the Nation's History', in Mikuláš Teich, Dušan Kováč and Martin D. Brown, eds, *Slovakia in History* (Cambridge: Cambridge University Press, 2011), pp. 206–28.

Press, Bernhard, *The Murder of the Jews in Latvia, 1941–1945*, trans. from German by Laimdota Mazzarins (Evanston, IL: Northwestern University Press, 2000 [1992]).

Pressac, Jean-Claude, with Robert-Jan van Pelt, 'The Machinery of Mass Murder at Auschwitz', in Yisrael Gutman and Michael Berenbaum, eds, *Anatomy of the Auschwitz Death Camp* (Bloomington, IN: Indiana University Press, 1994), pp. 183–245.

Prusin, Alexander, 'A Community of Violence: The SiPo/SD and its Role in the Nazi Terror System in Generalbezirk Kiew', *Holocaust and Genocide Studies*, vol. 21, no. 1 (spring 2007), pp. 1–30.

Rauh, Philipp, 'Der Krieg gegen die "nutzlosen Esser". Psychiatriepatienten als Opfer der NS-"Euthanasie"', in Christoph Dieckmann and Babette Quinkert, eds, *Kriegführung und Hunger 1939–1945. Zum Verhältnis von militärischen, wirtschaftlichen und politischen Interessen* (Göttingen: Wallstein, 2015), pp. 33–58.

Reid, Anna, *Leningrad: Tragedy of a City under Siege, 1941–44* (London: Bloomsbury, 2011).

Richie, Alexandra, *Warsaw 1944: Hitler, Himmler, and the Warsaw Uprising* (New York: Farrar, Straus and Giroux, 2013).

Richter, Timm C., 'Belarusian Partisans and German Reprisals', in Timothy Snyder and Ray Brandon, eds, *Stalin and Europe: Imitation and Domination, 1928–1953* (Oxford/New York: Oxford University Press, 2014), pp. 207–32.

Rieß, Volker, *Die Anfänge der Vernichtung 'lebensunwerten Lebens' in den Reichsgauen Danzig-Westpreußen und Wartheland 1939/40* (Frankfurt am Main: Peter Lang, 1995).

Robel, Gert, 'Sowjetunion', in Wolfgang Benz, ed., *Dimension des Völkermords. Die Zahl der jüdischen Opfer des Nationalsozialismus* (Munich: Oldenbourg, 1991), pp. 499–560.

Römer, Felix, *Comrades: The Wehrmacht from Within*, trans. from German by Alex J. Kay (Oxford: Oxford University Press, 2019).

Römer, Felix, *Der Kommissarbefehl: Wehrmacht und NS-Verbrechen an der Ostfront 1941/42* (Paderborn: Ferdinand Schöningh, 2008).

Römer, Felix, 'Gewaltsame Geschlechterordnung. Wehrmacht und "Flintenweiber" an der Ostfront 1941/42', in Klaus Latzel, Franka Maubach and Silke Satjukow, eds, *Soldatinnen. Gewalt und Geschlecht im Krieg vom Mittelalter bis heute* (Paderborn: Ferdinand Schöningh, 2011), pp. 331–51.

Römer, Felix, 'The Wehrmacht in the War of Ideologies: The Army and Hitler's Criminal Orders on the Eastern Front', in Alex J. Kay, Jeff Rutherford and David Stahel, eds, *Nazi Policy on the Eastern Front, 1941: Total War, Genocide, and Radicalization* (Rochester, NY: University of Rochester Press, 2012), pp. 73–100.

Rossino, Alexander B., *Hitler Strikes Poland: Blitzkrieg, Ideology, and Atrocity* (Lawrence, KS: University Press of Kansas, 2003).

Rossino, Alexander B., 'Nazi Anti-Jewish Policy during the Polish Campaign: The Case of the Einsatzgruppe von Woyrsch', *German Studies Review*, vol. 24, no. 1 (February 2001), pp. 35–53.

Roth, Karl Heinz, '"Generalplan Ost" – "Gesamtplan Ost": Forschungsstand, Quellenprobleme, neue Ergebnisse', in Mechthild Rössler and Sabine Schleiermacher, eds, *Der 'Generalplan Ost': Hauptlinien der nationalsozialistischen Planungs- und Vernichtungspolitik* (Berlin: Akademie, 1993), pp. 25–95.

Rutherford, Jeff, *Combat and Genocide on the Eastern Front: The German Infantry's War, 1941-1944* (Cambridge: Cambridge University Press, 2014).

Rutherford, Jeff, 'The Radicalization of German Occupation Policies: The Wirtschaftsstab Ost and the 121st Infantry Division in Pavlovsk, 1941', in Alex J. Kay, Jeff Rutherford and David Stahel, eds, *Nazi Policy on the Eastern Front, 1941: Total War, Genocide, and Radicalization* (Rochester, NY: University of Rochester Press, 2012), pp. 130–54.

Rutherford, Philip T., *Prelude to the Final Solution: The Nazi Program for Deporting Ethnic Poles, 1939-1941* (Lawrence, KS: University Press of Kansas, 2007).

Sandner, Peter, *Verwaltung des Krankenmordes. Der Bezirksverband Nassau im Nationalsozialismus* (Gießen: Psychosozial-Verlag, 2003).

Schaller, Dominik J., 'From Lemkin to Clooney: The Development and State of Genocide Studies', *Genocide Studies and Prevention: An International Journal*, vol. 6, no. 3 (2011), pp. 245–56.

Schaller, Dominik J., and Jürgen Zimmerer, eds, *The Origins of Genocide: Raphael Lemkin as a Historian of Mass Violence* (Abingdon, Oxon: Routledge, 2009).

Scheck, Raffael, *Hitler's African Victims: The German Army Massacres of Black French Soldiers in 1940* (New York: Cambridge University Press, 2006).

Schelvis, Jules, *Sobibor: A History of a Nazi Death Camp*, trans. from Dutch by Karin Dixon (London: Bloomsbury, 2014).

Schlarp, Karl-Heinz, *Wirtschaft und Besatzung in Serbien, 1941-1944. Ein Beitrag zur nationalsozialistischen Wirtschaftspolitik in Südosteuropa* (Wiesbaden: Franz Steiner, 1986).

Schlögel, Karl, *Entscheidung in Kiew. Ukrainische Lektionen* (Munich: Carl Hanser, 2015).

Schmider, Klaus, *Partisanenkrieg in Jugoslawien 1941-1944* (Hamburg: Mittler, 2002).

Schmidt, Gerhard, *Selektion in der Heilanstalt 1939-1945. Neuausgabe mit ergänzenden Texten*, ed. Frank Schneider (Berlin/Heidelberg: Springer, 2012).

Schmidt, Ulf, *Karl Brandt: The Nazi Doctor – Medicine and Power in the Third Reich* (London: Hambledon Continuum, 2007).

Schmidt, Ulf, 'Reassessing the Beginning of the "Euthanasia" Programme', *German History*, vol. 17, no. 4 (October 1999), pp. 543–50.

Schmuhl, Hans-Walter, '"Euthanasie" und Krankenmord', in Robert Jütte, Wolfgang U. Eckart, Hans-Walter Schmuhl and Winfried Süß, *Medizin und Nationalsozialismus. Bilanz und Perspektiven der Forschung* (Göttingen: Wallstein, 2011), pp. 214–55.

Shrira, Amit, Ravit Menashe and Moshe Bensimon, 'Filial Anxiety and Sense of Obligation among Offspring of Holocaust Survivors', *Aging & Mental Health*, vol. 23, no. 6 (2019), pp. 752–61.

Schulte, Jan Erik, 'Vom Arbeits- zum Vernichtungslager. Die Entstehungsgeschichte von Auschwitz-Birkenau 1941/42', *Vierteljahrshefte für Zeitgeschichte*, vol. 50, no. 1 (January 2002), pp. 41–69.

Schwanninger, Florian, 'Hartheim 1940–1944', in Günter Morsch and Bertrand Perz, eds, *Neue Studien zu nationalsozialistischen Massentötungen durch Giftgas. Historische Bedeutung, technische Entwicklung, revisionistische Leugnung* (Berlin: Metropol, 2011), pp. 118–30.

Schwindt, Barbara, *Das Konzentrations- und Vernichtungslager Majdanek: Funktionswandel im Kontext der 'Endlösung'* (Würzburg: Königshausen & Neumann, 2005).

Scianna, Bastian Matteo, 'A Predisposition to Brutality? German Practices against Civilians and *francs-tireurs* during the Franco-Prussian War 1870–1871 and their Relevance for the German "Military *Sonderweg*" Debate', *Small Wars & Insurgencies*, vol. 30, nos 4–5 (2019), pp. 968–93.

Seidel, Robert, *Deutsche Besatzungspolitik in Polen: Der Distrikt Radom 1939–1945* (Paderborn: Ferdinand Schöningh, 2006).

Shepherd, Ben, 'Bloodier than Boehme: The 342nd Infantry Division in Serbia', in Ben Shepherd and Juliette Pattinson, eds, *War in a Twilight World: Partisan and Anti-Partisan Warfare in Eastern Europe, 1939–45* (Houndmills: Palgrave Macmillan, 2010), pp. 189–209.

Shepherd, Ben, *Terror in the Balkans: German Armies and Partisan Warfare* (Cambridge, MA: Harvard University Press, 2012).

Shepherd, Ben, *War in the Wild East: The German Army and Soviet Partisans* (Cambridge, MA: Harvard University Press, 2004).

Shepherd, Ben H., *Hitler's Soldiers: The German Army in the Third Reich* (New Haven, CT/ London: Yale University Press, 2016).

Shooman, Yasemin, 'Die Rotunde von Zamość', in Wolfgang Benz and Barbara Distel, eds, *Der Ort des Terrors. Geschichte der nationalsozialistischen Konzentrationslager, Band 9* (Munich: C.H. Beck, 2009), pp. 497–510.

Sichrovsky, Peter, *Born Guilty: Children of Nazi Families*, trans. from German by Jean Steinberg (New York: Basic Books, 1988).

Siemen, Hans-Ludwig, 'Die bayerischen Heil- und Pflegeanstalten während des Nationalsozialismus', in Michael von Cranach and Hans-Ludwig Siemen, eds, *Psychiatrie im Nationalsozialismus. Die Bayerischen Heil- und Pflegeanstalten zwischen 1933 und 1945* (Munich: Oldenbourg, 2012), pp. 417–74.

Šindelářová, Lenka, *Finale der Vernichtung. Die Einsatzgruppe H in der Slowakei 1944/1945* (Darmstadt: Wissenschaftliche Buchgesellschaft, 2013).

Skorobohatov, A.V., *Kharkiv u chasy nimets'koï okupatsiï (1941–1943)* (Kharkiv: Prapor, 2004).

Snyder, Timothy, *Bloodlands: Europe between Stalin and Hitler* (New York: Basic Books, 2010).

Snyder, Timothy, 'Hitler vs. Stalin: Who Killed More?', *New York Review of Books*, 10 March 2011.

Stahel, David, *Kiev 1941: Hitler's Battle for Supremacy in the East* (Cambridge: Cambridge University Press, 2012).

Stahel, David, *Operation Barbarossa and Germany's Defeat in the East* (Cambridge: Cambridge University Press, 2009).

Stahel, David, 'Radicalizing Warfare: The German Command and the Failure of Operation Barbarossa', in Alex J. Kay, Jeff Rutherford and David Stahel, eds, *Nazi Policy on the Eastern Front, 1941: Total War, Genocide, and Radicalization* (Rochester, NY: University of Rochester Press, 2012), pp. 19–44.

Staub, Ervin, *Overcoming Evil: Genocide, Violent Conflict, and Terrorism* (Oxford/New York: Oxford University Press, 2011).

Steinbacher, Sybille, *Auschwitz. Geschichte und Nachgeschichte* (Munich: C.H. Beck, 2004).

Steinbacher, Sybille, *'Musterstadt' Auschwitz. Germanisierungspolitik und Judenmord in Ostoberschlesien* (Munich: K.G. Saur, 2000).

Stone, Dan, ed., *The Historiography of Genocide* (Houndmills: Palgrave Macmillan, 2008).

Stone, Lewi, 'Quantifying the Holocaust: Hyperintense Kill Rates during the Genocide', *Science Advances*, vol. 5, no. 1 (January 2019), pp. 1–10.

Streim, Alfred, *Die Behandlung sowjetischer Kriegsgefangener im 'Fall Barbarossa'. Eine Dokumentation* (Heidelberg/Karlsruhe: C.F. Müller Juristischer, 1981).

Streit, Christian, *Keine Kameraden. Die Wehrmacht und die sowjetischen Kriegsgefangenen 1941–1945*, 4th rev. edn (Bonn: Dietz, 1997 [1978]).

Streit, Christian, 'Keine Kameraden. Die Wehrmacht und die sowjetischen Kriegsgefangenen', in Verein 'KONTAKTE-КОНТАКТЫ' e.V., ed., *'Ich werde es nie vergessen'. Briefe sowjetischer Kriegsgefangener 2004–2006* (Berlin: Ch. Links, 2007), pp. 11–21.

Su, Yang, *Collective Killings in Rural China during the Cultural Revolution* (Cambridge/New York: Cambridge University Press, 2011).

Su, Yang, 'Mass Killings in the Cultural Revolution: A Study of Three Provinces', in Joseph Esherick, Paul Pickowicz and Andrew George Walder, eds, *The Chinese Cultural Revolution as History* (Stanford, CA: Stanford University Press, 2006), pp. 96–123.

Süß, Winfried, *Der 'Volkskörper' im Krieg. Gesundheitspolitik, Gesundheitsverhältnisse und Krankenmord im nationalsozialistischen Deutschland 1939–1945* (Munich: Oldenbourg, 2003).

Süß, Winfried, 'Dezentralisierter Krankenmord. Zum Verhältnis von Zentralgewalt und Regionalgewalten in der "Euthanasie" seit 1942', in Horst Möller, Jürgen John and Thomas Schaarschmidt, eds, *NS-Gaue – regionale Mittelinstanzen im zentralistischen 'Führerstaat'* (Munich: Oldenbourg, 2007), pp. 123–35.

Swaan, Abram de, *The Killing Compartments: The Mentality of Mass Murder* (New Haven, CT: Yale University Press, 2015).

Sydnor, Charles, 'Auschwitz I Main Camp', in Geoffrey P. Megargee, ed., *The United States Holocaust Memorial Museum Encyclopedia of Camps and Ghettos, 1933–1945, Vol. I: Early Camps, Youth Camps, and Concentration Camps and Subcamps under the SS-Business Administration Main Office (WVHA), Part A* (Bloomington, IN: Indiana University Press, 2009), pp. 204–8.

Tarach, Tilman, *Der ewige Sündenbock. Heiliger Krieg, die 'Protokolle der Weisen von Zion' und die Verlogenheit der sogenannten Linken im Nahostkonflikt*, 3rd rev. edn (Freiburg/Zurich: Edition Telok, 2010).

Terry, Nicholas, 'Covering Up Chelmno: Nazi Attempts to Obfuscate and Obliterate a Nazi Extermination Camp', *Dapim: Studies on the Holocaust*, vol. 32, no. 3 (2018), pp. 188–205.

Terry, Nicholas, 'The German Army Group Centre and the Soviet Civilian Population, 1942–1944: Forced Labour, Hunger and Population Displacement on the Eastern Front', unpublished PhD thesis, King's College London, 2005.

Topp, Sascha, Petra Fuchs, Gerrit Hohendorf, Paul Richter and Maike Rotzoll, 'Die Provinz Ostpreußen und die nationalsozialistische "Euthanasie": SS-"Aktion Lange" und "Aktion T4"', *Medizinhistorisches Journal*, vol. 43, no. 1 (2008), pp. 20–55.

Tyaglyy, Mikhail, 'Were the "Chingene" Victims of the Holocaust? Nazi Policy toward the Crimean Roma, 1941–1944', *Holocaust and Genocide Studies*, vol. 23, no. 1 (spring 2009), pp. 26–53.

Vasold, Manfred, 'Medizin', in Wolfgang Benz, Hermann Graml and Hermann Weiß, eds, *Enzyklopädie des Nationalsozialismus* (Munich: dtv, 2001 [1997]), pp. 235–50.

Viola, Lynne, 'The Question of the Perpetrator in Soviet History', *Slavic Review*, vol. 72, no. 1 (spring 2013), pp. 1–23.

Voglis, Polymeris, 'Surviving Hunger: Life in the Cities and the Countryside during the Occupation', in Robert Gildea, Olivier Wieviorka and Anette Warring, eds, *Surviving Hitler and Mussolini: Daily Life in Occupied Europe* (Oxford/New York: Berg, 2006), pp. 16–41.

Volkmann, Hans-Erich, ed., *Das Russlandbild im Dritten Reich* (Cologne: Böhlau, 1994).

Wachsmann, Nikolaus, *Hitler's Prisons: Legal Terror in Nazi Germany* (New Haven, CT/London: Yale University Press, 2004).

Wachsmann, Nikolaus, *KL: A History of the Nazi Concentration Camps* (London: Little, Brown, 2015).

Wachsmann, Nikolaus, 'The Dynamics of Destruction: The Development of the Concentration Camps, 1933–1945', in Jane Caplan and Nikolaus Wachsmann, eds, *Concentration Camps in Nazi Germany: The New Histories* (Abingdon, Oxon: Routledge, 2010), pp. 17–43.

Wagenaar, Aad, *Settela*, new edn, trans. from Dutch by Janna Eliot (Marshwood: Lamorna Publications, 2016).

Wardzyńska, Maria, *Był rok 1939. Operacja niemieckiej policji bezpieczeństwa w Polsce – Intelligenzaktion* (Warsaw: Instytut Pamięci Narodowej, 2009).

Weisbrod, Bernd, 'Generation und Generationalität in der Neueren Geschichte', *Aus Politik und Zeitgeschichte*, vol. 8 (2005), pp. 3–9.

Weiss-Wendt, Anton, 'Introduction', in Anton Weiss-Wendt, ed., *The Nazi Genocide of the Roma: Reassessment and Commemoration* (New York/Oxford: Berghahn Books, 2013), pp. 1–26.

Weitbrecht, Dorothee, 'Ermächtigung zur Vernichtung. Die Einsatzgruppen in Polen im Herbst 1939', in Klaus-Michael Mallmann and Bogdan Musial, eds, *Genesis des Genozids. Polen 1939–1941* (Darmstadt: Wissenschaftliche Buchgesellschaft, 2004), pp. 57–70.

Welzer, Harald, *Täter. Wie aus ganz normalen Menschen Massenmörder werden* (Frankfurt am Main: S. Fischer, 2005).

Wheatcroft, Stephen, 'The Scale and Nature of German and Soviet Repression and Mass Killings, 1930–45', *Europe-Asia Studies*, vol. 48, no. 8 (December 1996), pp. 1319–53.

Wildt, Michael, *Generation des Unbedingten. Das Führungskorps des Reichssicherheitshauptamtes*, rev. edn (Hamburg: Hamburger Edition, 2003 [2002]).

Winkler, Ulrike, and Gerrit Hohendorf, '"Nun ist Mogiljow frei von Verrückten". Die Ermordung der PsychiatriepatientInnen in Mogilew 1941/42', in Babette Quinkert, Philipp Rauh and Ulrike Winkler, eds, *Krieg und Psychiatrie 1914–1950* (Göttingen: Wallstein, 2010), pp. 75–103.

Winkler, Ulrike, and Gerrit Hohendorf, 'The Murder of Psychiatric Patients by the SS and the Wehrmacht in Poland and the Soviet Union, Especially in Mogilev, 1939–1945', in Alex J. Kay and David Stahel, eds, *Mass Violence in Nazi-Occupied Europe* (Bloomington, IN: Indiana University Press, 2018), pp. 147–70.

Wippermann, Wolfgang, '"The Definitive Solution to the Gypsy Question": The Pan-European Genocide of the European Roma', in Alex J. Kay and David Stahel, eds, *Mass Violence in Nazi-Occupied Europe* (Bloomington, IN: Indiana University Press, 2018), pp. 81–93.

Witte, Peter, and Stephen Tyas, 'A New Document on the Deportation and Murder of Jews during "Einsatz Reinhardt" 1942', *Holocaust and Genocide Studies*, vol. 15, no. 3 (winter 2001), pp. 468–86.

Wróbel, Karolina, 'The Roma Inside the Warsaw Ghetto's Walls', *Czas Kultury/English*, vol. 6 (2009), pp. 92–103.

Zamoiski, Andrei, 'Einheimische Mediziner und die nationalsozialistischen Krankenmorde in der Stadt Mahilëŭ', in Alexander Friedman and Rainer Hudeman, eds, *Diskriminiert – vernichtet – vergessen. Behinderte in der Sowjetunion, unter nationalsozialistischer Besatzung und im Ostblock 1917–1991* (Stuttgart: Franz Steiner, 2016), pp. 415–22.

Zarusky, Jürgen, 'Timothy Snyders "Bloodlands". Kritische Anmerkungen zur Konstruktion einer Geschichtslandschaft', *Vierteljahreshefte für Zeitgeschichte*, vol. 60, no. 1 (January 2012), pp. 1–31.

Zimmerer, Jürgen, 'Climate Change, Environmental Violence and Genocide', *The International Journal of Human Rights*, vol. 18, no. 3 (2014), pp. 265–80.

Zimmerer, Jürgen, *Deutsche Herrschaft über Afrikaner. Staatlicher Machtanspruch und Wirklichkeit im kolonialen Namibia* (Münster: LIT, 2001).

Zimmermann, Michael, *Rassenutopie und Genozid. Die nationalsozialistische 'Lösung der Zigeunerfrage'* (Hamburg: Christians, 1996).

Zwarte, Ingrid de, *The Hunger Winter: Fighting Famine in the Occupied Netherlands, 1944–1945* (Cambridge: Cambridge University Press, 2020).

INDEX